RAVE MASTER

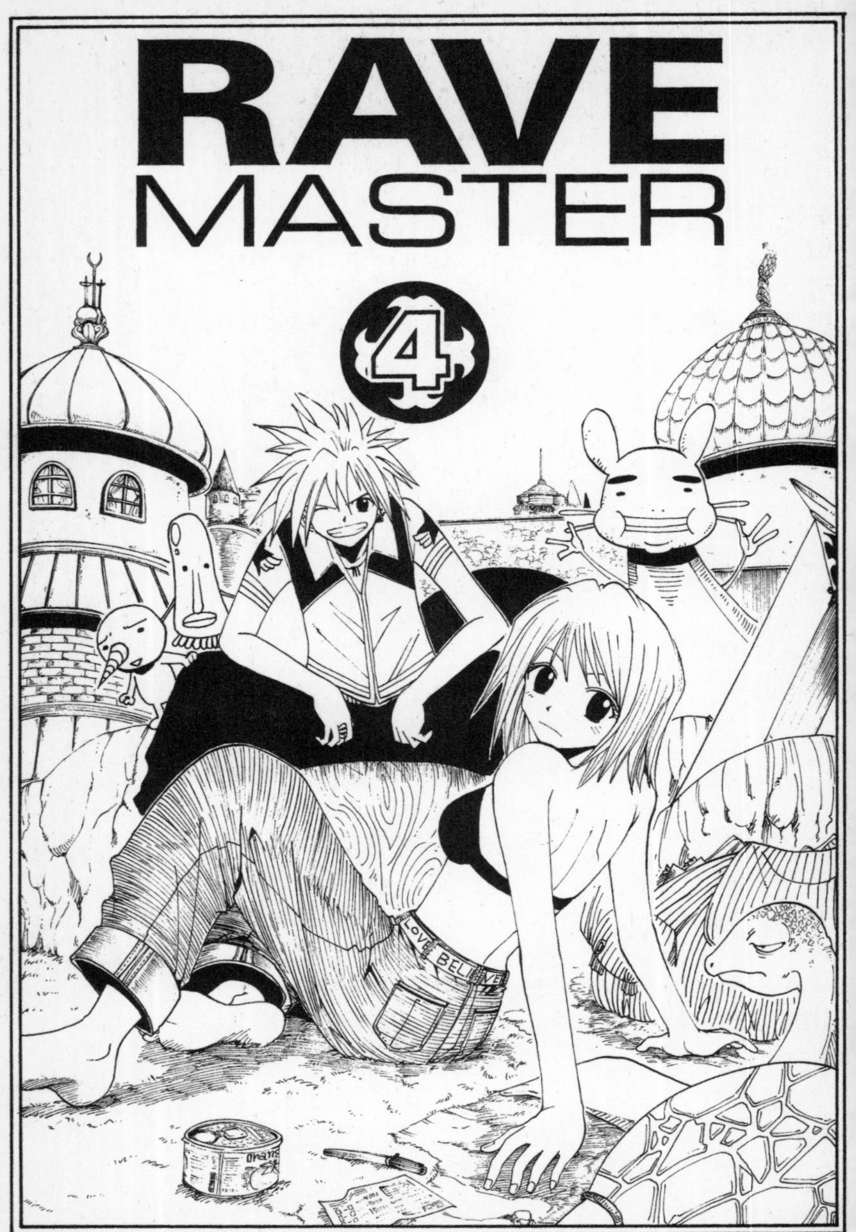
4

ALSO AVAILABLE FROM 🔲 TOKYOPOP®

MANGA

.HACK//LEGEND OF THE TWILIGHT (September 2003)
@LARGE (COMING SOON)
ANGELIC LAYER*
BABY BIRTH* (September 2003)
BATTLE ROYALE*
BRAIN POWERED*
BRIGADOON* (August 2003)
CARDCAPTOR SAKURA
CARDCAPTOR SAKURA: MASTER OF THE CLOW*
CHOBITS*
CHRONICLES OF THE CURSED SWORD
CLAMP SCHOOL DETECTIVES*
CLOVER
CONFIDENTIAL CONFESSIONS*
CORRECTOR YUI
COWBOY BEBOP*
COWBOY BEBOP: SHOOTING STAR*
DEMON DIARY
DIGIMON*
DRAGON HUNTER
DRAGON KNIGHTS*
DUKLYON: CLAMP SCHOOL DEFENDERS*
ERICA SAKURAZAWA*
FAKE*
FLCL* (September 2003)
FORBIDDEN DANCE* (August 2003)
GATE KEEPERS*
G GUNDAM*
GRAVITATION*
GTO*
GUNDAM WING
GUNDAM WING: BATTLEFIELD OF PACIFISTS
GUNDAM WING: ENDLESS WALTZ*
GUNDAM WING: THE LAST OUTPOST*
HAPPY MANIA*
HARLEM BEAT
I.N.V.U.
INITIAL D*
ISLAND
JING: KING OF BANDITS*
JULINE
KARE KANO*
KINDAICHI CASE FILES, THE*
KING OF HELL
KODOCHA: SANA'S STAGE*
LOVE HINA*
LUPIN III*
MAGIC KNIGHT RAYEARTH* (August 2003)
MAGIC KNIGHT RAYEARTH II* (COMING SOON)

MAN OF MANY FACES*
MARMALADE BOY*
MARS*
MIRACLE GIRLS
MIYUKI-CHAN IN WONDERLAND* (October 2003)
MONSTERS, INC.
PARADISE KISS*
PARASYTE
PEACH GIRL
PEACH GIRL: CHANGE OF HEART*
PET SHOP OF HORRORS*
PLANET LADDER*
PLANETES* (October 2003)
PRIEST
RAGNAROK
RAVE MASTER*
REALITY CHECK
REBIRTH
REBOUND*
RISING STARS OF MANGA
SABER MARIONETTE J*
SAILOR MOON
SAINT TAIL
SAMURAI DEEPER KYO*
SAMURAI GIRL: REAL BOUT HIGH SCHOOL*
SCRYED*
SHAOLIN SISTERS*
SHIRAHIME-SYO: SNOW GODDESS TALES* (Dec. 2003)
SHUTTERBOX (November 2003)
SORCERER HUNTERS
THE SKULL MAN*
THE VISION OF ESCAFLOWNE
TOKYO MEW MEW*
UNDER THE GLASS MOON
VAMPIRE GAME*
WILD ACT*
WISH*
WORLD OF HARTZ (COMING SOON)
X-DAY* (August 2003)
ZODIAC P.I. *

For more information visit www.TOKYOPOP.com

*INDICATES 100% AUTHENTIC MANGA (RIGHT-TO-LEFT FORMAT)

CINE-MANGA™

CARDCAPTORS
JACKIE CHAN ADVENTURES (COMING SOON)
JIMMY NEUTRON (September 2003)
KIM POSSIBLE
LIZZIE MCGUIRE
POWER RANGERS: NINJA STORM (August 2003)
SPONGEBOB SQUAREPANTS (September 2003)
SPY KIDS 2

NOVELS

KARMA CLUB (April 2004)
SAILOR MOON

TOKYOPOP KIDS

STRAY SHEEP (September 2003)

ART BOOKS

CARDCAPTOR SAKURA*
MAGIC KNIGHT RAYEARTH*

ANIME GUIDES

COWBOY BEBOP ANIME GUIDES
GUNDAM TECHNICAL MANUALS
SAILOR MOON SCOUT GUIDES

6-5-03

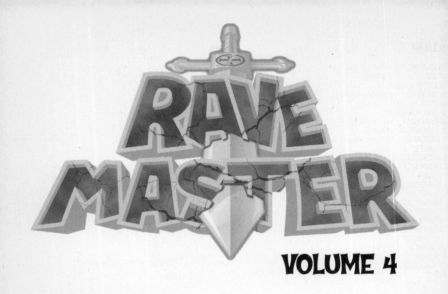

VOLUME 4

Story and Art by
HIRO MASHIMA

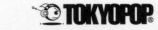 **TOKYOPOP®**

Los Angeles · Tokyo · London

Translator - Amy Forsyth
English Adaptation - James Lucas Jones
Editor - Jake Forbes
Copy Editors - Jennifer Wagner & Paul Morrissey
Retouch and Lettering - Vivian Choi
Cover Artist - Pauline Sims
Cover Layout - Raymond Makowski

Managing Editor - Jill Freshney
Production Coordinator - Antonio DePietro
Production Manager - Jennifer Miller
Art Director - Matt Alford
Editorial Director - Jeremy Ross
VP of Production - Ron Klamert
President & C.O.O. - John Parker
Publisher & C.E.O. - Stuart Levy

Email: editor@TOKYOPOP.com
Come visit us online at www.TOKYOPOP.com

A 🐸 **TOKYOPOP**® Manga

TOKYOPOP® is an imprint of Mixx Entertainment, Inc.
5900 Wilshire Blvd. Suite 2000, Los Angeles, CA 90036

ISBN: 1-59182-211-4

T 252151

First TOKYOPOP® printing: August 2003

10 9 8 7 6 5 4 3

Printed in the USA

CONTENTS

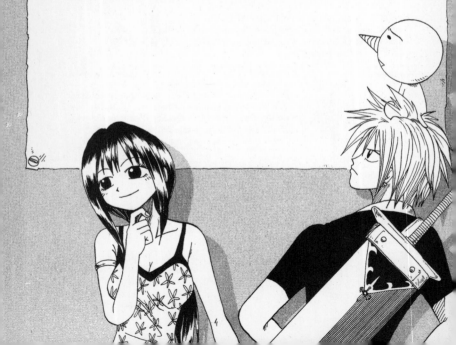

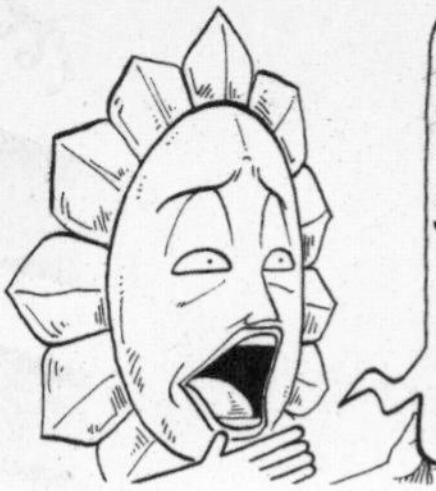

The Story So Far...

HARU GLORY is the RAVE MASTER, the only one capable of wielding RAVE and stopping the evil society DEMON CARD. His Guide is PLUE, a strange creature who can track down the four missing Raves. They are joined by ELIE, a girl in search of her memories. When last we left our team, they had arrived at Ska Village while searching for a "fallen star" that just might be one of the missing Raves. Ska Village has been drenched by nonstop rain for years due to the influence of the "Thunder-Man." Could it be the work of Demon Card, or perhaps the mysterious man of Elie's past? Three heroes...two quests...one destiny.

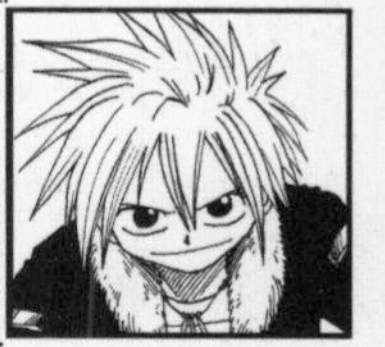

HARU GLORY: The Rave Master. Haru is the heir to Rave, the only one capable of wielding it and destroying Dark Bring. Impulsive and headstrong, he's not afraid to put himself in danger to do what is right. His father disappeared in search of Rave when he was very young.

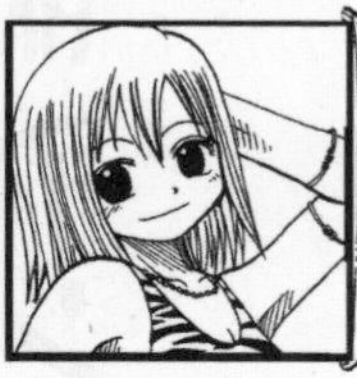

ELIE: A Girl with no past. Elie travels the world in search of the key to her forgotten memories. Outwardly cheerful, she hides a great sadness from her past. She's hot-headed, so when she pulls out her explosive Tonfa Blasters, bad guys watch out!

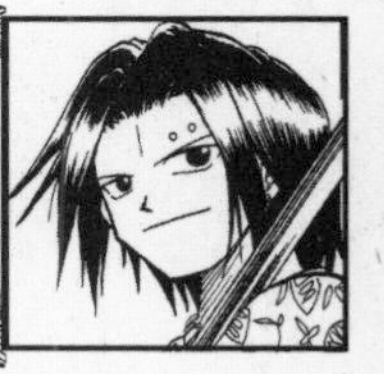

MUSICA: Leader of the Silver Rhythm Gang. An orphan whose family was slaughtered when he was a baby, Musica became a street-fighting petty thief, but he has a good heart.

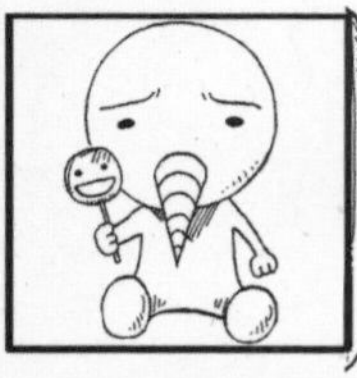

PLUE: The Rave Bearer. Plue is supposed to be Haru's guide in finding the Rave Stones, but so far he's just gotten him in and out of trouble. No one knows exactly what Plue is, but he seems to have healing abilities and is smarter than your average...whatever he is.

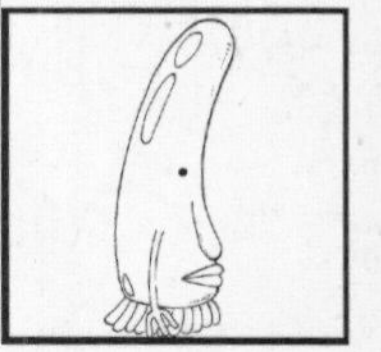

GRIFF: Don't even ask what this thing is. His full name is Griffon Kato, but he just goes by Griff. He works as a cart driver and is hired to transport Haru and friends across the Continent of Song. His body can stretch like rubber and he's got a crush on Elie.

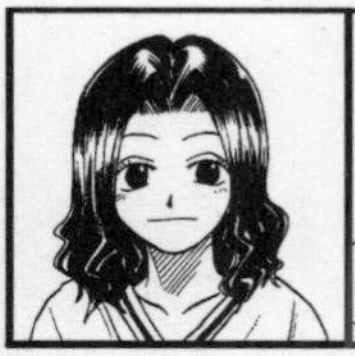

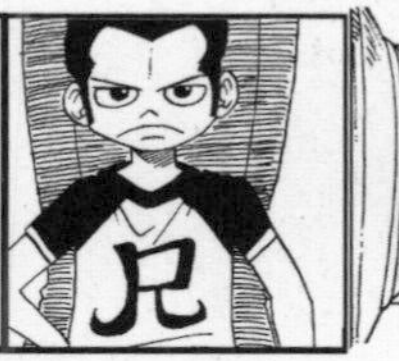

LASAGNA & CHINO: Lasagna runs the hotel in Ska Village where Haru and Elie stayed. Chino is her son, who, because of the constant rain, has never seen a sunny day.

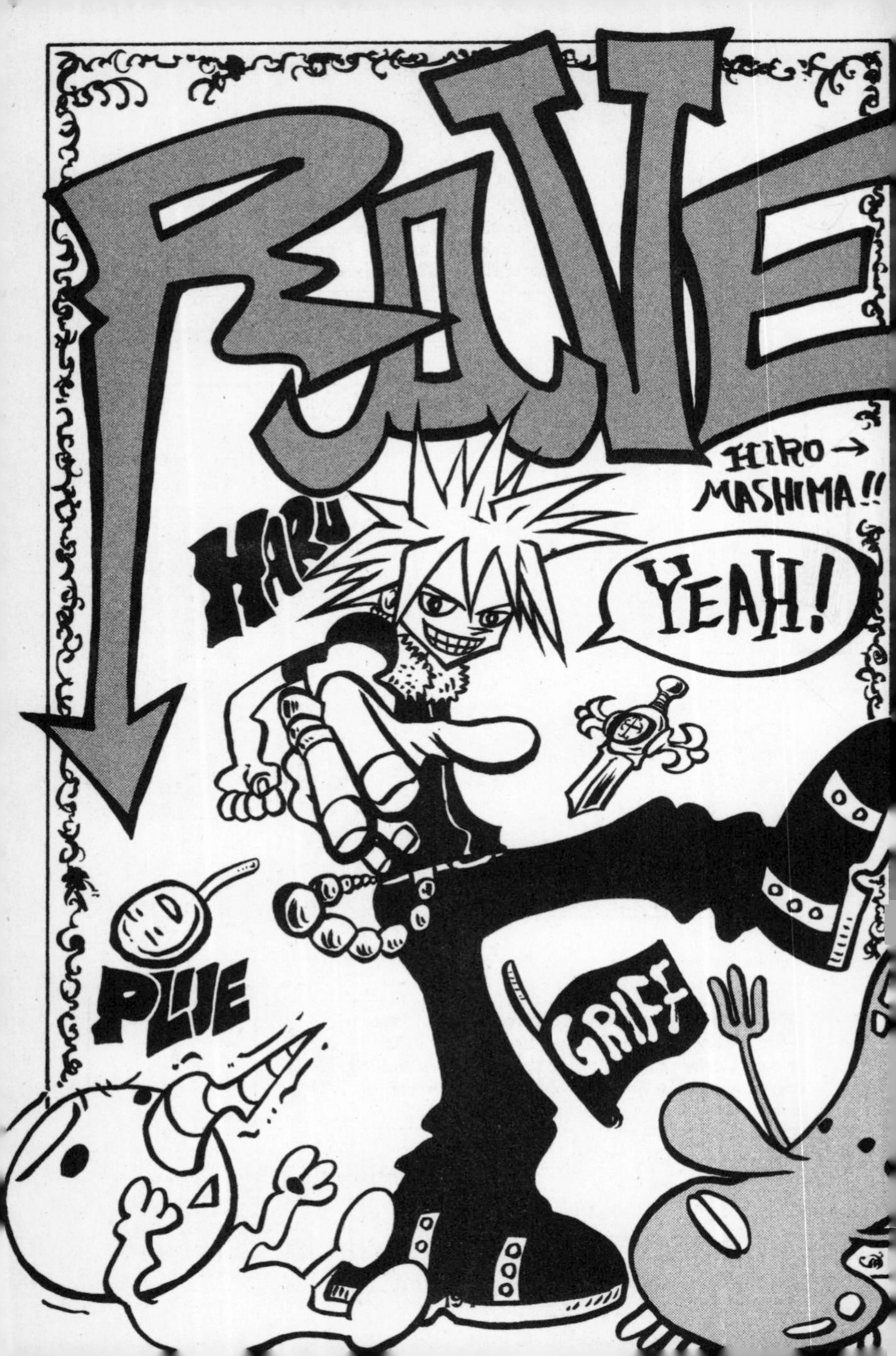
RAVE
HIRO → MASHIMA!!
HARU
YEAH!
PLUE
GRIFF

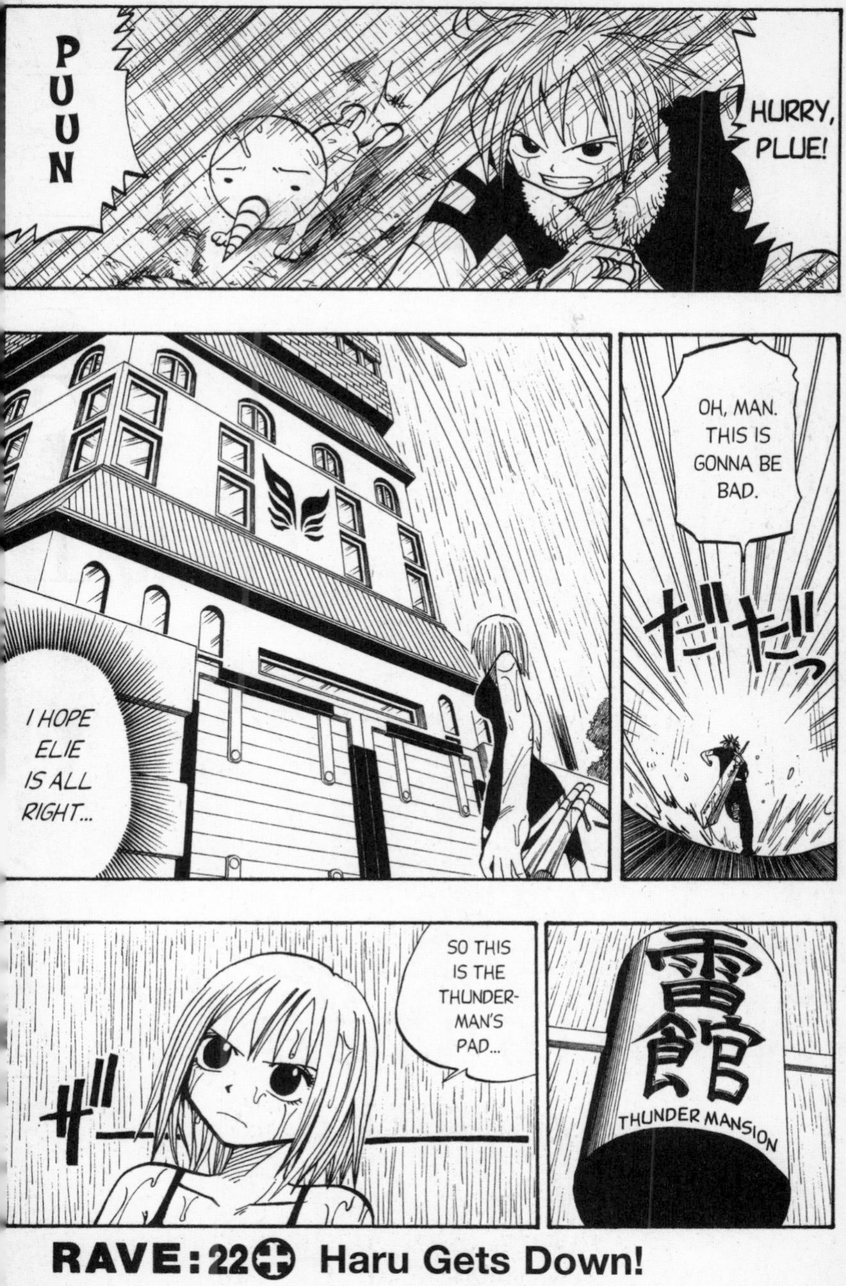
HURRY, PLUE!
PUUN
OH, MAN. THIS IS GONNA BE BAD.
だだっ
I HOPE ELIE IS ALL RIGHT...
雷館
THUNDER MANSION
SO THIS IS THE THUNDER-MAN'S PAD...
ザー

RAVE: 22 Haru Gets Down!

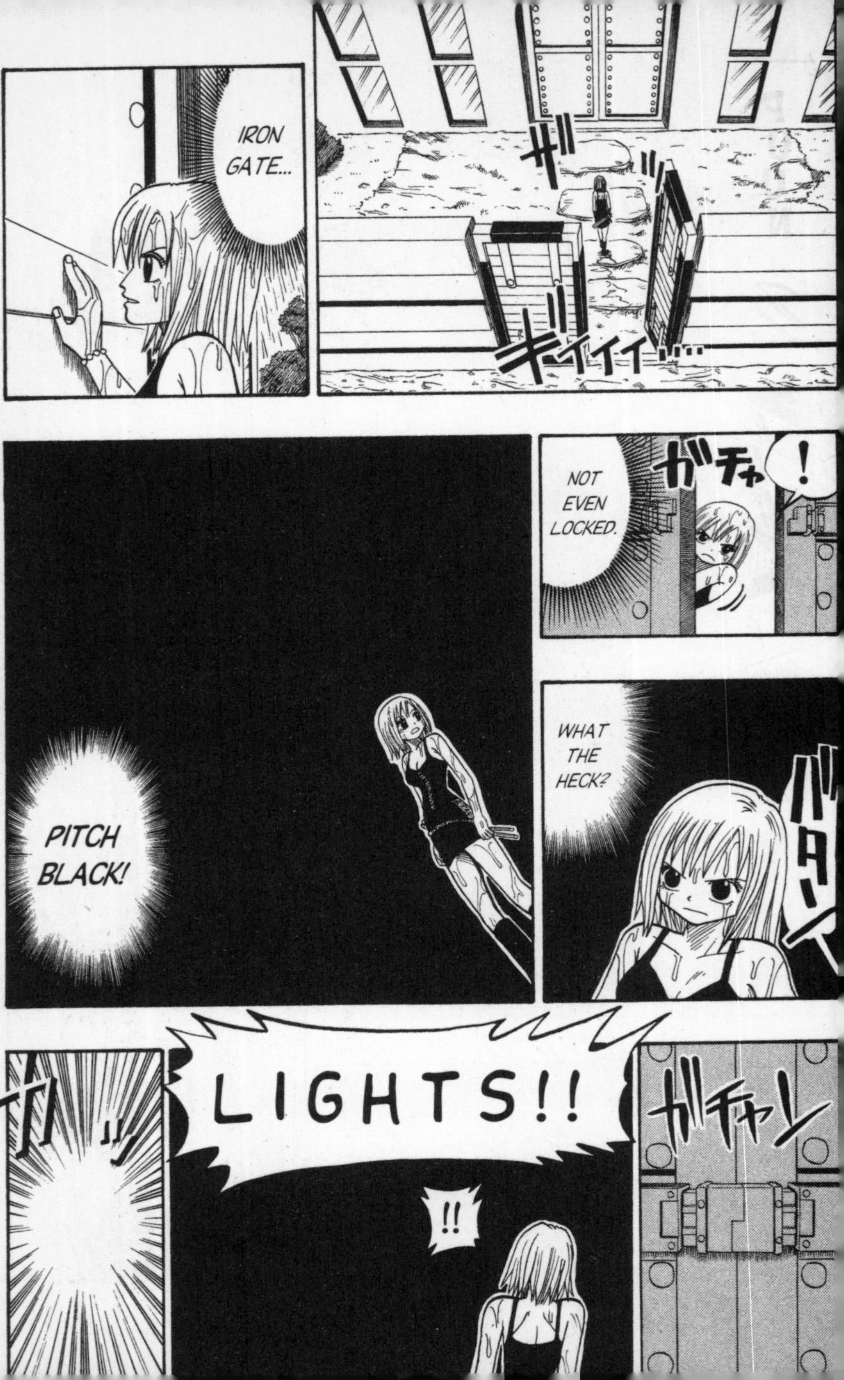
ギイイイ…
IRON GATE...
ガチャ
!
NOT EVEN LOCKED.
バタン
WHAT THE HECK?
PITCH BLACK!
ガチャン
LIGHTS!!
!!
パッ

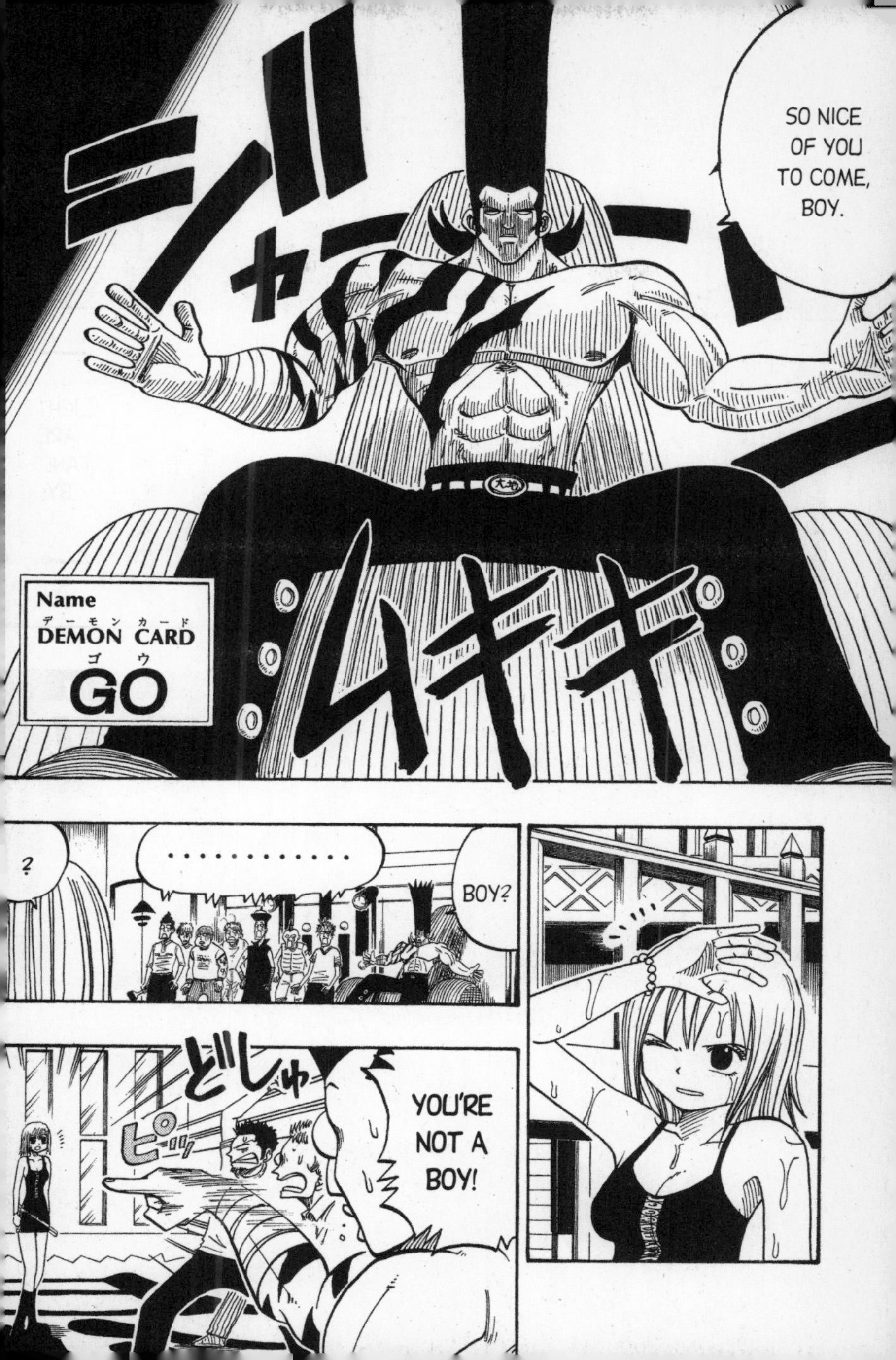
SO NICE OF YOU TO COME, BOY.
Name
DEMON CARD
GO
BOY?
....
?
YOU'RE NOT A BOY!

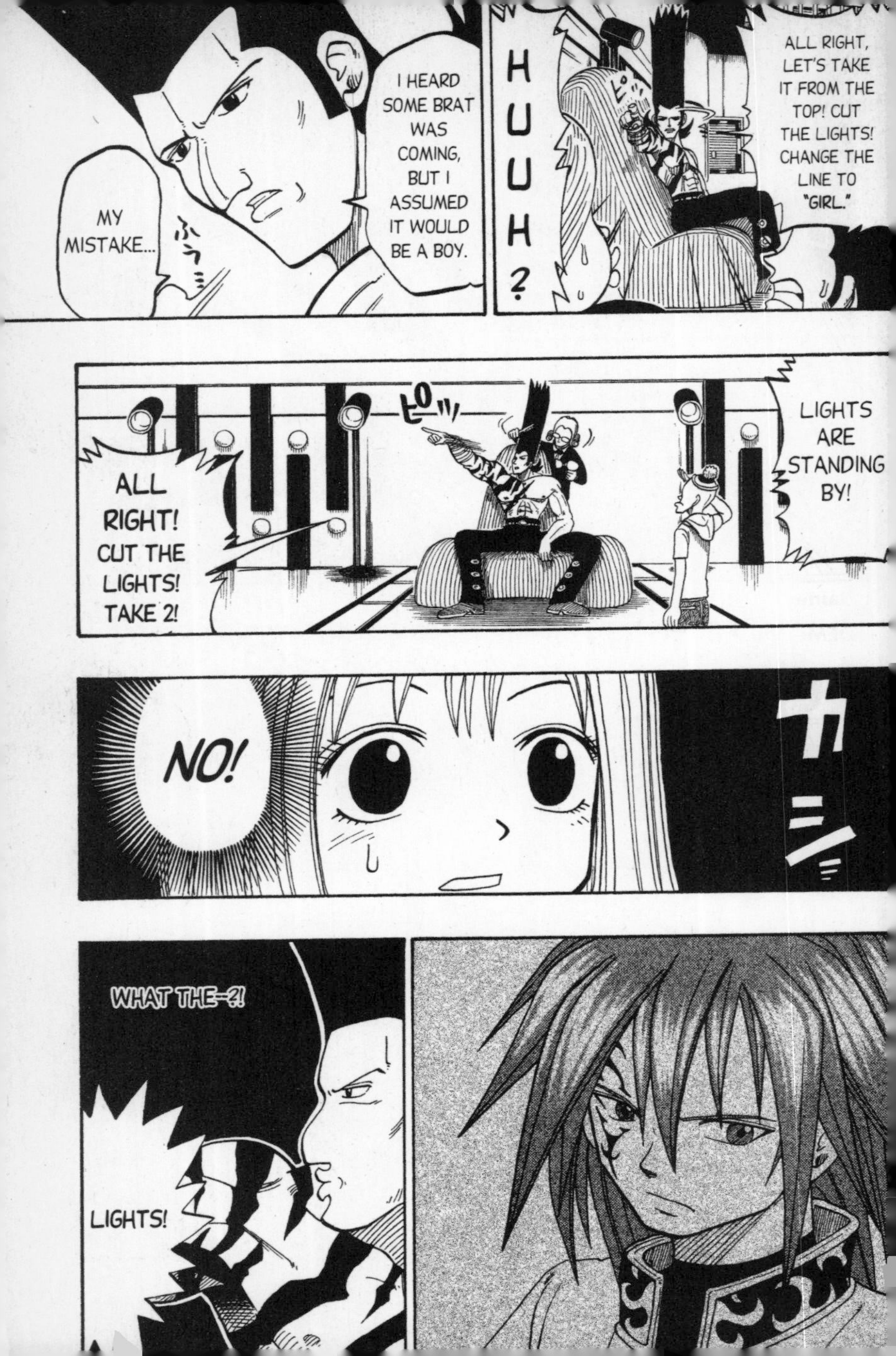
ALL RIGHT, LET'S TAKE IT FROM THE TOP! CUT THE LIGHTS! CHANGE THE LINE TO "GIRL."
HUUH?
I HEARD SOME BRAT WAS COMING, BUT I ASSUMED IT WOULD BE A BOY.
MY MISTAKE...
LIGHTS ARE STANDING BY!
ALL RIGHT! CUT THE LIGHTS! TAKE 2!
NO!
WHAT THE--?!
LIGHTS!

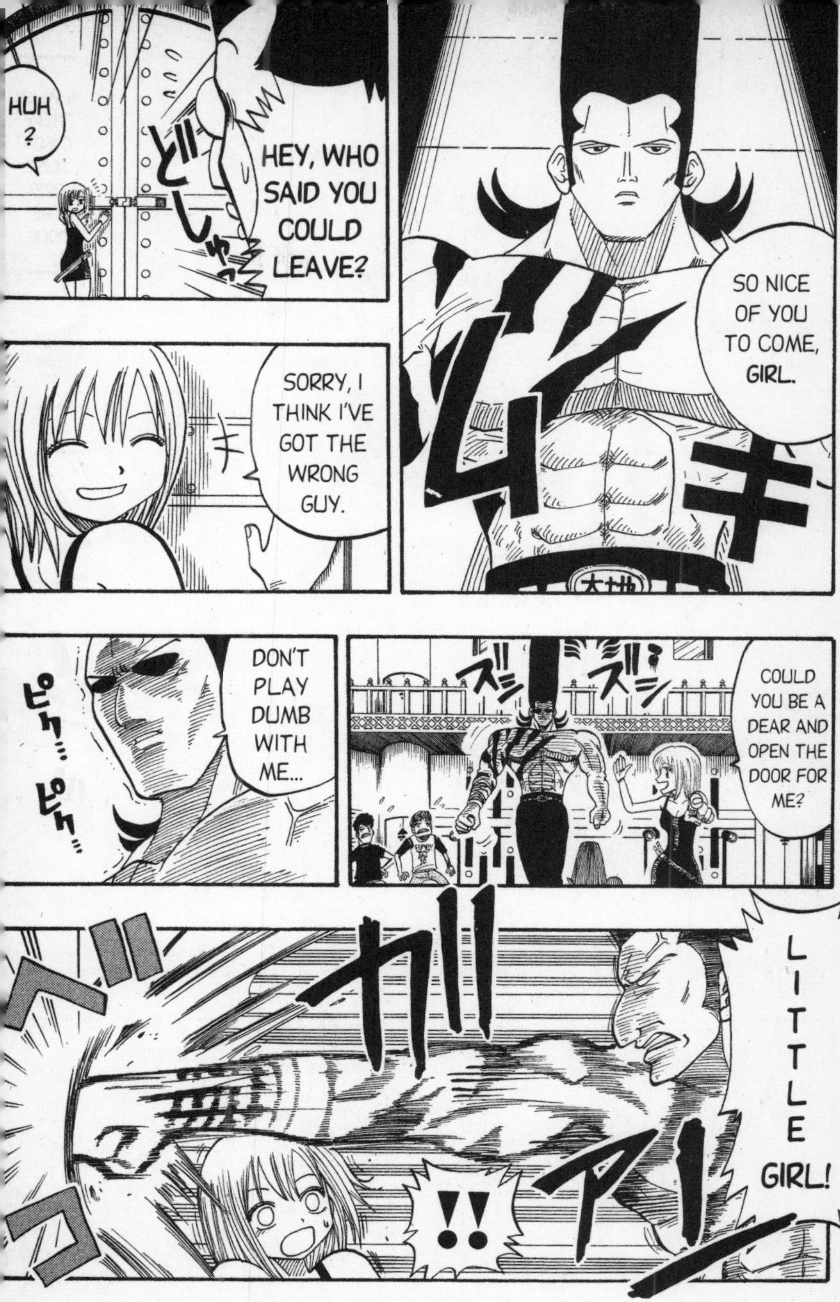
SO NICE OF YOU TO COME, GIRL.
HEY, WHO SAID YOU COULD LEAVE?
HUH ?
SORRY, I THINK I'VE GOT THE WRONG GUY.
COULD YOU BE A DEAR AND OPEN THE DOOR FOR ME?
DON'T PLAY DUMB WITH ME...
LITTLE GIRL!
!!

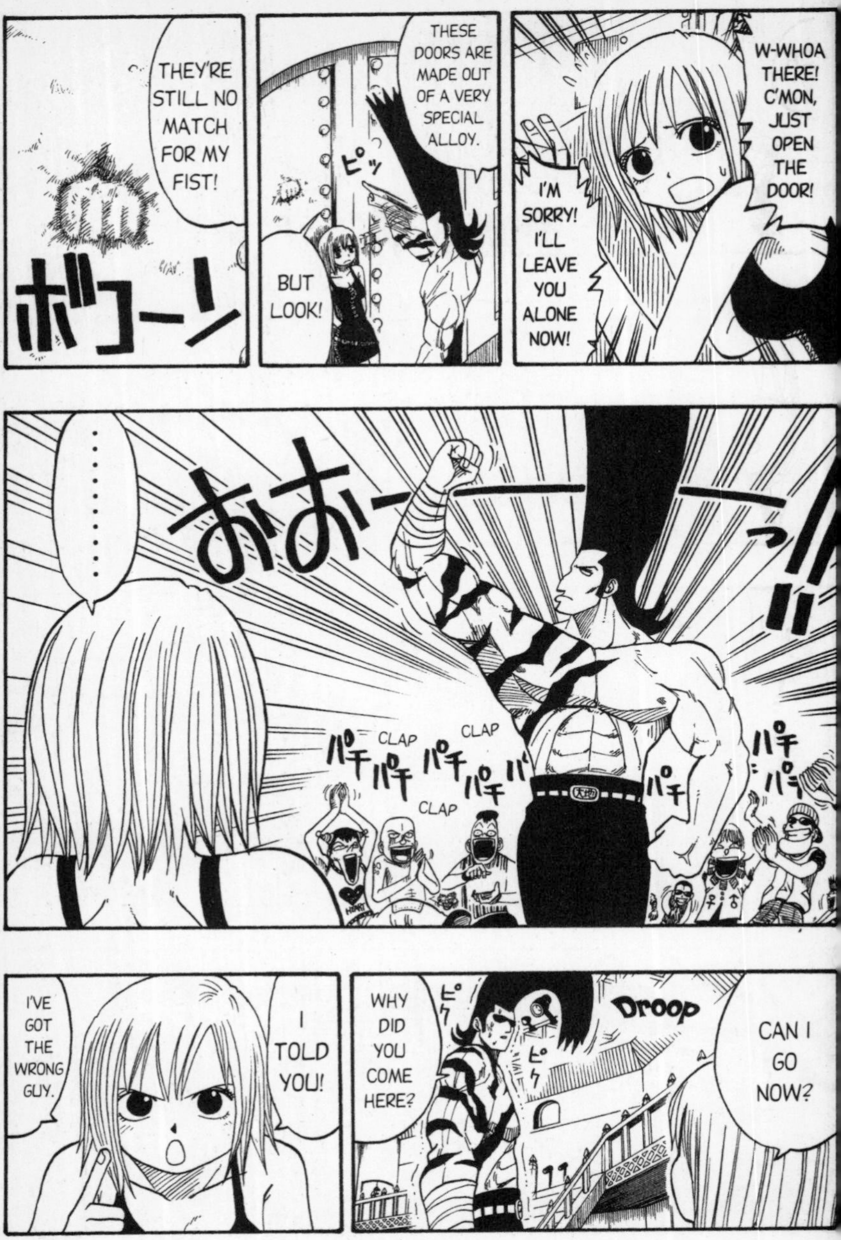

W-WHOA THERE! C'MON, JUST OPEN THE DOOR!
I'M SORRY! I'LL LEAVE YOU ALONE NOW!
THESE DOORS ARE MADE OUT OF A VERY SPECIAL ALLOY.
ピッ
BUT LOOK!
THEY'RE STILL NO MATCH FOR MY FIST!
ボゴーン
おおーーーーっ!!
......
パチパチ
CLAP
パチパチ
CLAP
CLAP
パチパチパチ
パチパチ
CAN I GO NOW?
Droop
ピク
ピク
WHY DID YOU COME HERE?
I TOLD YOU!
I'VE GOT THE WRONG GUY.

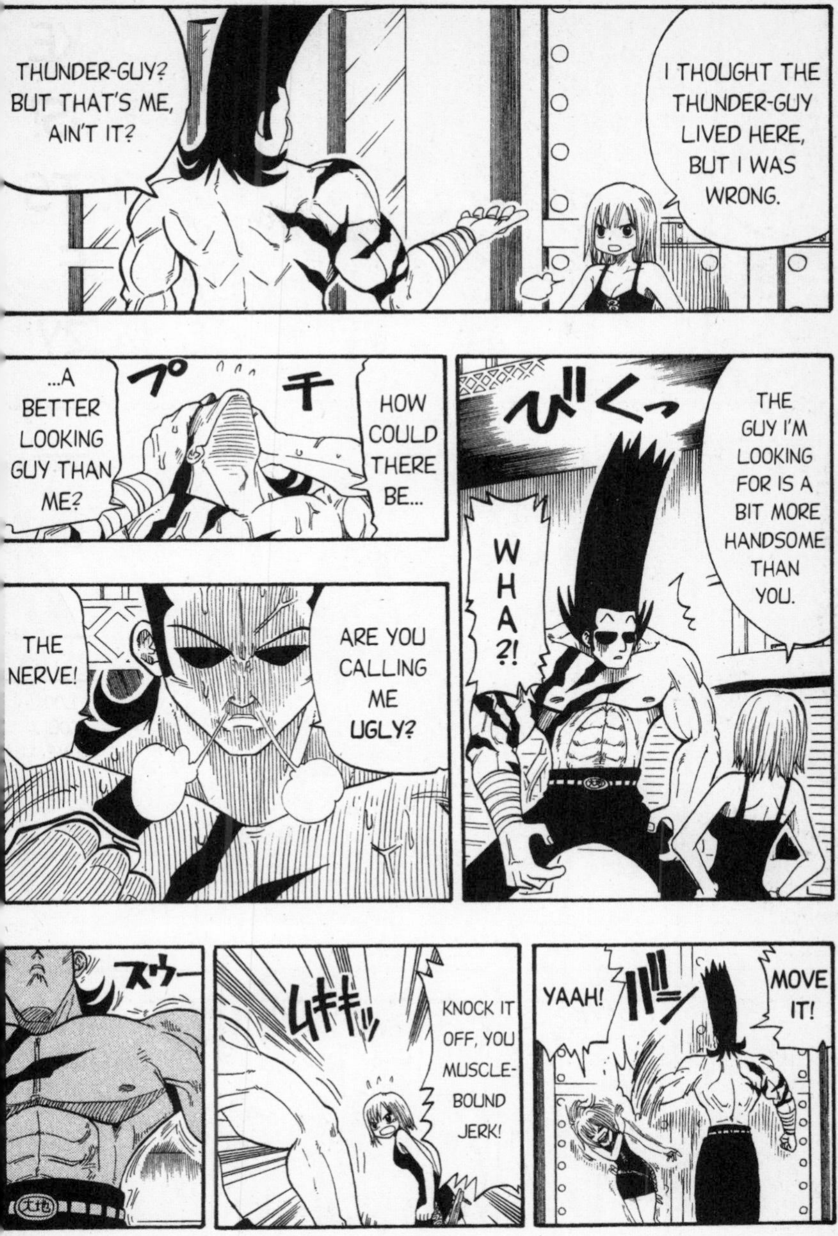

I THOUGHT THE THUNDER-GUY LIVED HERE, BUT I WAS WRONG.
THUNDER-GUY? BUT THAT'S ME, AIN'T IT?
びくっ
THE GUY I'M LOOKING FOR IS A BIT MORE HANDSOME THAN YOU.
WHA?!
HOW COULD THERE BE...
プチ
...A BETTER LOOKING GUY THAN ME?
ARE YOU CALLING ME UGLY?
THE NERVE!
MOVE IT!
バッ
YAAH!
KNOCK IT OFF, YOU MUSCLE-BOUND JERK!
ムキキッ
スウー

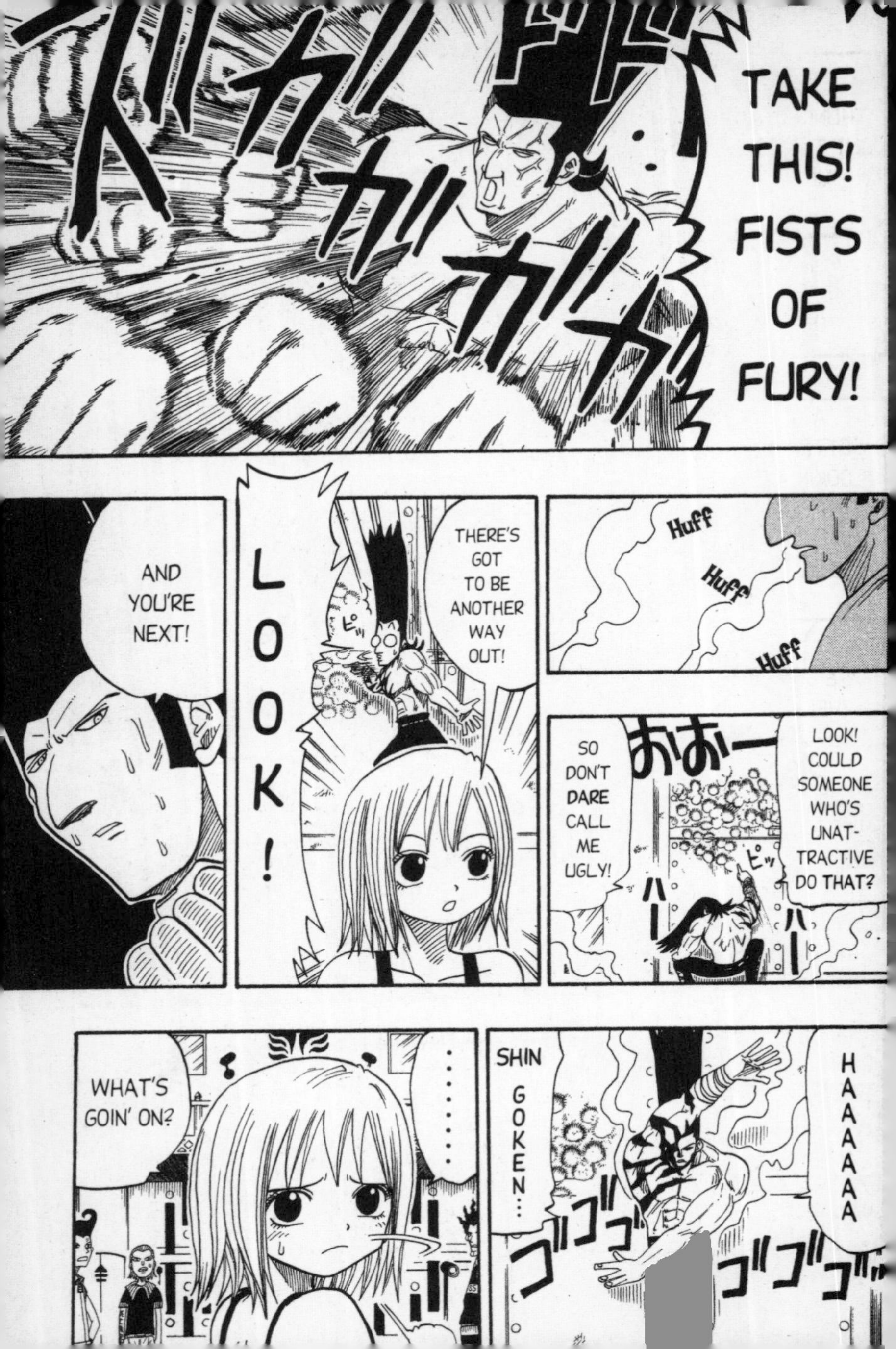

TAKE THIS! FISTS OF FURY!
Huff
Huff
Huff
LOOK! COULD SOMEONE WHO'S UNAT-TRACTIVE DO THAT?
おおー
SO DON'T DARE CALL ME UGLY!
THERE'S GOT TO BE ANOTHER WAY OUT!
LOOK!
AND YOU'RE NEXT!
HAAAAAAA
SHIN GOKEN...
......
WHAT'S GOIN' ON?

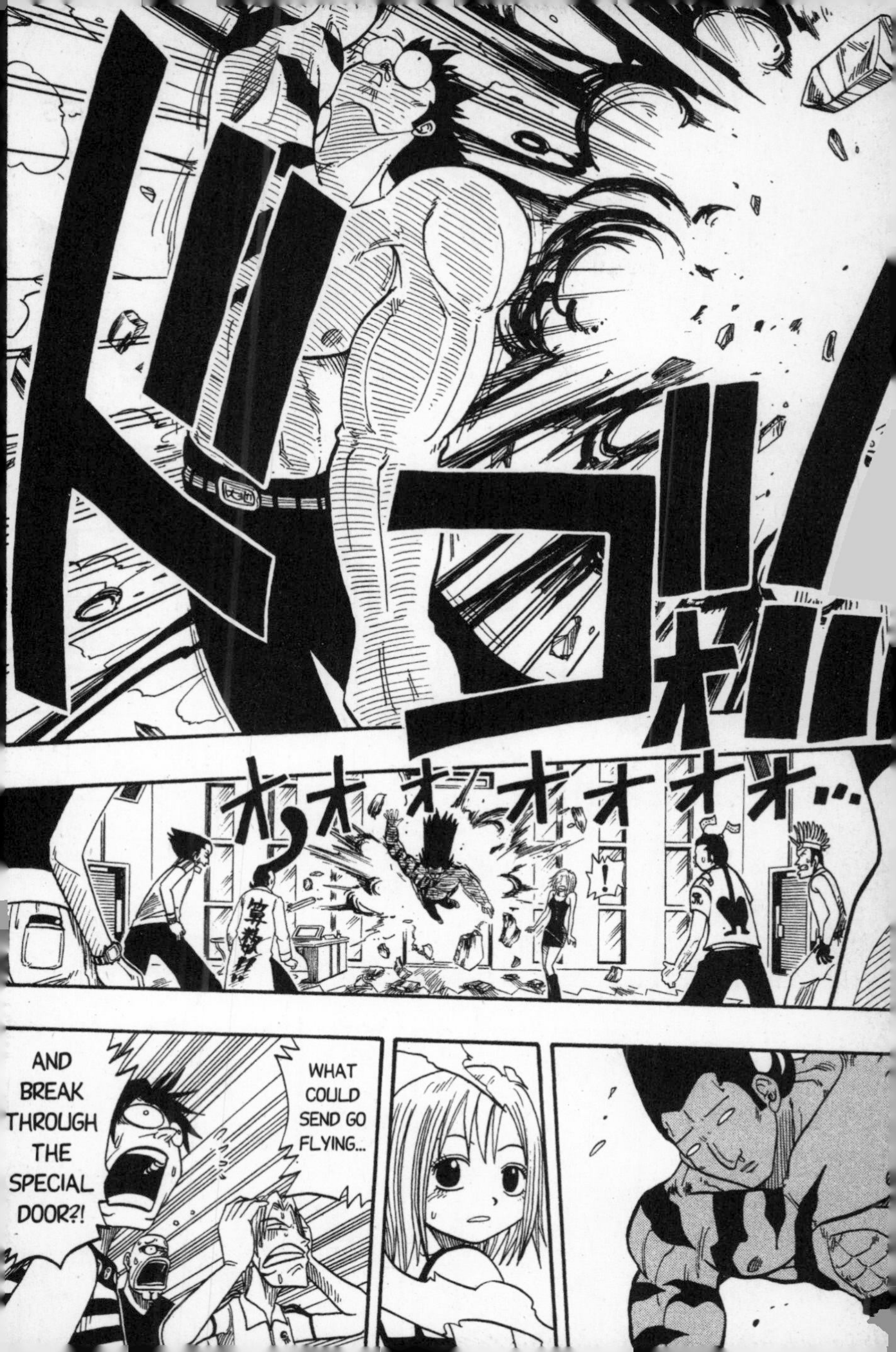
WHAT COULD SEND GO FLYING...
AND BREAK THROUGH THE SPECIAL DOOR?!

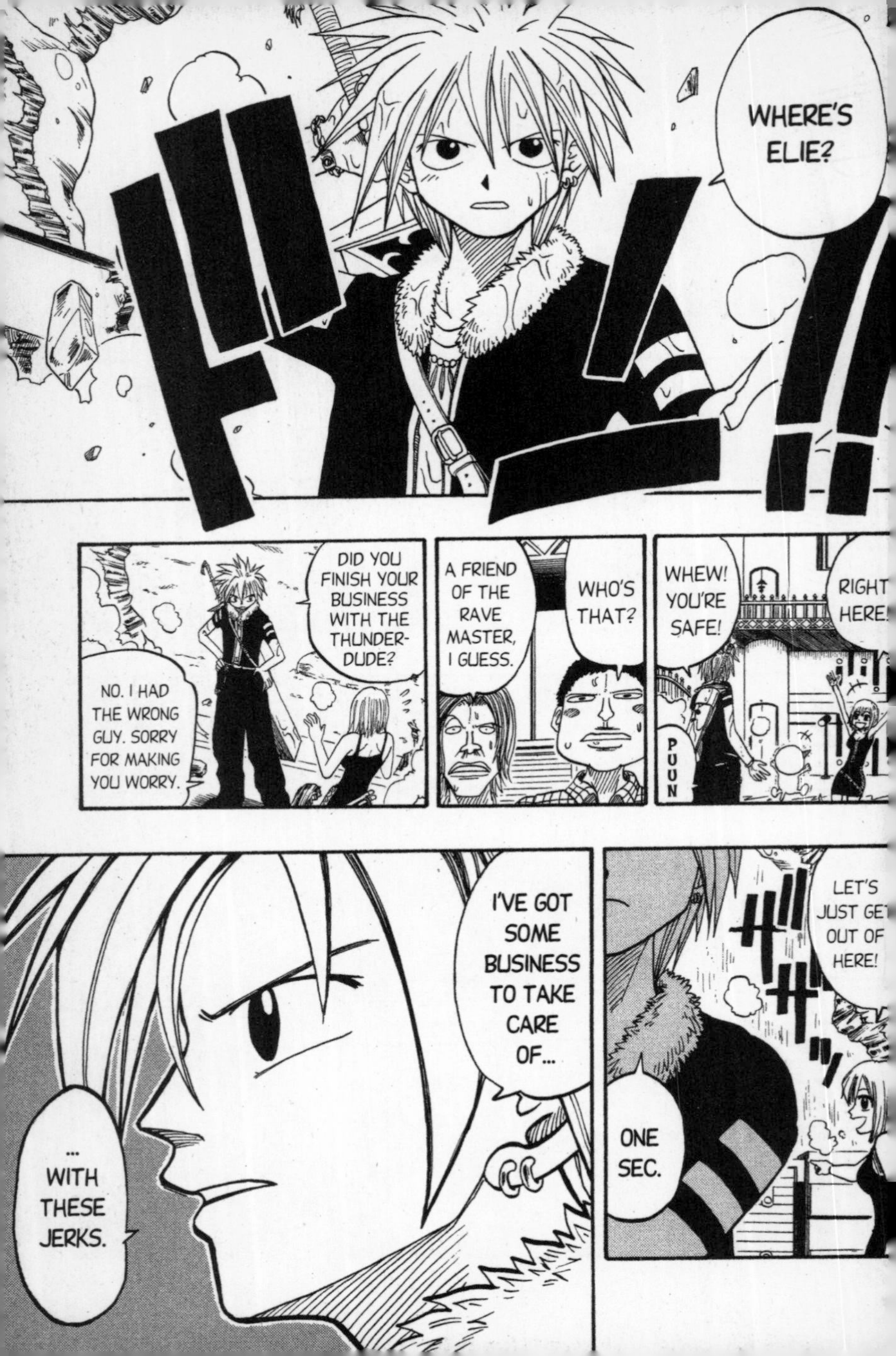
WHERE'S ELIE?
RIGHT HERE!
WHEW! YOU'RE SAFE!
PUUN
WHO'S THAT?
A FRIEND OF THE RAVE MASTER, I GUESS.
DID YOU FINISH YOUR BUSINESS WITH THE THUNDER-DUDE?
NO. I HAD THE WRONG GUY. SORRY FOR MAKING YOU WORRY.
LET'S JUST GET OUT OF HERE!
ONE SEC.
I'VE GOT SOME BUSINESS TO TAKE CARE OF...
... WITH THESE JERKS.

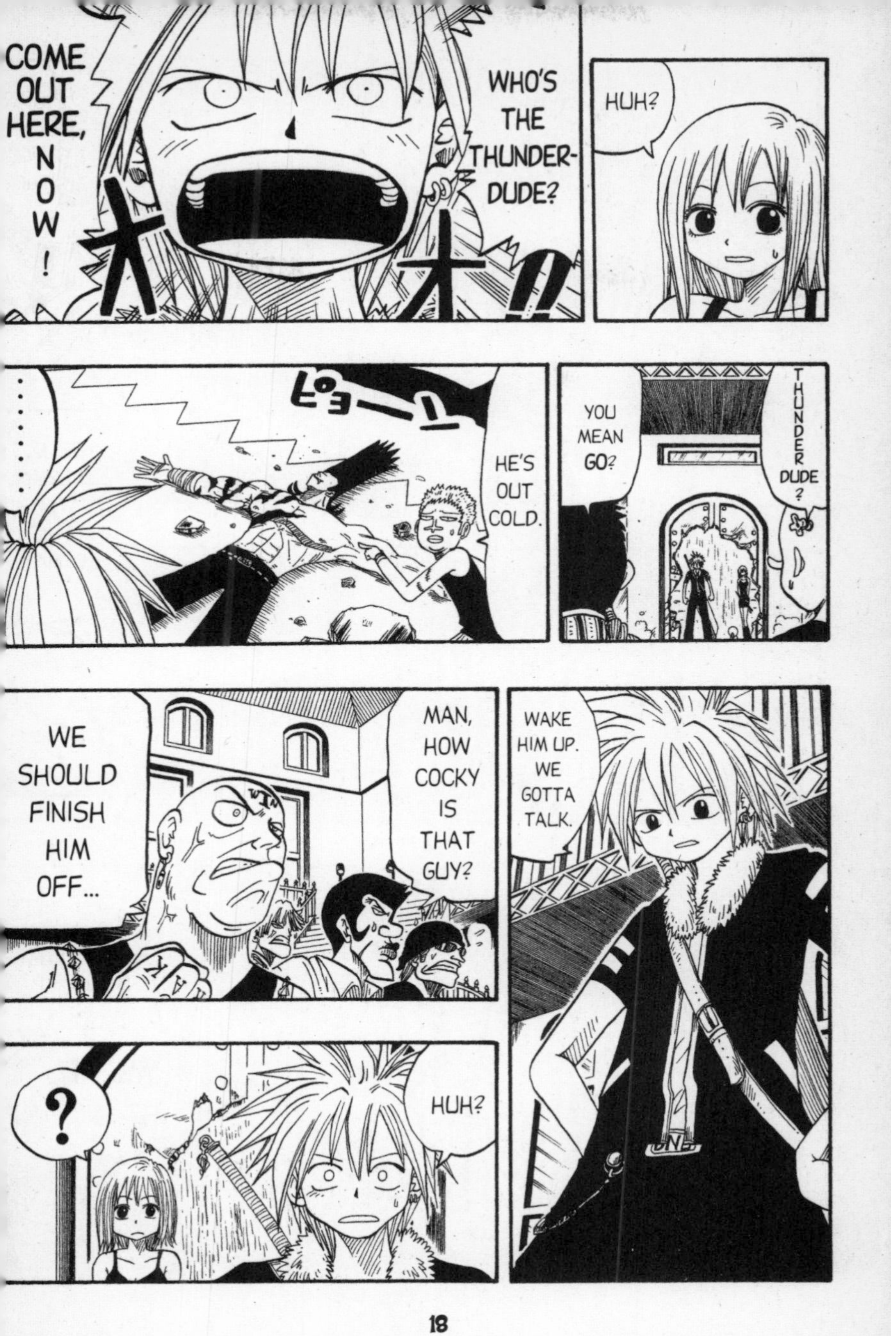
HUH?
WHO'S THE THUNDER-DUDE?
COME OUT HERE, NOW!
THUNDER DUDE?
YOU MEAN GO?
HE'S OUT COLD.
......
WAKE HIM UP. WE GOTTA TALK.
MAN, HOW COCKY IS THAT GUY?
WE SHOULD FINISH HIM OFF...
HUH?
?

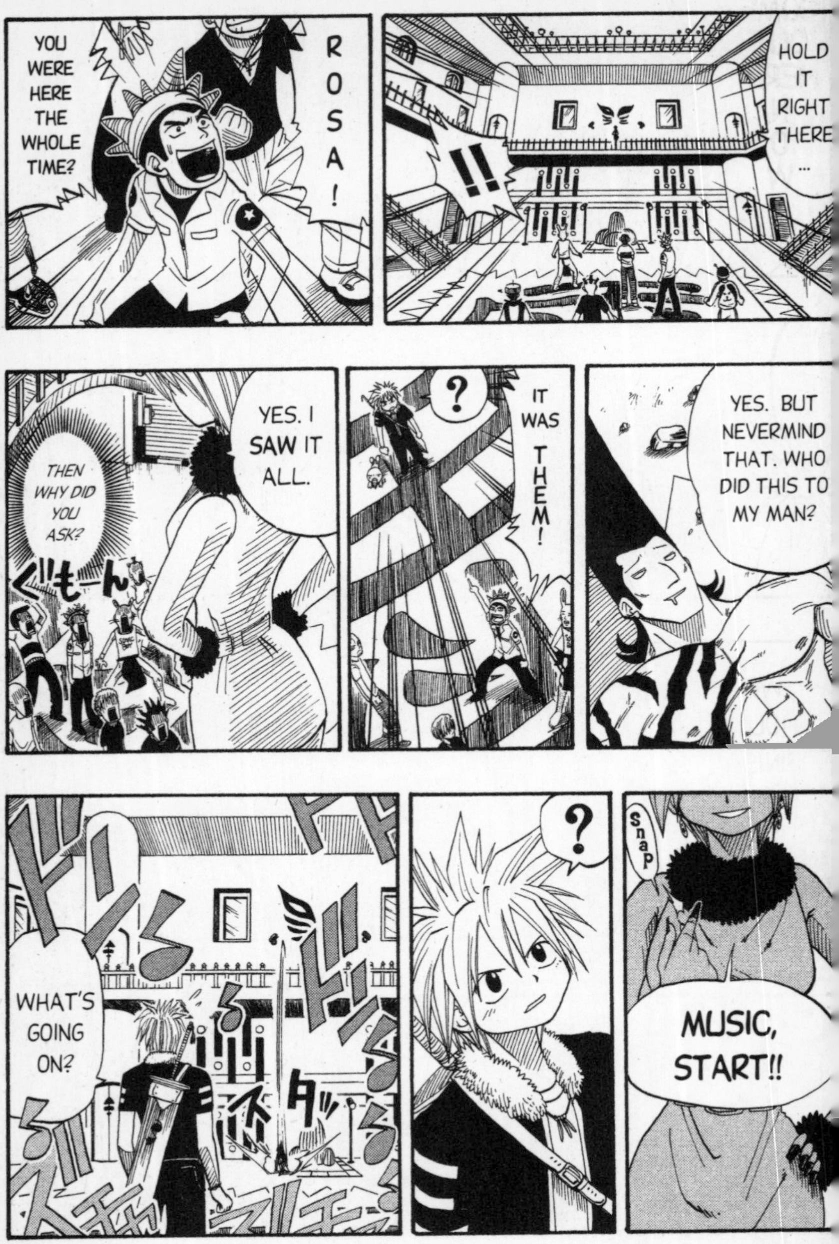

HOLD IT RIGHT THERE ...
!!
ROSA!
YOU WERE HERE THE WHOLE TIME?
YES. BUT NEVERMIND THAT. WHO DID THIS TO MY MAN?
?
IT WAS THEM!
YES. I SAW IT ALL.
THEN WHY DID YOU ASK?
ぐもーん
snap
MUSIC, START!!
?
WHAT'S GOING ON?

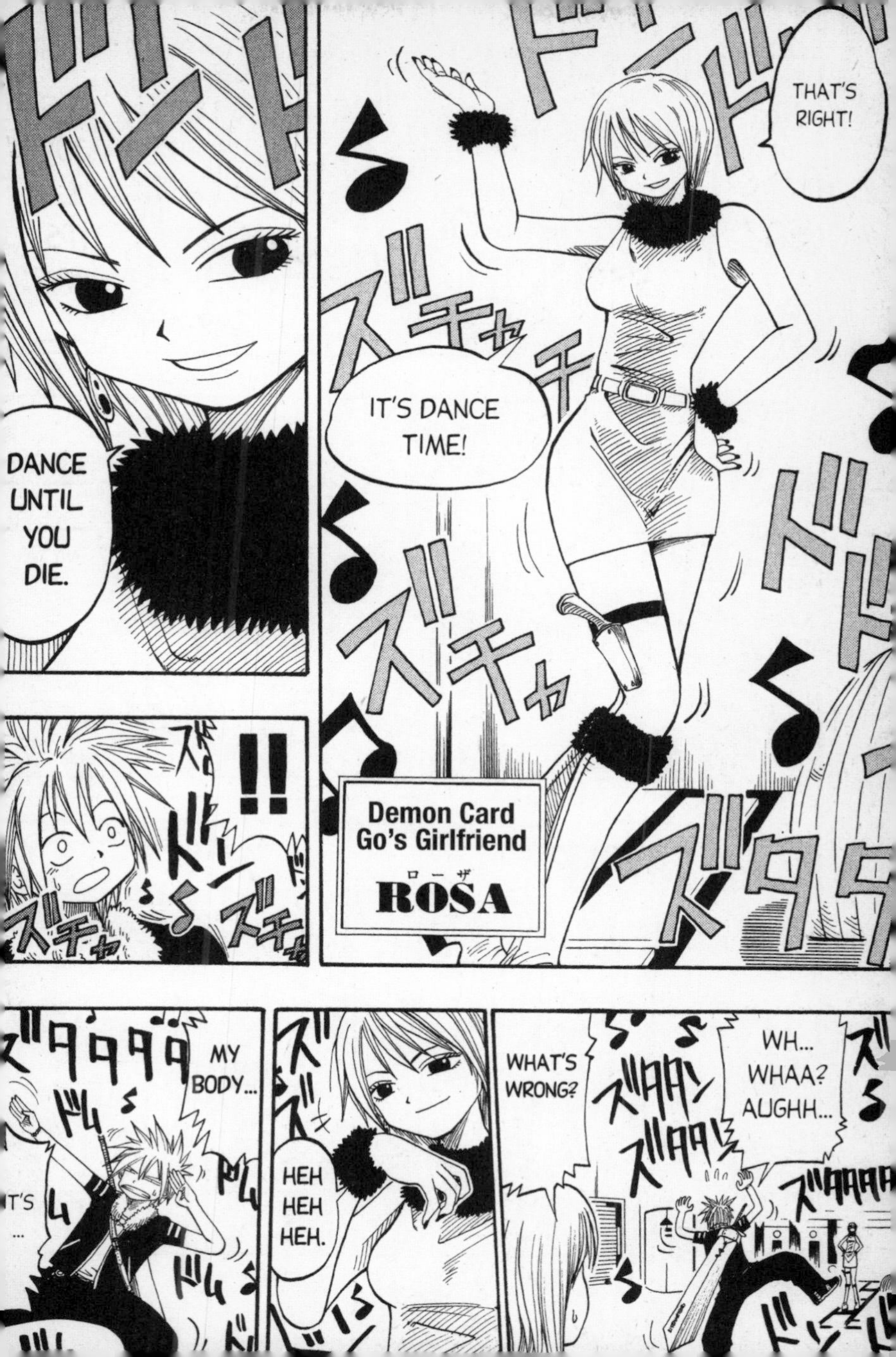
THAT'S RIGHT!
IT'S DANCE TIME!
Demon Card Go's Girlfriend
ローザ
ROSA
DANCE UNTIL YOU DIE.
!!
WH... WHAA? AUGHH...
WHAT'S WRONG?
HEH HEH HEH.
MY BODY...
IT'S ...

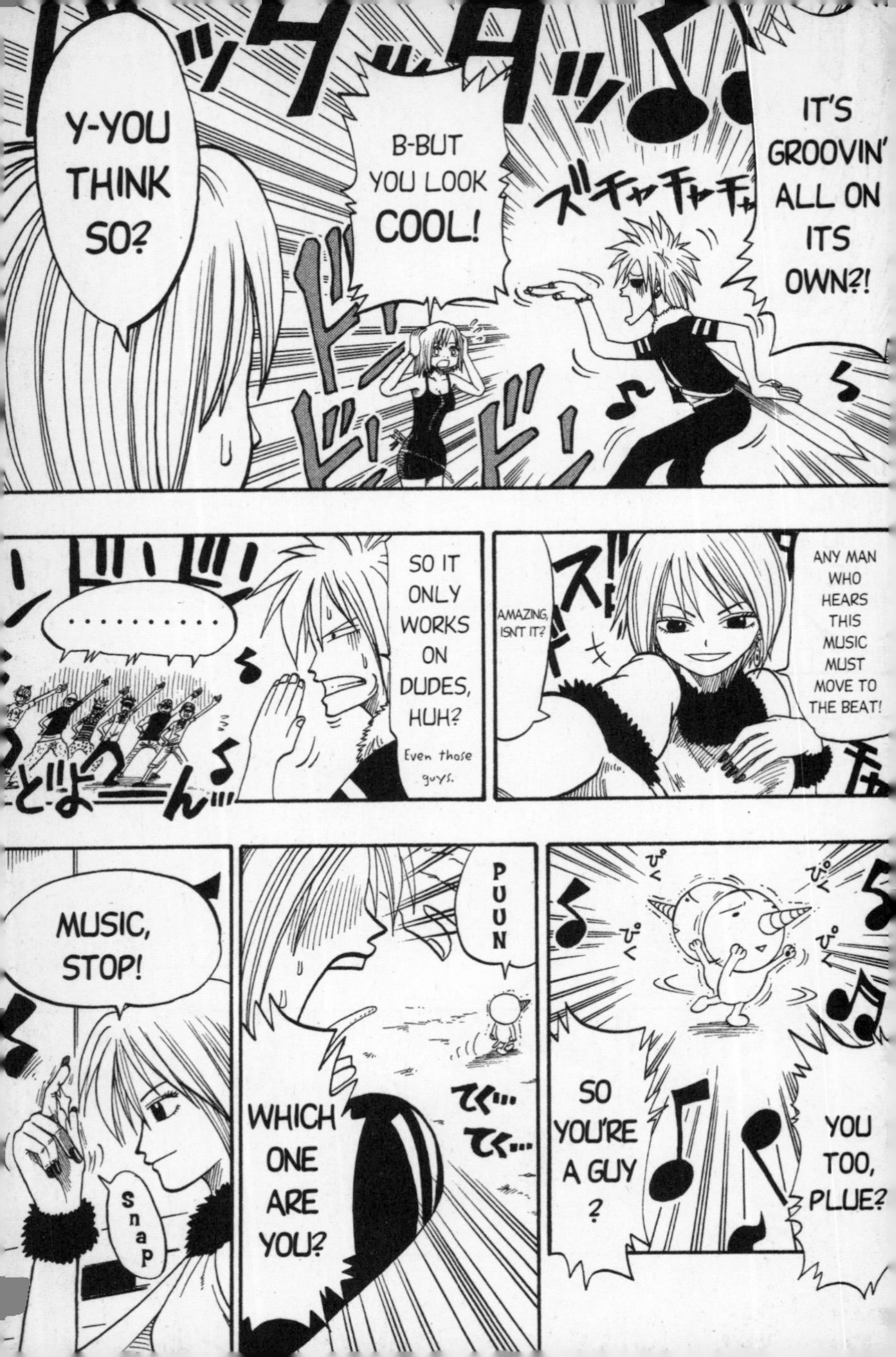
IT'S GROOVIN' ALL ON ITS OWN?!
B-BUT YOU LOOK COOL!
Y-YOU THINK SO?
ANY MAN WHO HEARS THIS MUSIC MUST MOVE TO THE BEAT!
AMAZING, ISN'T IT?
SO IT ONLY WORKS ON DUDES, HUH?
Even those guys.
....
YOU TOO, PLUE?
SO YOU'RE A GUY?
PUUN
WHICH ONE ARE YOU?
MUSIC, STOP!
snap

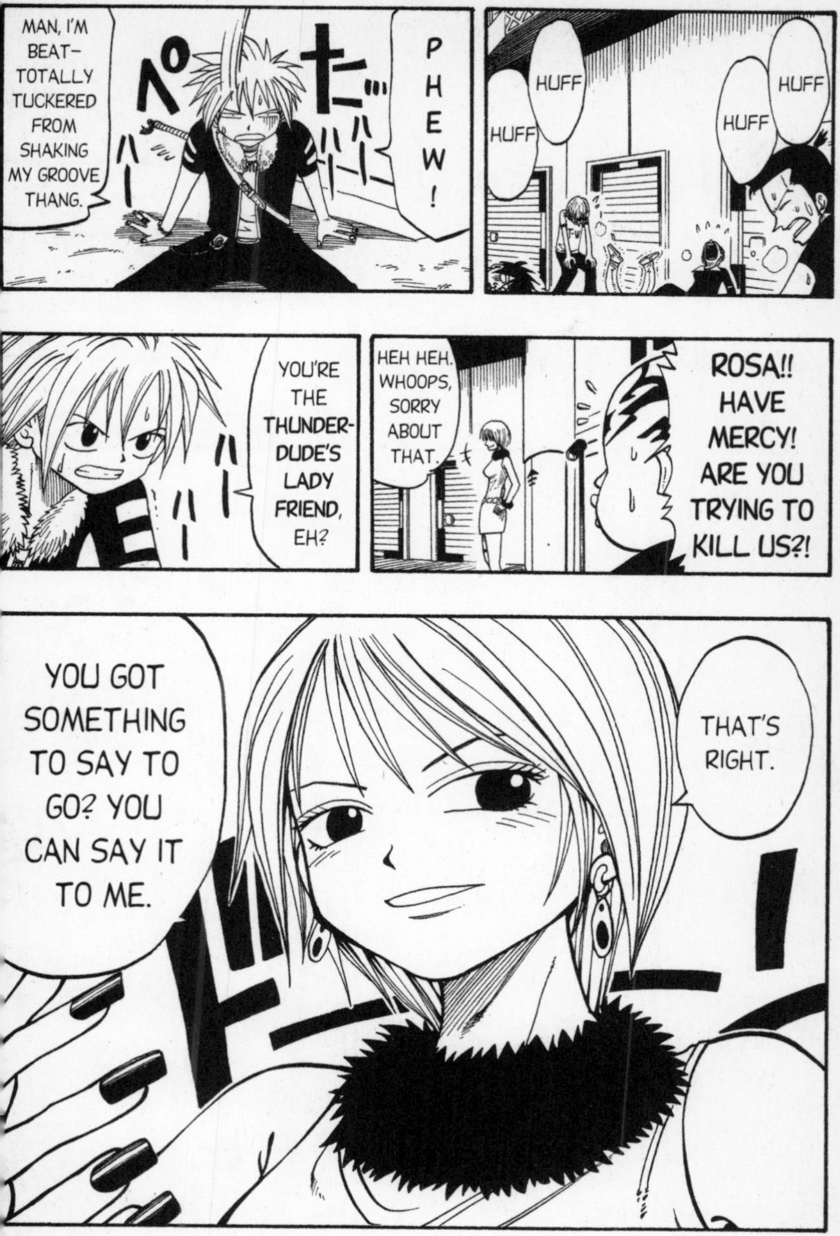
HUFF
HUFF
HUFF
HUFF
PHEW!
MAN, I'M BEAT— TOTALLY TUCKERED FROM SHAKING MY GROOVE THANG.
ROSA!! HAVE MERCY! ARE YOU TRYING TO KILL US?!
HEH HEH. WHOOPS, SORRY ABOUT THAT.
YOU'RE THE THUNDER-DUDE'S LADY FRIEND, EH?
THAT'S RIGHT.
YOU GOT SOMETHING TO SAY TO GO? YOU CAN SAY IT TO ME.

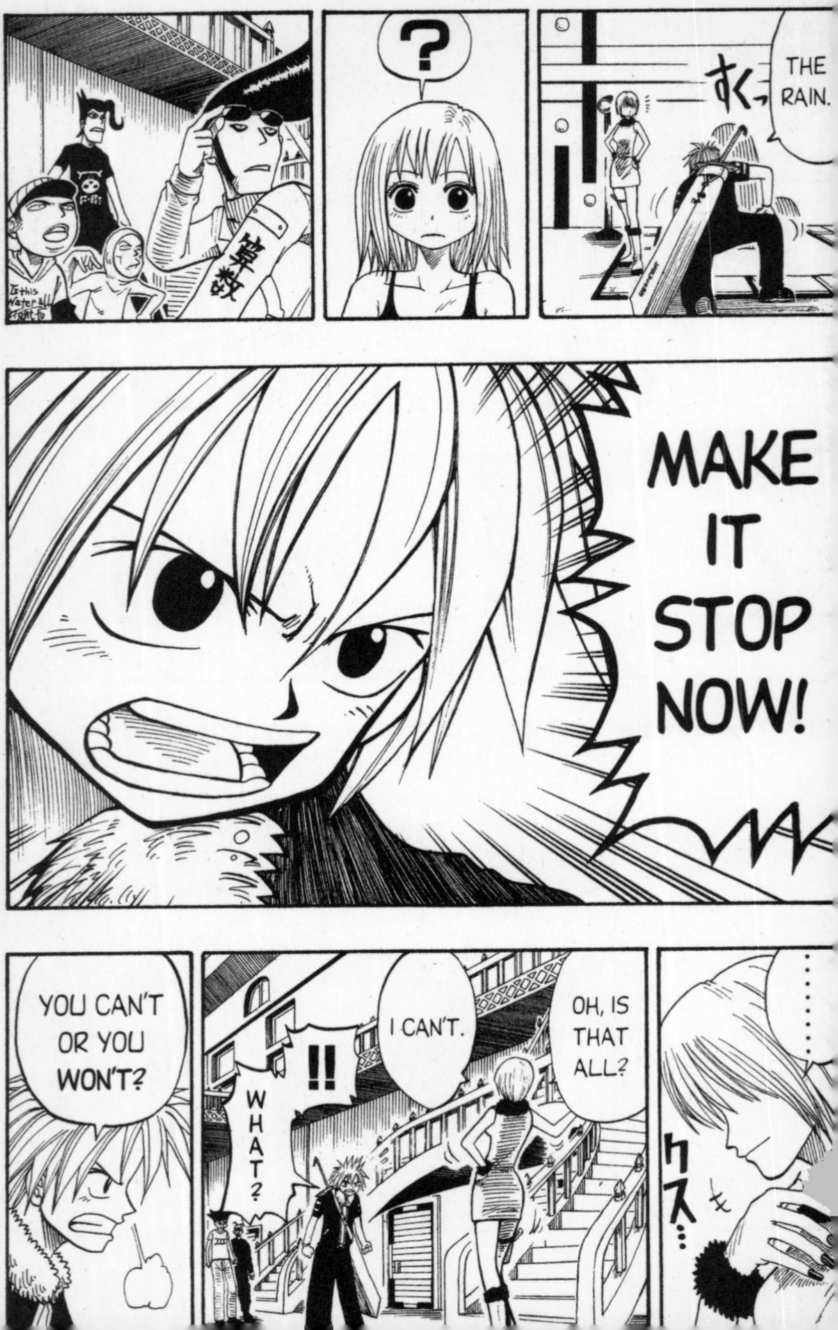
THE RAIN.
すくっ
?
算数
Is this Water all Right to
MAKE IT STOP NOW!
......
クス...
OH, IS THAT ALL?
I CAN'T.
!!
WHAT?
YOU CAN'T OR YOU WON'T?

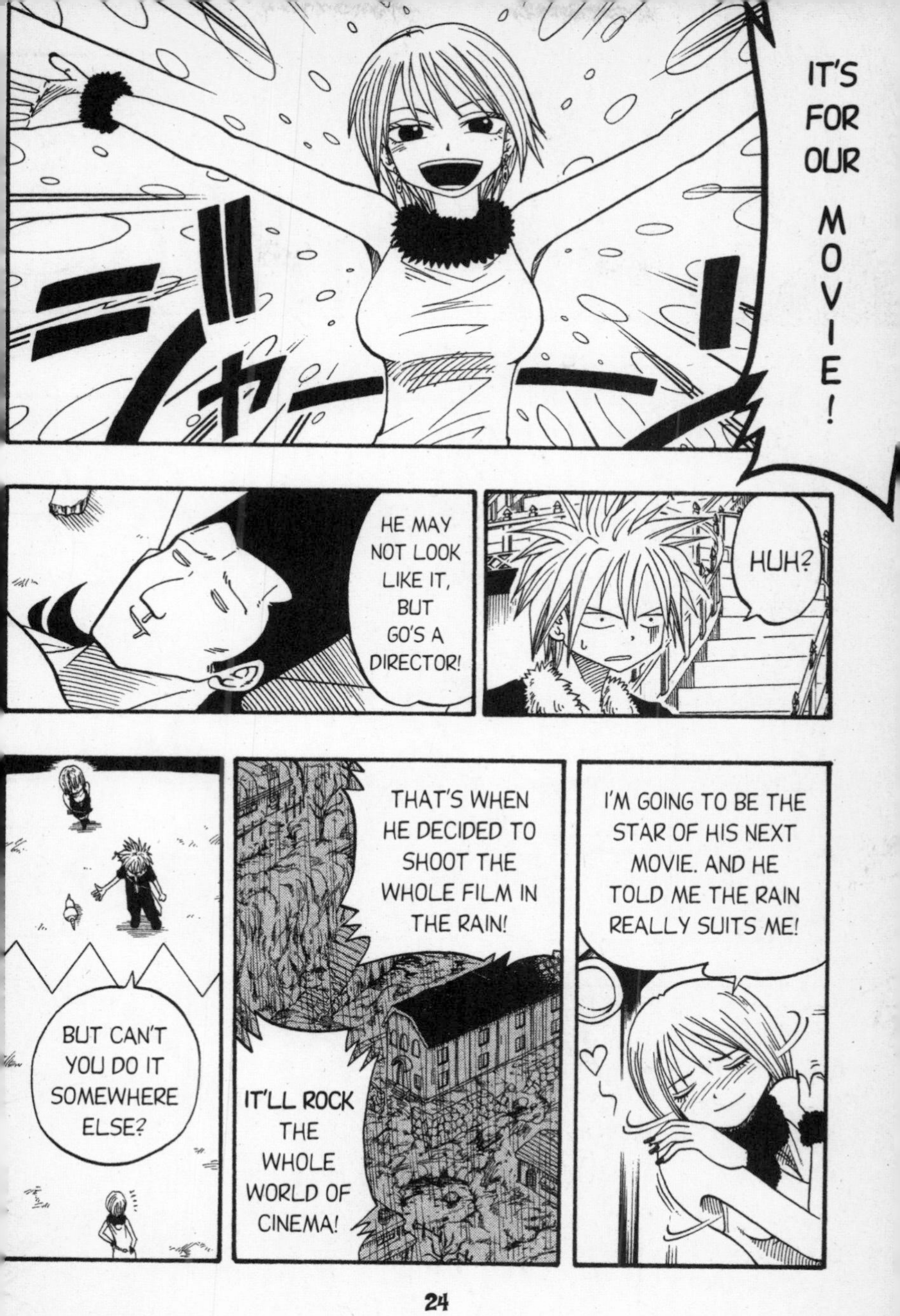
IT'S FOR OUR MOVIE!
HUH?
HE MAY NOT LOOK LIKE IT, BUT GO'S A DIRECTOR!
I'M GOING TO BE THE STAR OF HIS NEXT MOVIE. AND HE TOLD ME THE RAIN REALLY SUITS ME!
THAT'S WHEN HE DECIDED TO SHOOT THE WHOLE FILM IN THE RAIN!
IT'LL ROCK THE WHOLE WORLD OF CINEMA!
BUT CAN'T YOU DO IT SOMEWHERE ELSE?

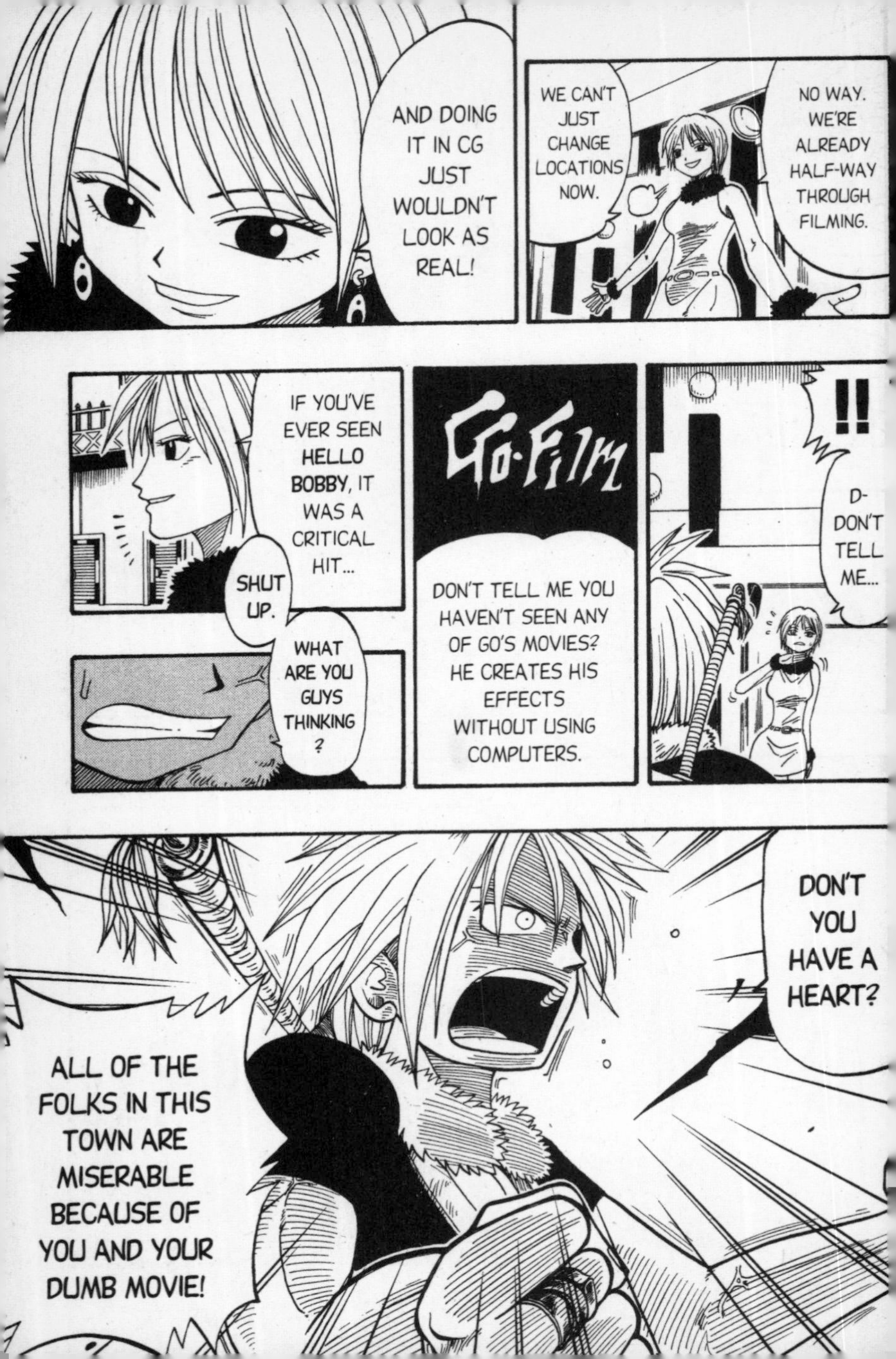
NO WAY. WE'RE ALREADY HALF-WAY THROUGH FILMING.
WE CAN'T JUST CHANGE LOCATIONS NOW.
AND DOING IT IN CG JUST WOULDN'T LOOK AS REAL!
!!
D- DON'T TELL ME...
Go-Film
DON'T TELL ME YOU HAVEN'T SEEN ANY OF GO'S MOVIES? HE CREATES HIS EFFECTS WITHOUT USING COMPUTERS.
IF YOU'VE EVER SEEN HELLO BOBBY, IT WAS A CRITICAL HIT...
SHUT UP.
WHAT ARE YOU GUYS THINKING?
DON'T YOU HAVE A HEART?
ALL OF THE FOLKS IN THIS TOWN ARE MISERABLE BECAUSE OF YOU AND YOUR DUMB MOVIE!

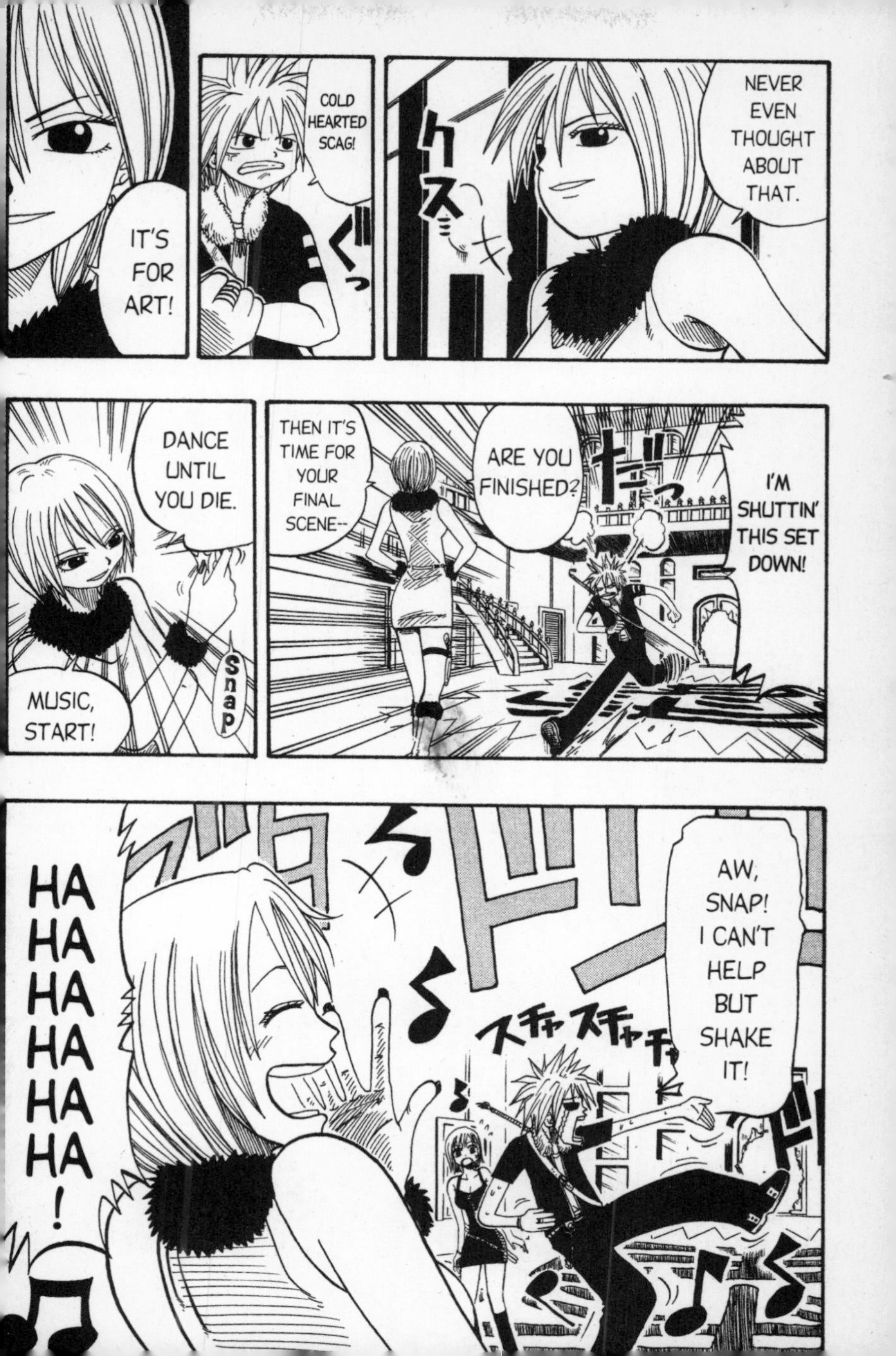

NEVER EVEN THOUGHT ABOUT THAT.
クス
COLD HEARTED SCAG!
ぐっ
IT'S FOR ART!
ARE YOU FINISHED?
ダッ
I'M SHUTTIN' THIS SET DOWN!
THEN IT'S TIME FOR YOUR FINAL SCENE--
DANCE UNTIL YOU DIE.
Snap
MUSIC, START!
AW, SNAP! I CAN'T HELP BUT SHAKE IT!
スチャスチャチャ
HA HA HA HA HA HA HA HA!

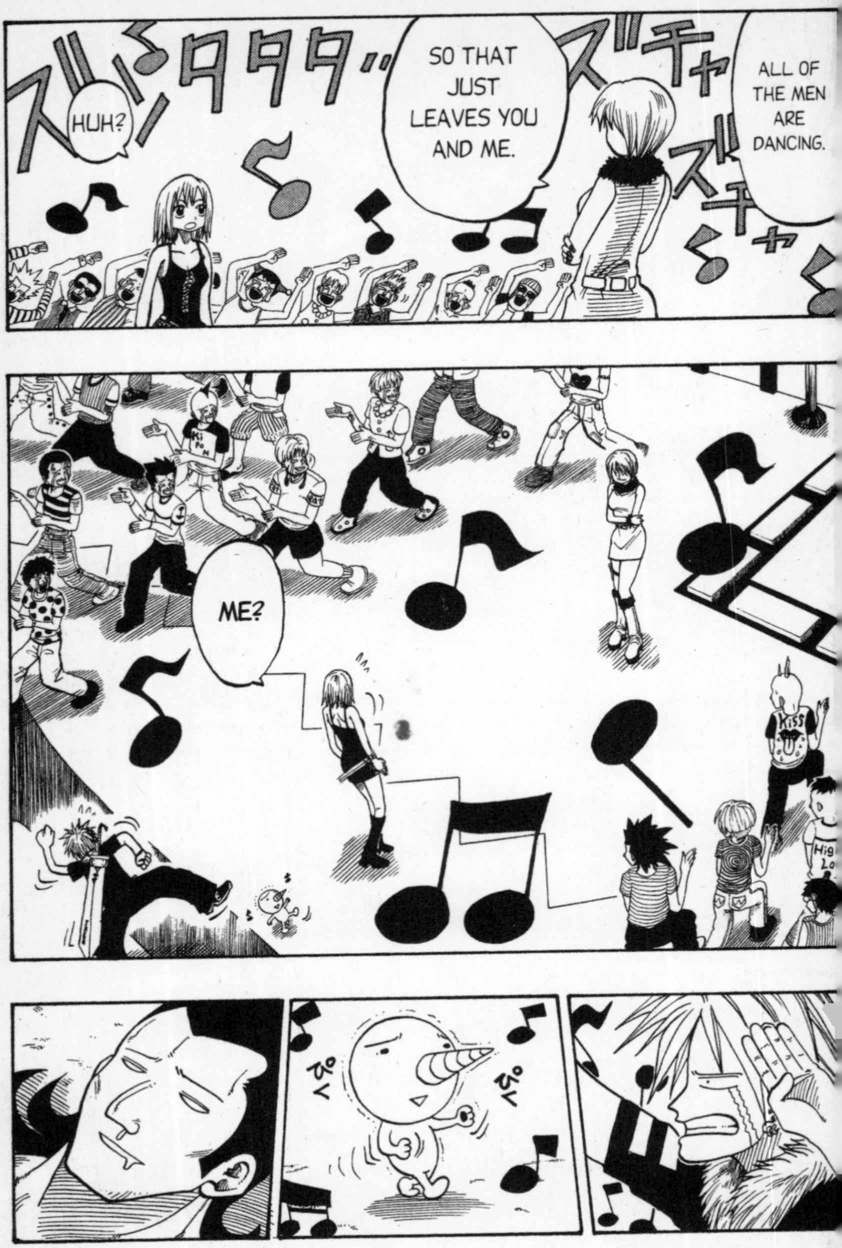
ALL OF THE MEN ARE DANCING.
ズチャ
ズチャ
SO THAT JUST LEAVES YOU AND ME.
ズンタタタ
HUH?
ME?
ぴく
ぴく

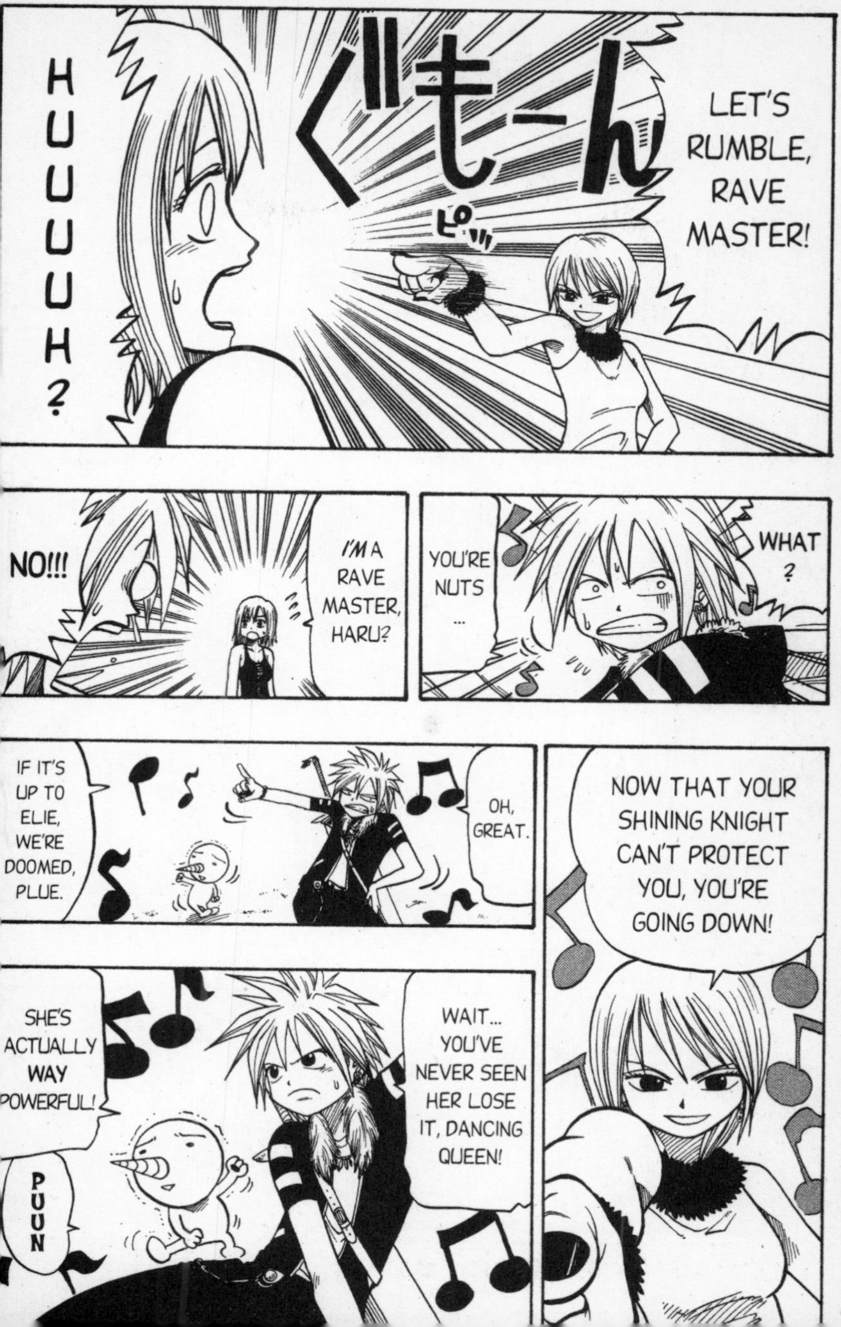

LET'S RUMBLE, RAVE MASTER!
ぐもーん
ピッ
HUUUUUH?
WHAT?
YOU'RE NUTS...
I'M A RAVE MASTER, HARU?
NO!!!
NOW THAT YOUR SHINING KNIGHT CAN'T PROTECT YOU, YOU'RE GOING DOWN!
OH, GREAT.
IF IT'S UP TO ELIE, WE'RE DOOMED, PLUE.
WAIT... YOU'VE NEVER SEEN HER LOSE IT, DANCING QUEEN!
SHE'S ACTUALLY WAY POWERFUL!
PUUN

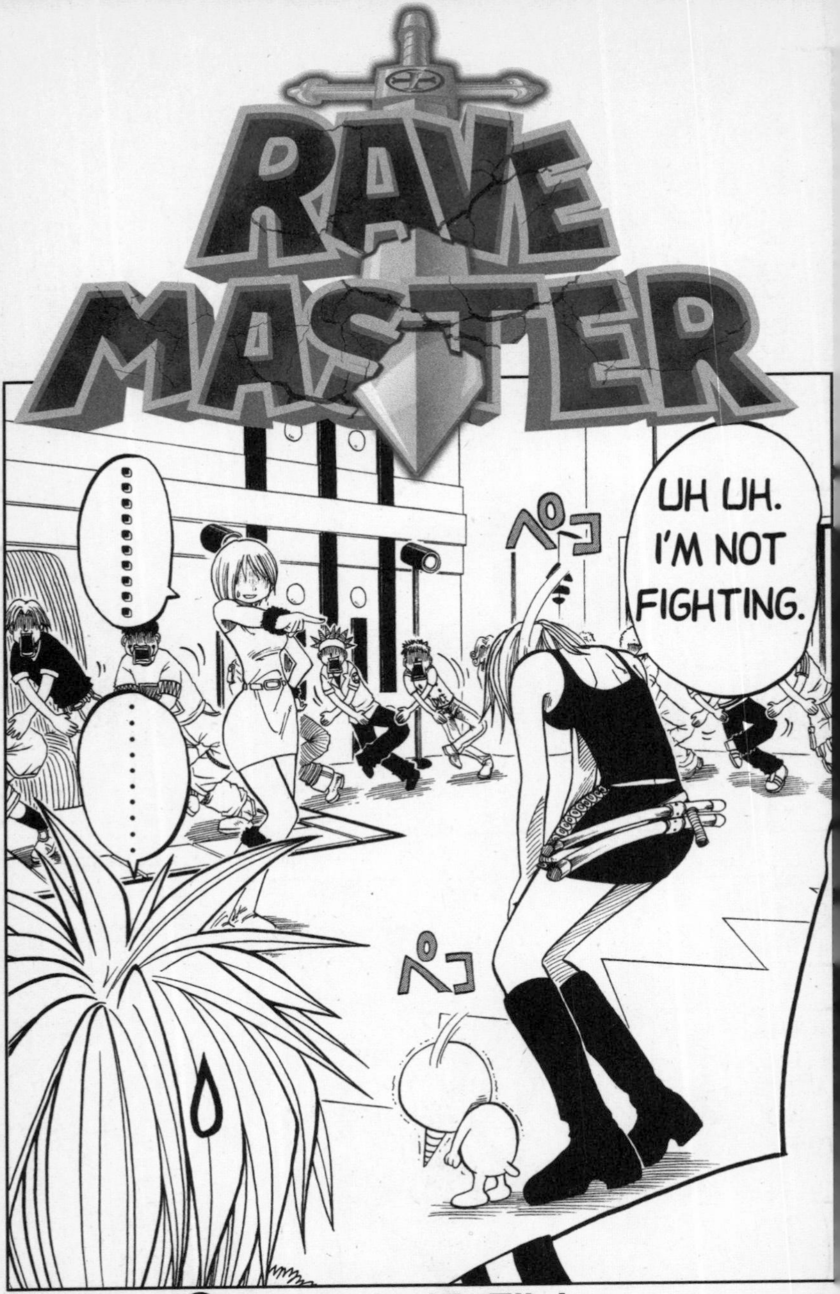
RAVE MASTER
ペコ
UH UH. I'M NOT FIGHTING.
ペコ

RAVE:23 ✥ **Boppin' with Elie!**

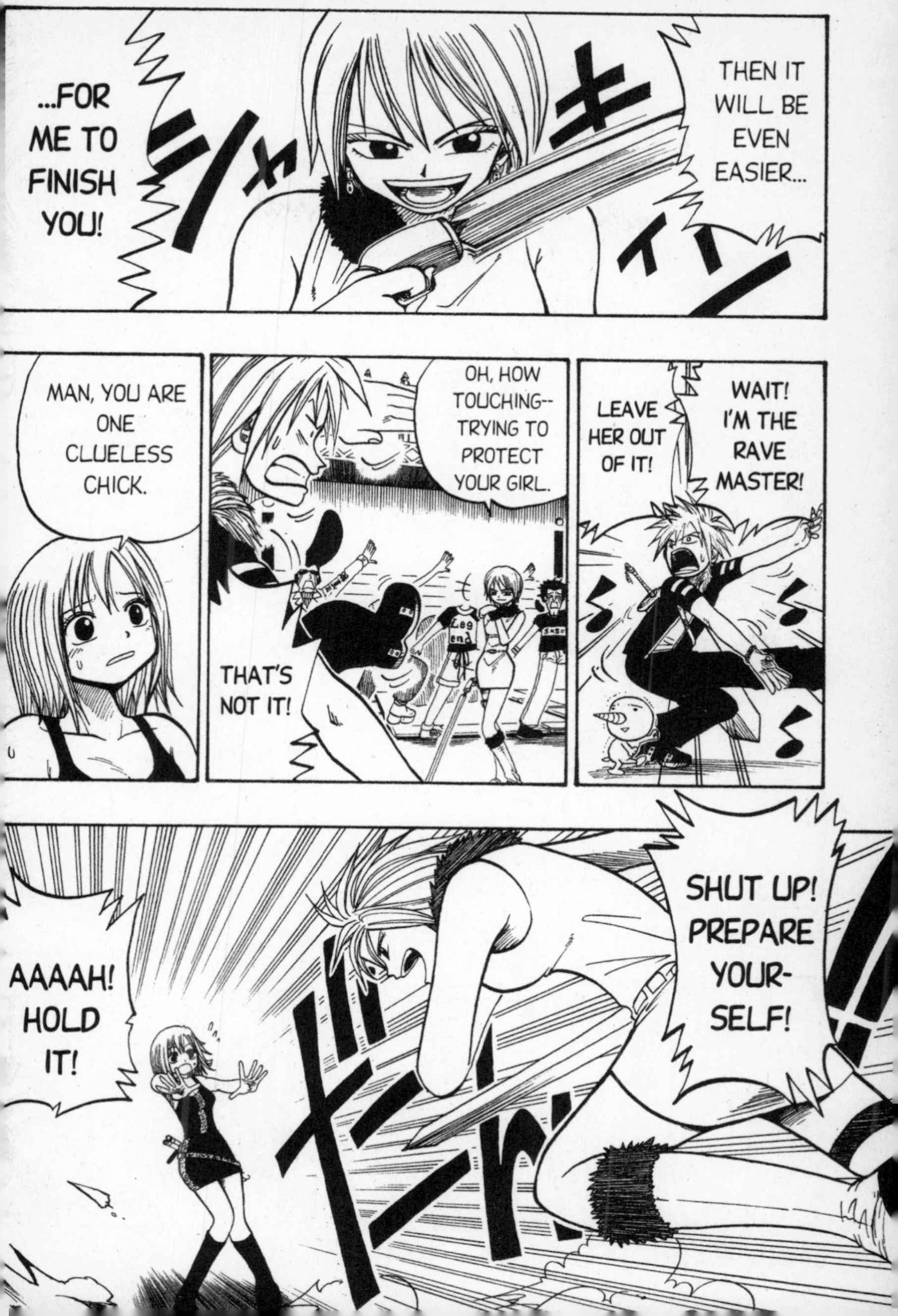
THEN IT WILL BE EVEN EASIER...
...FOR ME TO FINISH YOU!
シャキィン
WAIT! I'M THE RAVE MASTER!
LEAVE HER OUT OF IT!
OH, HOW TOUCHING-- TRYING TO PROTECT YOUR GIRL.
THAT'S NOT IT!
MAN, YOU ARE ONE CLUELESS CHICK.
SHUT UP! PREPARE YOUR-SELF!
AAAAH! HOLD IT!

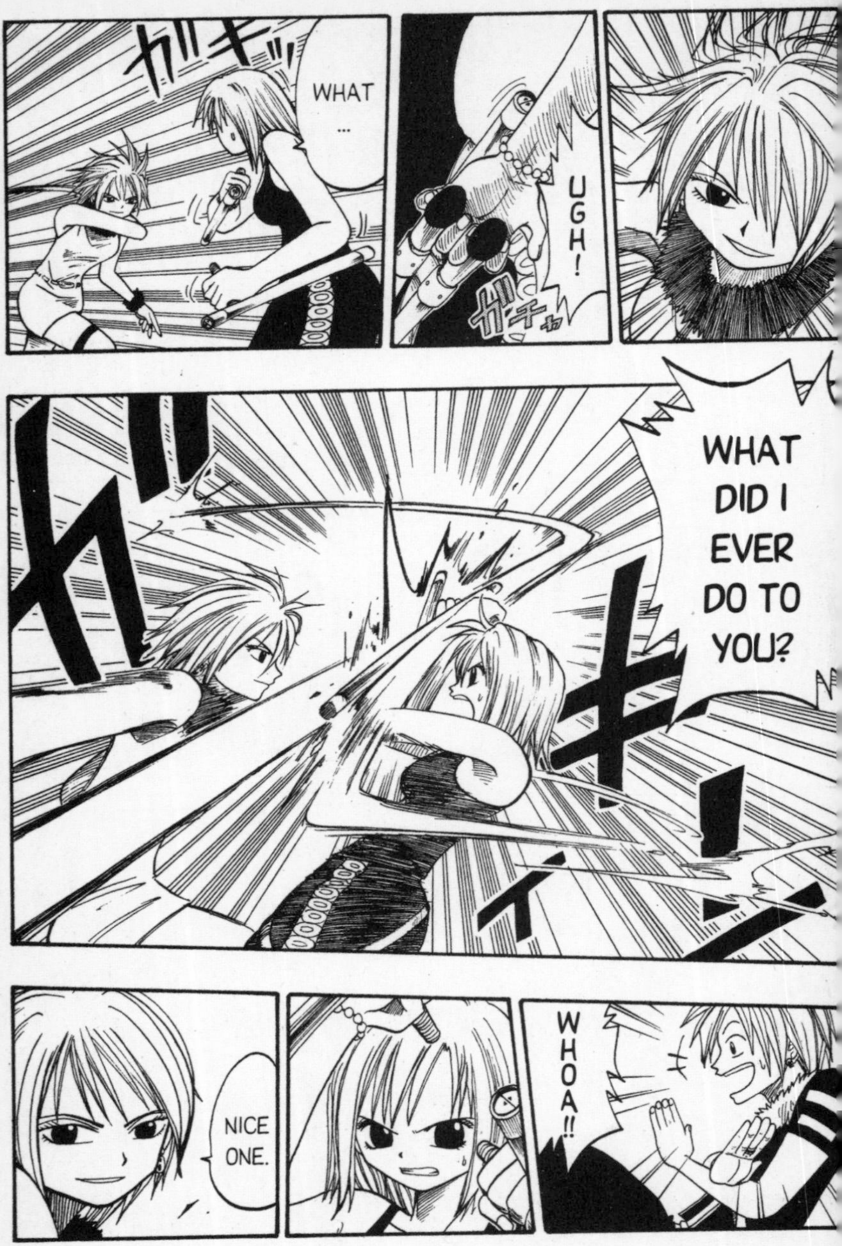
UGH!
WHAT ...
WHAT DID I EVER DO TO YOU?
WHOA!!
NICE ONE.

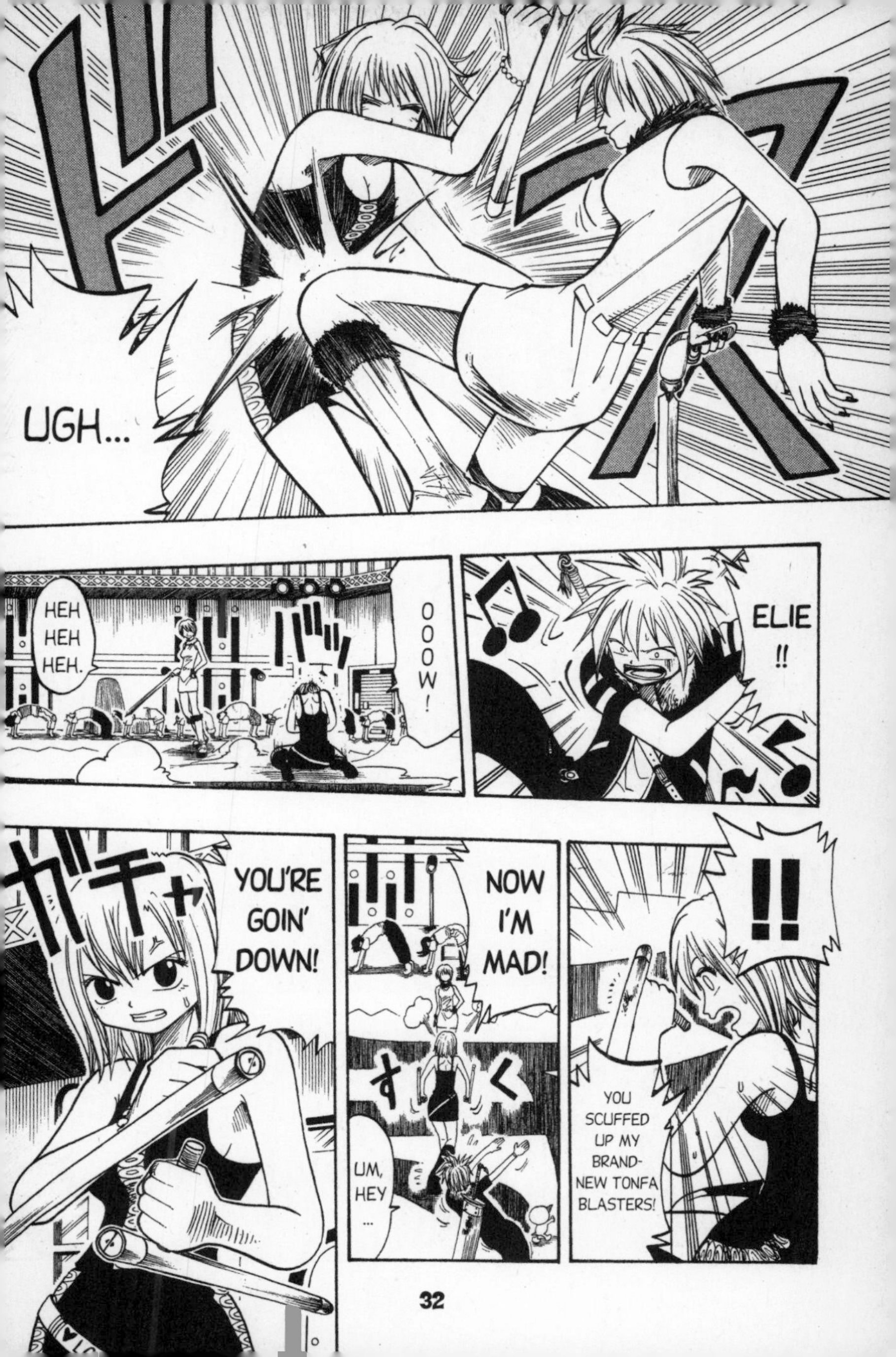
UGH...
ELIE !!
OOOW!
HEH HEH HEH.
!!
YOU SCUFFED UP MY BRAND-NEW TONFA BLASTERS!
NOW I'M MAD!
UM, HEY ...
YOU'RE GOIN' DOWN!

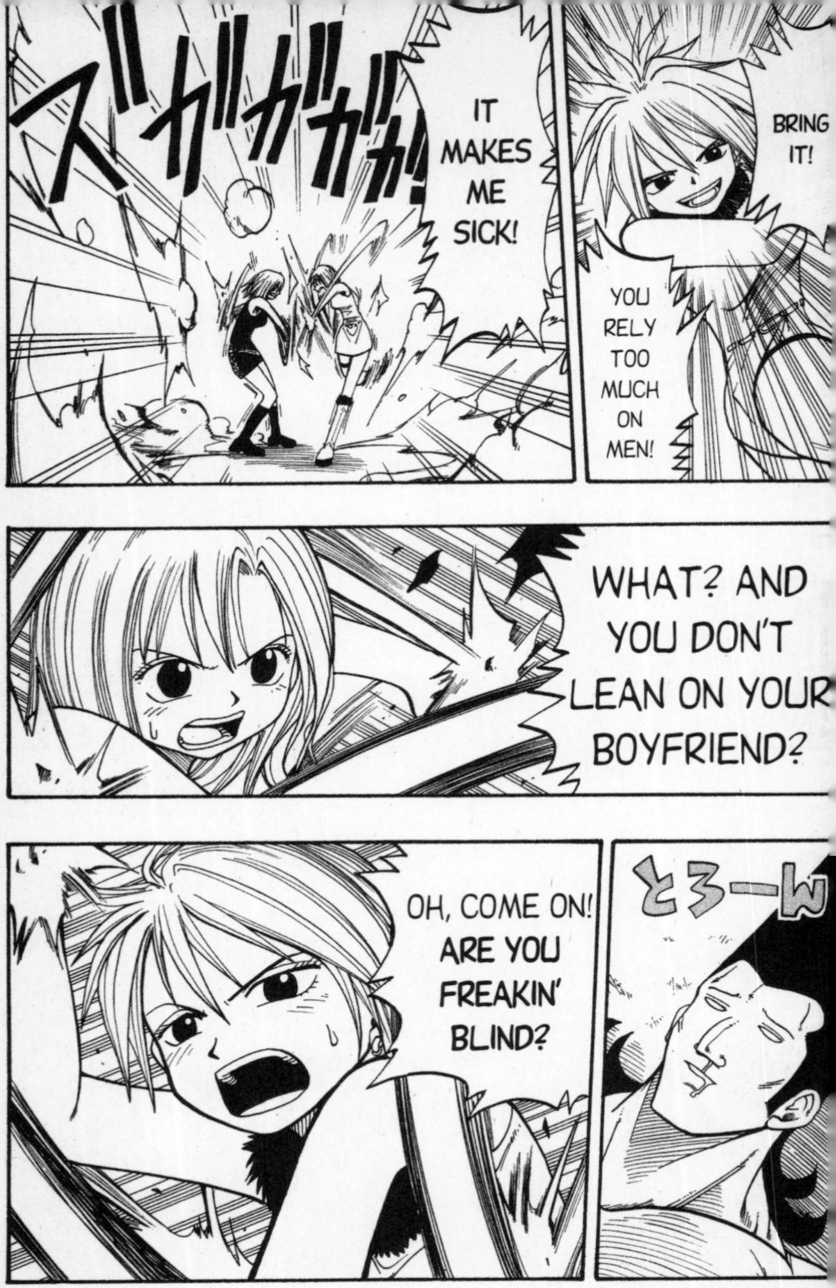
BRING IT!
YOU RELY TOO MUCH ON MEN!
ズガガガガ!!
IT MAKES ME SICK!
WHAT? AND YOU DON'T LEAN ON YOUR BOYFRIEND?
とろーん
OH, COME ON! ARE YOU FREAKIN' BLIND?

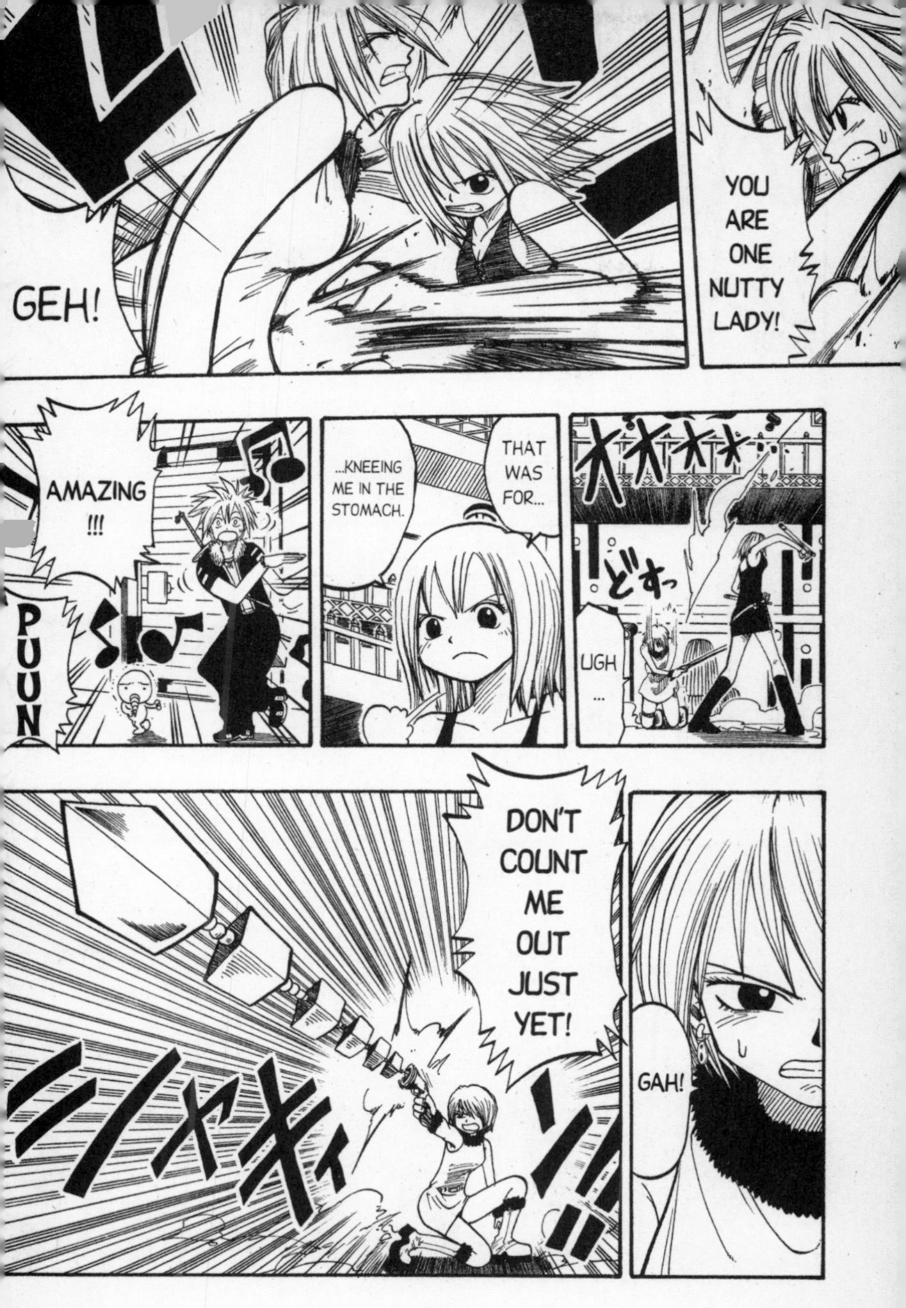
YOU ARE ONE NUTTY LADY!
GEH!
どすっ
UGH ...
THAT WAS FOR...
...KNEEING ME IN THE STOMACH.
AMAZING !!!
PUUN
GAH!
DON'T COUNT ME OUT JUST YET!

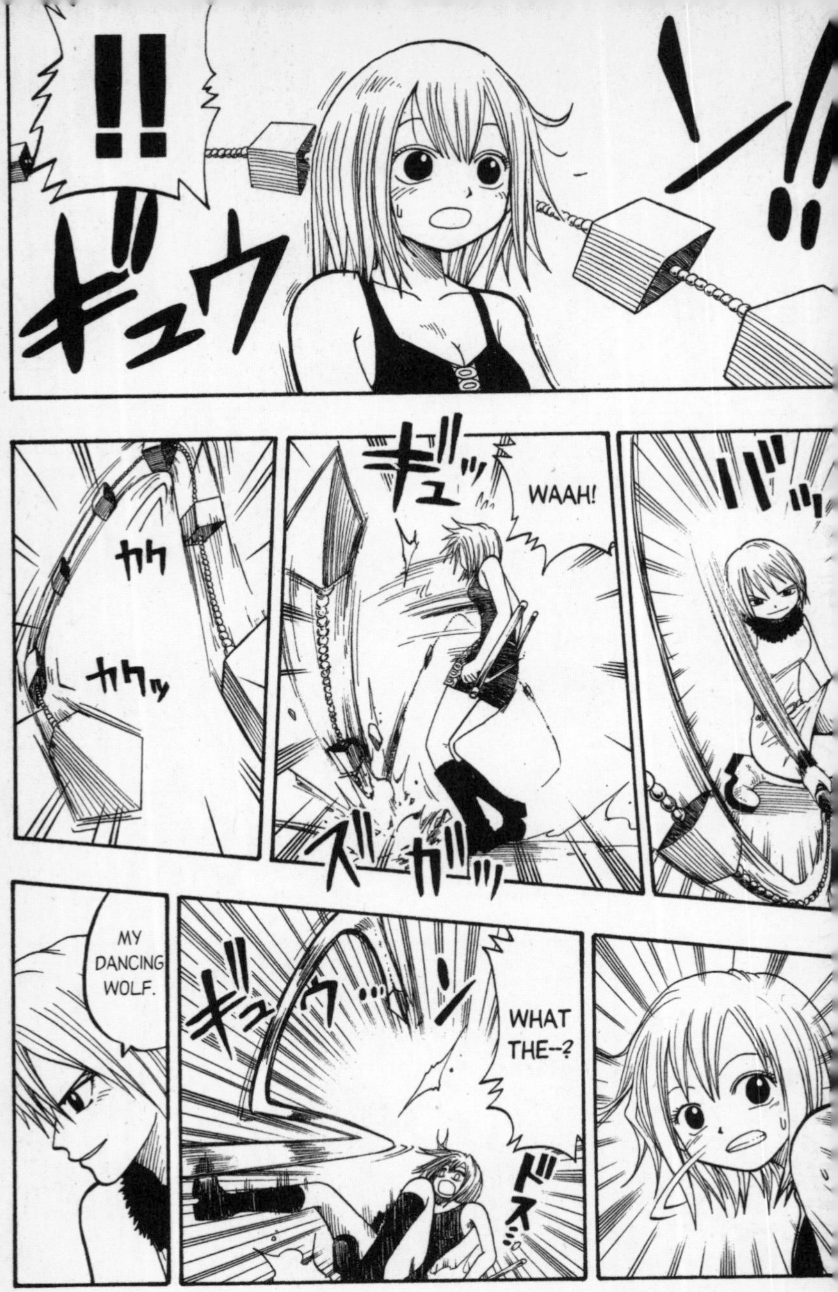

!!
ギュウ
バッ
ギュッ
WAAH!
ズガッ
カク
カクッ
ギュウ…
WHAT THE--?
ドス…
MY DANCING WOLF.

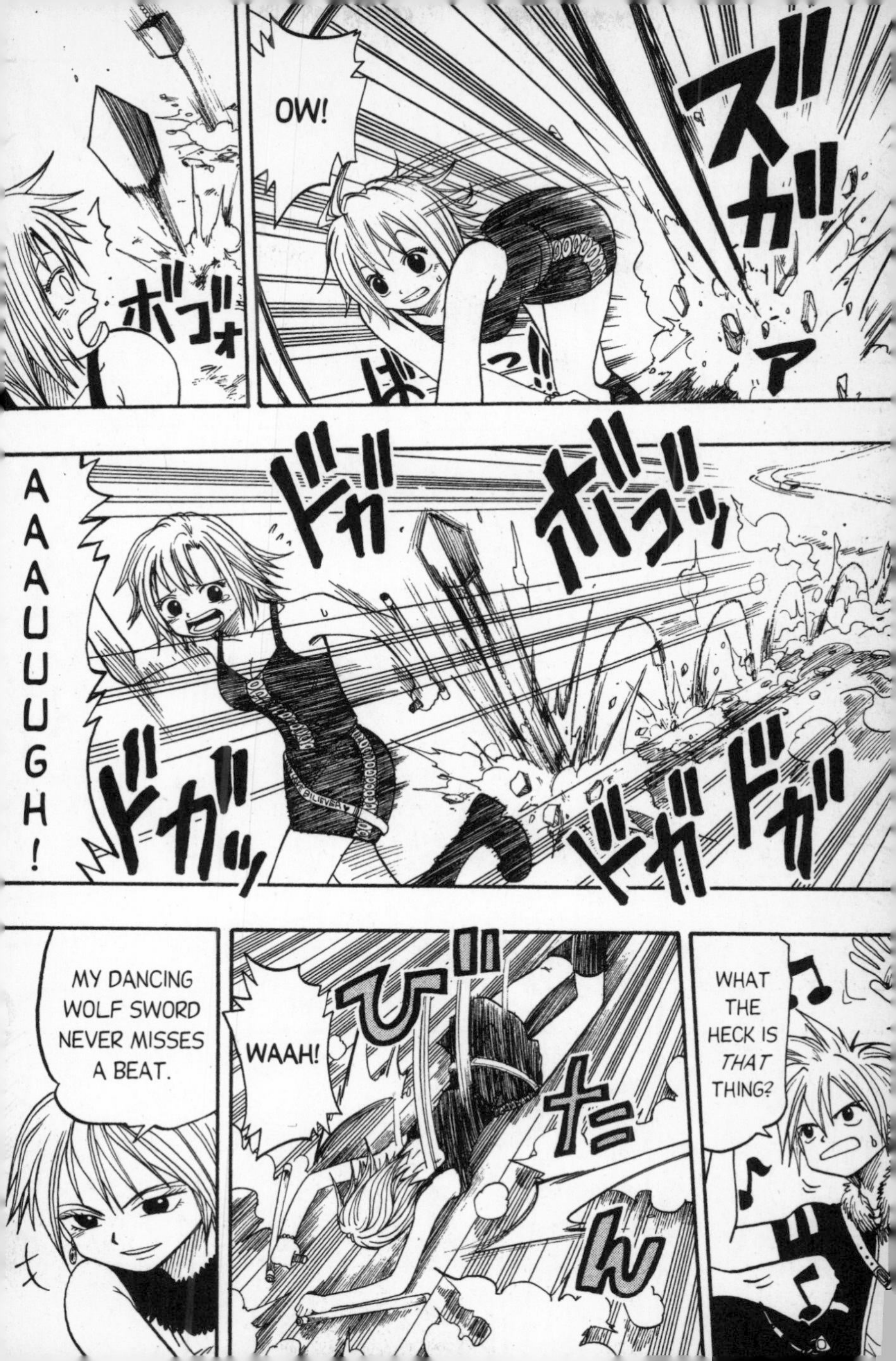

ズガガァ
OW!
ボゴォ
AAAUUUGH!
ボゴッ
ドガ
ドガドガ
ドガッ
WHAT THE HECK IS *THAT* THING?
WAAH!
MY DANCING WOLF SWORD NEVER MISSES A BEAT.

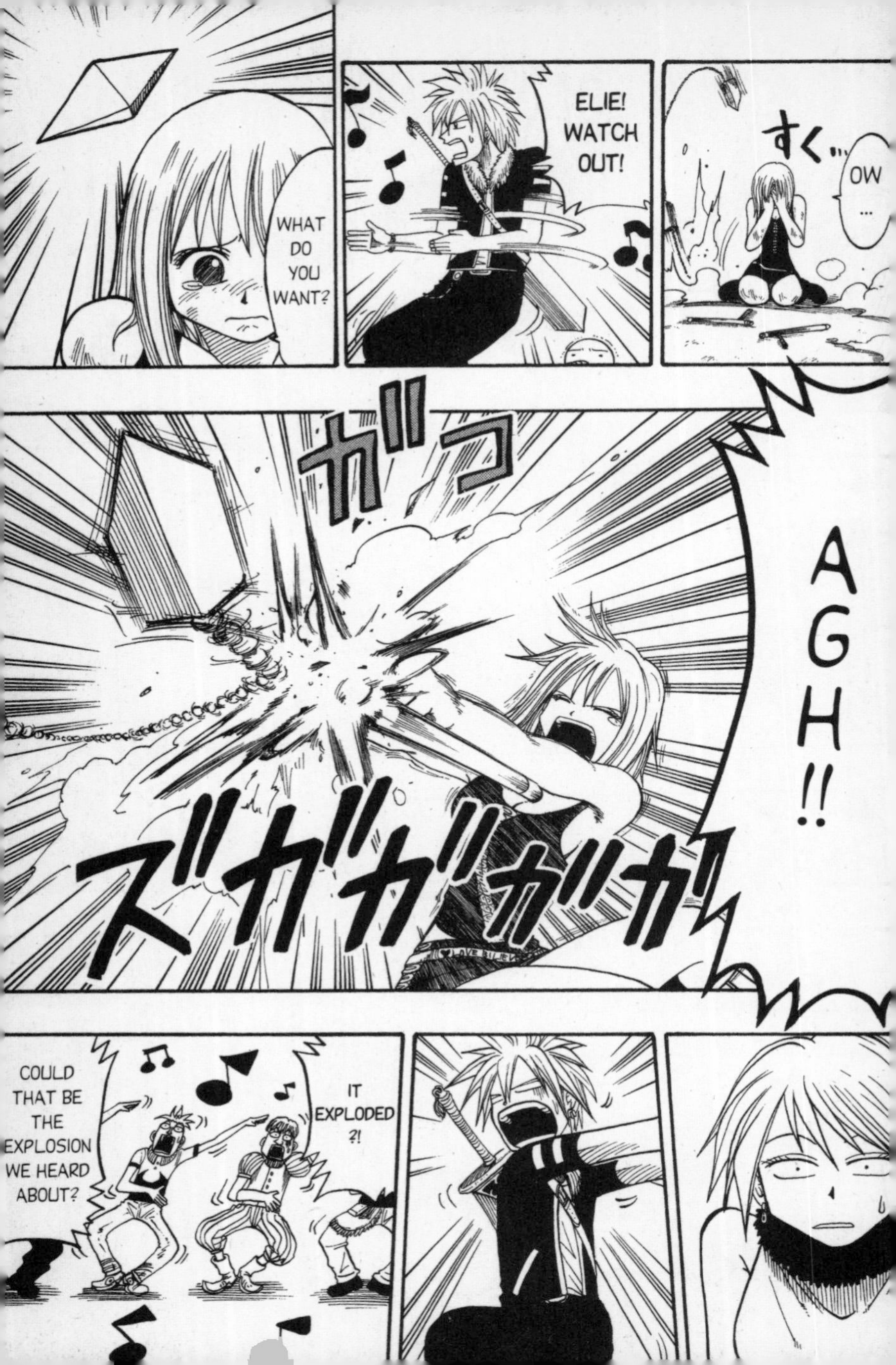
すく…
OW ...
ELIE! WATCH OUT!
WHAT DO YOU WANT?
ガッ
AGH!!
ズガガガッガ
IT EXPLODED ?!
COULD THAT BE THE EXPLOSION WE HEARD ABOUT?

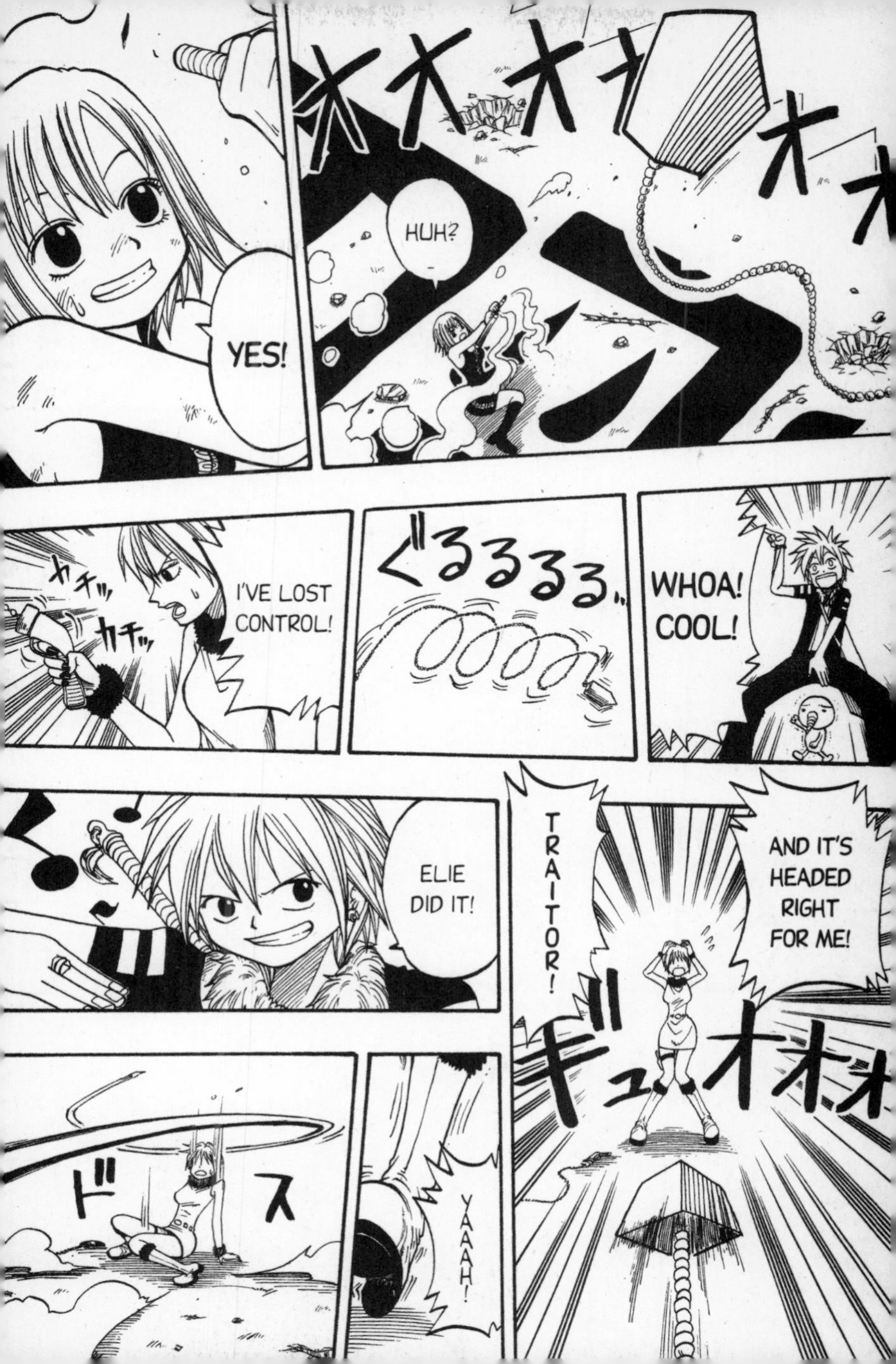

HUH?
オオオオオ
YES!
WHOA! COOL!
ぐるるるる
I'VE LOST CONTROL!
カチッ
カチッ
AND IT'S HEADED RIGHT FOR ME!
TRAITOR!
ギュオオオ
ELIE DID IT!
YAAAH!
ドス

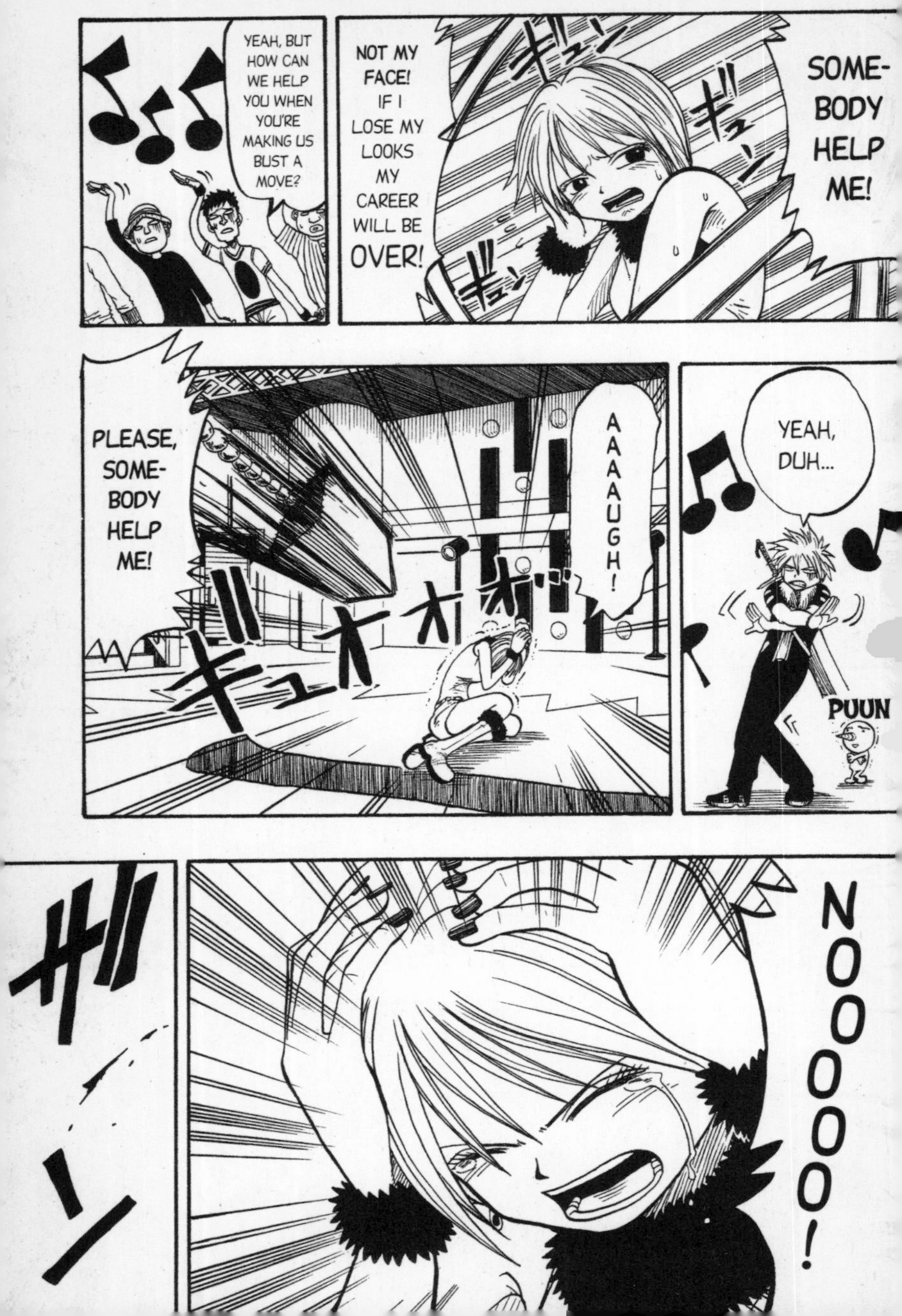
SOME-BODY HELP ME!
NOT MY FACE! IF I LOSE MY LOOKS MY CAREER WILL BE OVER!
YEAH, BUT HOW CAN WE HELP YOU WHEN YOU'RE MAKING US BUST A MOVE?
YEAH, DUH...
PUUN
AAAAAUGH!
PLEASE, SOME-BODY HELP ME!
NOOOOOO!

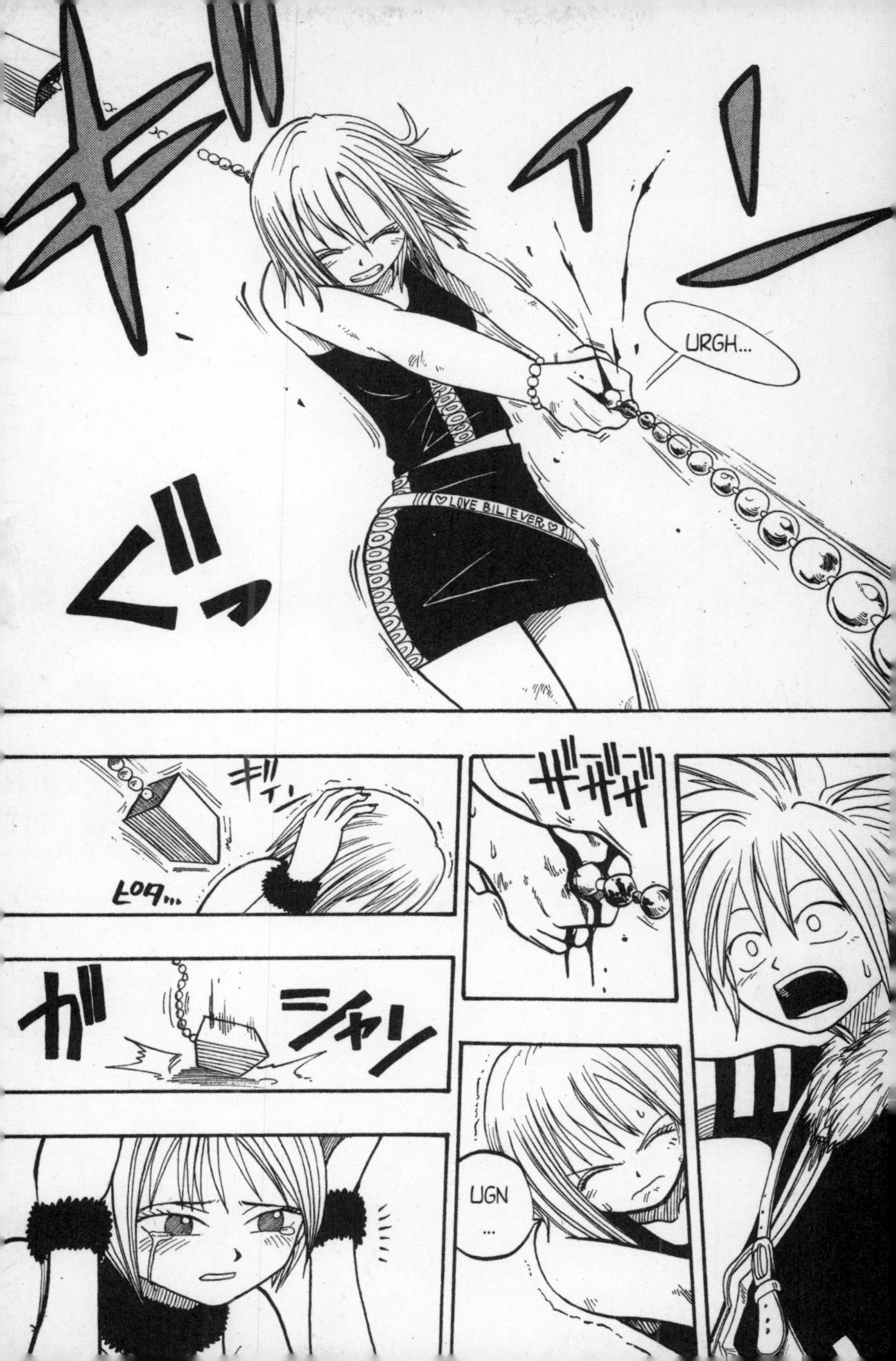
URGH...
ズイン
LOVE BILIEVER
ぐっ
ザザザ
ギィン
ヒクッ...
ガシャン
UGN
...

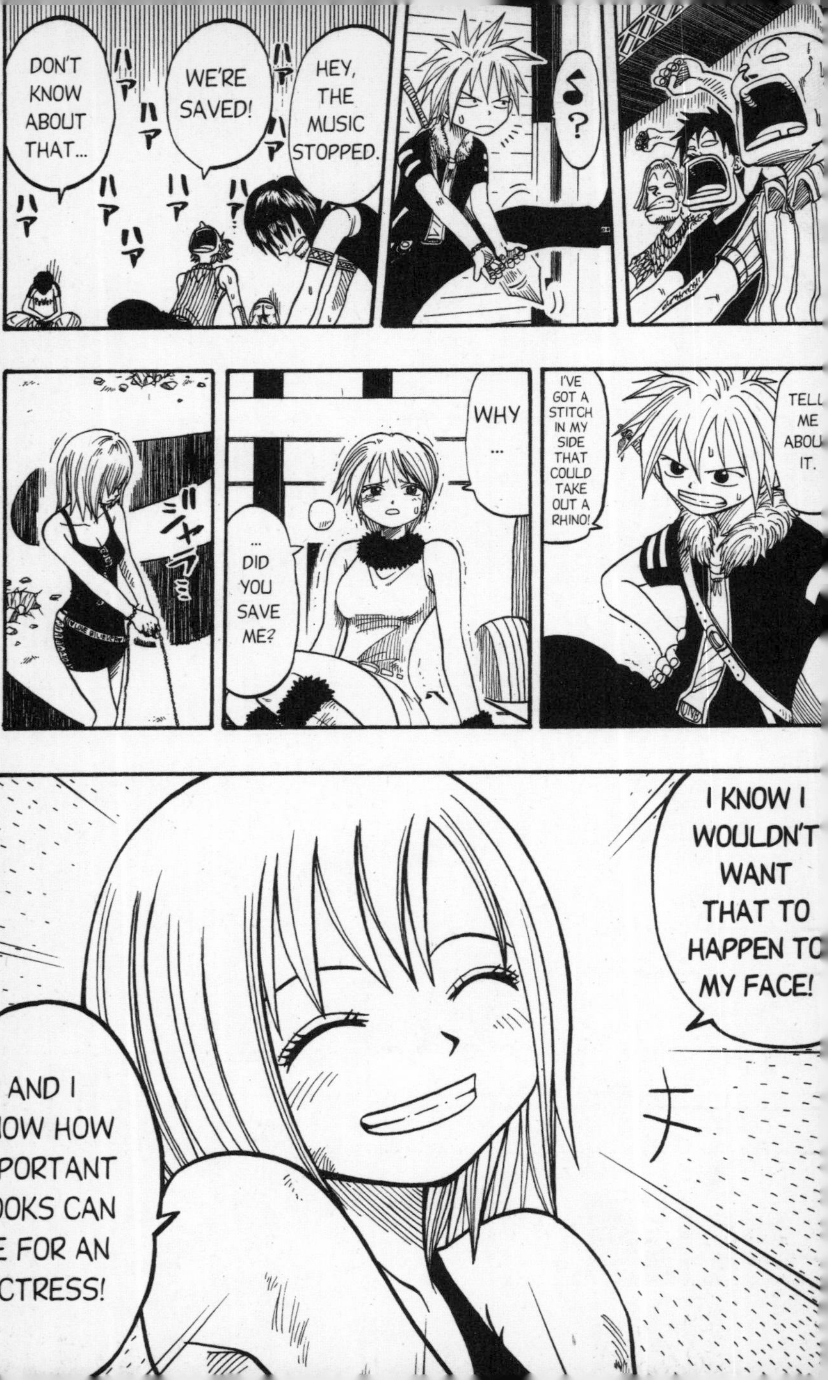
?
HEY, THE MUSIC STOPPED.
WE'RE SAVED!
DON'T KNOW ABOUT THAT...
TELL ME ABOU IT.
I'VE GOT A STITCH IN MY SIDE THAT COULD TAKE OUT A RHINO!
WHY ...
... DID YOU SAVE ME?
I KNOW I WOULDN'T WANT THAT TO HAPPEN TO MY FACE!
AND I KNOW HOW IMPORTANT LOOKS CAN BE FOR AN ACTRESS!

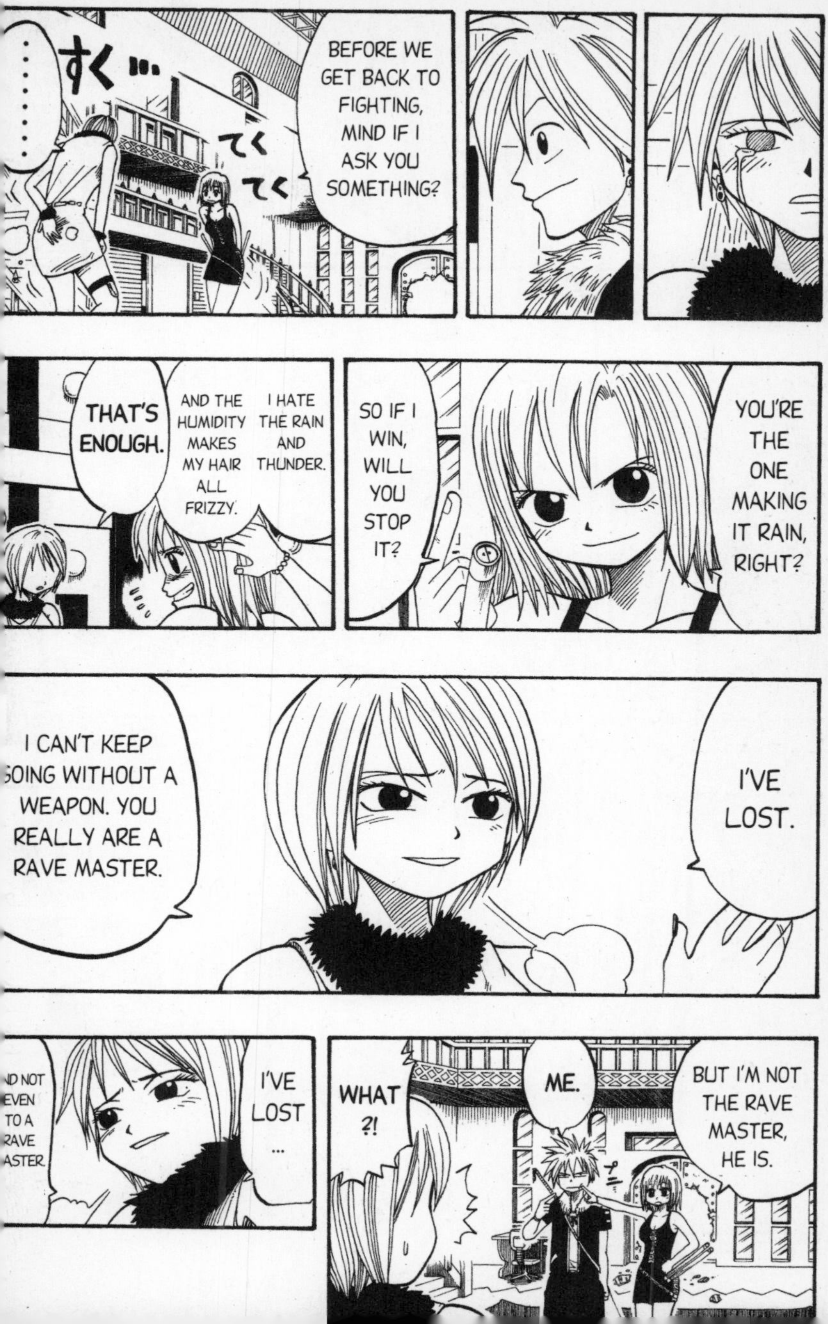

BEFORE WE GET BACK TO FIGHTING, MIND IF I ASK YOU SOMETHING?
てく てく
すく
......
YOU'RE THE ONE MAKING IT RAIN, RIGHT?
SO IF I WIN, WILL YOU STOP IT?
I HATE THE RAIN AND THUNDER.
AND THE HUMIDITY MAKES MY HAIR ALL FRIZZY.
THAT'S ENOUGH.
I'VE LOST.
I CAN'T KEEP GOING WITHOUT A WEAPON. YOU REALLY ARE A RAVE MASTER.
BUT I'M NOT THE RAVE MASTER, HE IS.
ME.
WHAT ?!
I'VE LOST ...
ND NOT EVEN TO A RAVE ASTER.

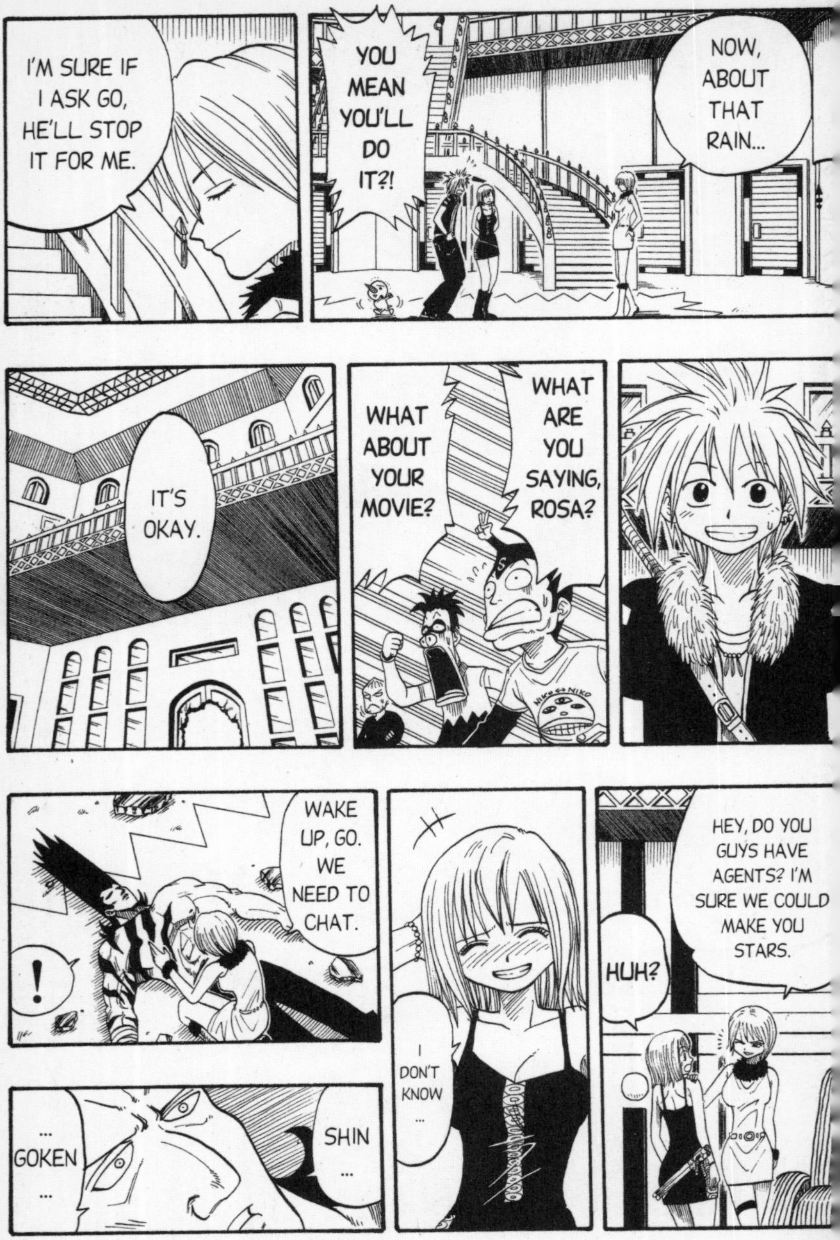
NOW, ABOUT THAT RAIN...
YOU MEAN YOU'LL DO IT?!
I'M SURE IF I ASK GO, HE'LL STOP IT FOR ME.
WHAT ARE YOU SAYING, ROSA?
WHAT ABOUT YOUR MOVIE?
NIKO NIKO
IT'S OKAY.
HEY, DO YOU GUYS HAVE AGENTS? I'M SURE WE COULD MAKE YOU STARS.
HUH?
I DON'T KNOW ...
WAKE UP, GO. WE NEED TO CHAT.
!
SHIN ...
... GOKEN ...

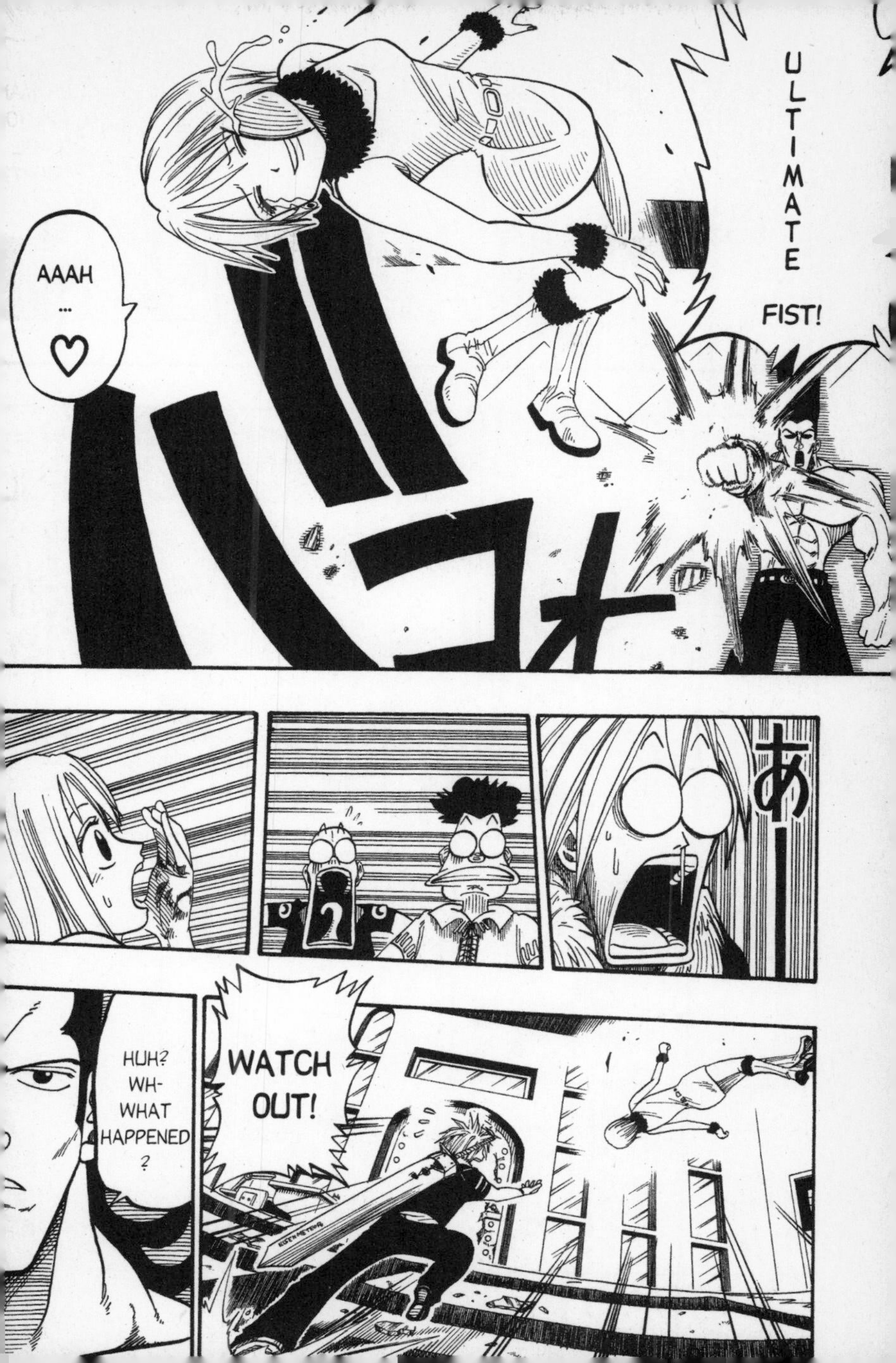
ULTIMATE
FIST!
AAAH ... ♡
あー
WATCH OUT!
HUH? WH-WHAT HAPPENED?

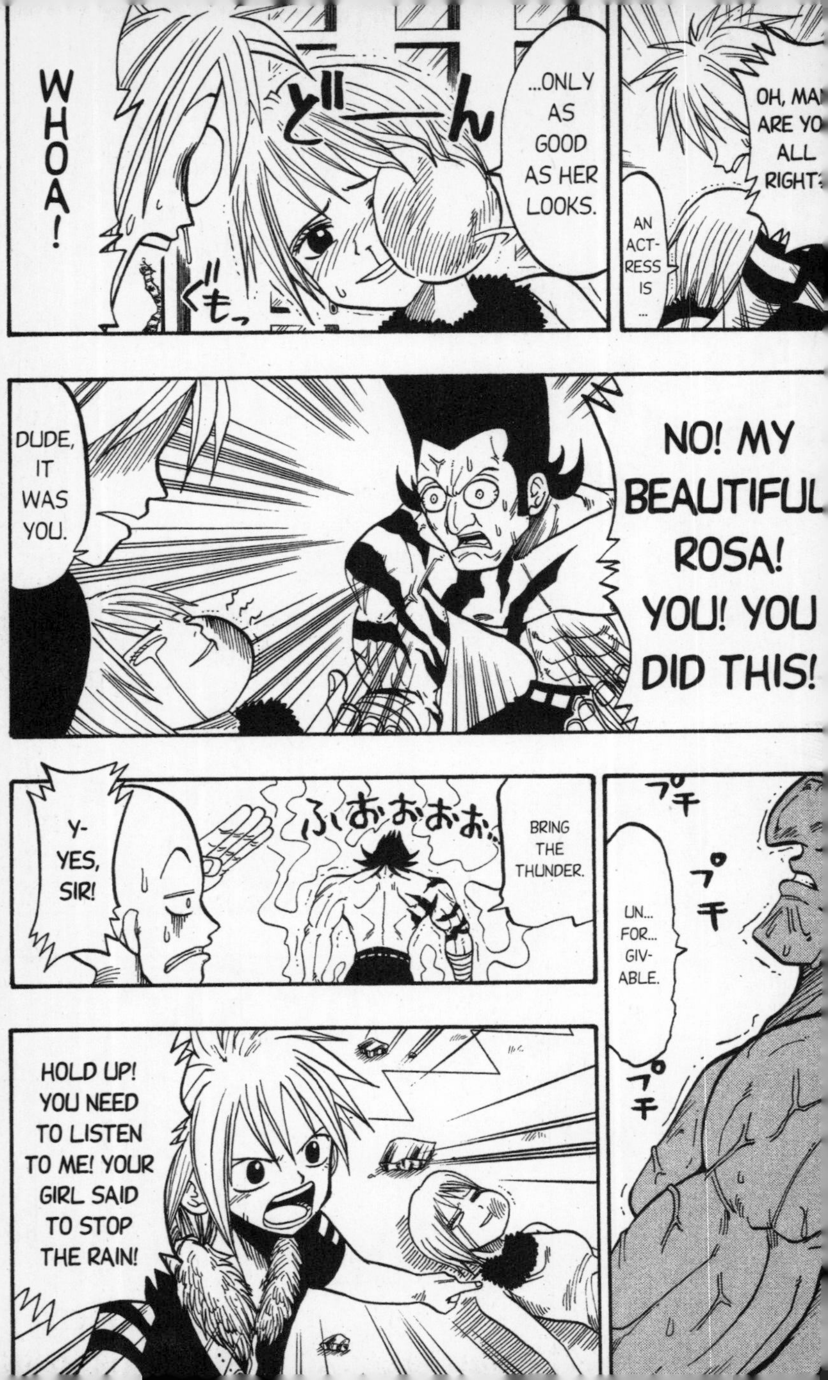
OH, MA ARE YO ALL RIGHT?
AN ACT-RESS IS ...
...ONLY AS GOOD AS HER LOOKS.
どーん
WHOA!
ぐもっ
NO! MY BEAUTIFUL ROSA! YOU! YOU DID THIS!
DUDE, IT WAS YOU.
プチ
プチ
UN... FOR... GIV-ABLE.
プチ
BRING THE THUNDER.
ふぉぉぉぉ
Y- YES, SIR!
HOLD UP! YOU NEED TO LISTEN TO ME! YOUR GIRL SAID TO STOP THE RAIN!

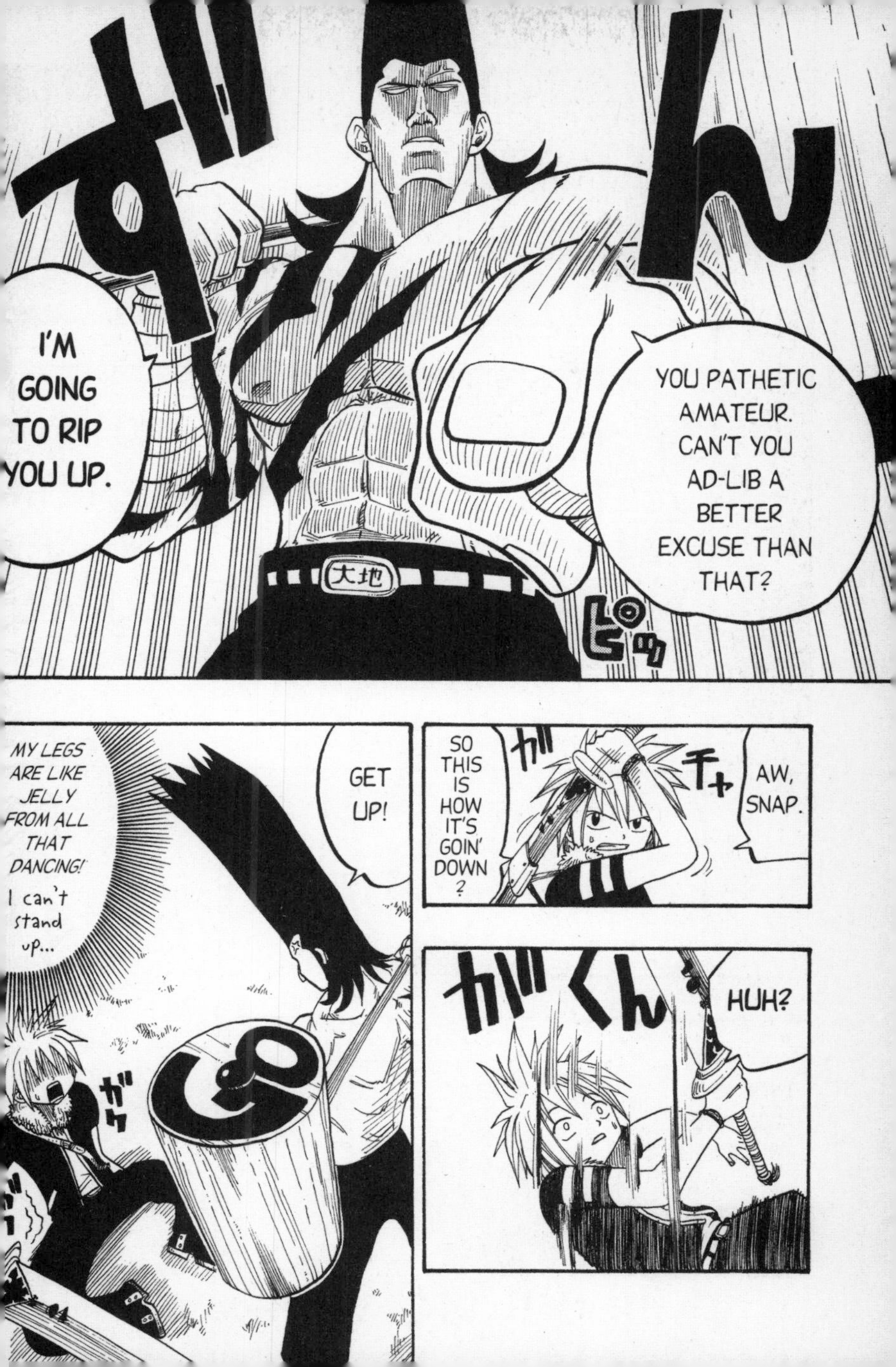
YOU PATHETIC AMATEUR. CAN'T YOU AD-LIB A BETTER EXCUSE THAN THAT?
I'M GOING TO RIP YOU UP.
AW, SNAP.
SO THIS IS HOW IT'S GOIN' DOWN?
HUH?
GET UP!
MY LEGS ARE LIKE JELLY FROM ALL THAT DANCING!
I can't stand up...

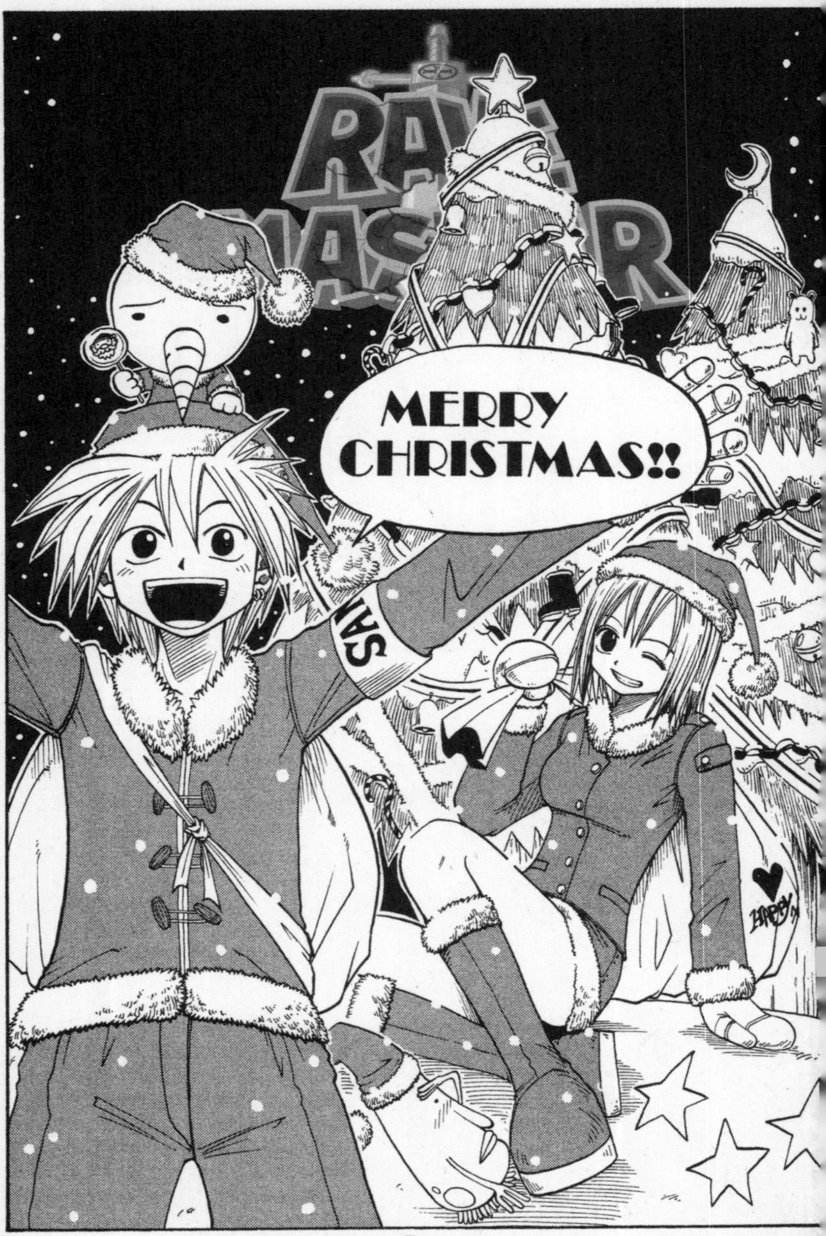
MERRY CHRISTMAS!!

RAVE:24+ Last Scene

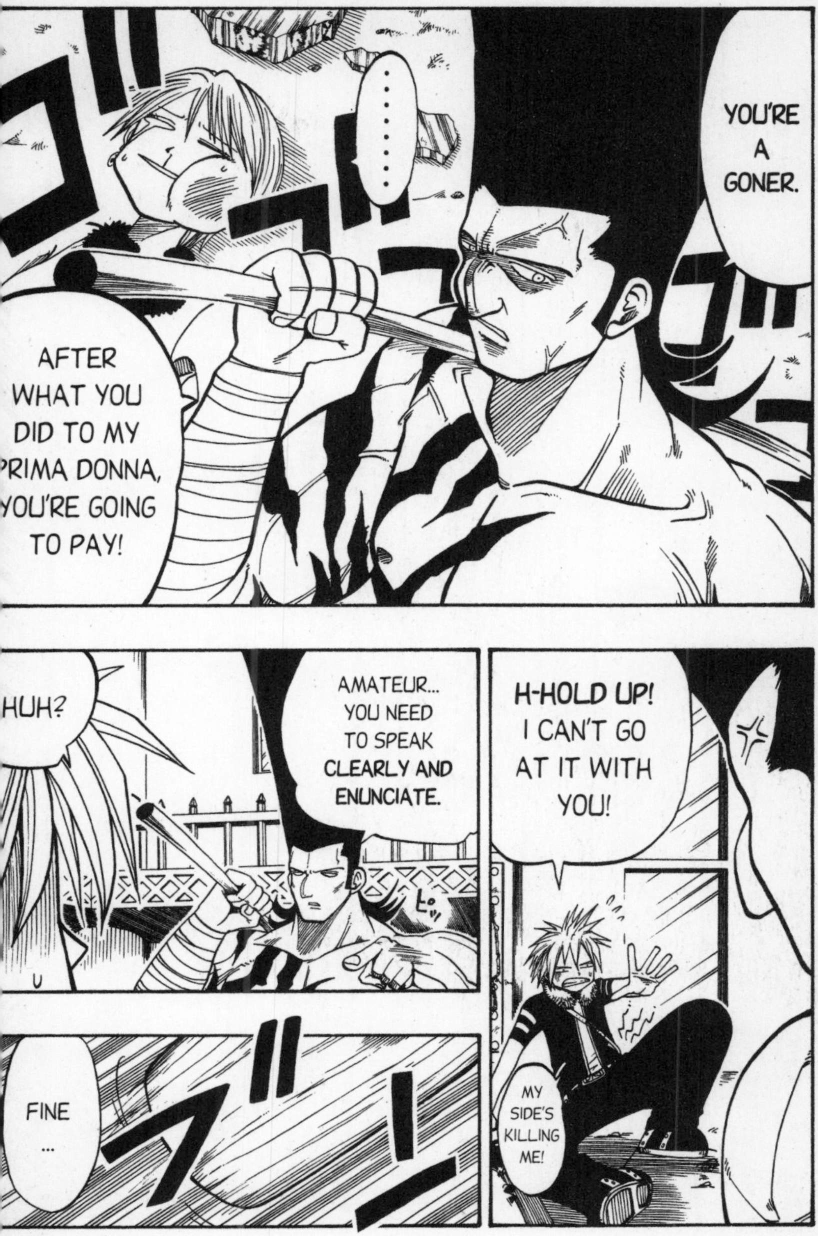
YOU'RE A GONER.
......
AFTER WHAT YOU DID TO MY RIMA DONNA, OU'RE GOING TO PAY!
H-HOLD UP! I CAN'T GO AT IT WITH YOU!
MY SIDE'S KILLING ME!
AMATEUR... YOU NEED TO SPEAK CLEARLY AND ENUNCIATE.
HUH?
FINE ...

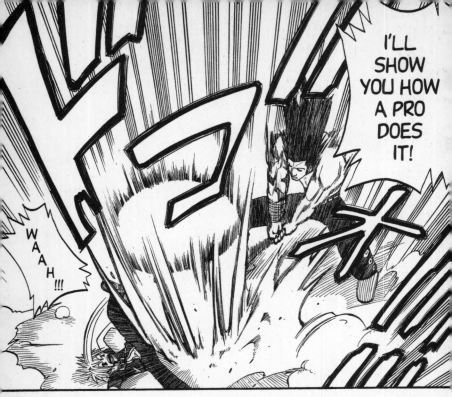

I'LL SHOW YOU HOW A PRO DOES IT!

WAAH!!!

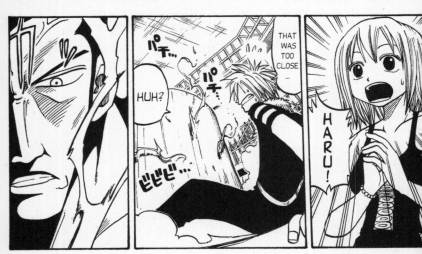

パチ…

HUH?

パチ…

ビビビ…

THAT WAS TOO CLOSE…

HARU!

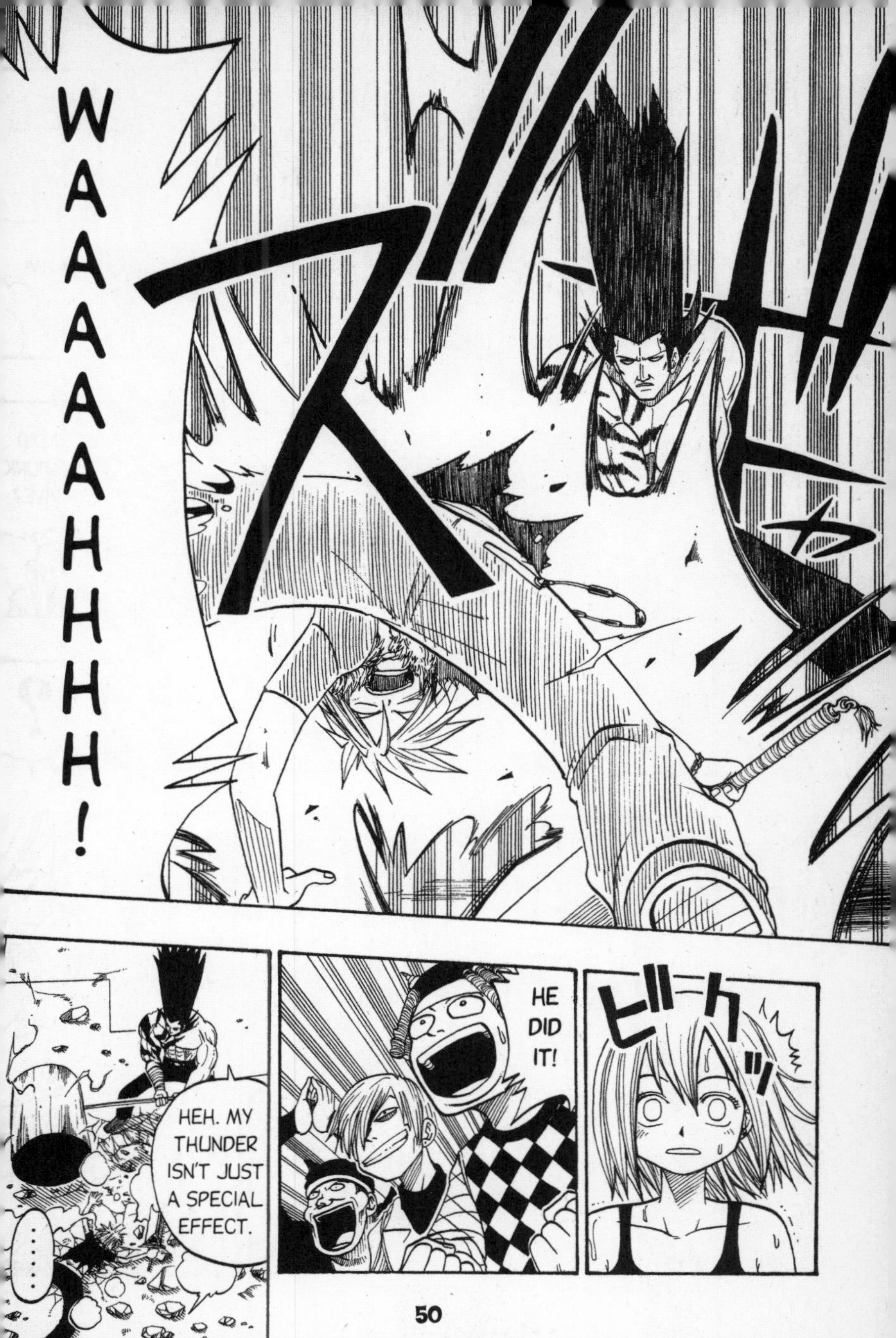
WAAAAAHHHHH!
HE DID IT!
HEH. MY THUNDER ISN'T JUST A SPECIAL EFFECT.
......

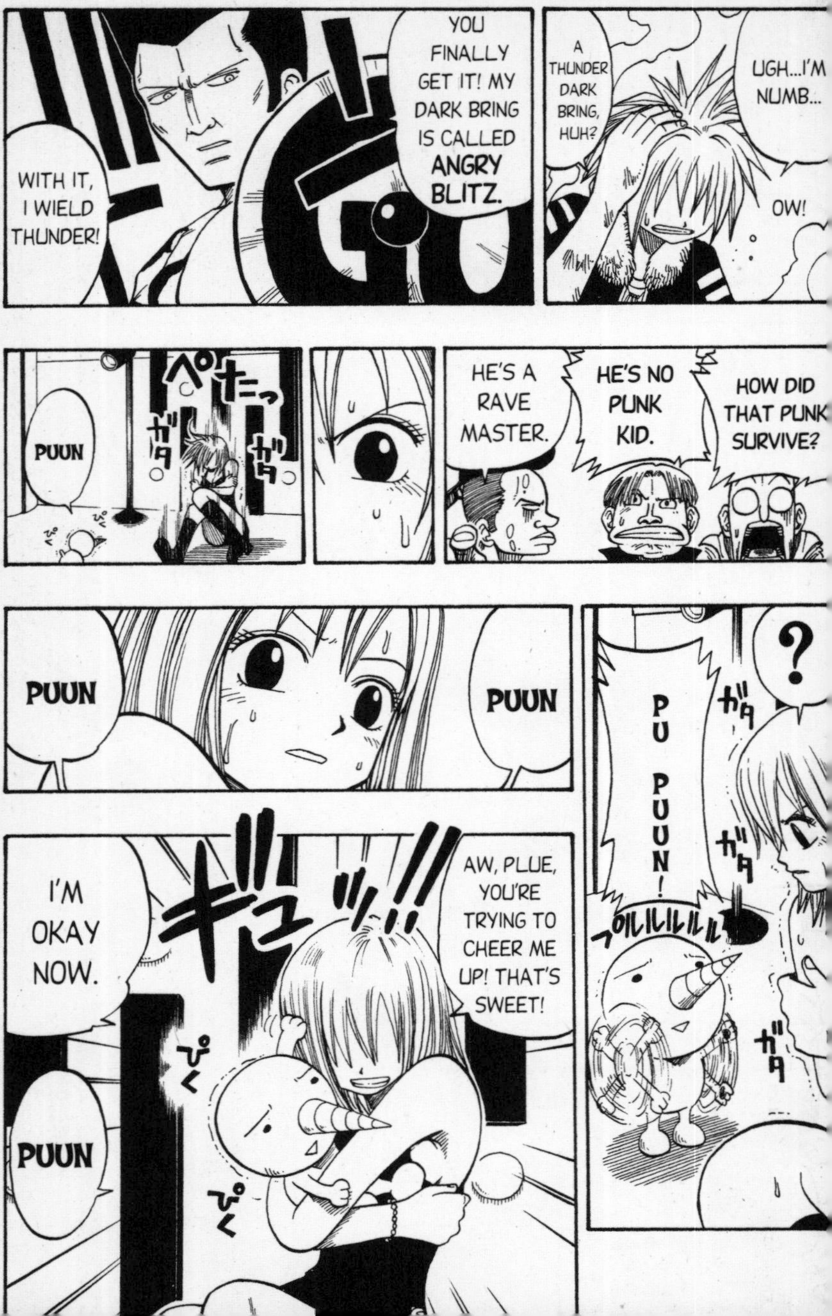
UGH...I'M NUMB...
OW!
A THUNDER DARK BRING, HUH?
YOU FINALLY GET IT! MY DARK BRING IS CALLED ANGRY BLITZ.
WITH IT, I WIELD THUNDER!
HOW DID THAT PUNK SURVIVE?
HE'S NO PUNK KID.
HE'S A RAVE MASTER.
ぺたっ
ガタ ガタ
PUUN
?
PU PU PUUN!
PUUN
PUUN
ギュッ!!
AW, PLUE, YOU'RE TRYING TO CHEER ME UP! THAT'S SWEET!
I'M OKAY NOW.
PUUN

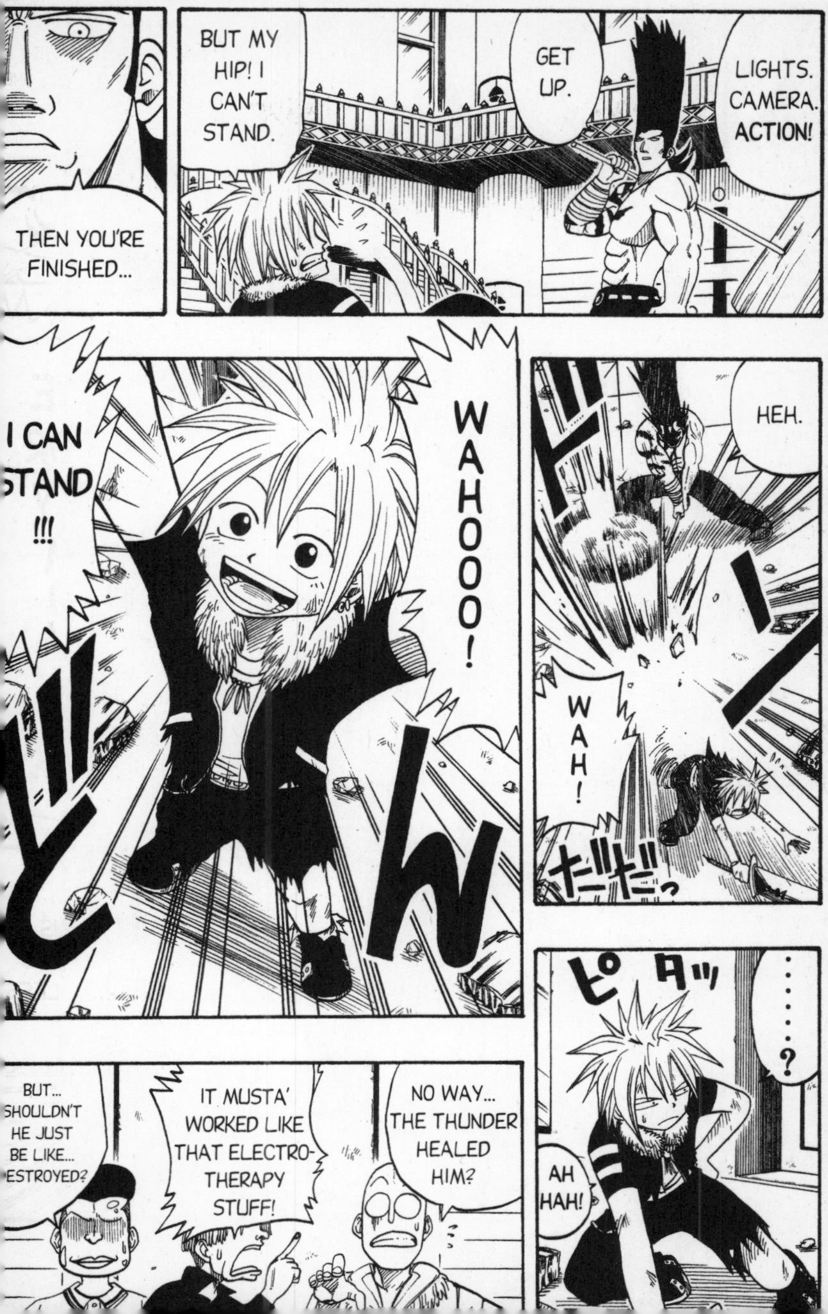
LIGHTS. CAMERA. ACTION!
GET UP.
BUT MY HIP! I CAN'T STAND.
THEN YOU'RE FINISHED...
HEH.
WAH!
WAHOOOO!
I CAN STAND!!!
......?
AH HAH!
NO WAY... THE THUNDER HEALED HIM?
IT MUSTA' WORKED LIKE THAT ELECTRO-THERAPY STUFF!
BUT... SHOULDN'T HE JUST BE LIKE... ESTROYED?

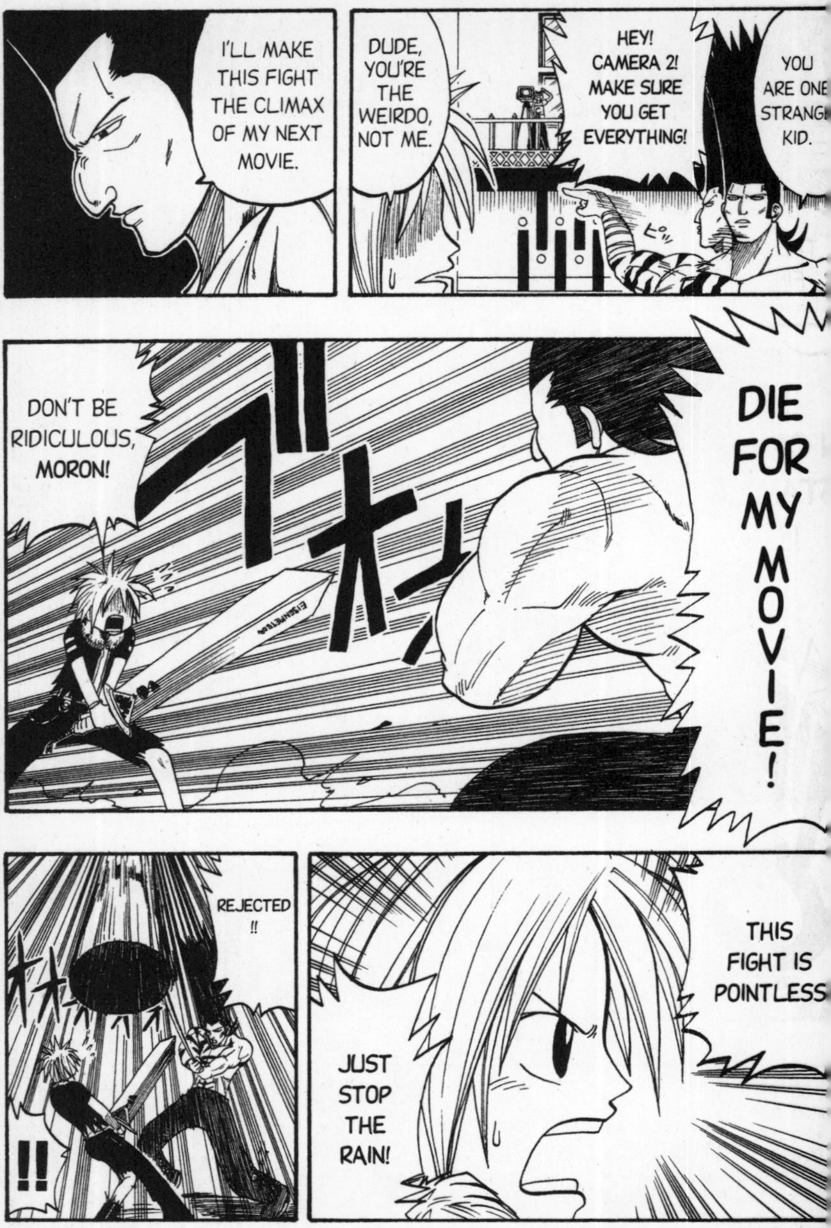
YOU ARE ONE STRANG KID.
HEY! CAMERA 2! MAKE SURE YOU GET EVERYTHING!
DUDE, YOU'RE THE WEIRDO, NOT ME.
I'LL MAKE THIS FIGHT THE CLIMAX OF MY NEXT MOVIE.
DIE FOR MY MOVIE!
DON'T BE RIDICULOUS, MORON!
THIS FIGHT IS POINTLESS
JUST STOP THE RAIN!
REJECTED !!
!!

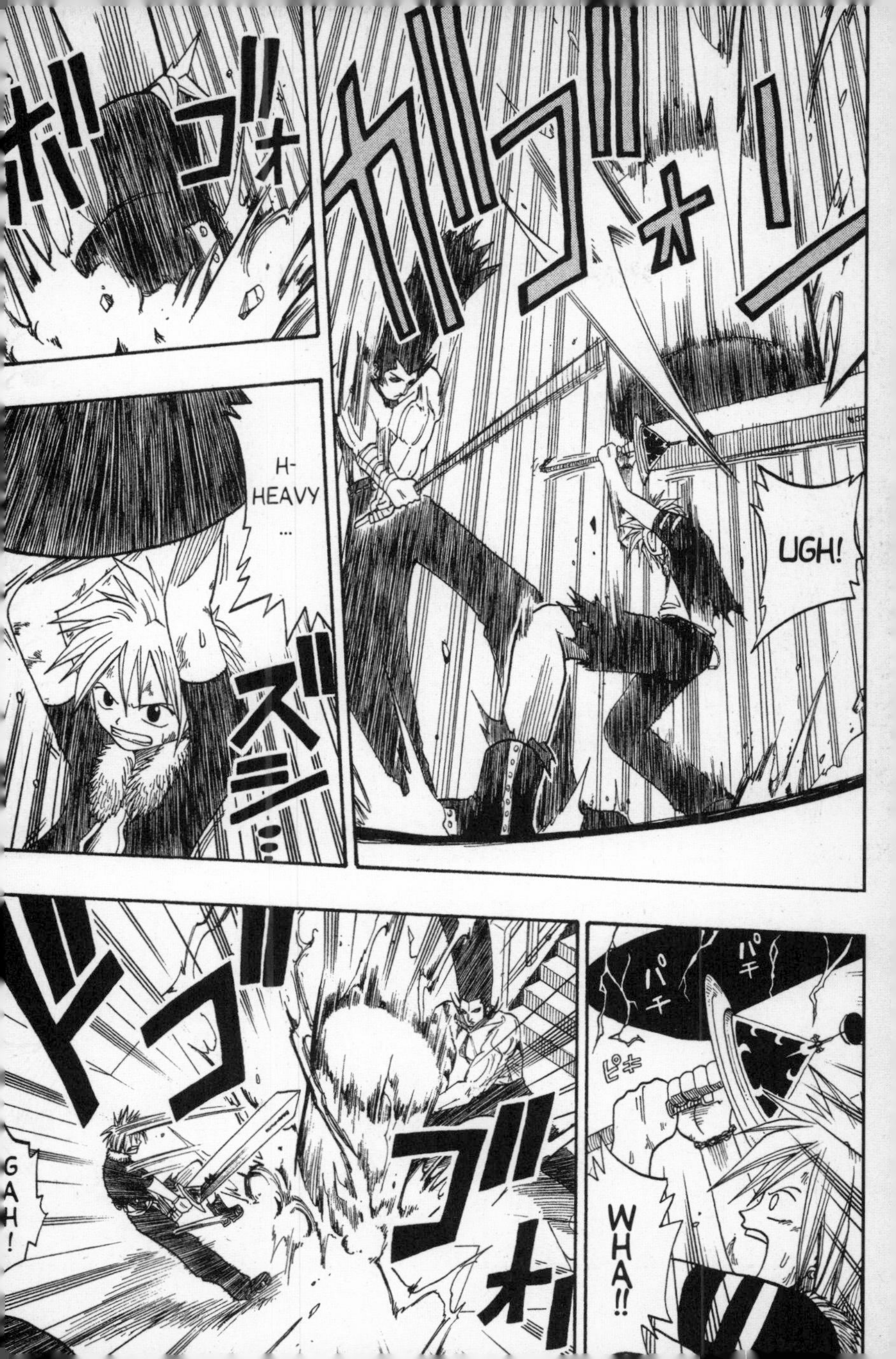
ガゴォーン
UGH!
ボゴォ
H-
HEAVY
...
ズシ…
パチ
パチ
ピキ
WHA!!
ドゴォ
GAH!

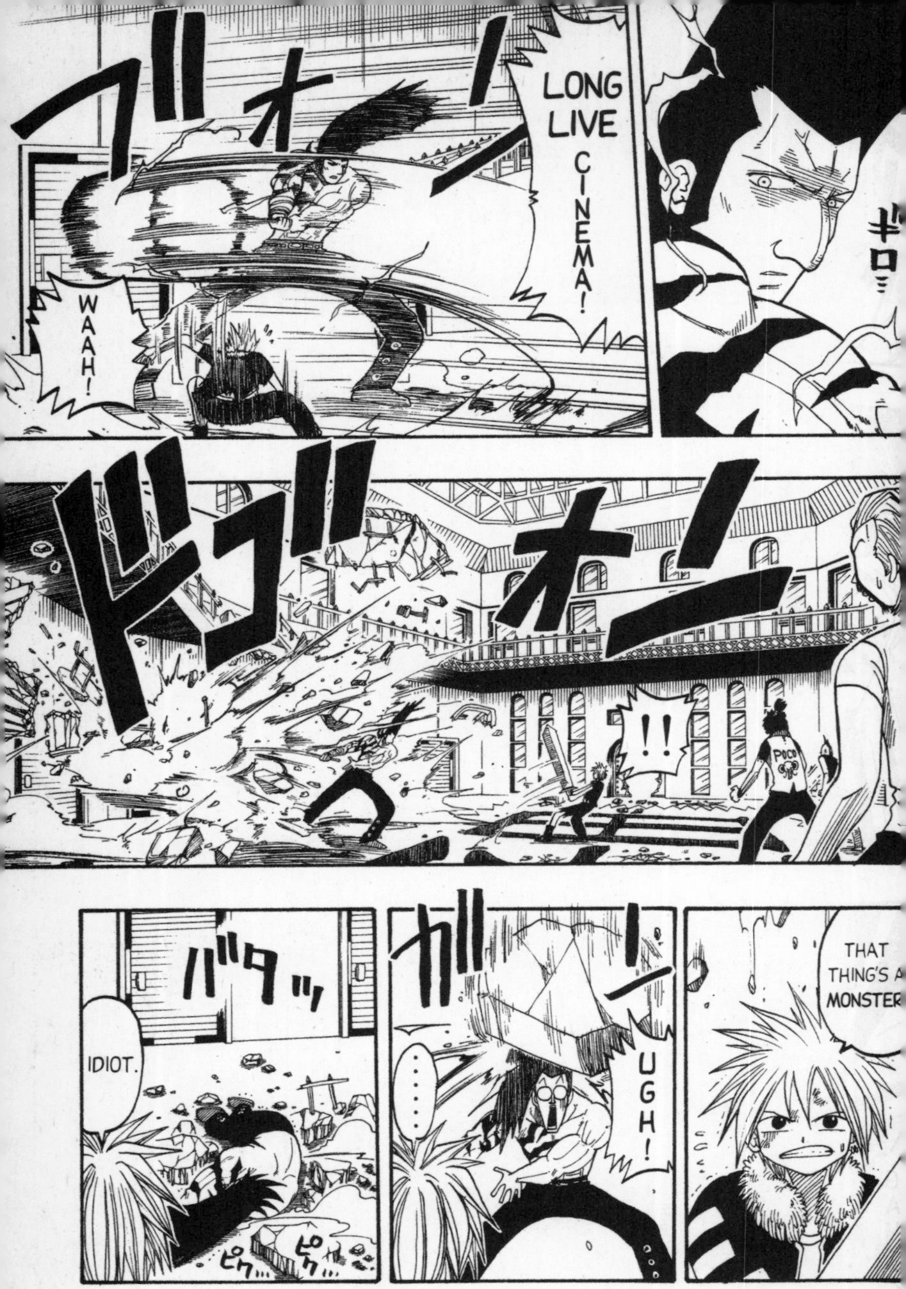
ギロ…
LONG LIVE CINEMA!
ブォーン
WAAH!
ドゴォーン
!!
THAT THING'S A MONSTER
ガーン
UGH!
……
バタッ
IDIOT.
ピクピク…

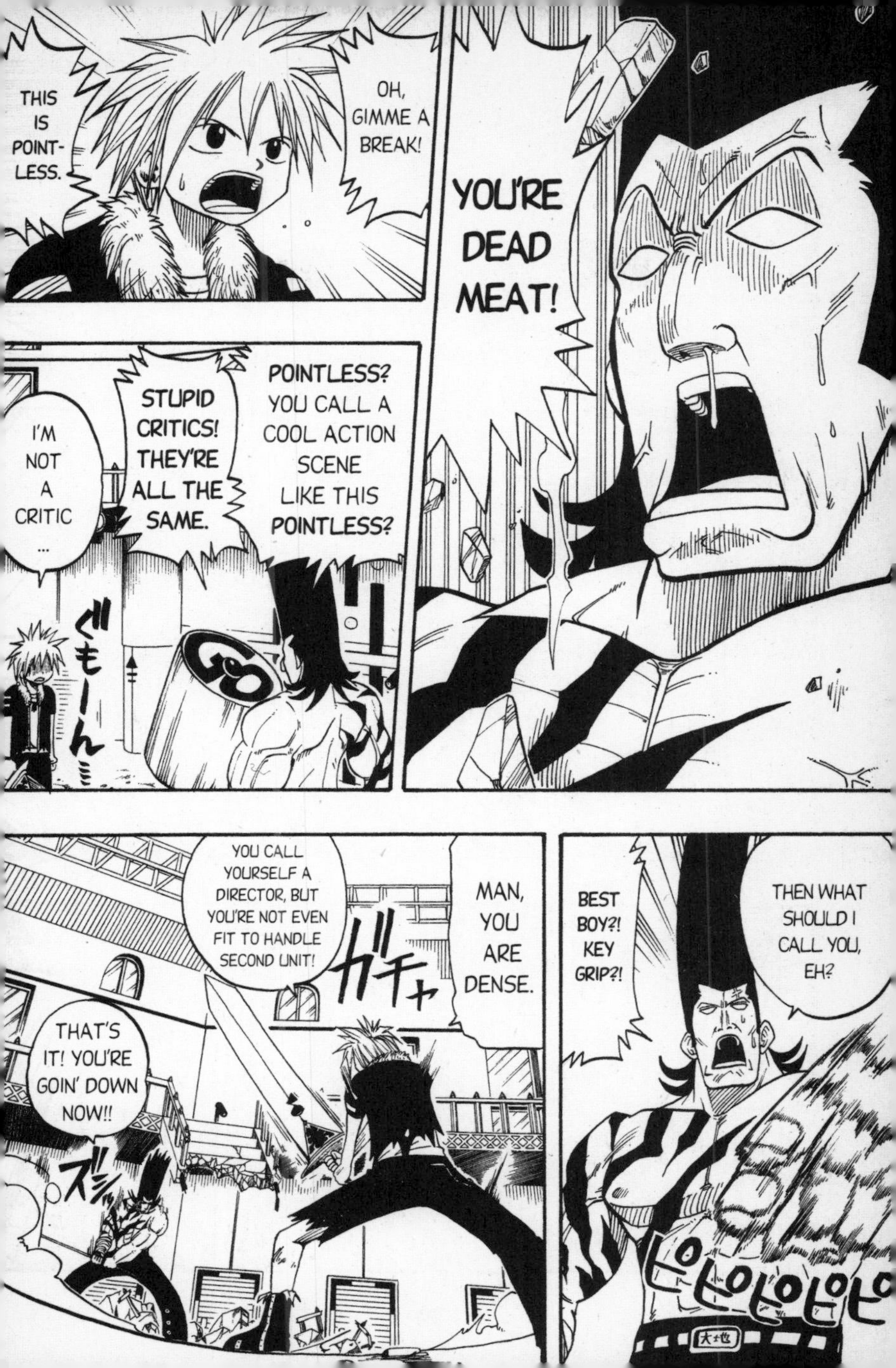
YOU'RE DEAD MEAT!
OH, GIMME A BREAK!
THIS IS POINTLESS.
POINTLESS? YOU CALL A COOL ACTION SCENE LIKE THIS POINTLESS?
STUPID CRITICS! THEY'RE ALL THE SAME.
I'M NOT A CRITIC ...
ぐもーん
THEN WHAT SHOULD I CALL YOU, EH?
BEST BOY?! KEY GRIP?!
MAN, YOU ARE DENSE.
YOU CALL YOURSELF A DIRECTOR, BUT YOU'RE NOT EVEN FIT TO HANDLE SECOND UNIT!
ガチャ
THAT'S IT! YOU'RE GOIN' DOWN NOW!!

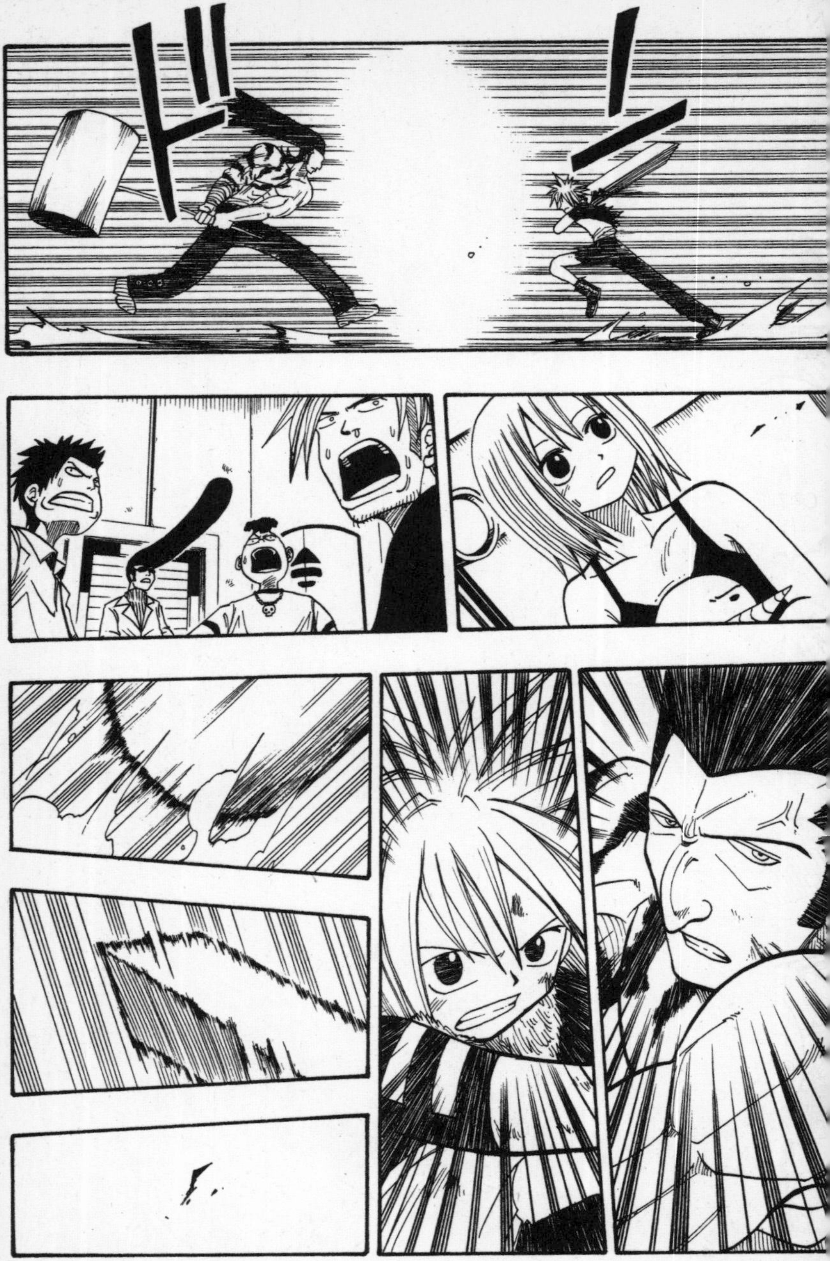
ド

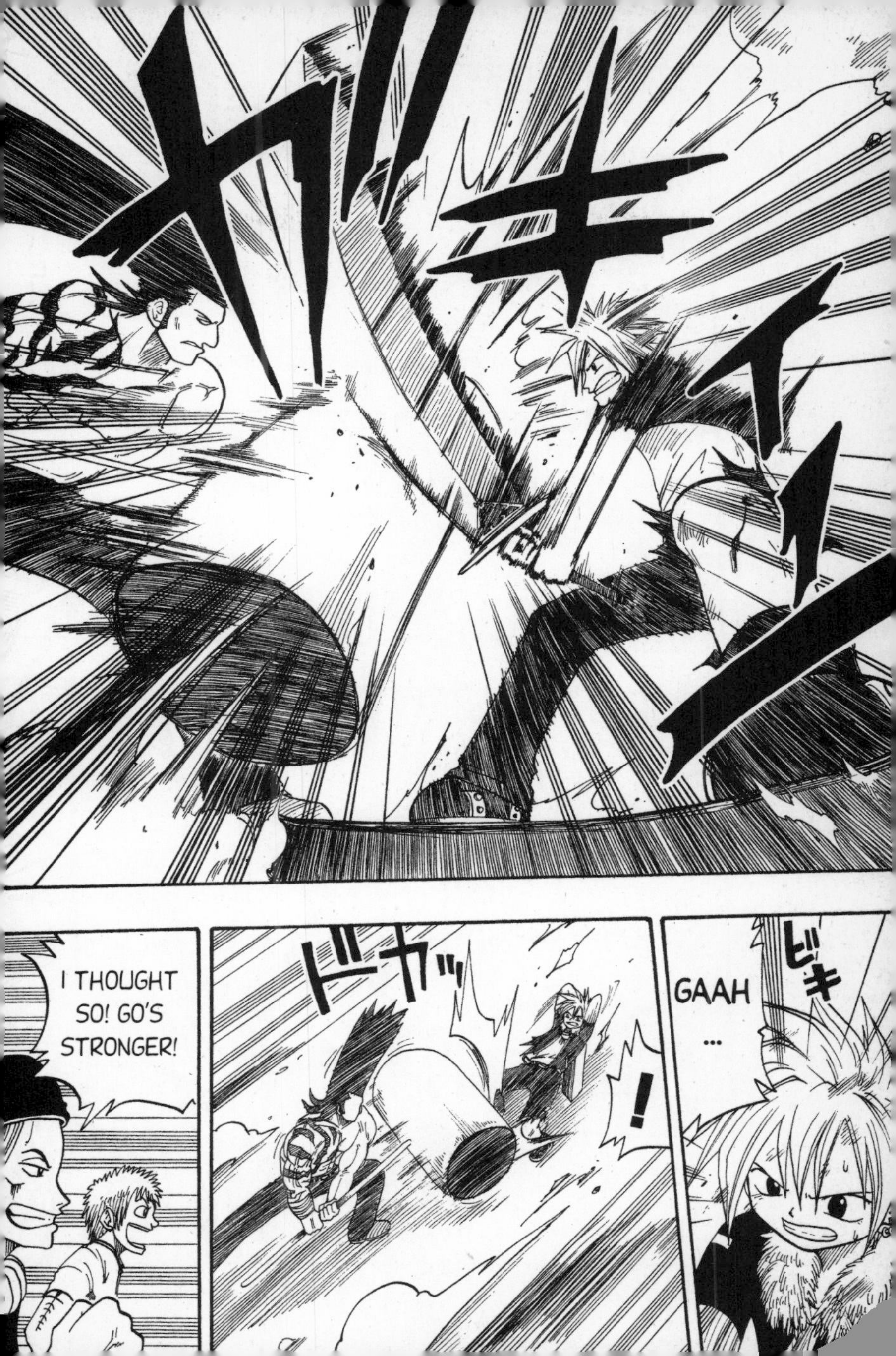
GAAH ...
ビキ
ドガッ
!
I THOUGHT SO! GO'S STRONGER!

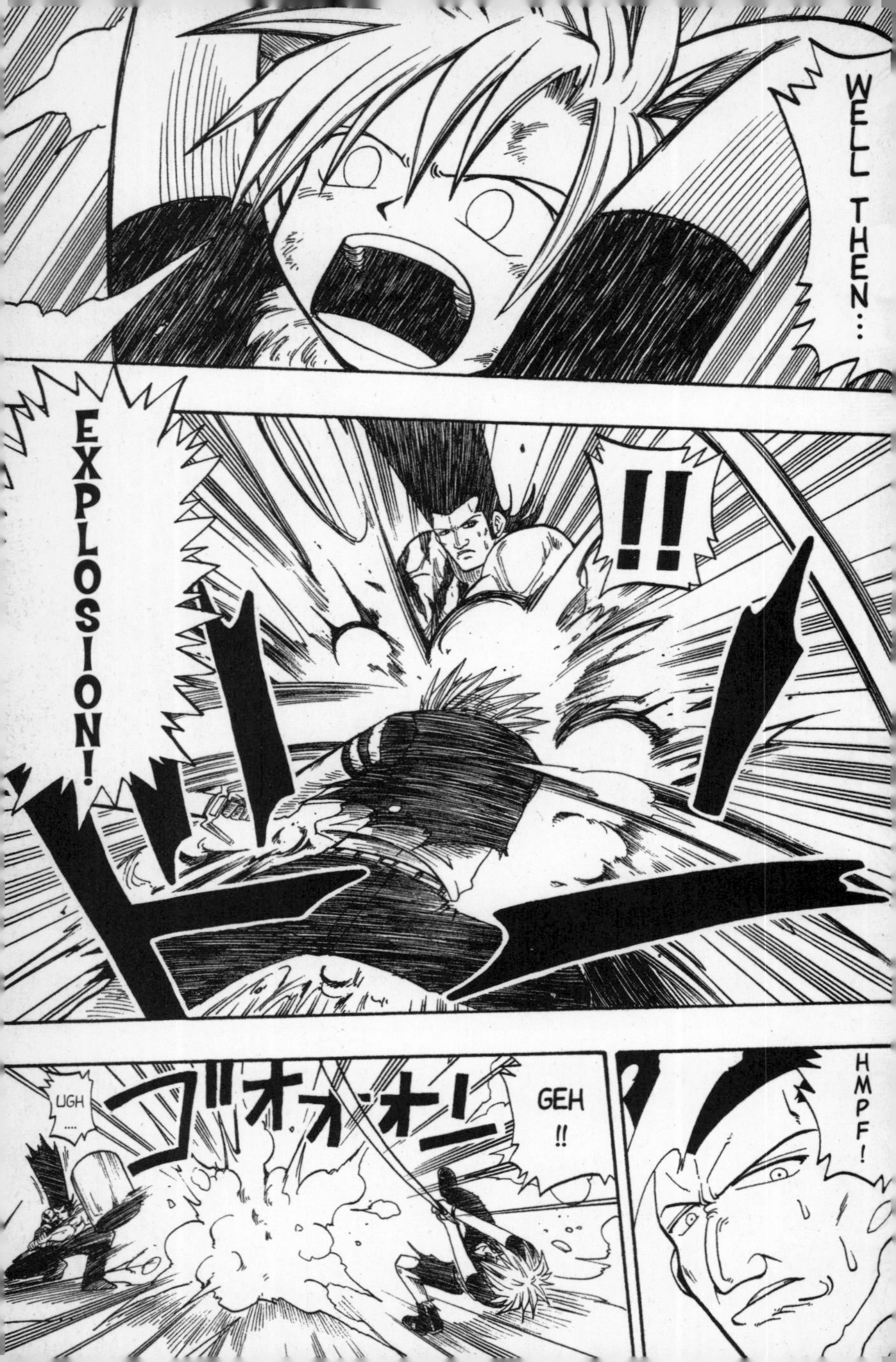
WELL THEN...
EXPLOSION!
!!
HMPF!
GEH !!
コ"オ・オ・オー
UGH ....

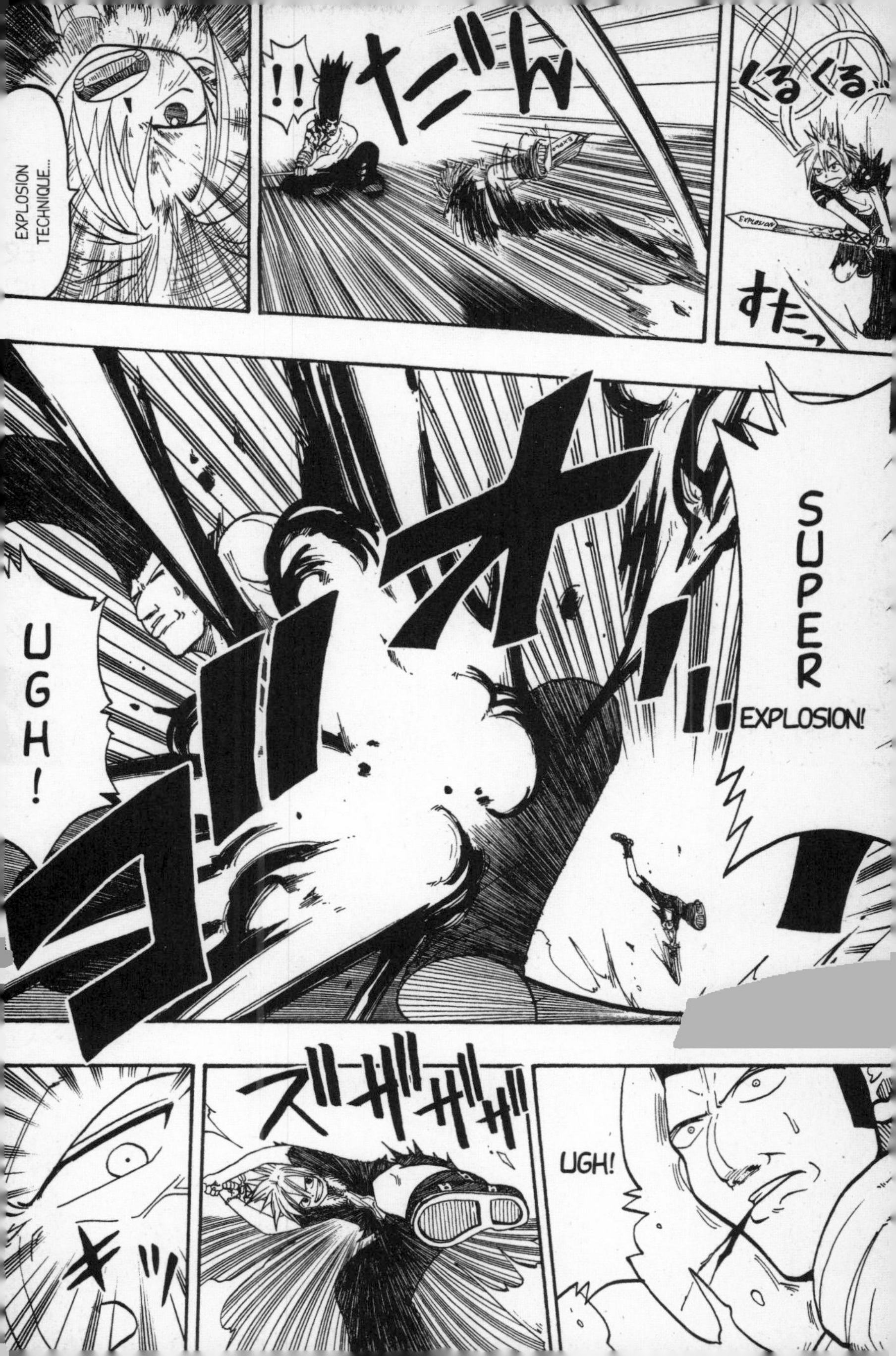
くるくる…
すたっ
!!
EXPLOSION TECHNIQUE…
SUPER EXPLOSION!
UGH!
UGH!
ズザザザ
キッ

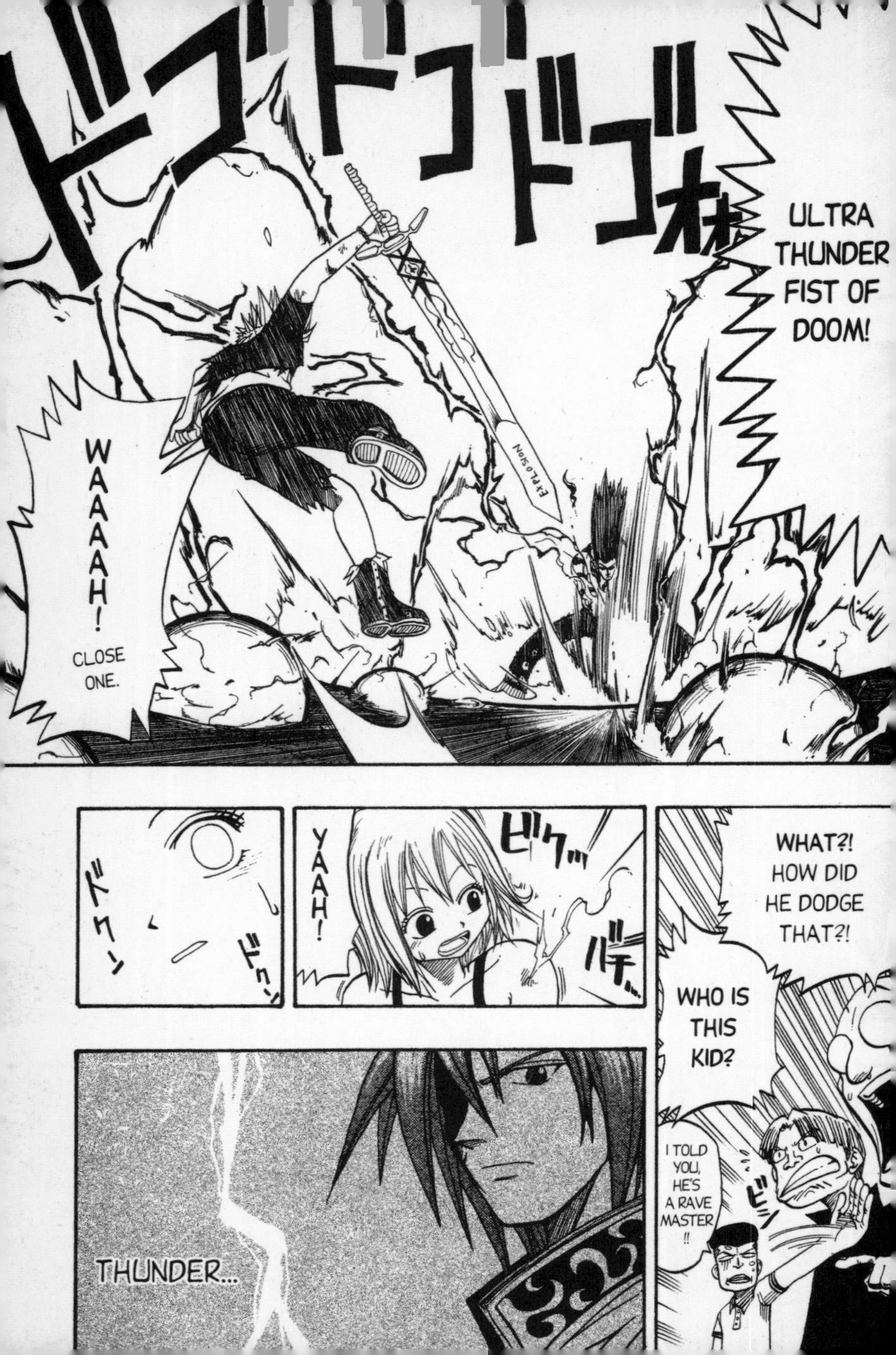

ドゴドゴドゴオォ
ULTRA THUNDER FIST OF DOOM!
EXPLOSION
WAAAAAH!
CLOSE ONE.
WHAT?! HOW DID HE DODGE THAT?!
WHO IS THIS KID?
I TOLD YOU, HE'S A RAVE MASTER!!
YAAAH!
ビクッ
バチ…
ドクン
ドクン
THUNDER...

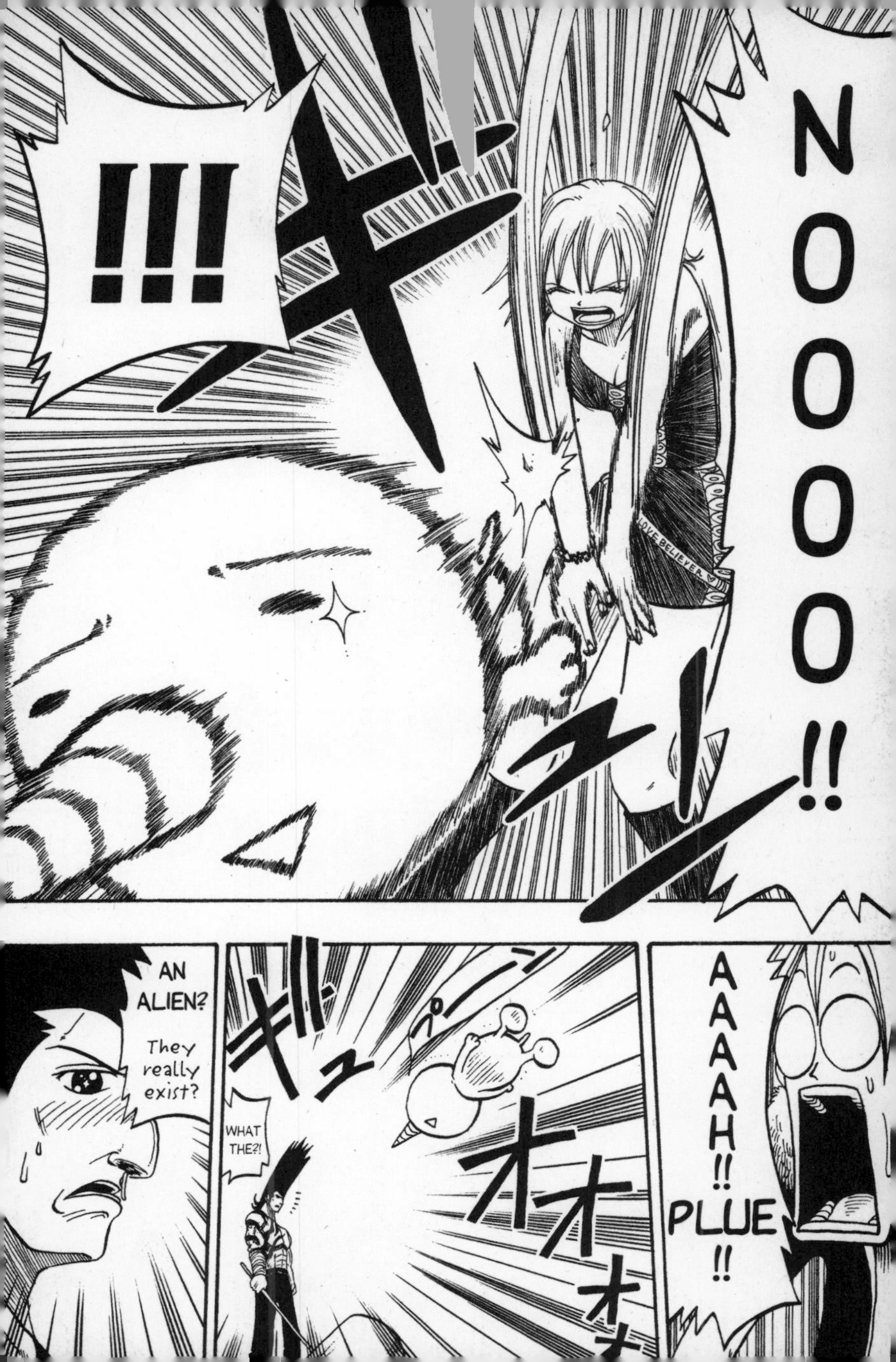

NOOOO!!
!!!
AAAAH!! PLUE!!
WHAT THE?!
AN ALIEN?
They really exist?

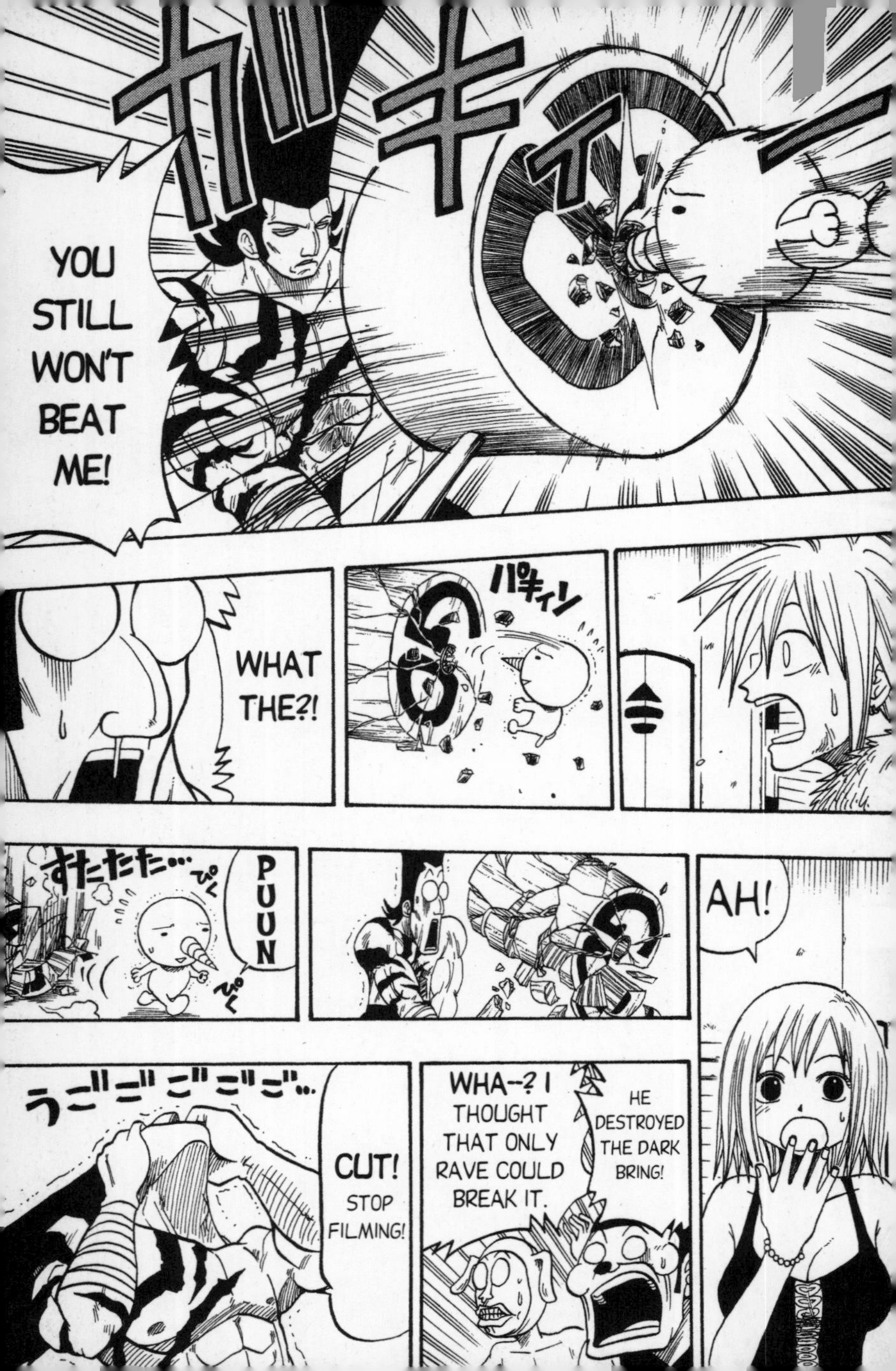

カッキィーン
YOU STILL WON'T BEAT ME!
パキィン
WHAT THE?!
AH!
すたたた…
ぴく
PUUN
ぴく
HE DESTROYED THE DARK BRING!
WHA--?! I THOUGHT THAT ONLY RAVE COULD BREAK IT.
うごごごご…
CUT! STOP FILMING!

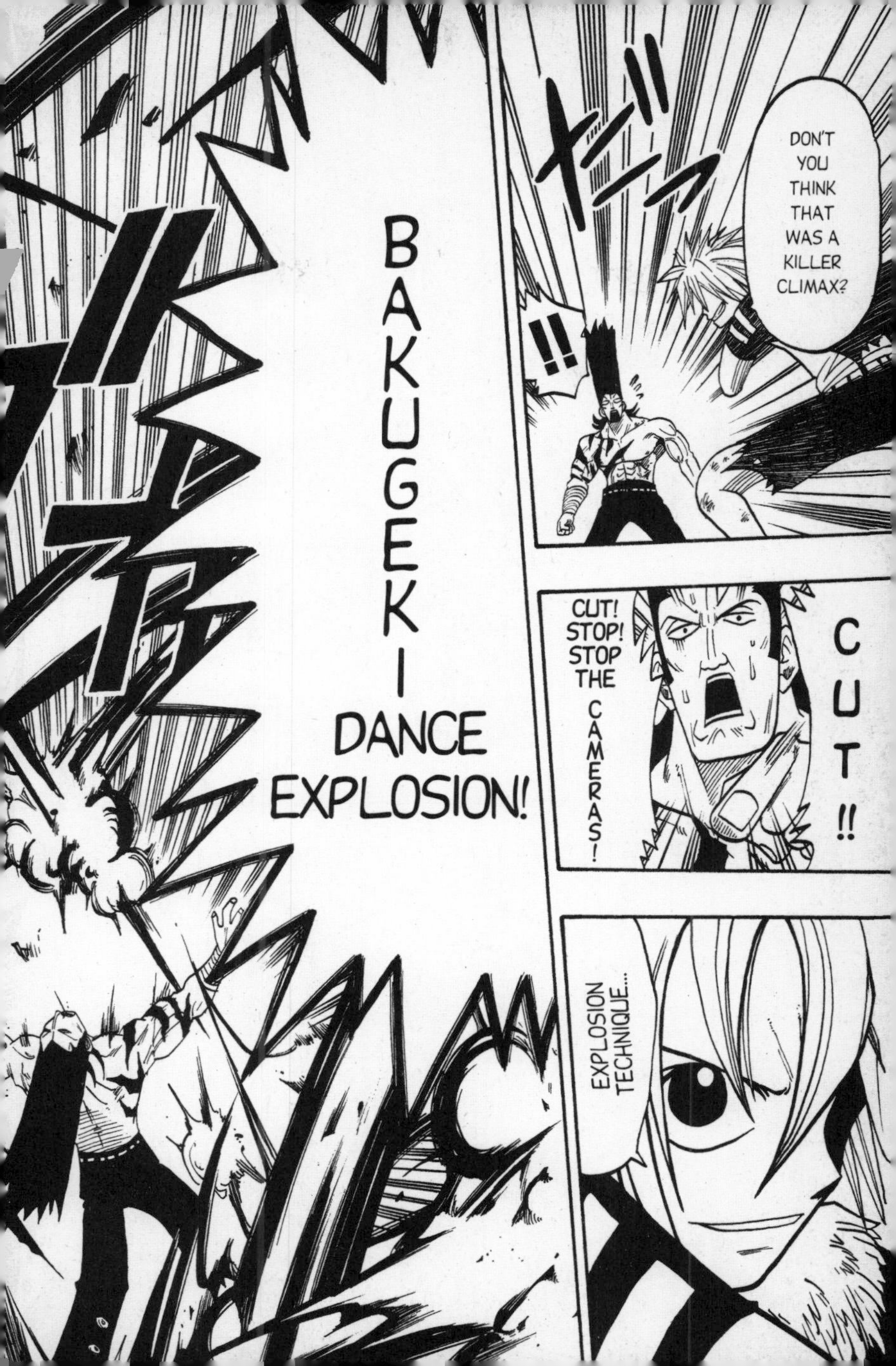
DON'T YOU THINK THAT WAS A KILLER CLIMAX?
!!
CUT !!
CUT! STOP! STOP THE CAMERAS!
EXPLOSION TECHNIQUE...
BAKUGEKI DANCE EXPLOSION!

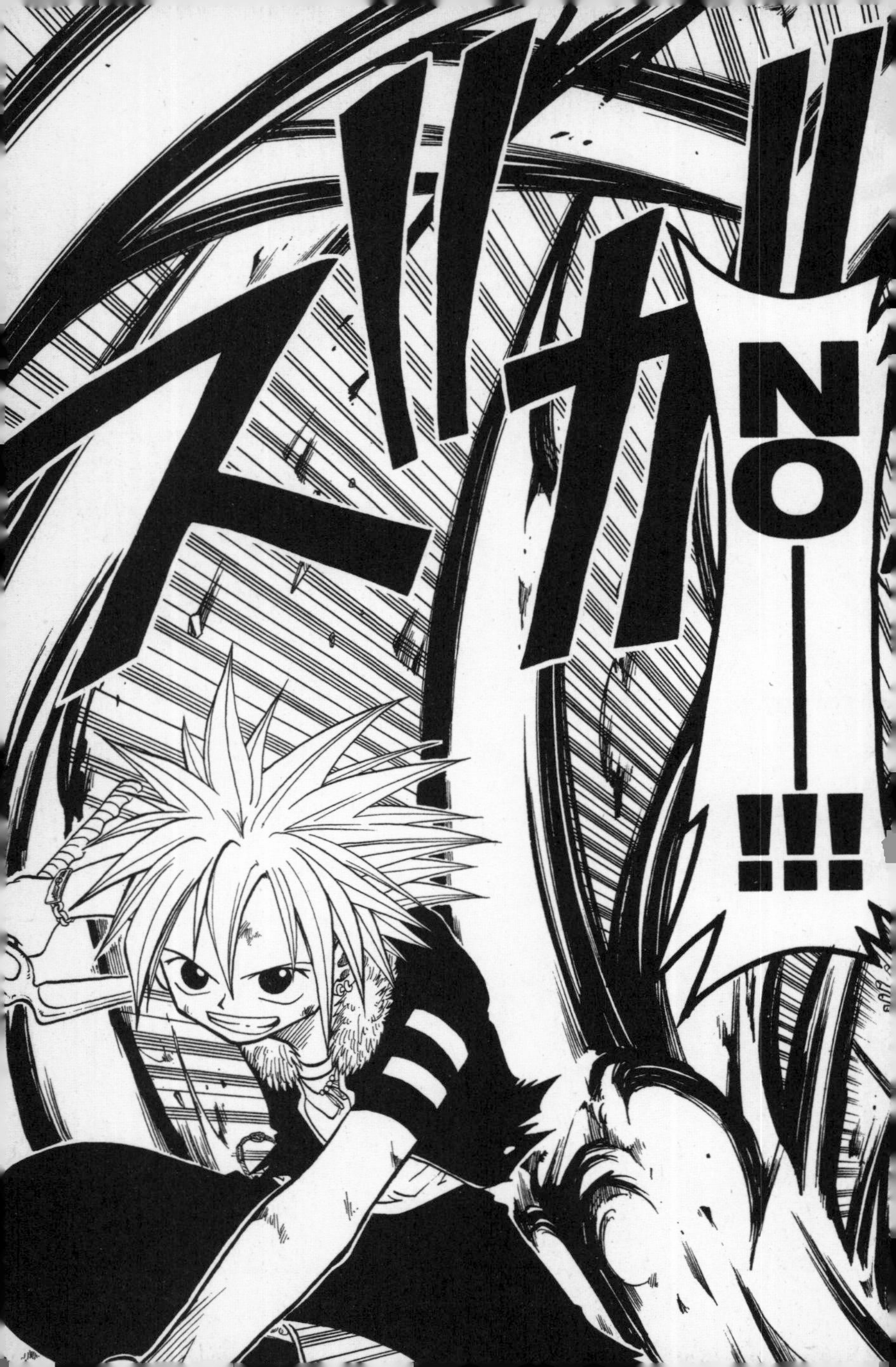
NO—!!!

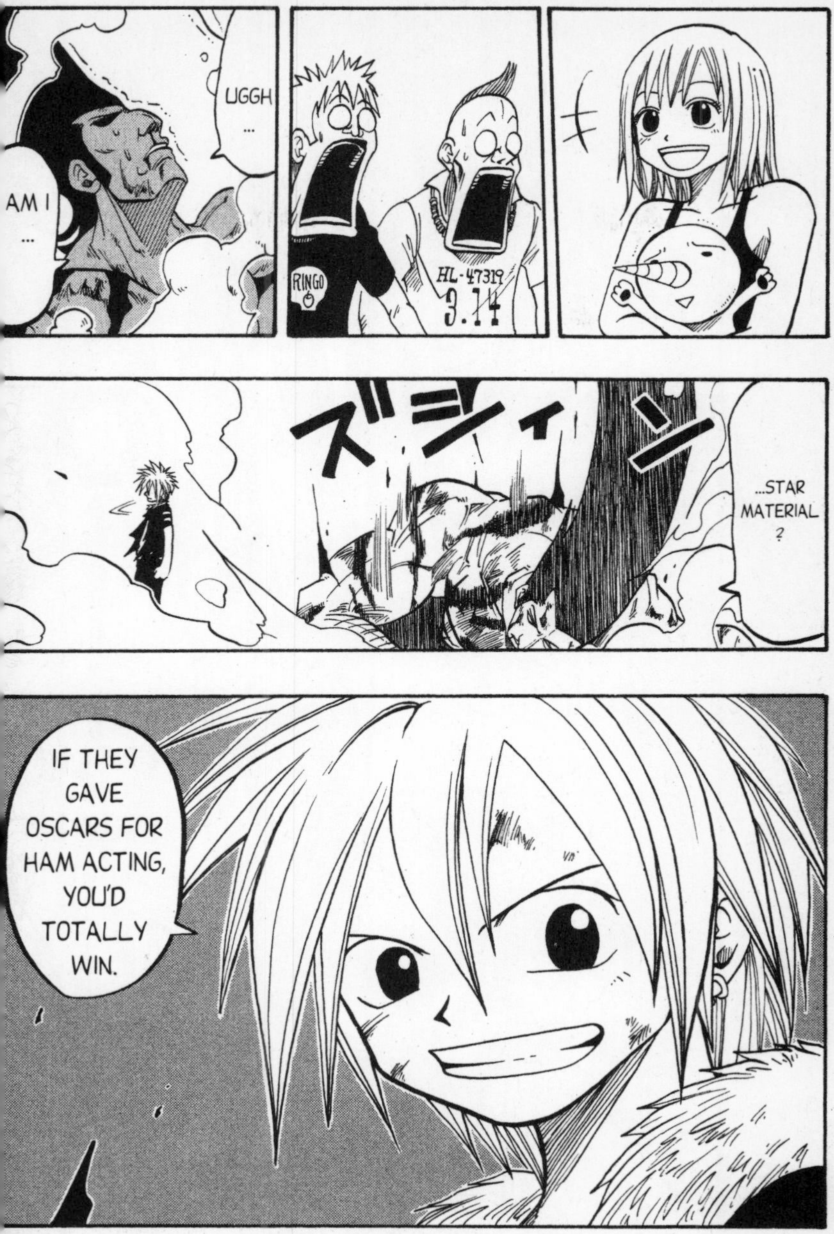
HL-47319
3.14
RINGO
UGGH ...
AM I ...
...STAR MATERIAL ?
IF THEY GAVE OSCARS FOR HAM ACTING, YOU'D TOTALLY WIN.

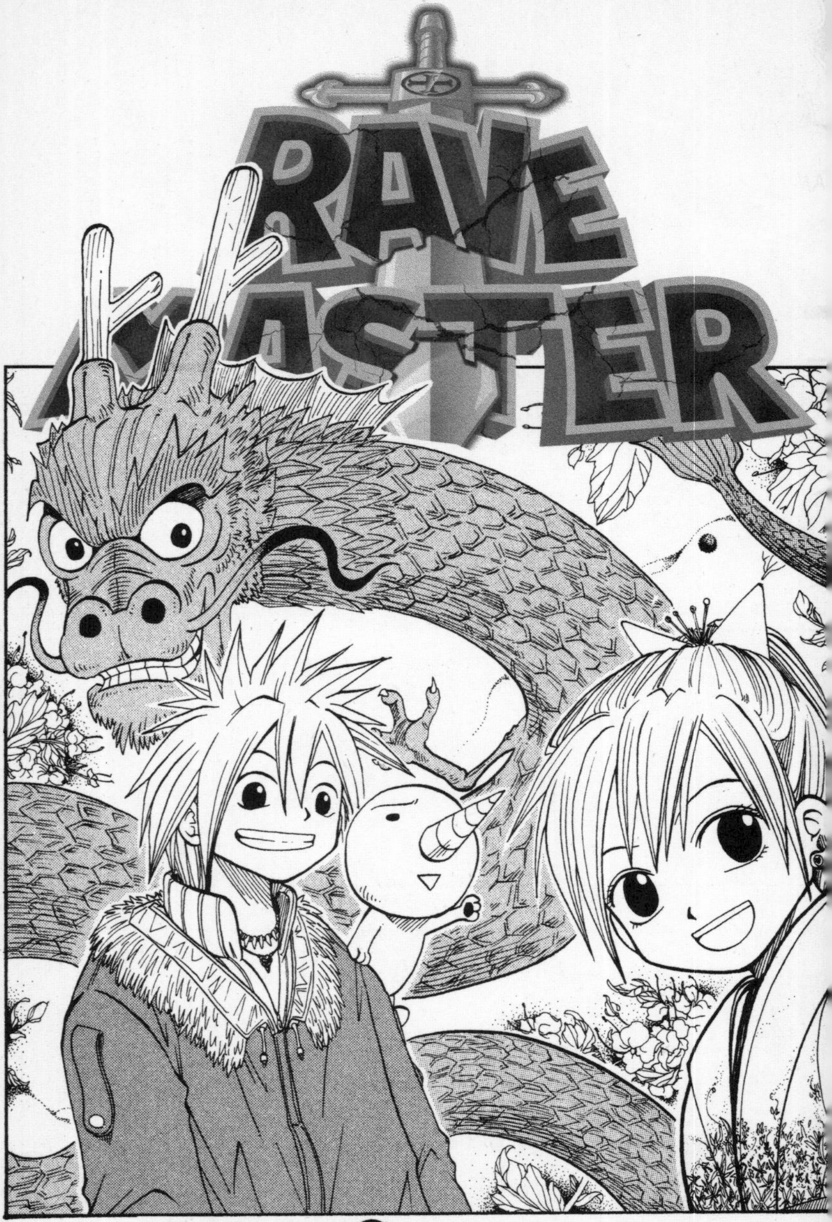
RAVE MASTER

RAVE: 25 ✠ Gentle Sunlight

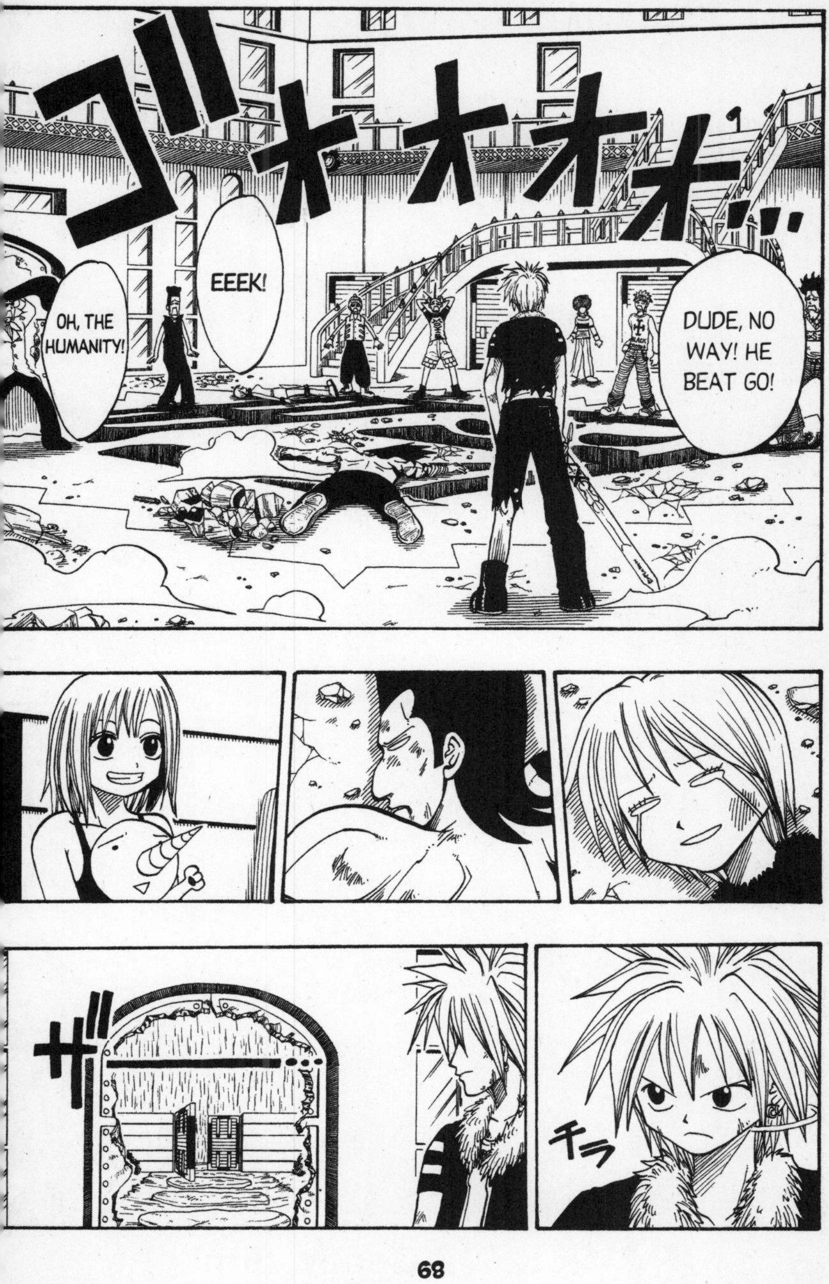

ゴオオオオ…
DUDE, NO WAY! HE BEAT GO!
EEEK!
OH, THE HUMANITY!
チラ
ザ

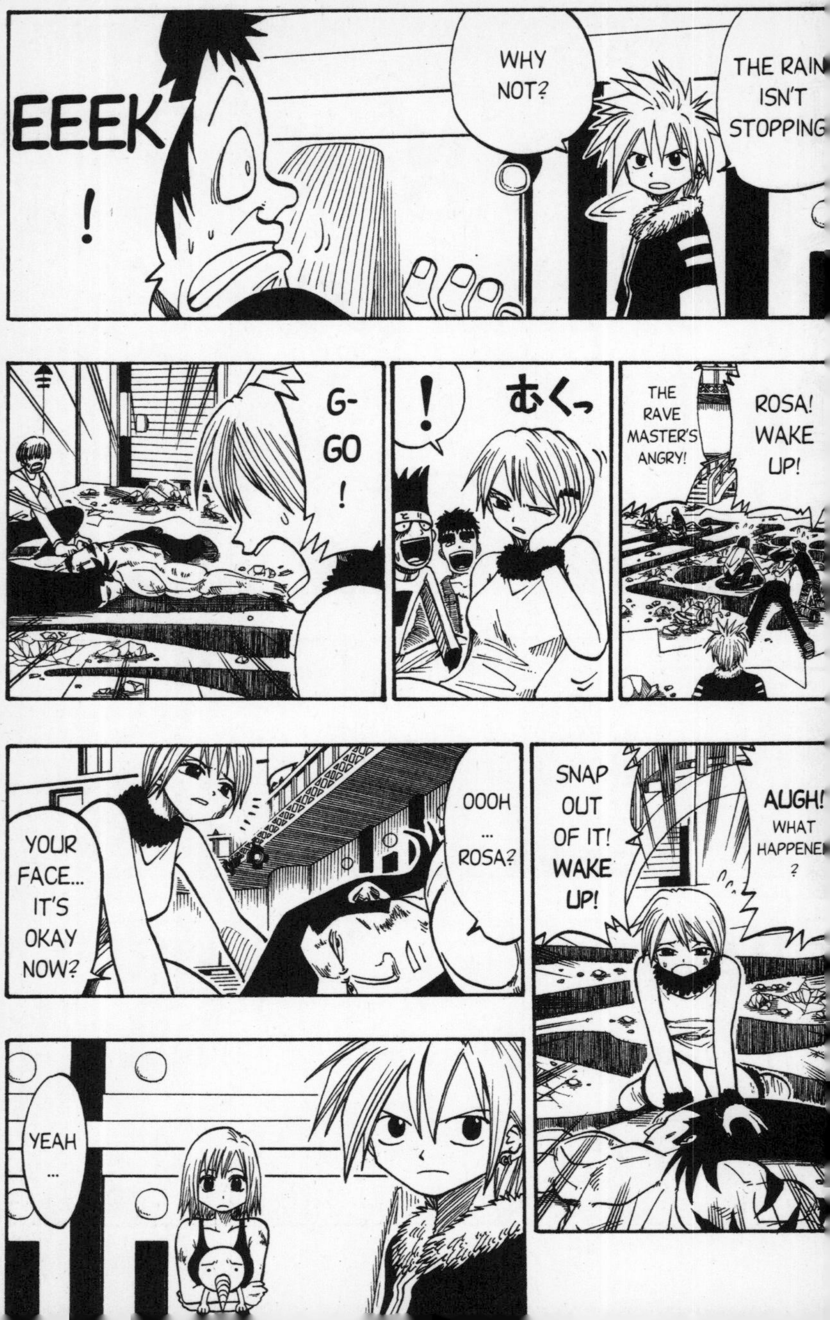
THE RAIN ISN'T STOPPING
WHY NOT?
EEEK
!
ROSA! WAKE UP!
THE RAVE MASTER'S ANGRY!
むくっ
!
G-GO!
AUGH! WHAT HAPPENE ?
SNAP OUT OF IT! WAKE UP!
OOOH ... ROSA?
YOUR FACE... IT'S OKAY NOW?
YEAH ...

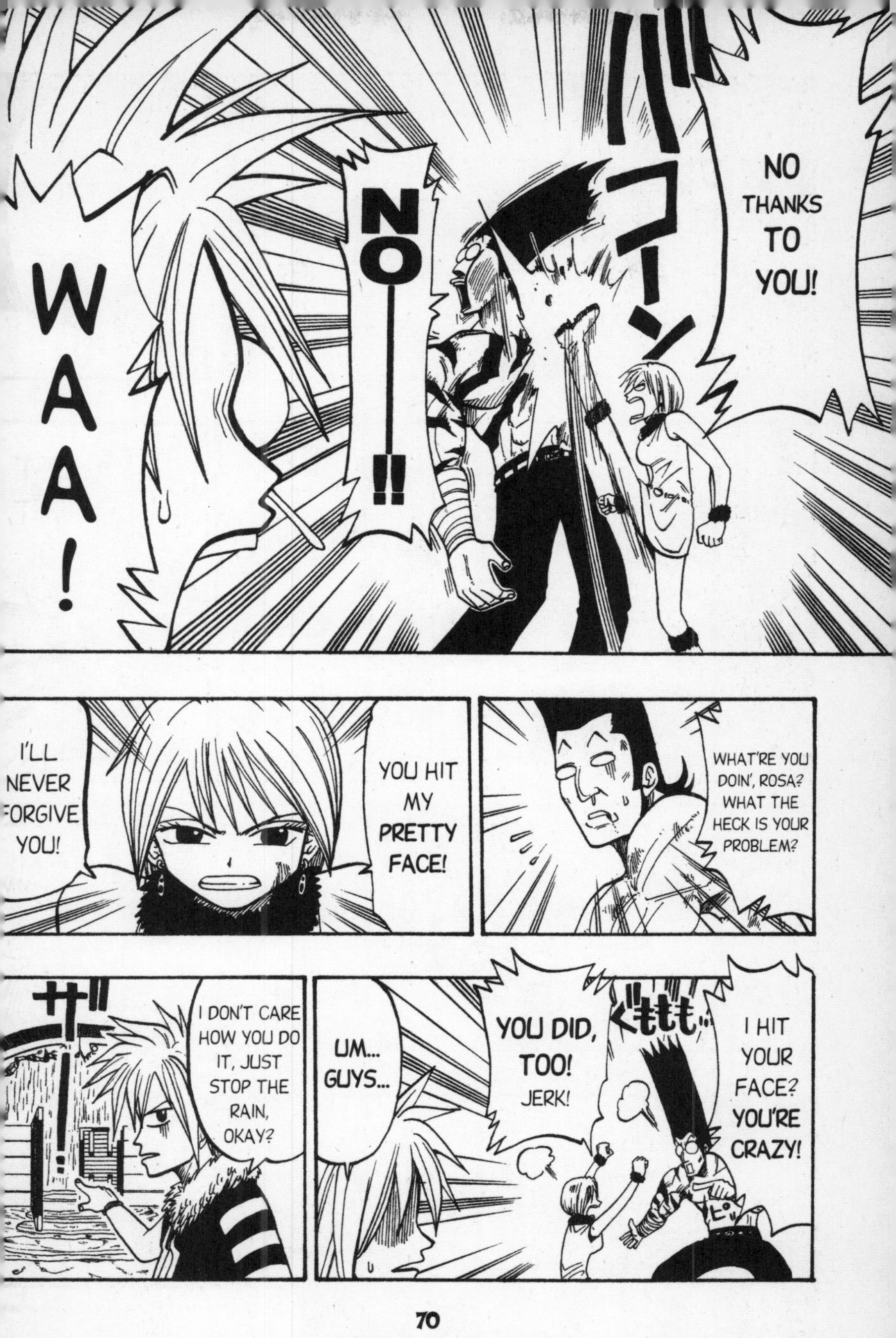
NO THANKS TO YOU!
バコーン
NO—!!
WAA!
WHAT'RE YOU DOIN', ROSA? WHAT THE HECK IS YOUR PROBLEM?
YOU HIT MY PRETTY FACE!
I'LL NEVER FORGIVE YOU!
I HIT YOUR FACE? YOU'RE CRAZY!
ぐももも
YOU DID, TOO! JERK!
UM... GUYS...
ザー
I DON'T CARE HOW YOU DO IT, JUST STOP THE RAIN, OKAY?

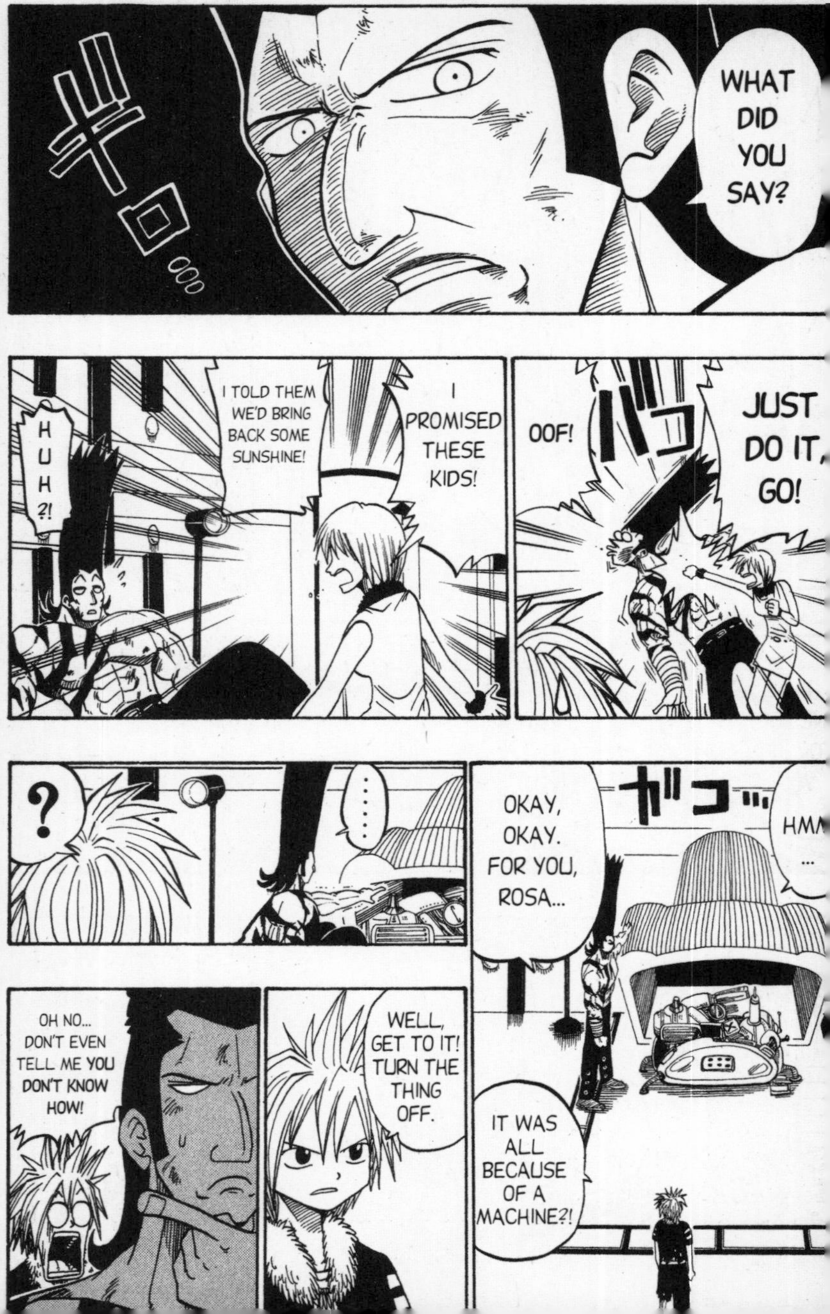

ギロ
WHAT DID YOU SAY?
JUST DO IT, GO!
バコ
OOF!
I PROMISED THESE KIDS!
I TOLD THEM WE'D BRING BACK SOME SUNSHINE!
HUH?!
HMM...
ガコッ
OKAY, OKAY. FOR YOU, ROSA...
IT WAS ALL BECAUSE OF A MACHINE?!
......
?
WELL, GET TO IT! TURN THE THING OFF.
OH NO... DON'T EVEN TELL ME YOU DON'T KNOW HOW!

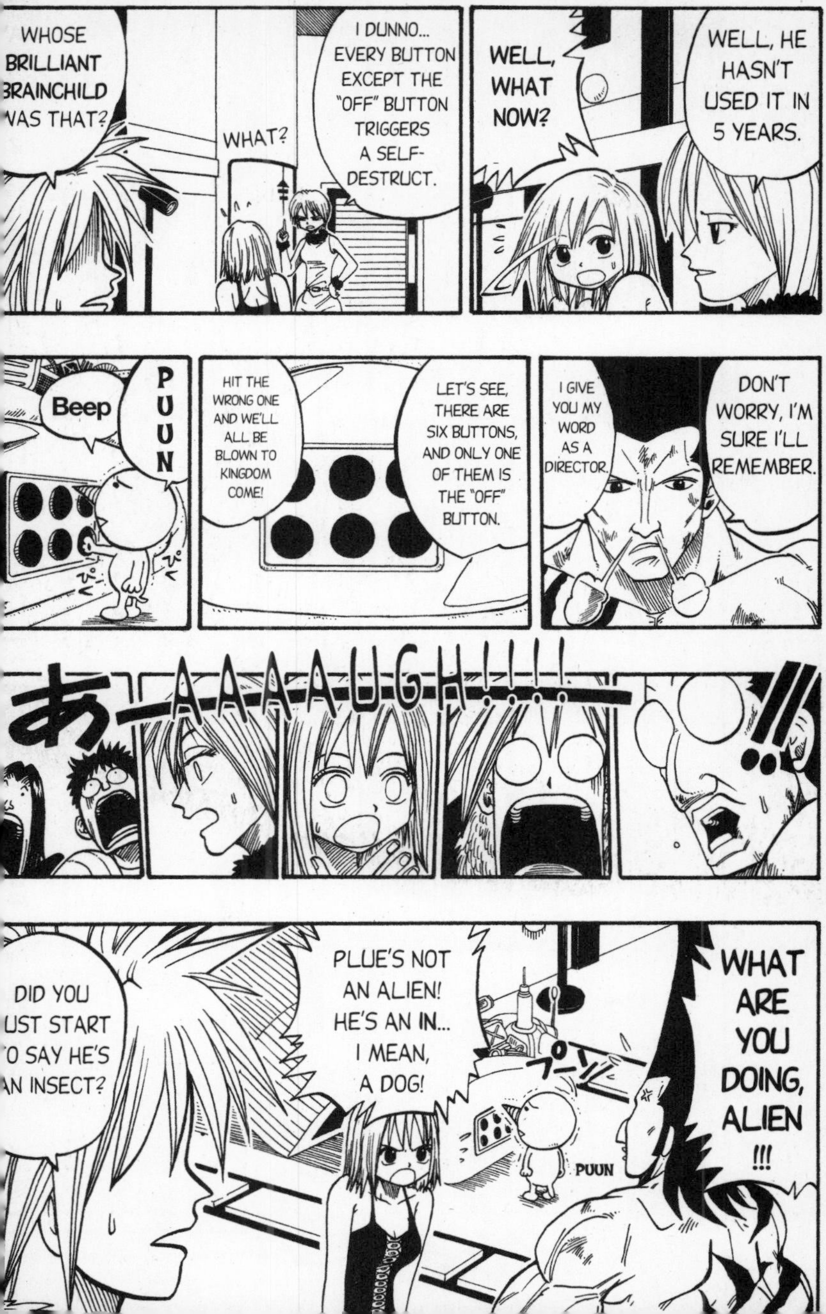

WELL, HE HASN'T USED IT IN 5 YEARS.
WELL, WHAT NOW?
I DUNNO... EVERY BUTTON EXCEPT THE "OFF" BUTTON TRIGGERS A SELF-DESTRUCT.
WHAT?
WHOSE BRILLIANT BRAINCHILD WAS THAT?
DON'T WORRY, I'M SURE I'LL REMEMBER.
I GIVE YOU MY WORD AS A DIRECTOR.
LET'S SEE, THERE ARE SIX BUTTONS, AND ONLY ONE OF THEM IS THE "OFF" BUTTON.
HIT THE WRONG ONE AND WE'LL ALL BE BLOWN TO KINGDOM COME!
PUUN
Beep
ぴく ぴく
あーAAAAUGH!!!!
WHAT ARE YOU DOING, ALIEN!!!
PUUN
プーン
PLUE'S NOT AN ALIEN! HE'S AN IN... I MEAN, A DOG!
DID YOU JUST START TO SAY HE'S AN INSECT?

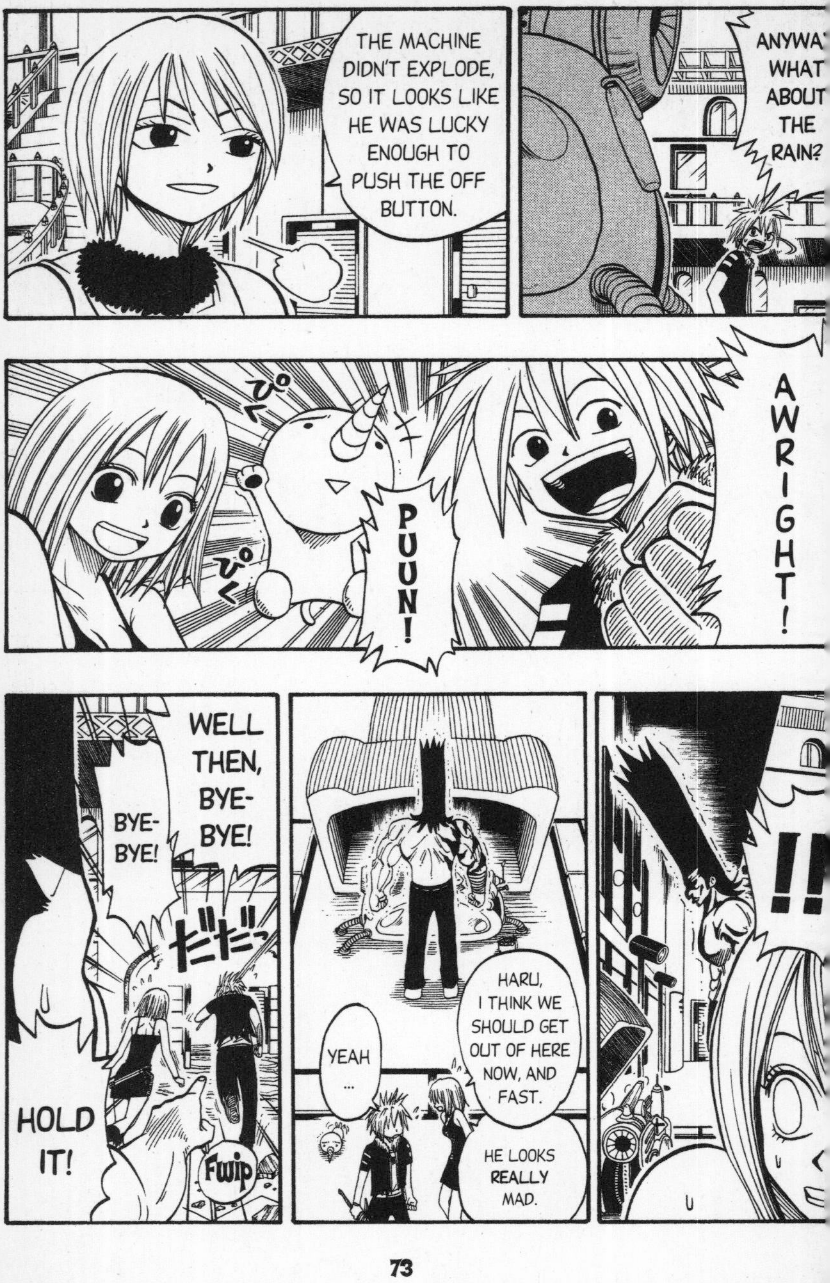
THE MACHINE DIDN'T EXPLODE, SO IT LOOKS LIKE HE WAS LUCKY ENOUGH TO PUSH THE OFF BUTTON.
ANYWA WHAT ABOUT THE RAIN?
ぴく
ぴく
PUUN!
AWRIGHT!
WELL THEN, BYE-BYE!
BYE-BYE!
だだっ
HOLD IT!
Fwip
HARU, I THINK WE SHOULD GET OUT OF HERE NOW, AND FAST.
YEAH ...
HE LOOKS REALLY MAD.
!!

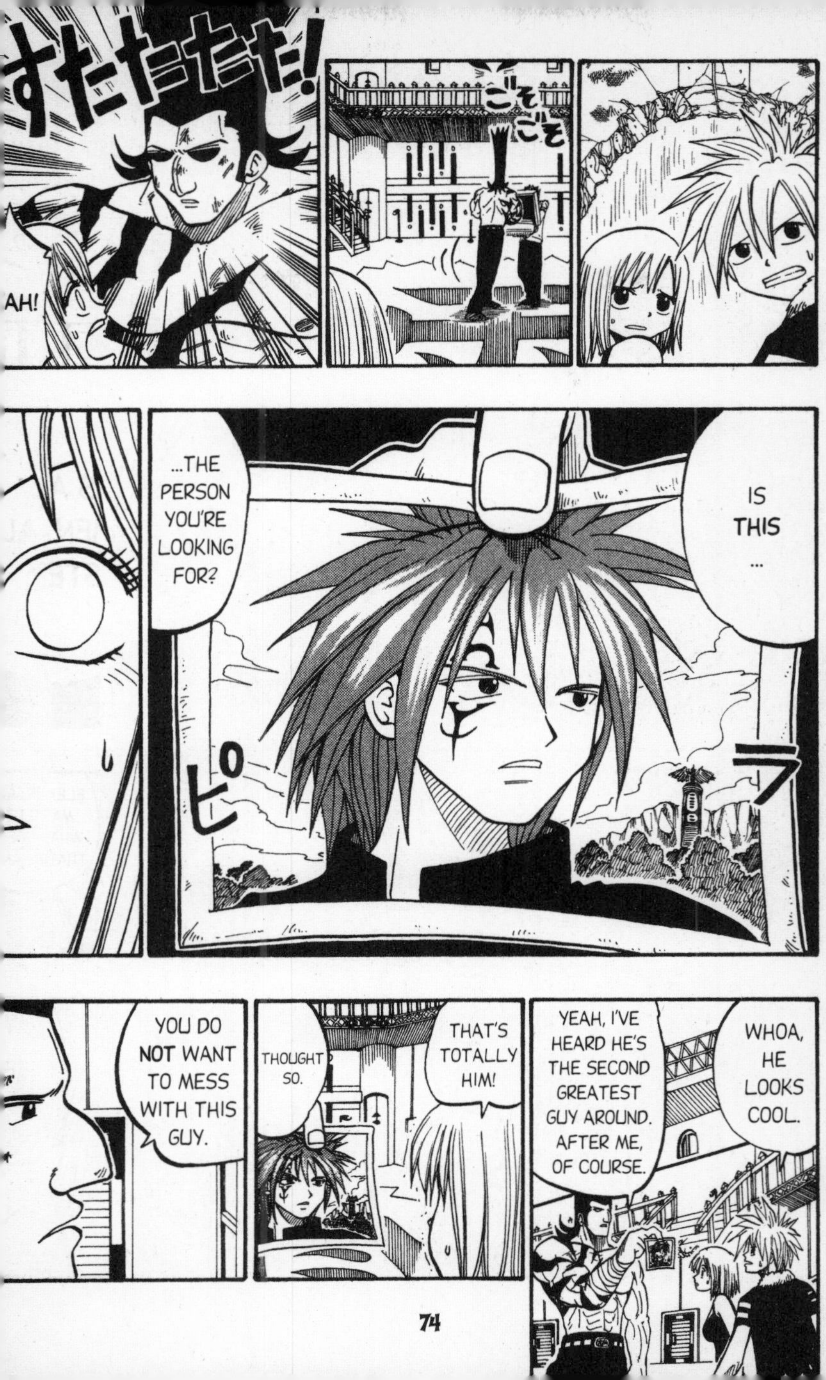
ごそごそ
すたたたた!
AH!
IS THIS ...
...THE PERSON YOU'RE LOOKING FOR?
ピラ
WHOA, HE LOOKS COOL.
YEAH, I'VE HEARD HE'S THE SECOND GREATEST GUY AROUND. AFTER ME, OF COURSE.
THAT'S TOTALLY HIM!
THOUGHT SO.
YOU DO **NOT** WANT TO MESS WITH THIS GUY.

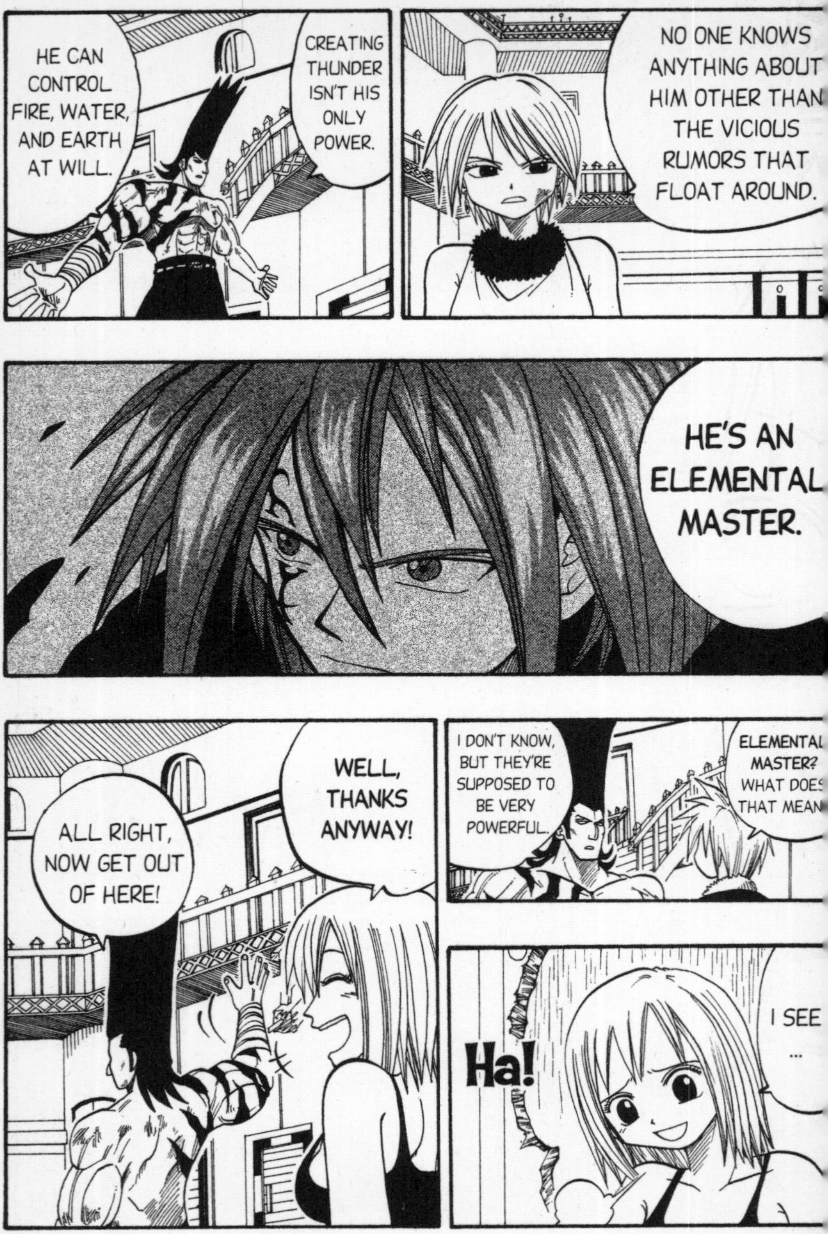
NO ONE KNOWS ANYTHING ABOUT HIM OTHER THAN THE VICIOUS RUMORS THAT FLOAT AROUND.
CREATING THUNDER ISN'T HIS ONLY POWER.
HE CAN CONTROL FIRE, WATER, AND EARTH AT WILL.
HE'S AN ELEMENTAL MASTER.
ELEMENTAL MASTER? WHAT DOES THAT MEAN
I DON'T KNOW, BUT THEY'RE SUPPOSED TO BE VERY POWERFUL.
I SEE ...
Ha!
WELL, THANKS ANYWAY!
ALL RIGHT, NOW GET OUT OF HERE!

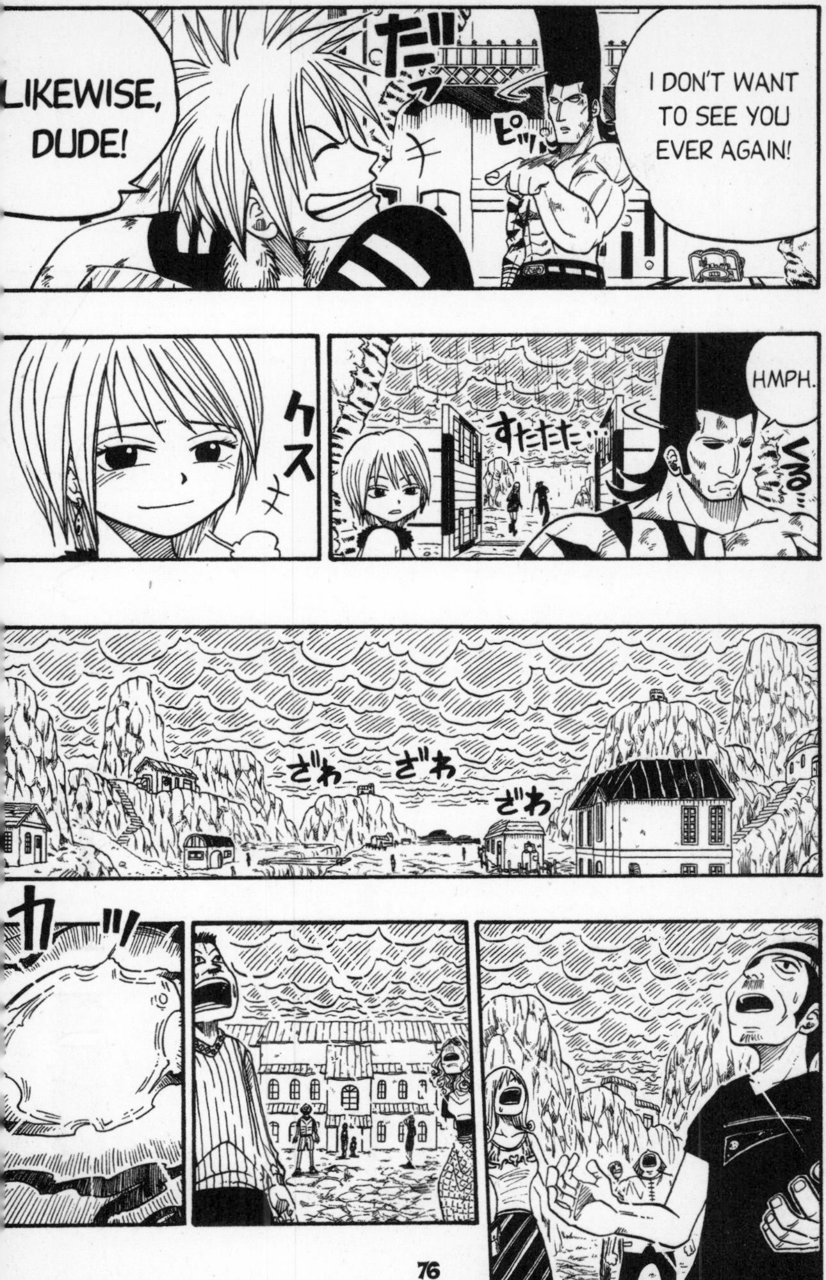
I DON'T WANT TO SEE YOU EVER AGAIN!
ピッ
だーッ
LIKEWISE, DUDE!
HMPH.
くる…
すたたた…
クスッ
ざわ
ざわ
ざわ
カーッ

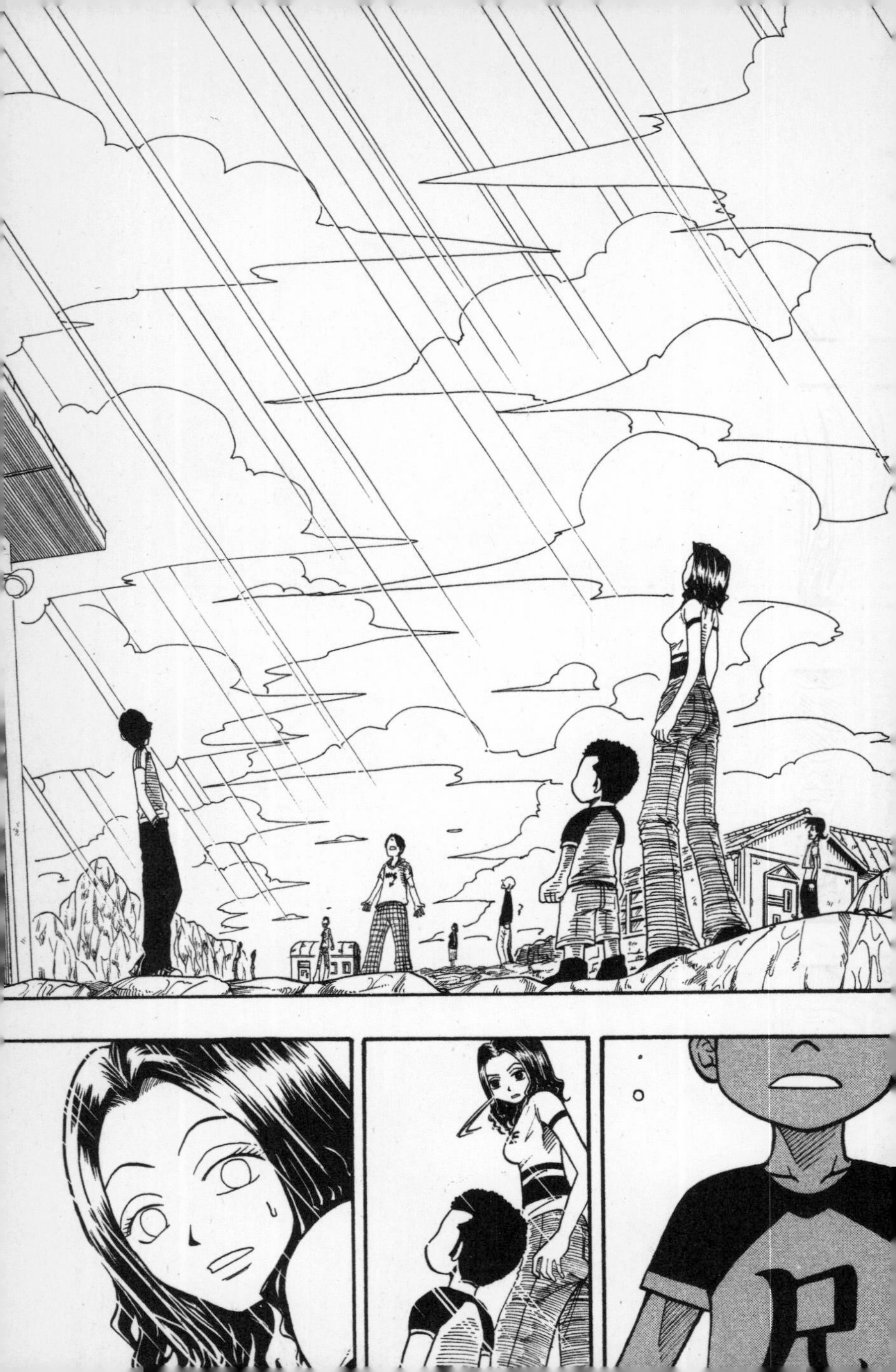

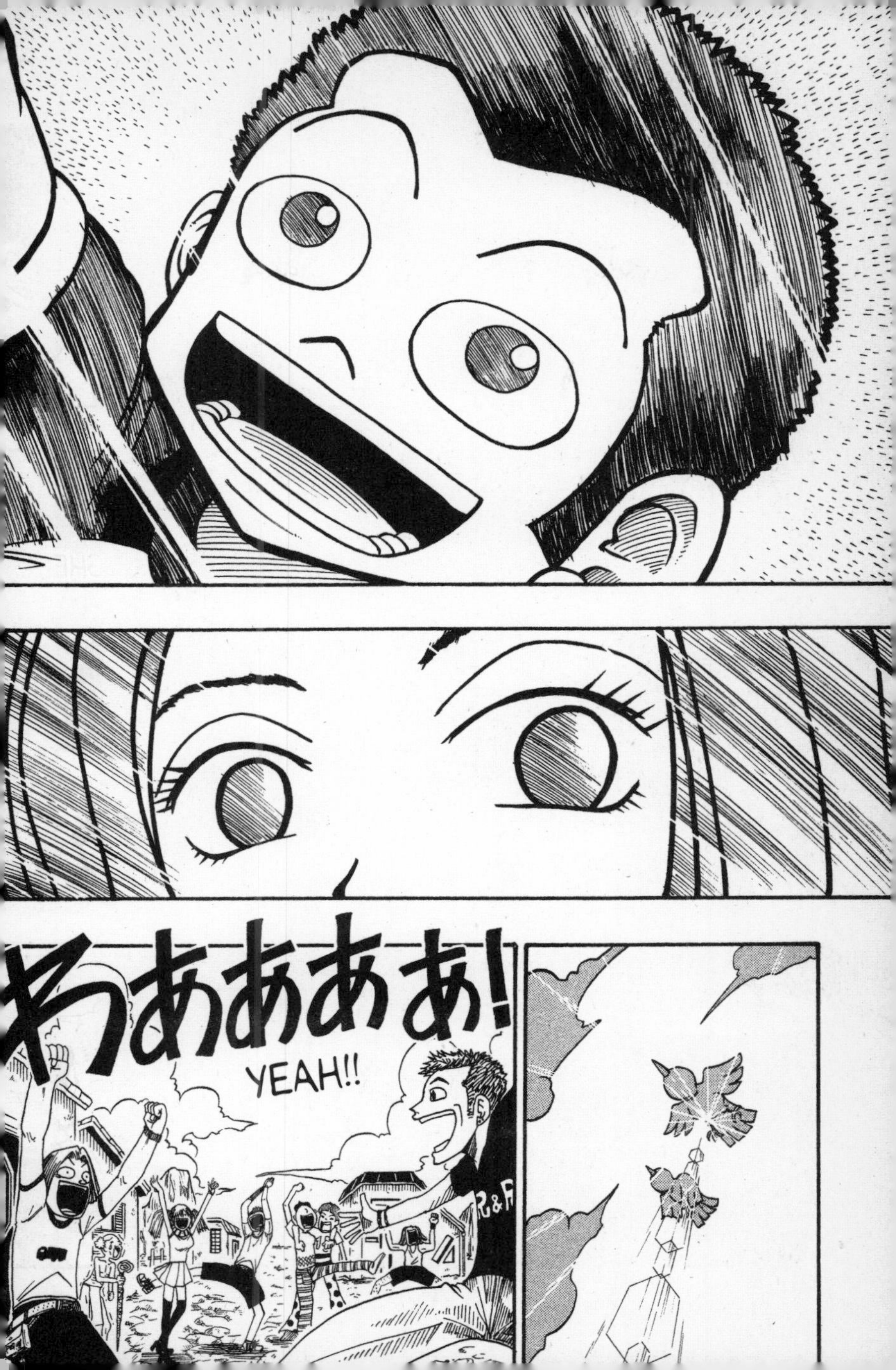
わあああああ!
YEAH!!

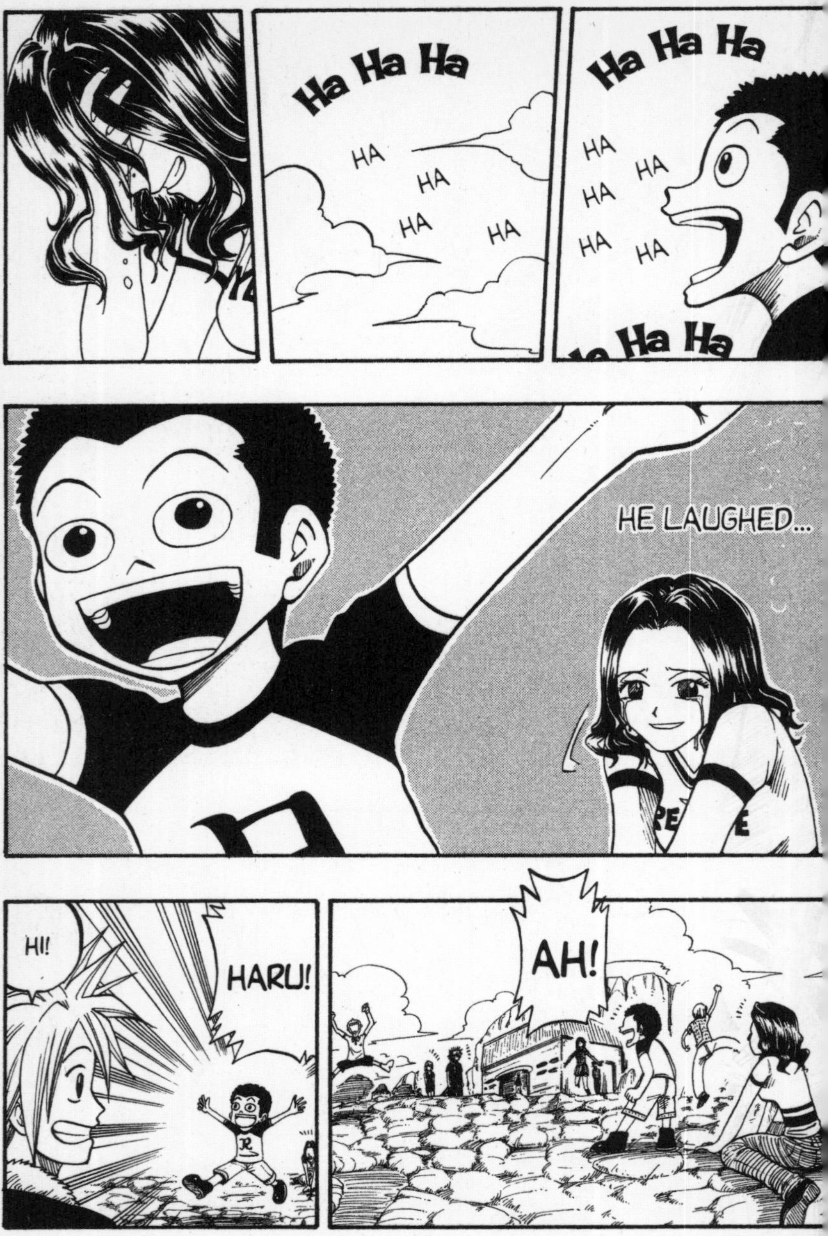
Ha Ha Ha
HA
HA
HA
HA
HA
HA
Ha Ha
Ha Ha Ha
HA
HA
HA
HA
HE LAUGHED...
AH!
HARU!
HI!

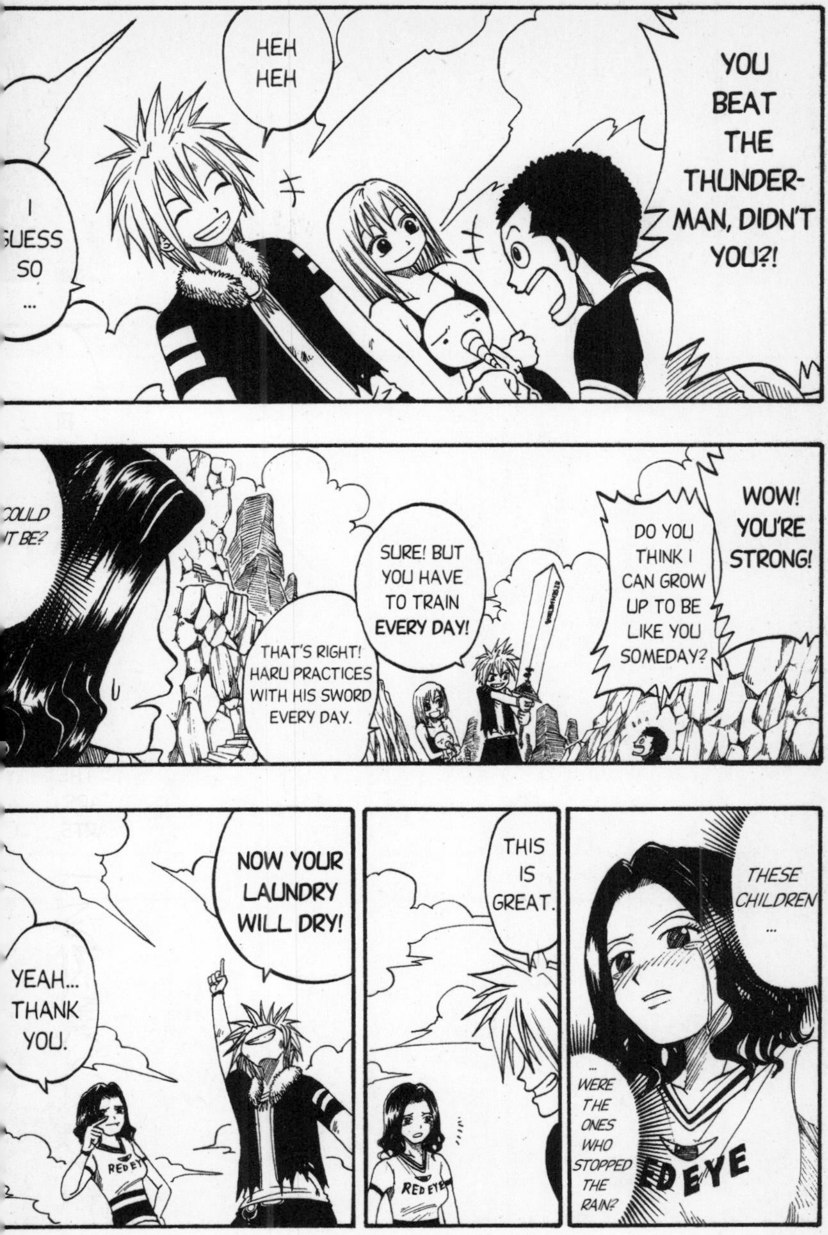
YOU BEAT THE THUNDER-MAN, DIDN'T YOU?!
HEH HEH
I GUESS SO ...
WOW! YOU'RE STRONG!
DO YOU THINK I CAN GROW UP TO BE LIKE YOU SOMEDAY?
SURE! BUT YOU HAVE TO TRAIN EVERY DAY!
THAT'S RIGHT! HARU PRACTICES WITH HIS SWORD EVERY DAY.
THESE CHILDREN ...
... WERE THE ONES WHO STOPPED THE RAIN?
THIS IS GREAT.
NOW YOUR LAUNDRY WILL DRY!
YEAH... THANK YOU.

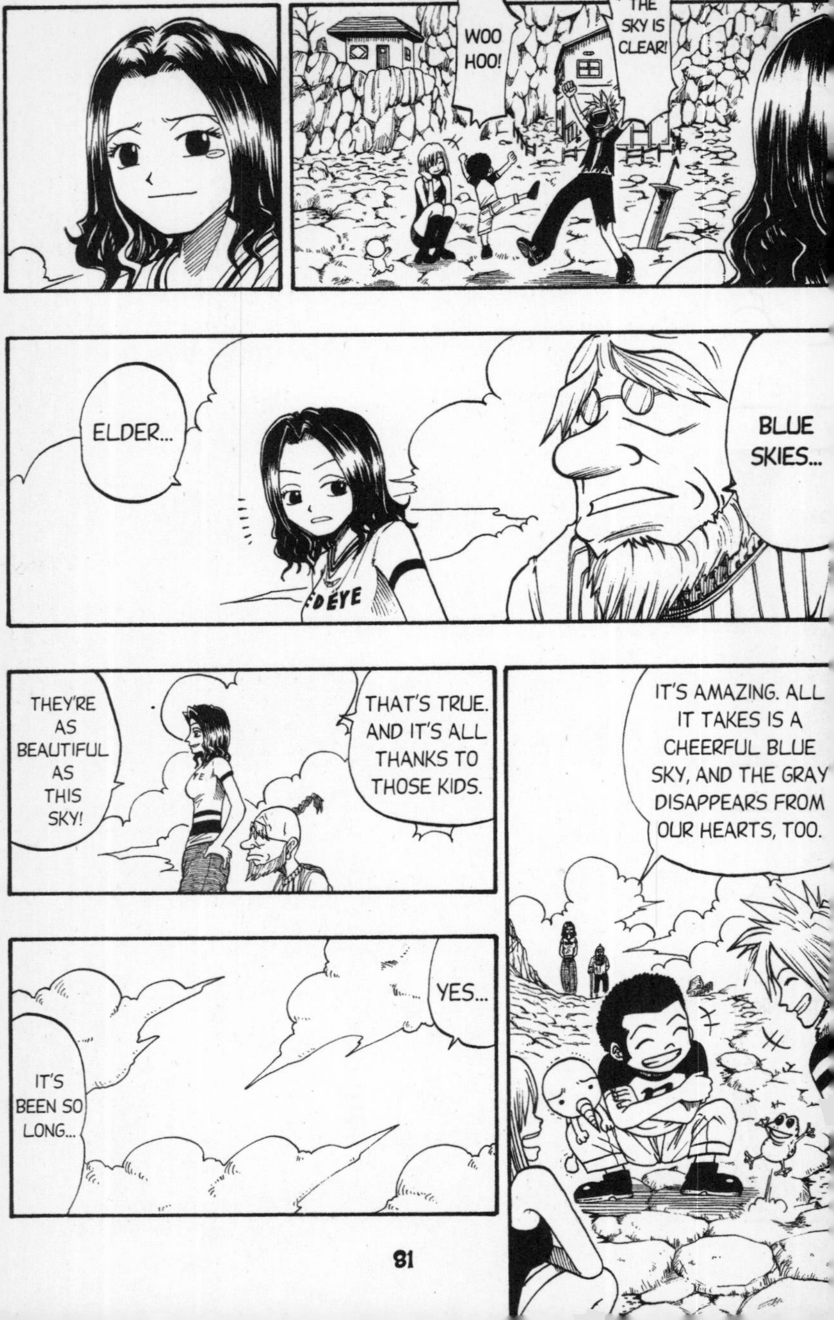
THE SKY IS CLEAR!
WOO HOO!
BLUE SKIES...
ELDER...
IT'S AMAZING. ALL IT TAKES IS A CHEERFUL BLUE SKY, AND THE GRAY DISAPPEARS FROM OUR HEARTS, TOO.
THAT'S TRUE. AND IT'S ALL THANKS TO THOSE KIDS.
THEY'RE AS BEAUTIFUL AS THIS SKY!
YES...
IT'S BEEN SO LONG...

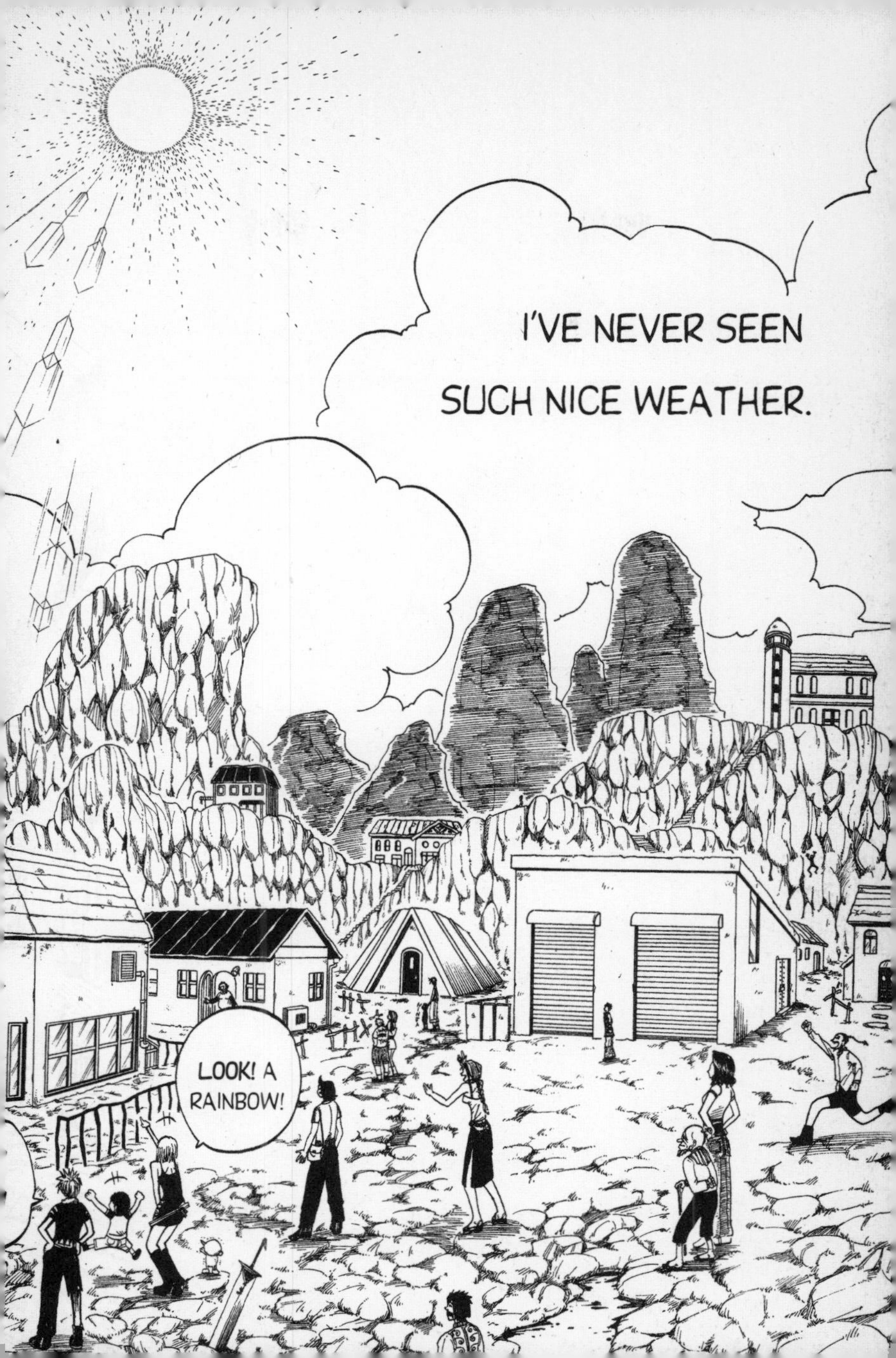
I'VE NEVER SEEN SUCH NICE WEATHER.
LOOK! A RAINBOW!

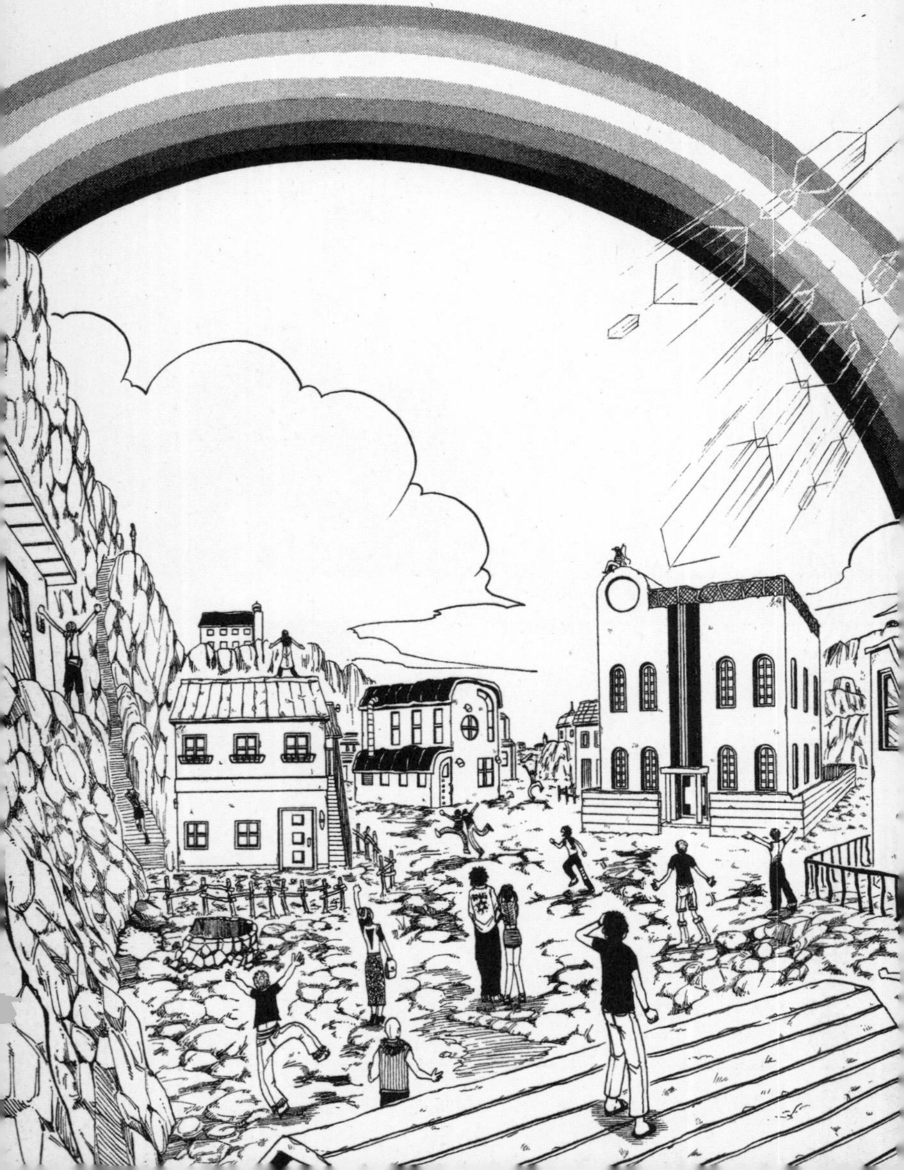

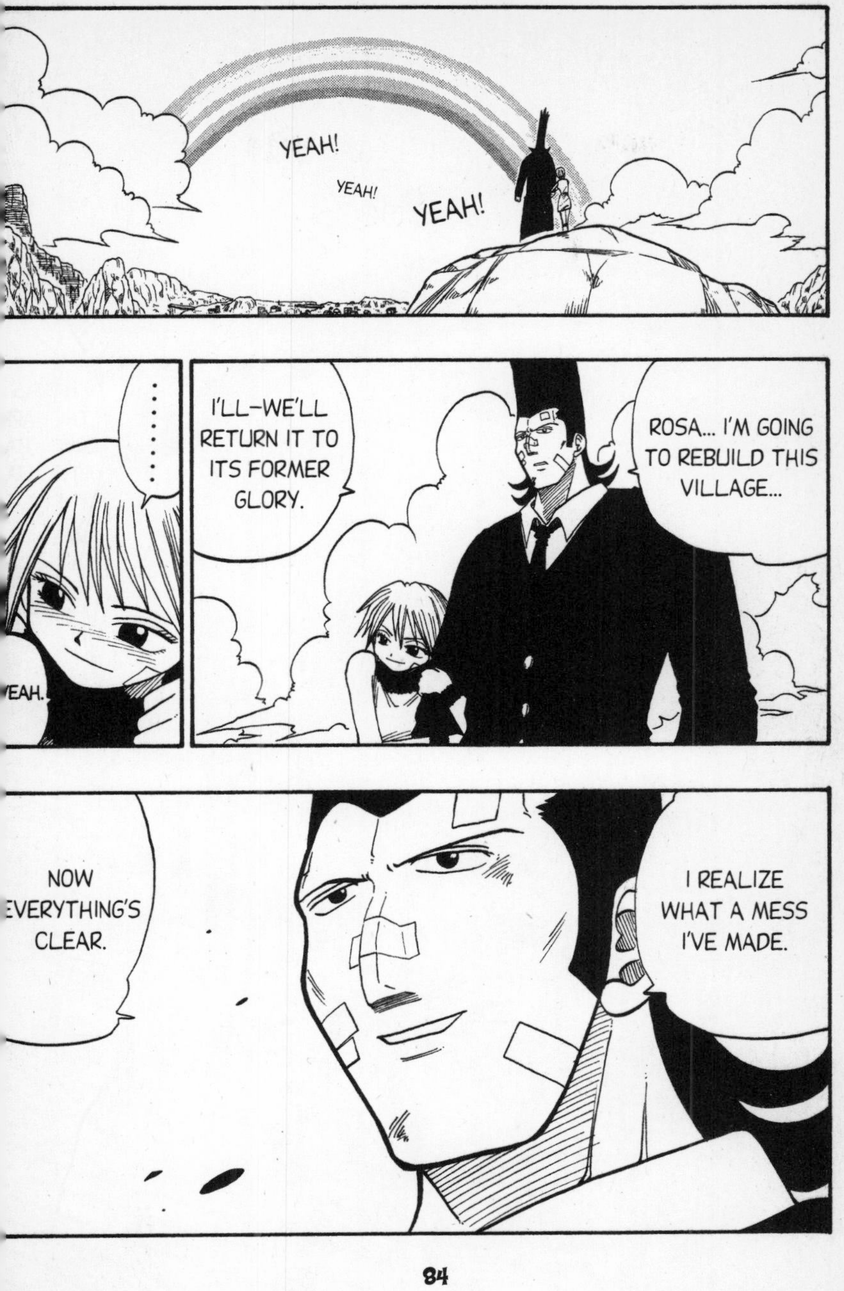
YEAH!
YEAH!
YEAH!
ROSA... I'M GOING TO REBUILD THIS VILLAGE...
I'LL-WE'LL RETURN IT TO ITS FORMER GLORY.
......
EAH.
I REALIZE WHAT A MESS I'VE MADE.
NOW EVERYTHING'S CLEAR.

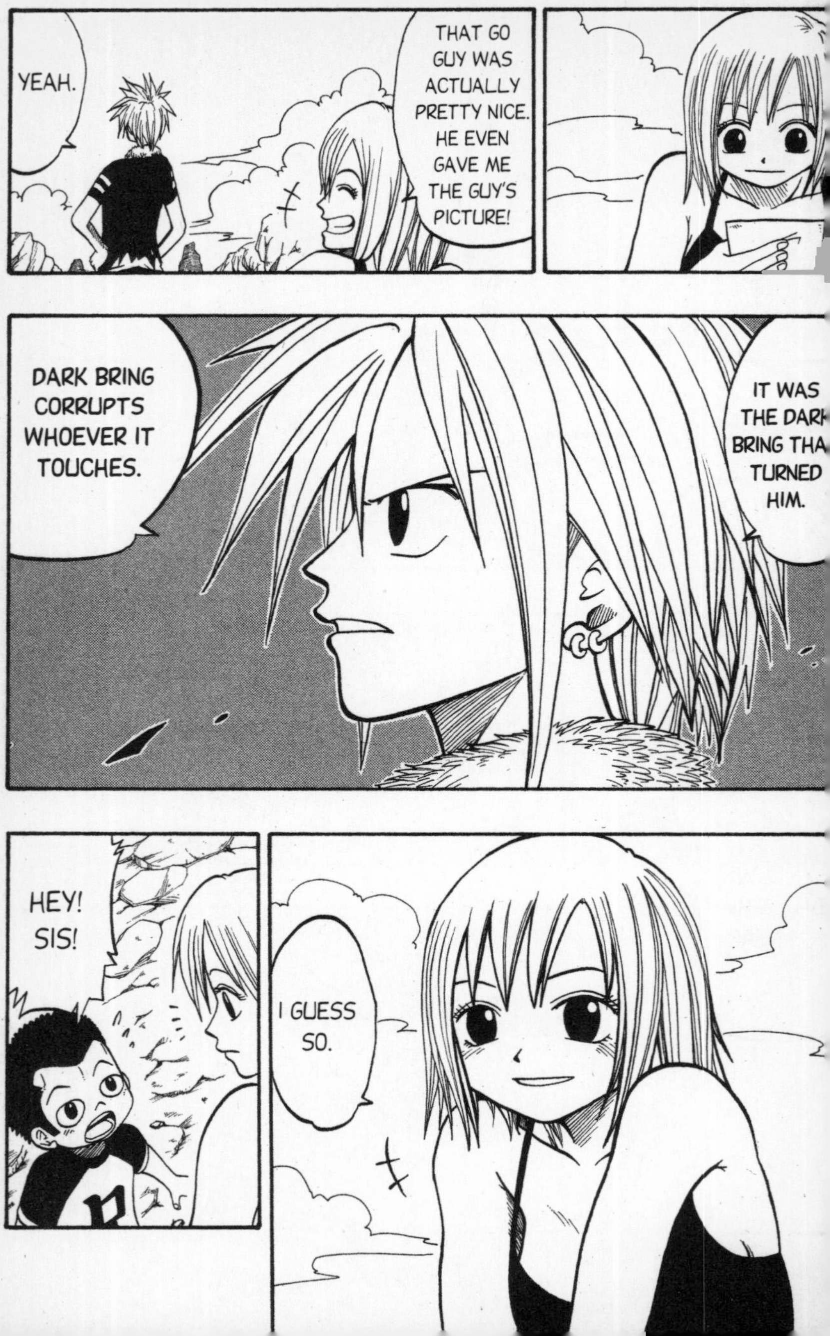
THAT GO GUY WAS ACTUALLY PRETTY NICE. HE EVEN GAVE ME THE GUY'S PICTURE!
YEAH.
IT WAS THE DARK BRING THA TURNED HIM.
DARK BRING CORRUPTS WHOEVER IT TOUCHES.
I GUESS SO.
HEY! SIS!

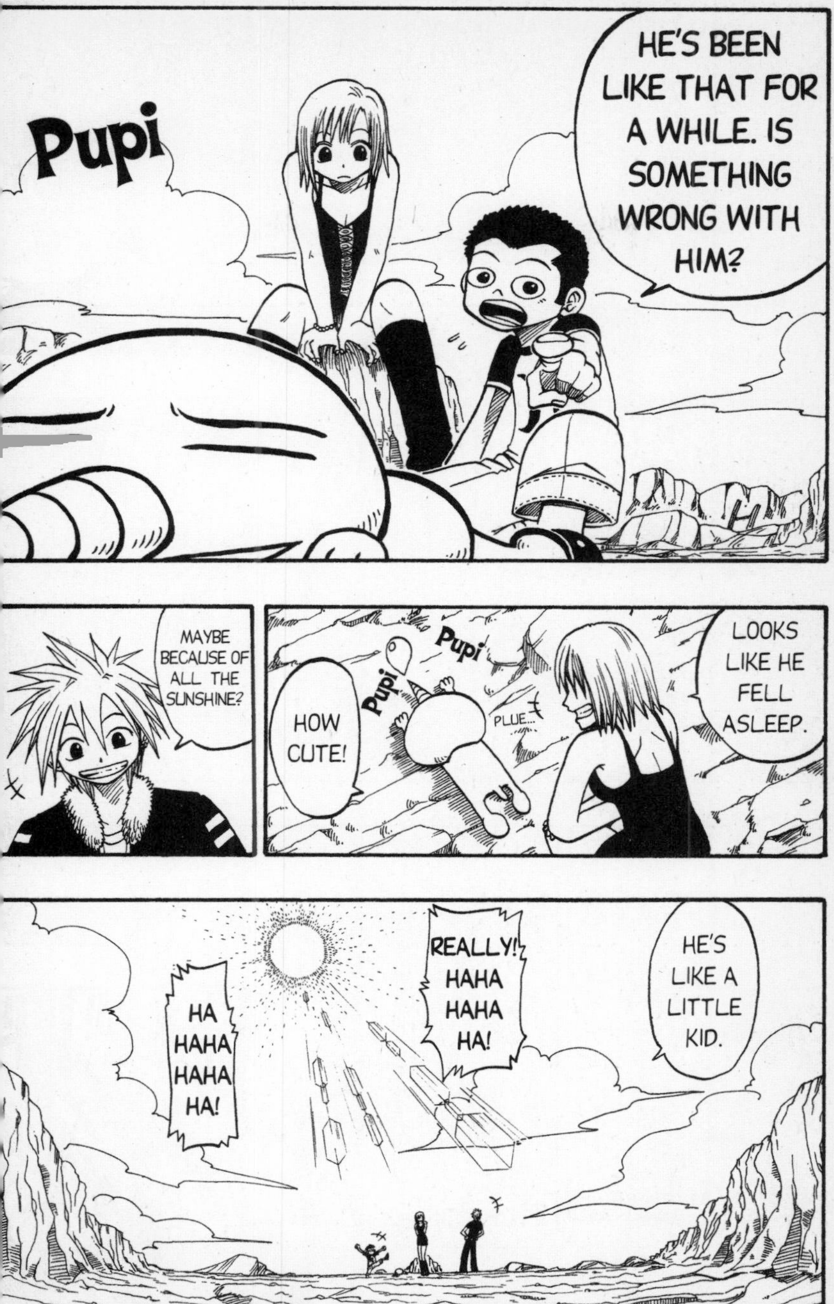
HE'S BEEN LIKE THAT FOR A WHILE. IS SOMETHING WRONG WITH HIM?
Pupi
LOOKS LIKE HE FELL ASLEEP.
Pupi
Pupi
PLUE...
HOW CUTE!
MAYBE BECAUSE OF ALL THE SUNSHINE?
HE'S LIKE A LITTLE KID.
REALLY! HAHA HAHA HA!
HA HAHA HAHA HA!

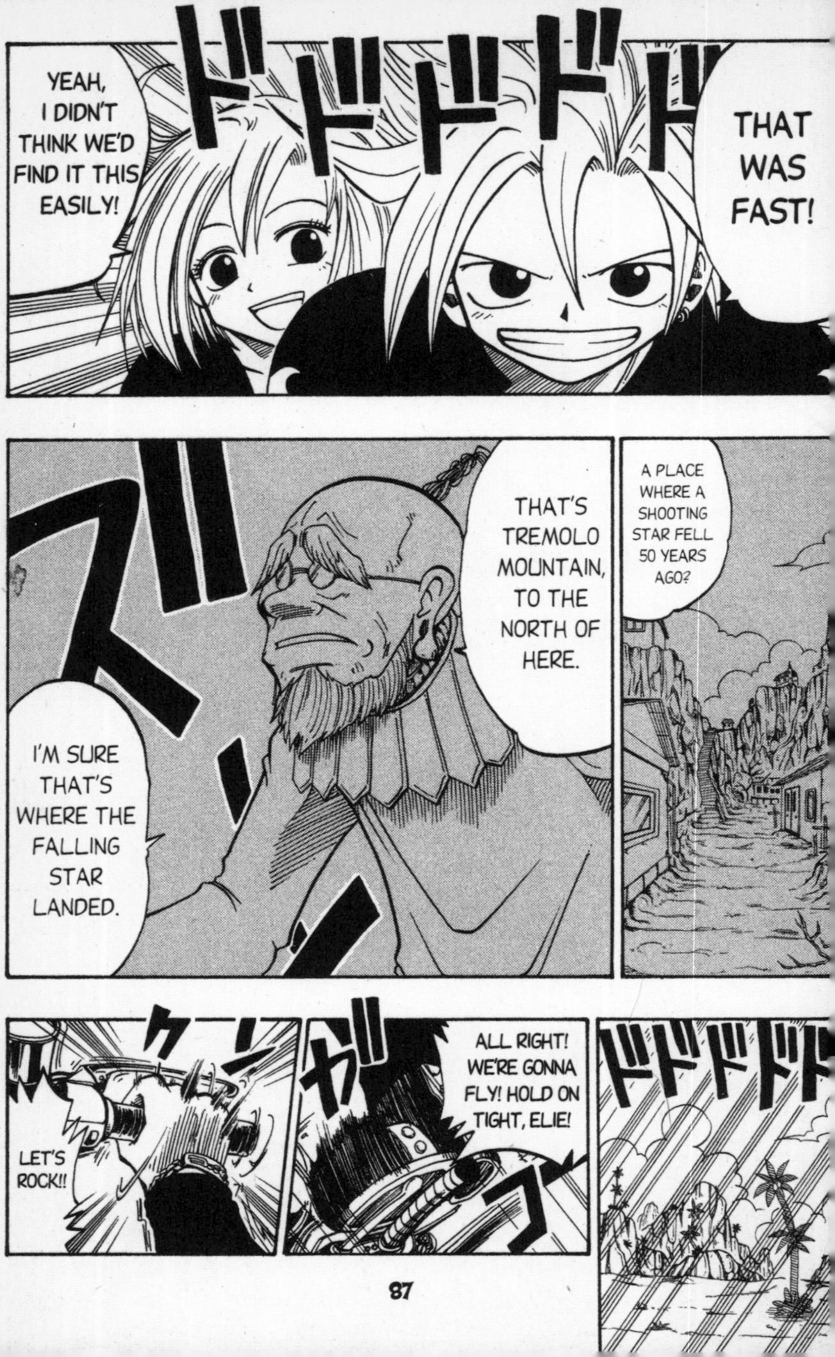
THAT WAS FAST!
YEAH, I DIDN'T THINK WE'D FIND IT THIS EASILY!
A PLACE WHERE A SHOOTING STAR FELL 50 YEARS AGO?
THAT'S TREMOLO MOUNTAIN, TO THE NORTH OF HERE.
I'M SURE THAT'S WHERE THE FALLING STAR LANDED.
ALL RIGHT! WE'RE GONNA FLY! HOLD ON TIGHT, ELIE!
LET'S ROCK!!

RAVE MASTER

RAVE:26 Viva la Labyrinth!

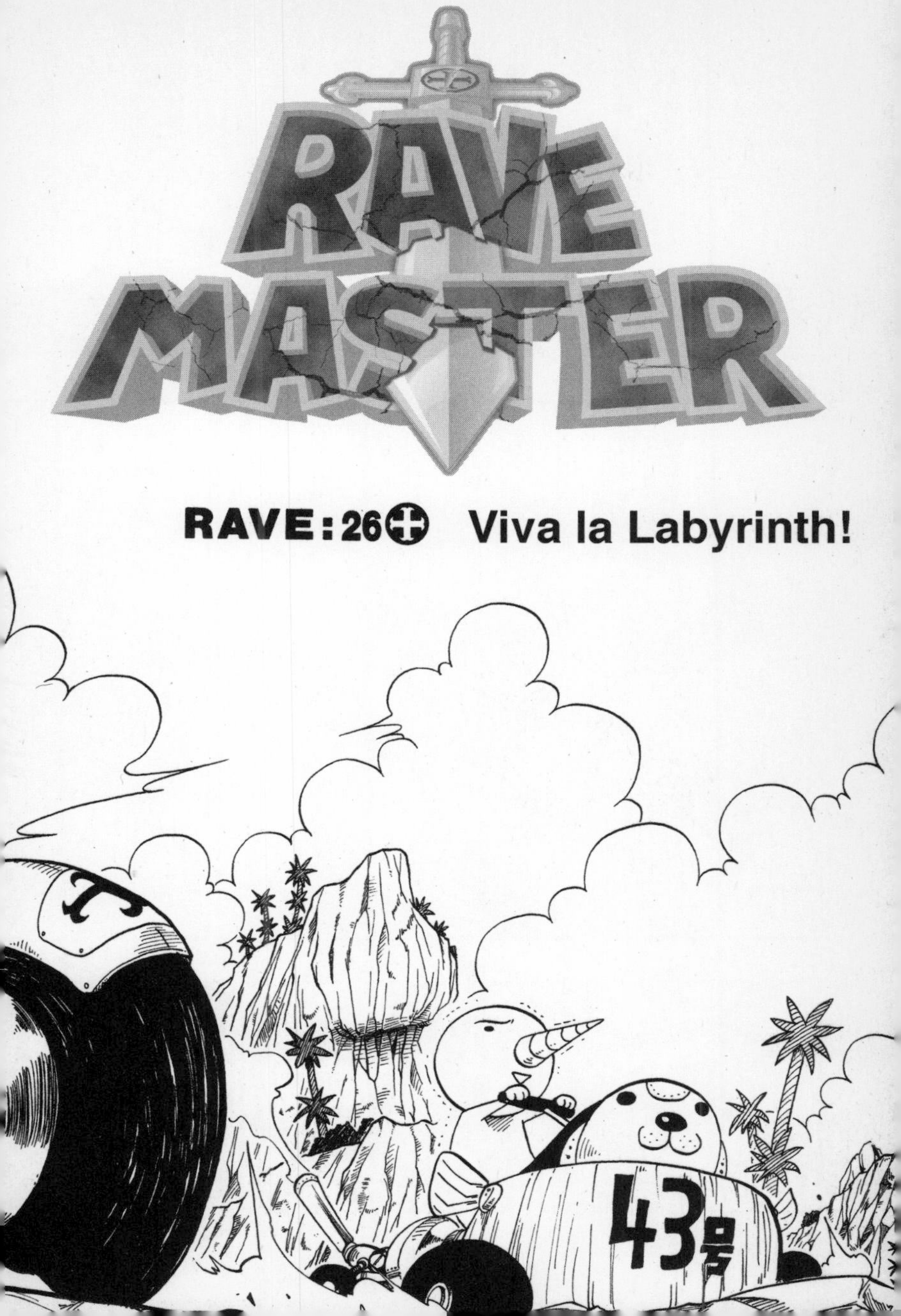
43号

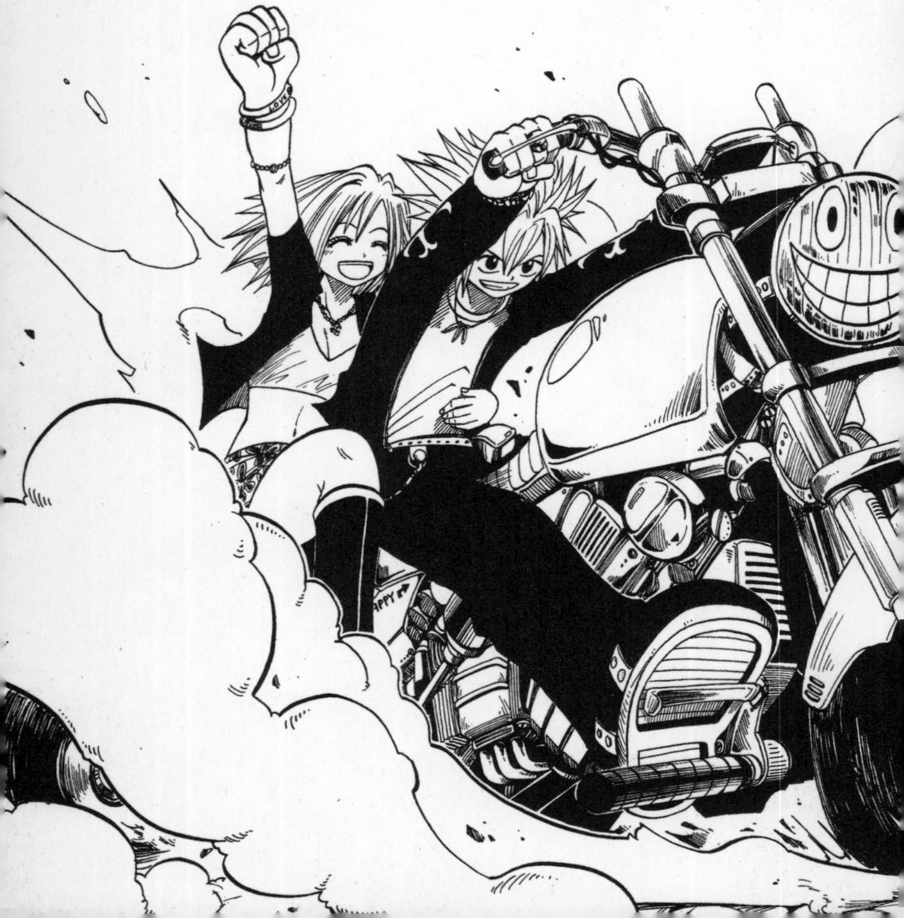

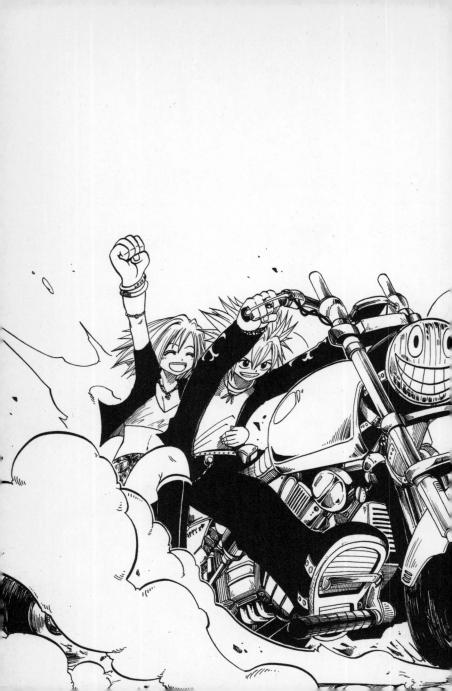

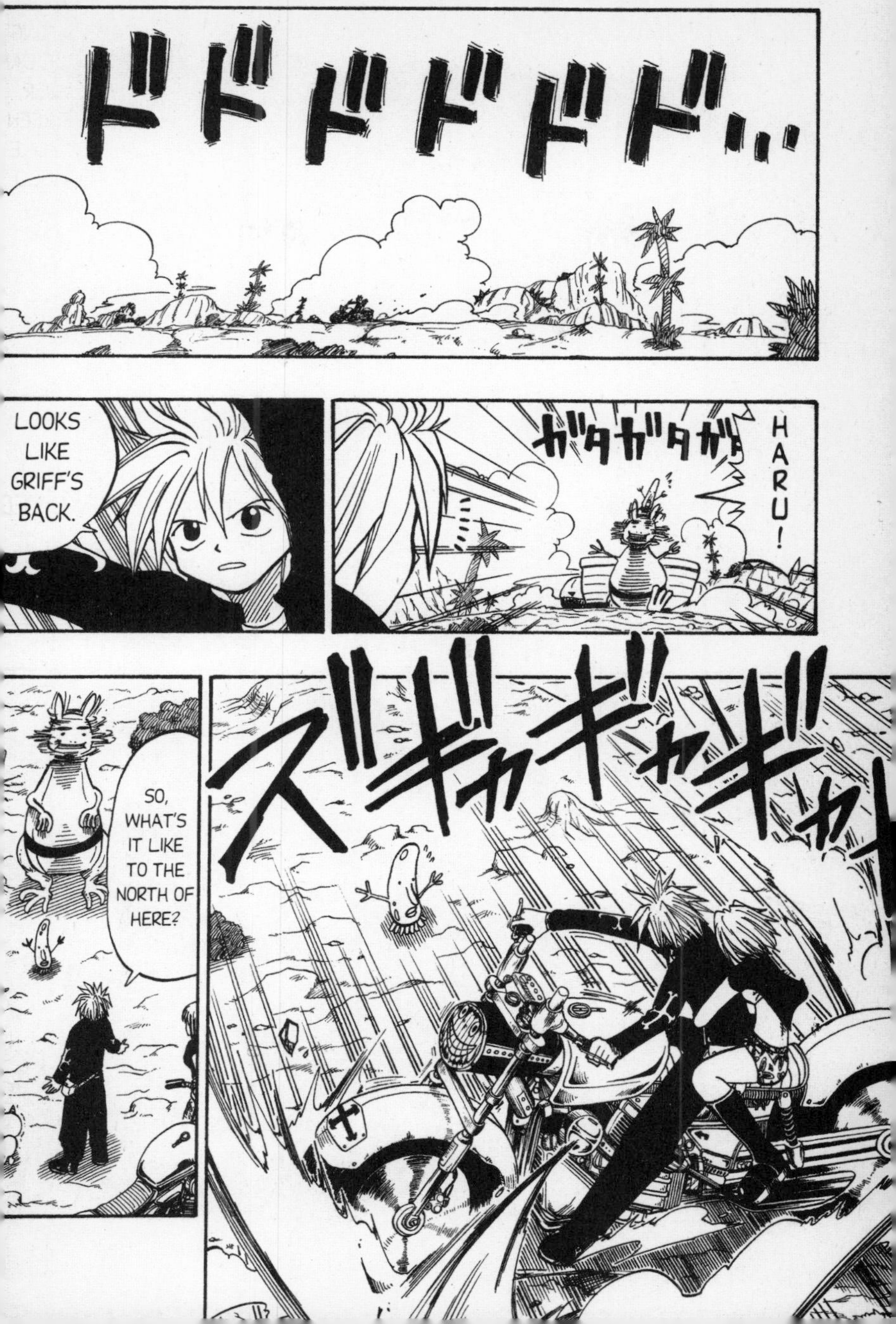
ドドドドドド‥
ガタガタガ
HARU!
LOOKS LIKE GRIFF'S BACK.
ズギャギャギャ
SO, WHAT'S IT LIKE TO THE NORTH OF HERE?

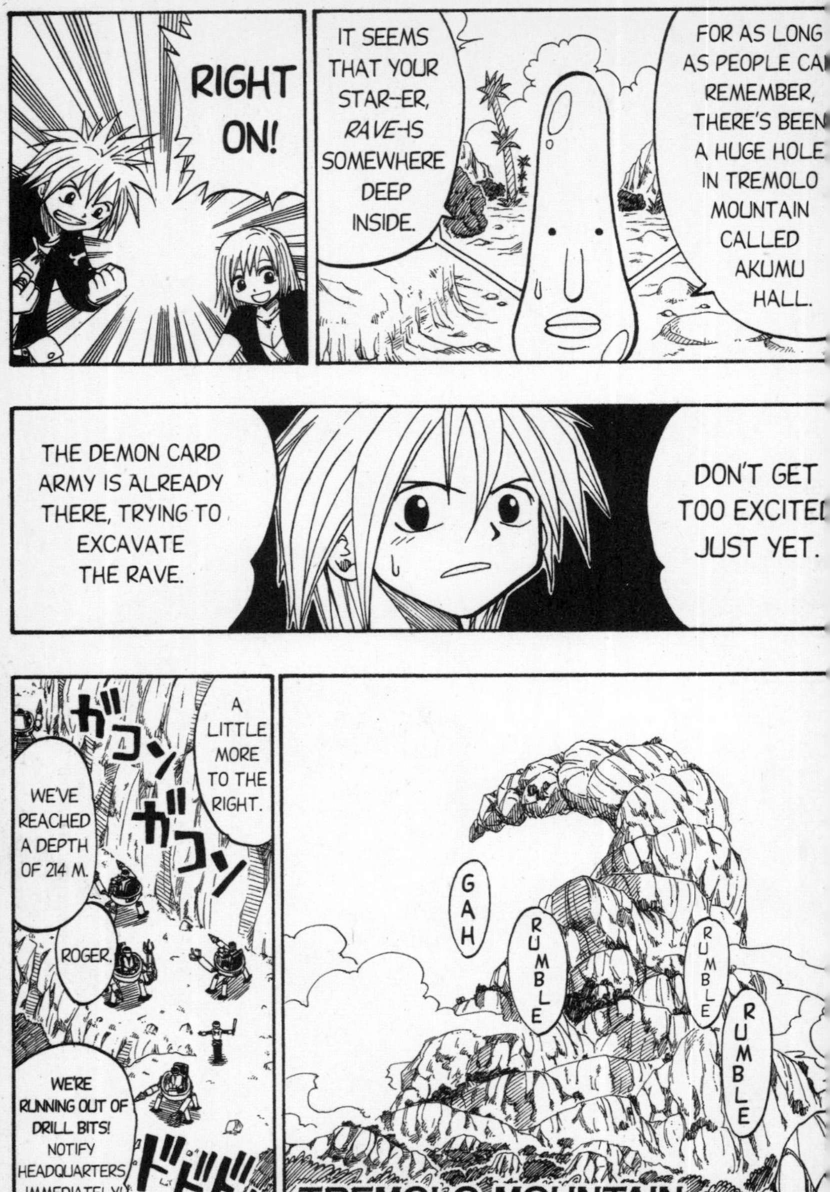
FOR AS LONG AS PEOPLE CA REMEMBER, THERE'S BEEN A HUGE HOLE IN TREMOLO MOUNTAIN CALLED AKUMU HALL.
IT SEEMS THAT YOUR STAR--ER, *RAVE*--IS SOMEWHERE DEEP INSIDE.
RIGHT ON!
DON'T GET TOO EXCITE JUST YET.
THE DEMON CARD ARMY IS ALREADY THERE, TRYING TO EXCAVATE THE RAVE.
RUMBLE
RUMBLE
RUMBLE
GAH
TREMOLO MOUNTAIN
A LITTLE MORE TO THE RIGHT.
ガコン
ガコン
WE'VE REACHED A DEPTH OF 214 M.
ROGER.
WE'RE RUNNING OUT OF DRILL BITS! NOTIFY HEADQUARTERS IMMEDIATELY!
ドドド…

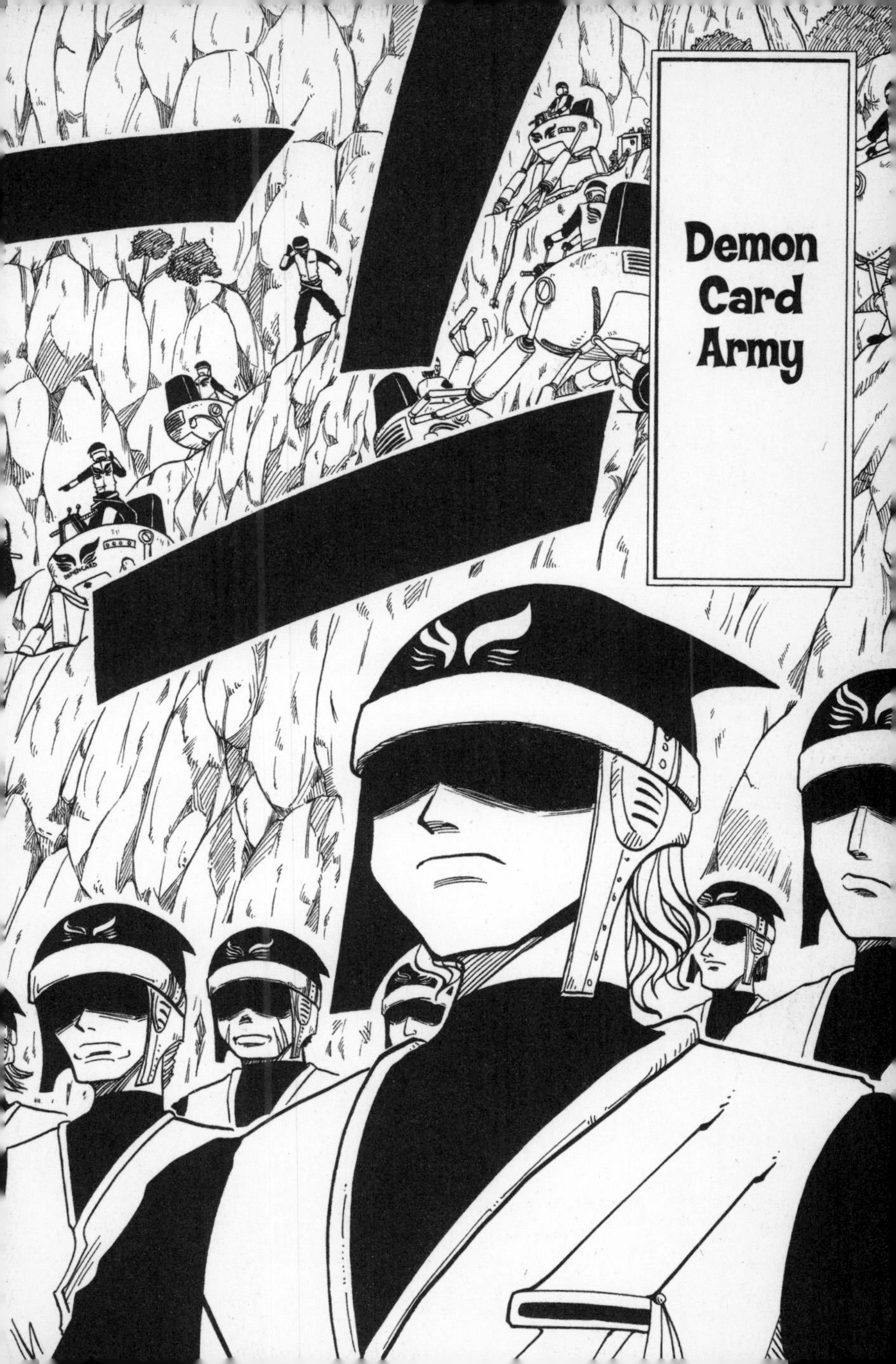
Demon
Card
Army

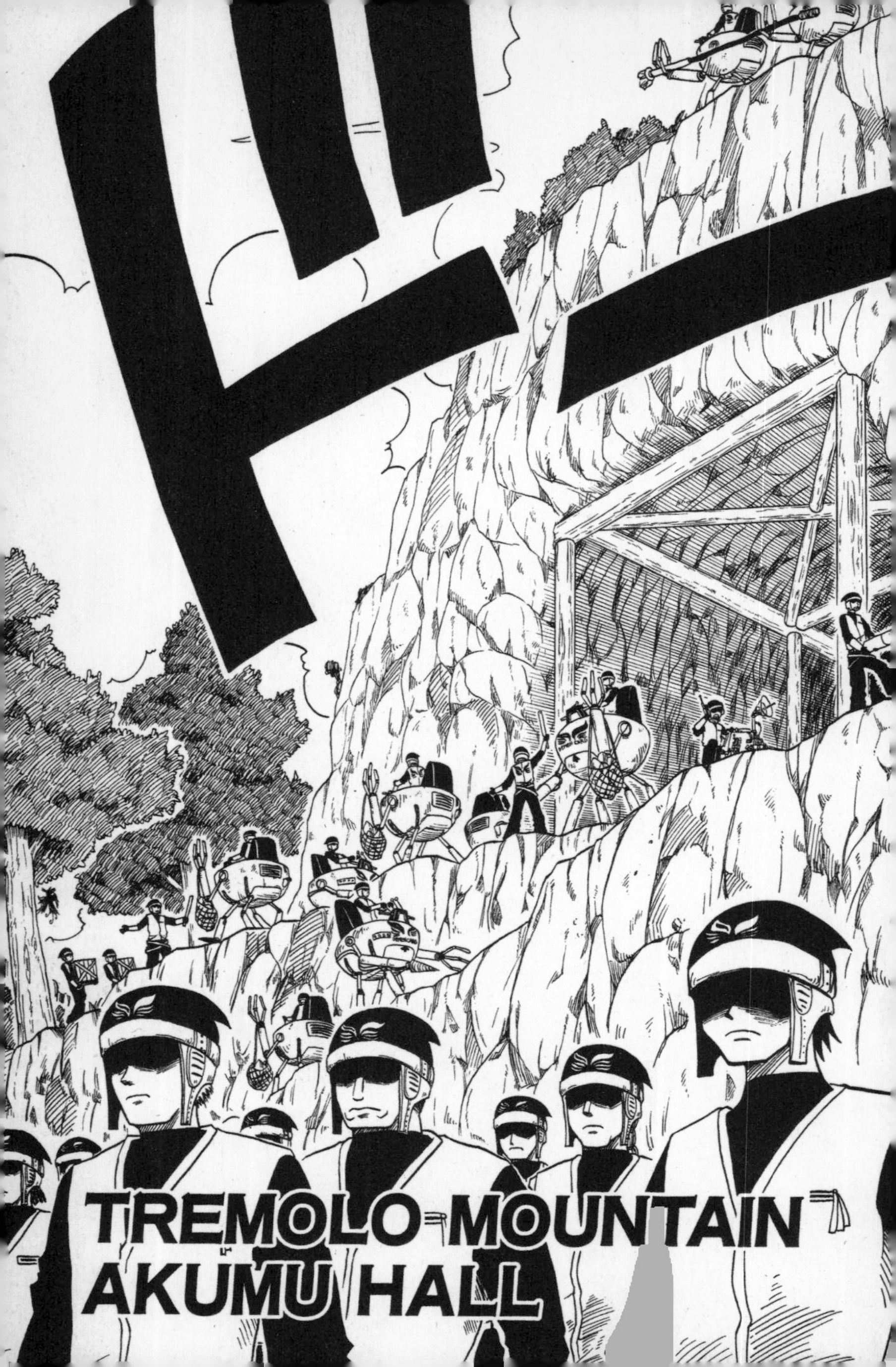
ドー
TREMOLO MOUNTAIN
AKUMU HALL

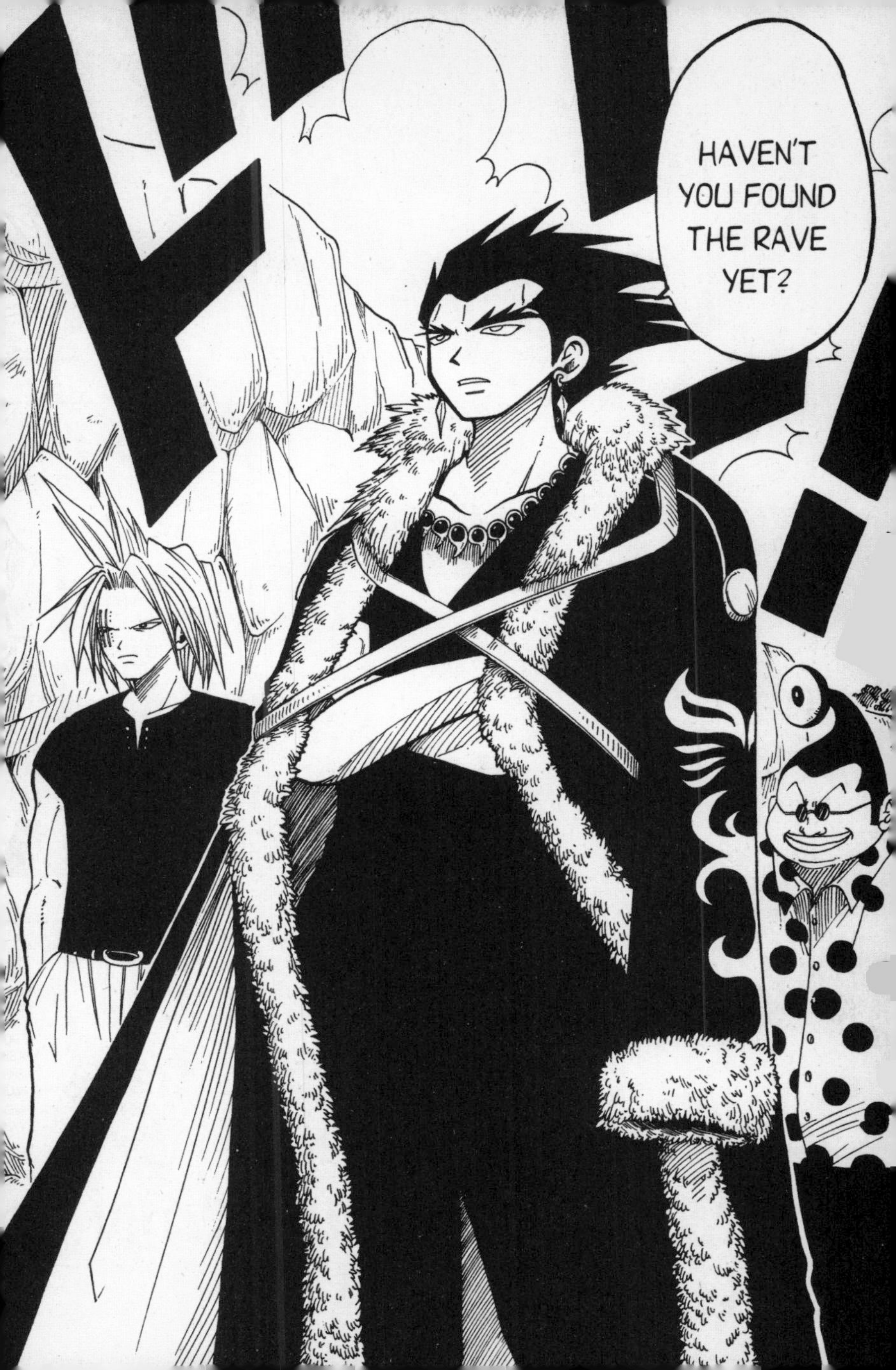
HAVEN'T YOU FOUND THE RAVE YET?

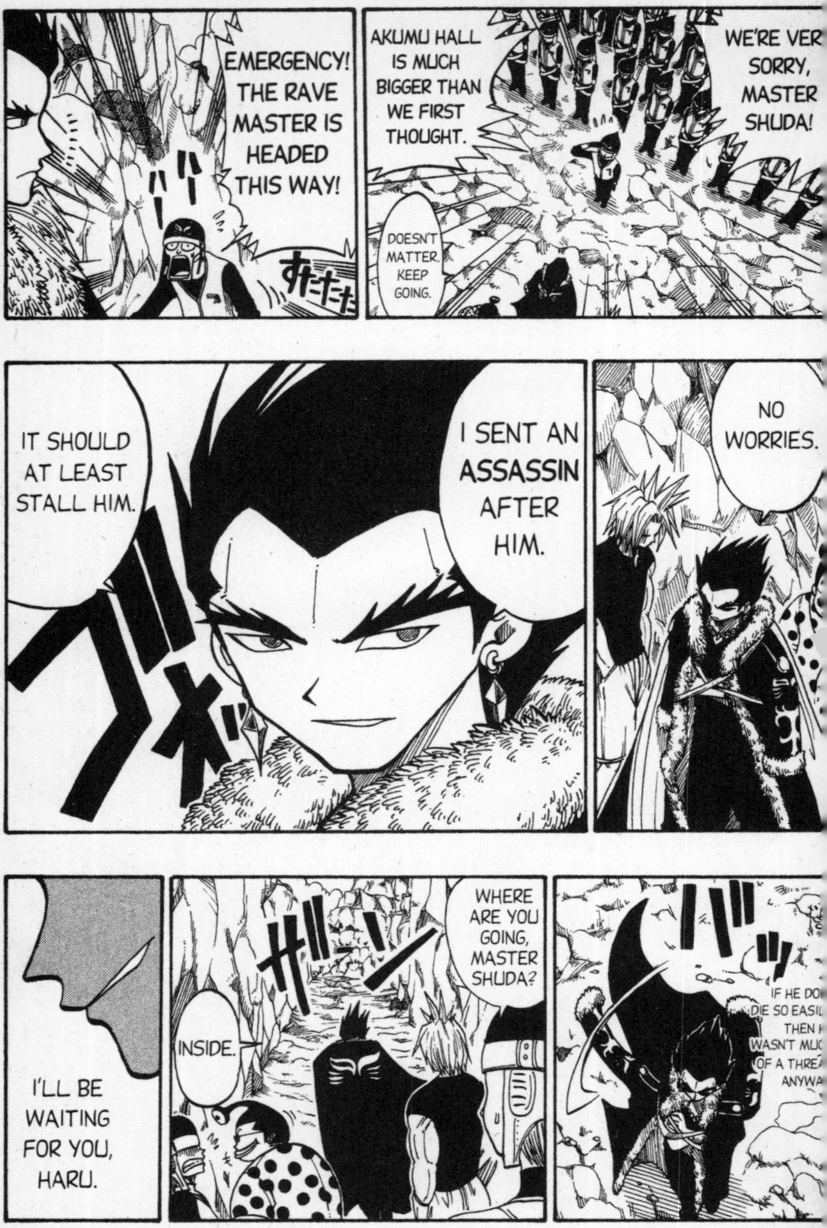
WE'RE VER SORRY, MASTER SHUDA!
AKUMU HALL IS MUCH BIGGER THAN WE FIRST THOUGHT.
DOESN'T MATTER. KEEP GOING.
EMERGENCY! THE RAVE MASTER IS HEADED THIS WAY!
NO WORRIES.
I SENT AN ASSASSIN AFTER HIM.
IT SHOULD AT LEAST STALL HIM.
IF HE DO DIE SO EASIL THEN WASN'T MUC OF A THREA ANYWA
WHERE ARE YOU GOING, MASTER SHUDA?
INSIDE.
I'LL BE WAITING FOR YOU, HARU.

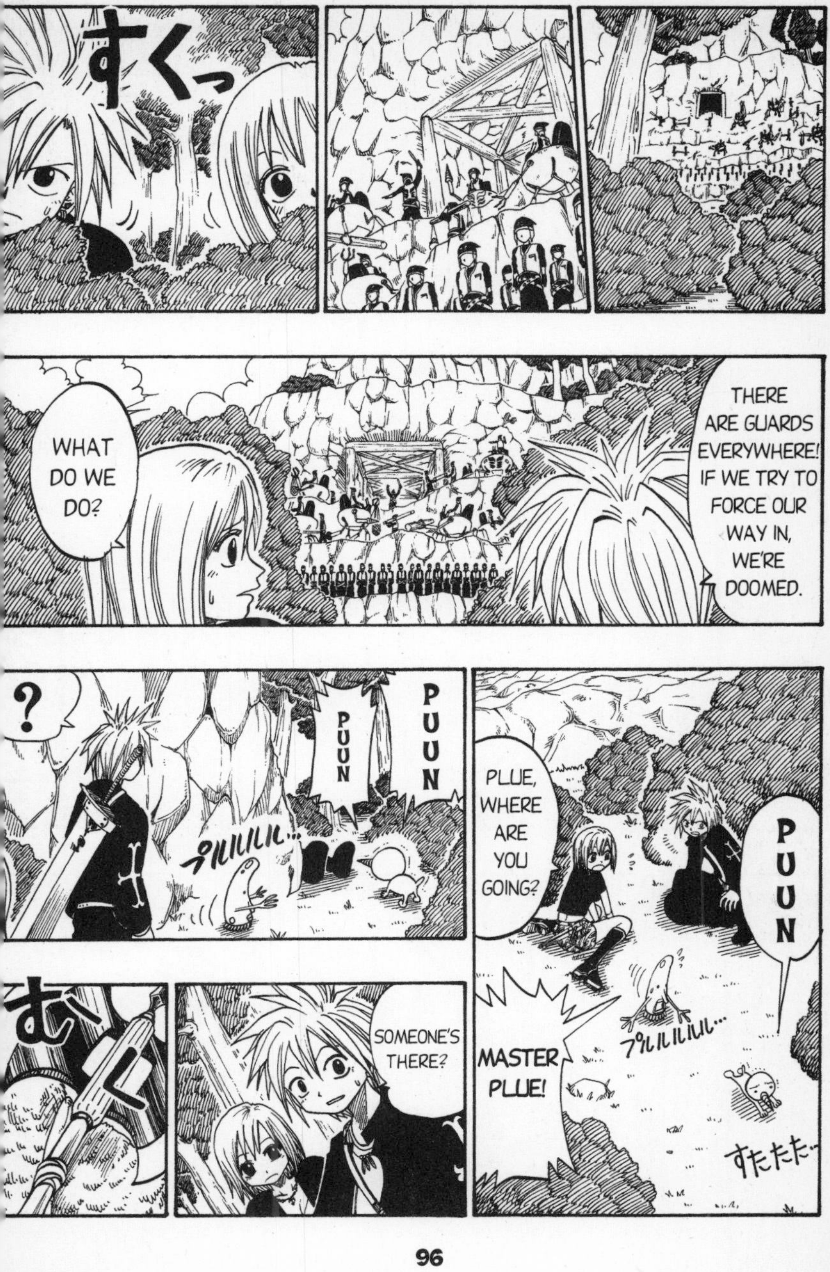
すくっ
THERE ARE GUARDS EVERYWHERE! IF WE TRY TO FORCE OUR WAY IN, WE'RE DOOMED.
WHAT DO WE DO?
PUUN
PLUE, WHERE ARE YOU GOING?
プルルルル…
MASTER PLUE!
すたたた…
PUUN
PUUN
?
プルルルル…
SOMEONE'S THERE?
むくっ

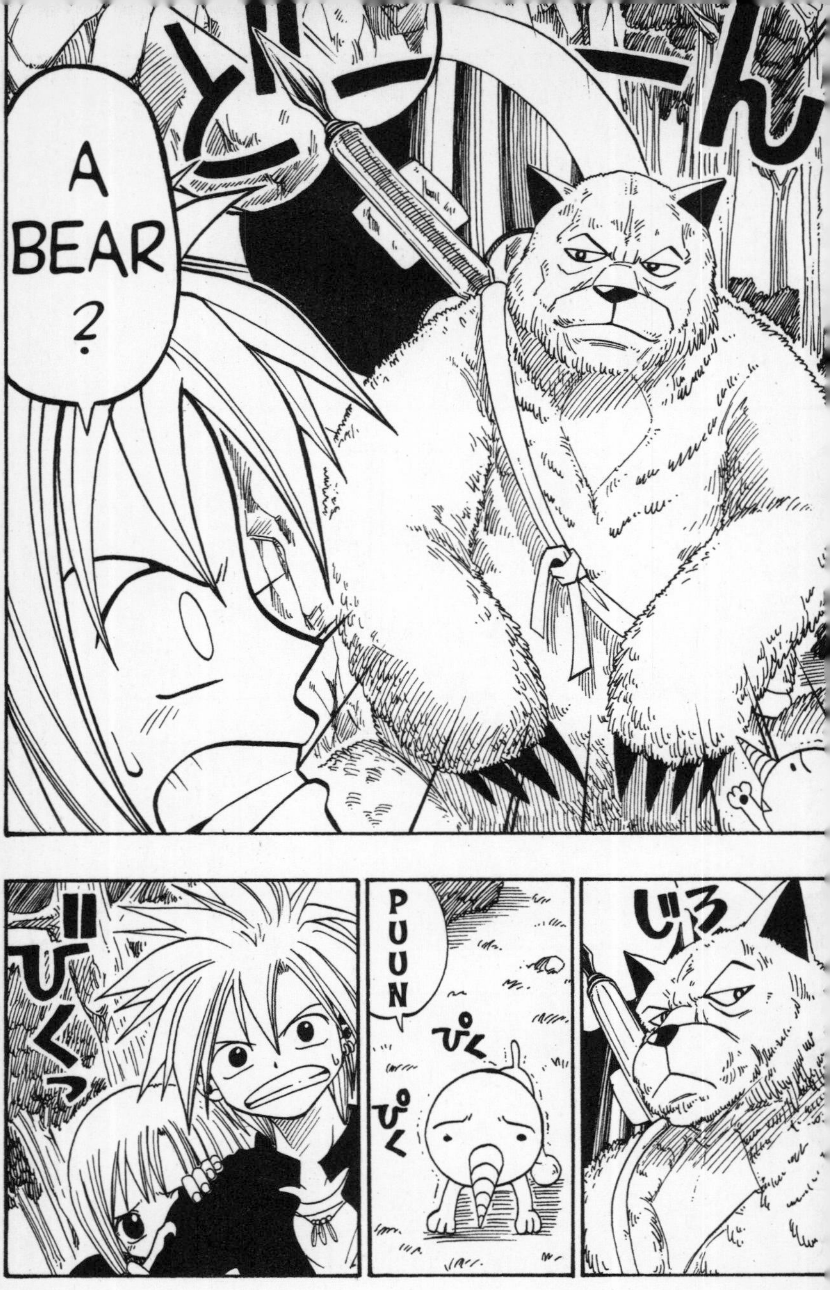
A BEAR?
じろ
PUUN
ぴく
ぴく
びくっ

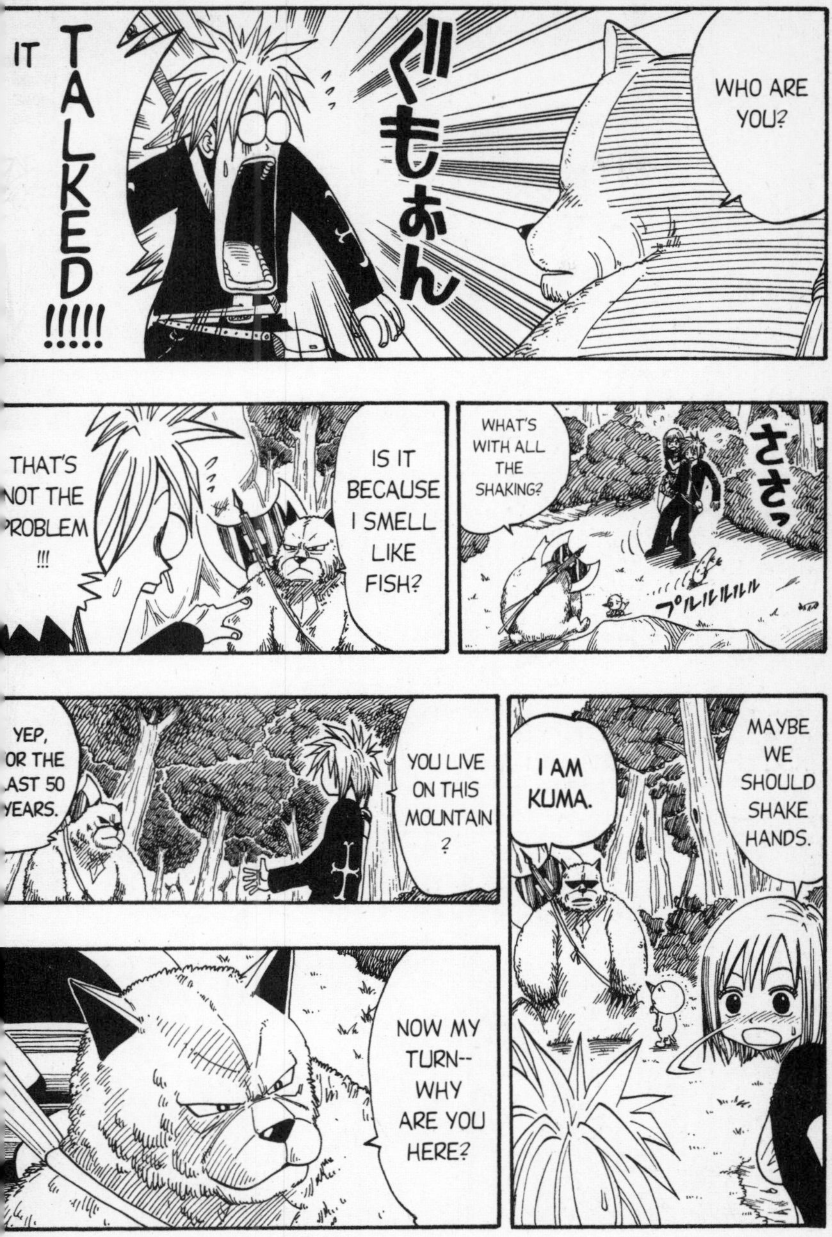
WHO ARE YOU?
ぐもぉん
IT TALKED!!!!!
ささっ
WHAT'S WITH ALL THE SHAKING?
プルルルルル
IS IT BECAUSE I SMELL LIKE FISH?
THAT'S NOT THE PROBLEM!!!
MAYBE WE SHOULD SHAKE HANDS.
I AM KUMA.
YOU LIVE ON THIS MOUNTAIN?
YEP, FOR THE LAST 50 YEARS.
NOW MY TURN-- WHY ARE YOU HERE?

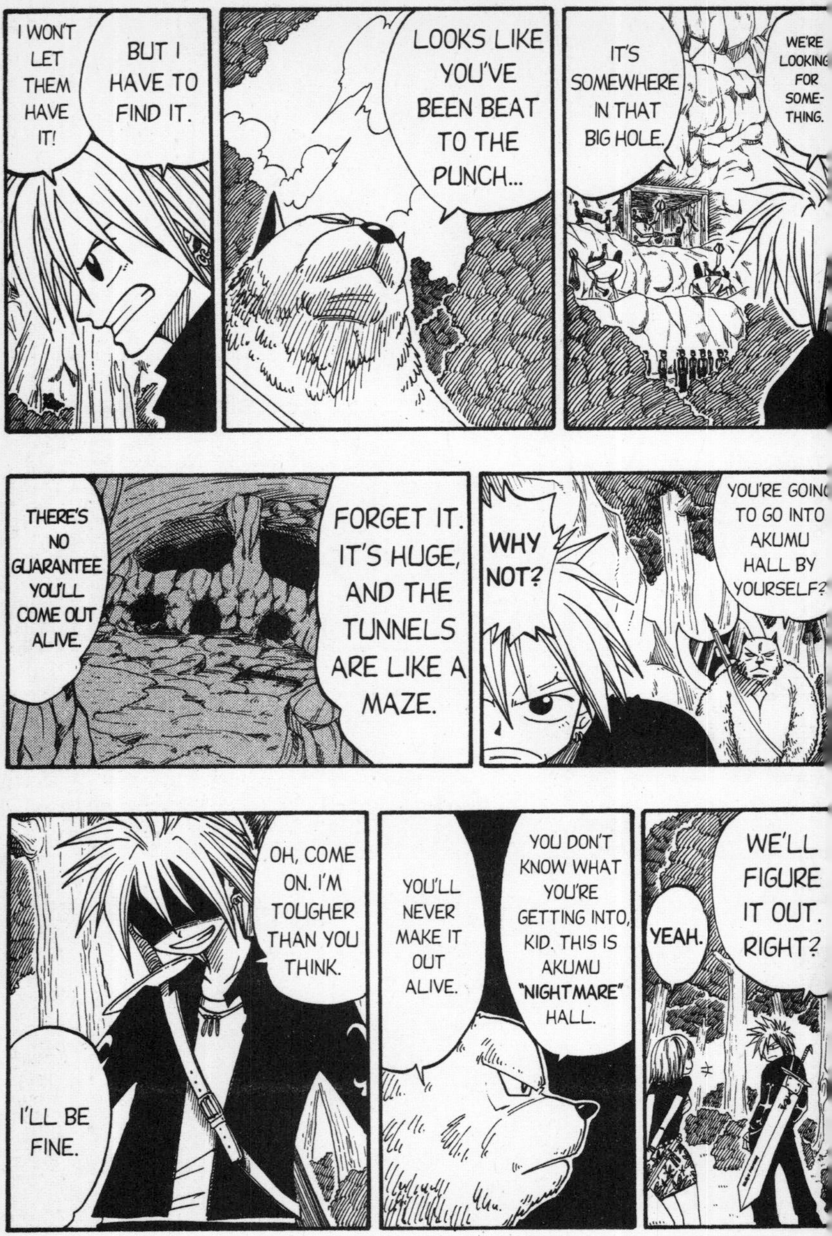
WE'RE LOOKING FOR SOME-THING.
IT'S SOMEWHERE IN THAT BIG HOLE.
LOOKS LIKE YOU'VE BEEN BEAT TO THE PUNCH...
BUT I HAVE TO FIND IT.
I WON'T LET THEM HAVE IT!
YOU'RE GOIN TO GO INTO AKUMU HALL BY YOURSELF?
WHY NOT?
FORGET IT. IT'S HUGE, AND THE TUNNELS ARE LIKE A MAZE.
THERE'S NO GUARANTEE YOU'LL COME OUT ALIVE.
WE'LL FIGURE IT OUT. RIGHT?
YEAH.
YOU DON'T KNOW WHAT YOU'RE GETTING INTO, KID. THIS IS AKUMU "NIGHTMARE" HALL.
YOU'LL NEVER MAKE IT OUT ALIVE.
OH, COME ON. I'M TOUGHER THAN YOU THINK.
I'LL BE FINE.

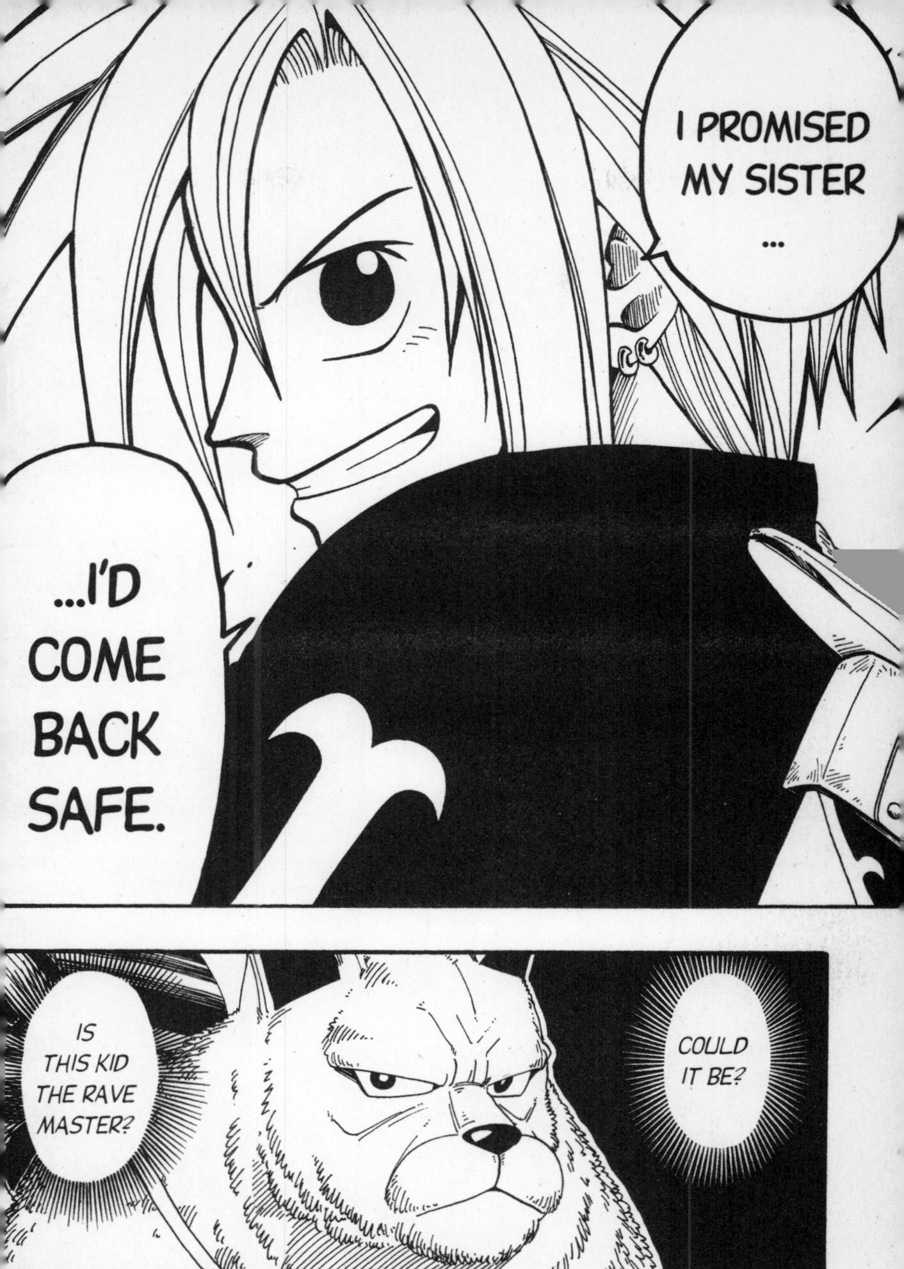
I PROMISED MY SISTER ...
...I'D COME BACK SAFE.
COULD IT BE?
IS THIS KID THE RAVE MASTER?

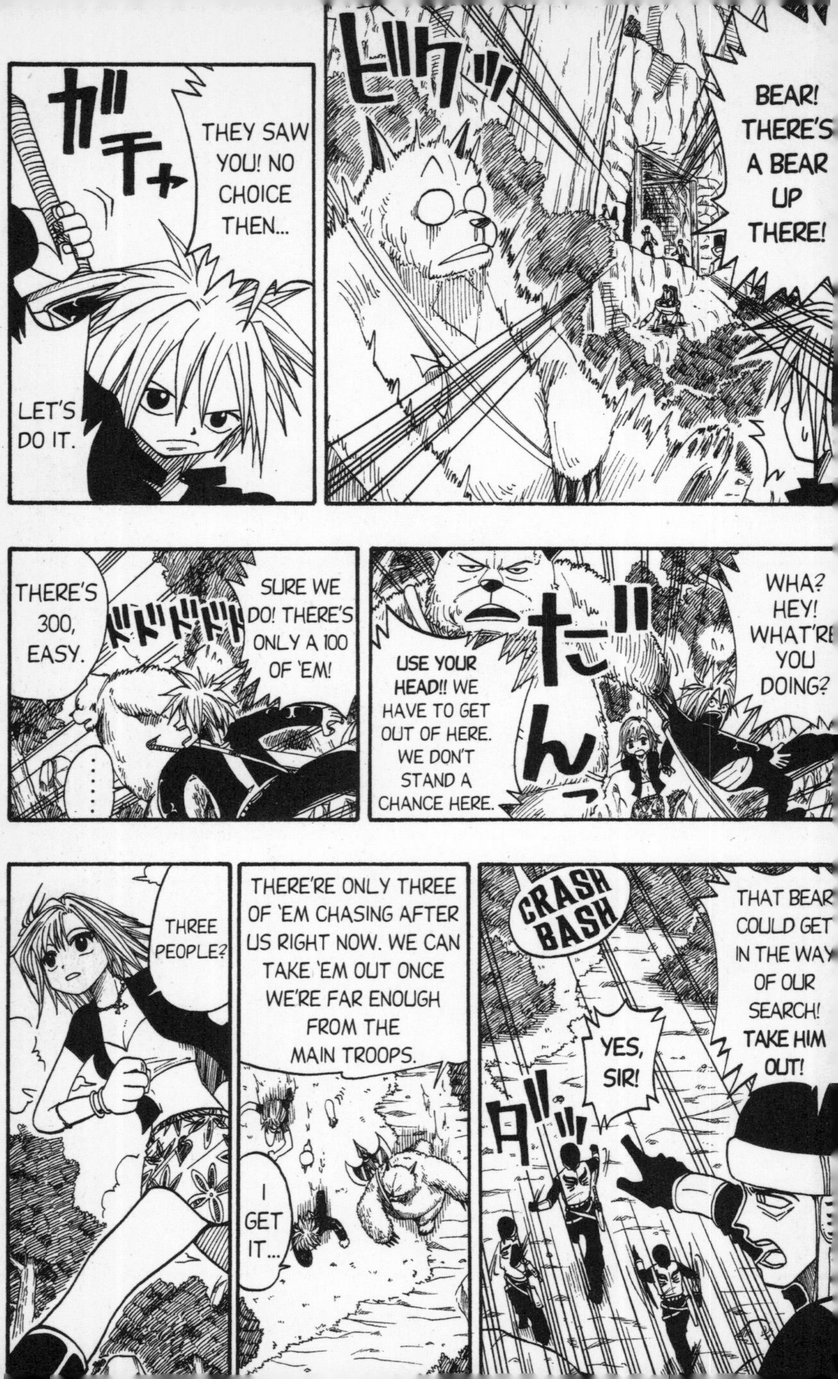
ビクッ
BEAR! THERE'S A BEAR UP THERE!
ガチャ
THEY SAW YOU! NO CHOICE THEN...
LET'S DO IT.
WHA? HEY! WHAT'RE YOU DOING?
だんっ
USE YOUR HEAD!! WE HAVE TO GET OUT OF HERE. WE DON'T STAND A CHANCE HERE.
SURE WE DO! THERE'S ONLY A 100 OF 'EM!
ドドドドド
THERE'S 300, EASY.
......
THAT BEAR COULD GET IN THE WAY OF OUR SEARCH! TAKE HIM OUT!
CRASH BASH
YES, SIR!
ダッ
THERE'RE ONLY THREE OF 'EM CHASING AFTER US RIGHT NOW. WE CAN TAKE 'EM OUT ONCE WE'RE FAR ENOUGH FROM THE MAIN TROOPS.
I GET IT...
THREE PEOPLE?

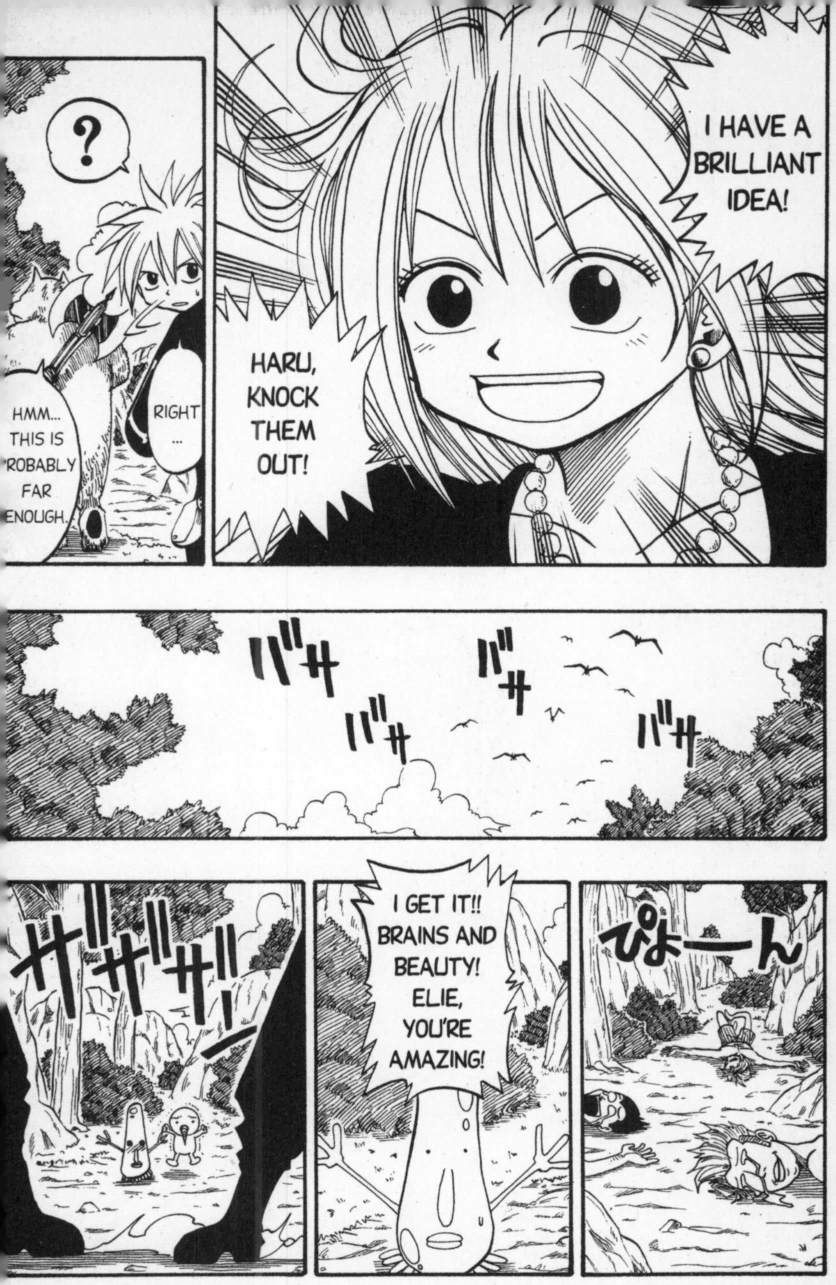
I HAVE A BRILLIANT IDEA!
HARU, KNOCK THEM OUT!
?
RIGHT ...
HMM... THIS IS ROBABLY FAR ENOUGH..
バサ
バサ
バサ
バサ
ぴよーん
I GET IT!! BRAINS AND BEAUTY! ELIE, YOU'RE AMAZING!
サザザー

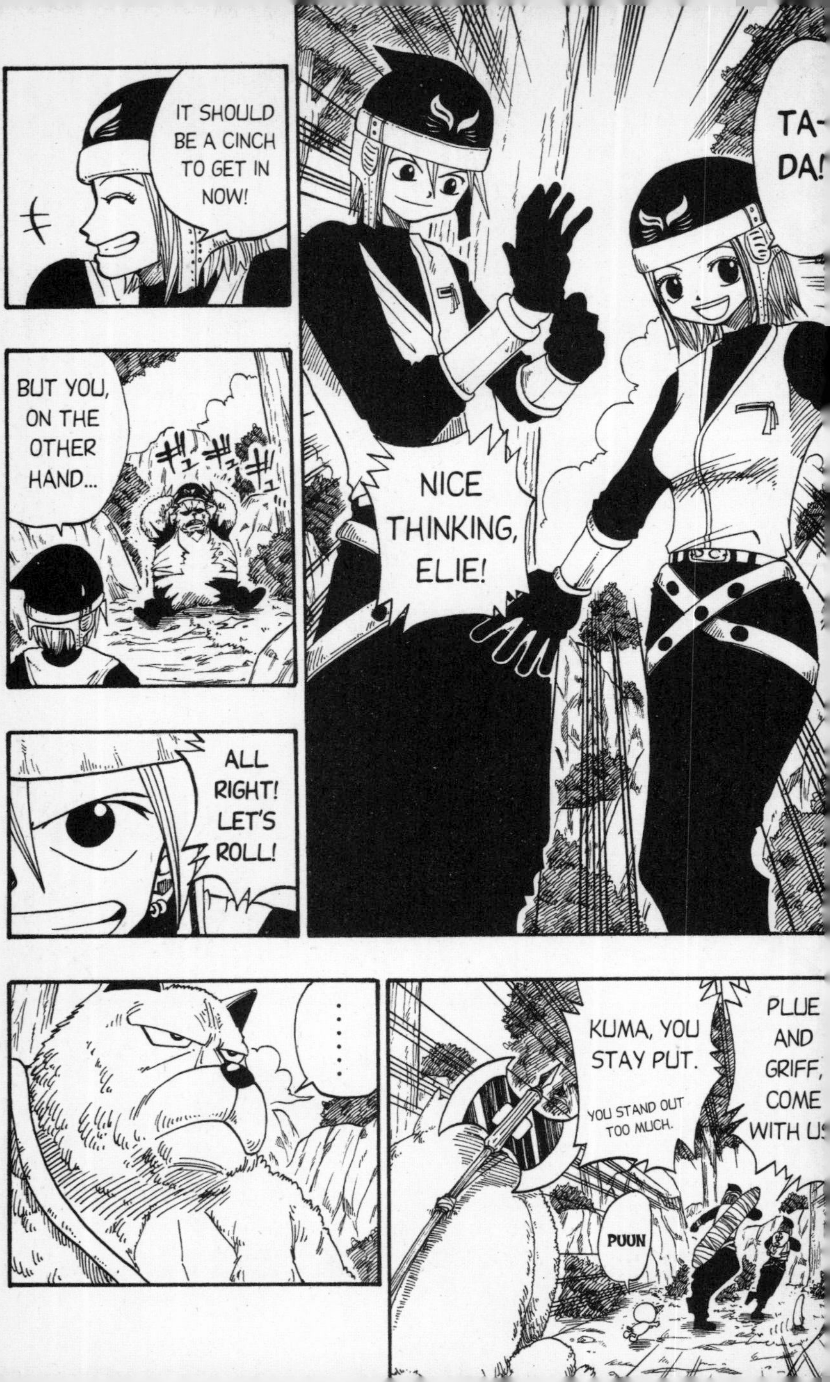
TA-DA!
NICE THINKING, ELIE!
IT SHOULD BE A CINCH TO GET IN NOW!
BUT YOU, ON THE OTHER HAND...
ギュ ギュ ギュ
ALL RIGHT! LET'S ROLL!
PLUE AND GRIFF, COME WITH US
KUMA, YOU STAY PUT.
YOU STAND OUT TOO MUCH.
PUUN
......

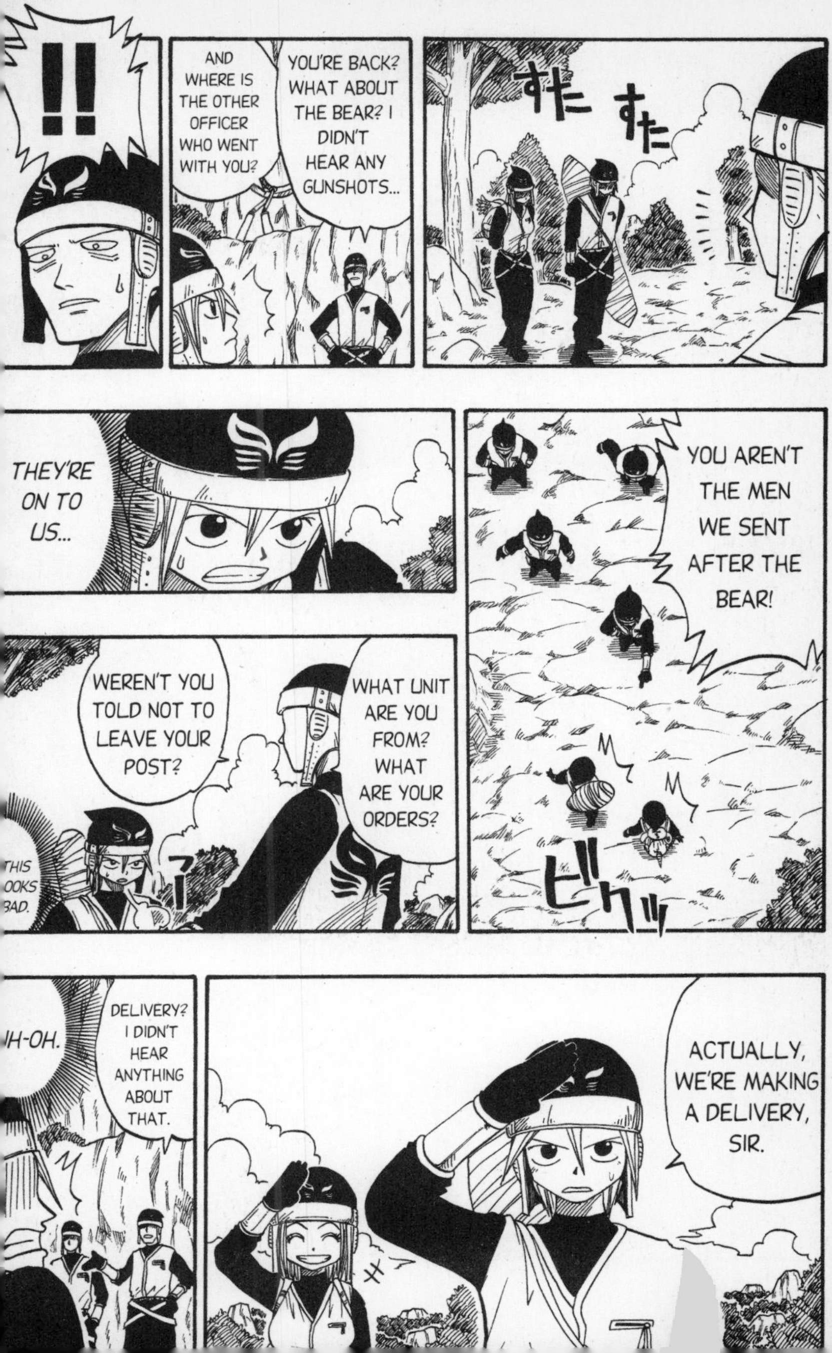
すた すた
YOU'RE BACK? WHAT ABOUT THE BEAR? I DIDN'T HEAR ANY GUNSHOTS...
AND WHERE IS THE OTHER OFFICER WHO WENT WITH YOU?
!!
YOU AREN'T THE MEN WE SENT AFTER THE BEAR!
M
M
ビクッ
THEY'RE ON TO US...
WHAT UNIT ARE YOU FROM? WHAT ARE YOUR ORDERS?
WEREN'T YOU TOLD NOT TO LEAVE YOUR POST?
THIS OOKS BAD.
ACTUALLY, WE'RE MAKING A DELIVERY, SIR.
DELIVERY? I DIDN'T HEAR ANYTHING ABOUT THAT.
H-OH.

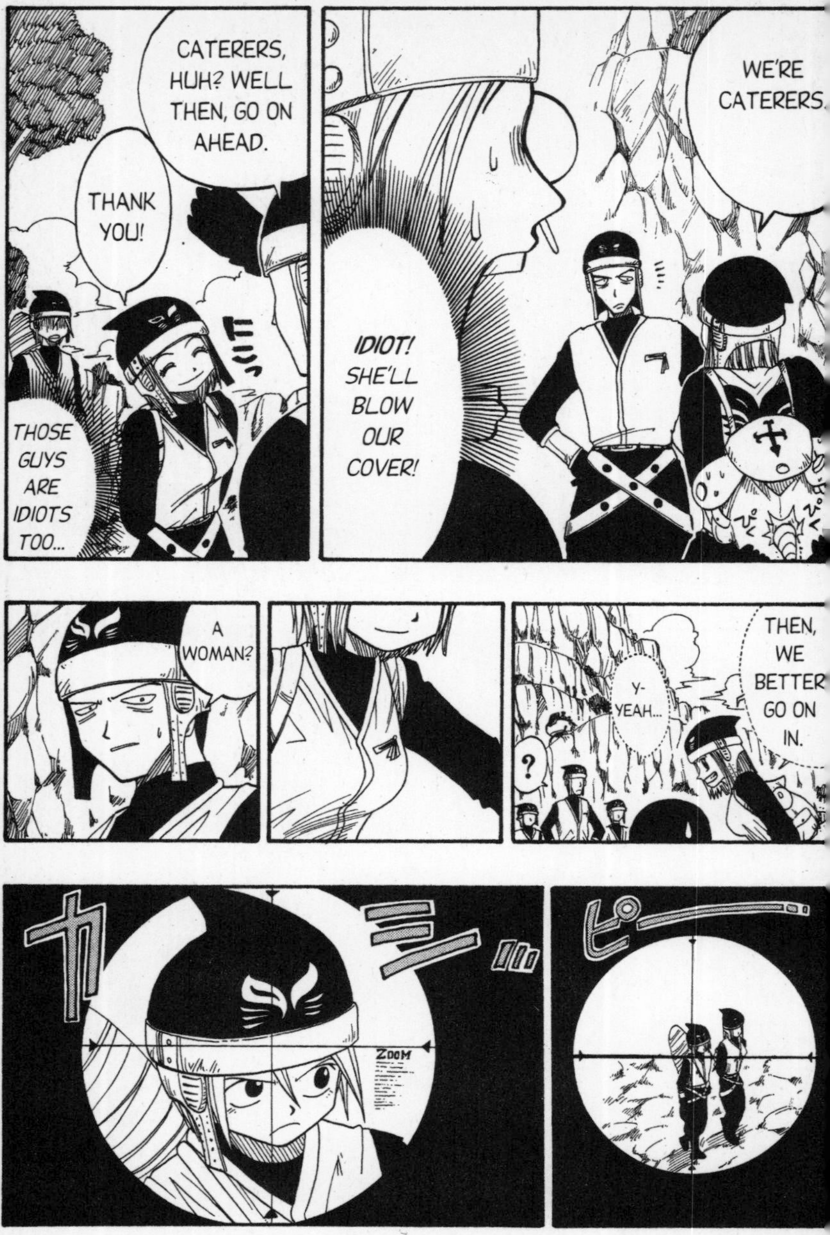
WE'RE CATERERS.
IDIOT! SHE'LL BLOW OUR COVER!
CATERERS, HUH? WELL THEN, GO ON AHEAD.
THANK YOU!
THOSE GUYS ARE IDIOTS TOO...
THEN, WE BETTER GO ON IN.
Y-YEAH...
?
A WOMAN?
ZOOM

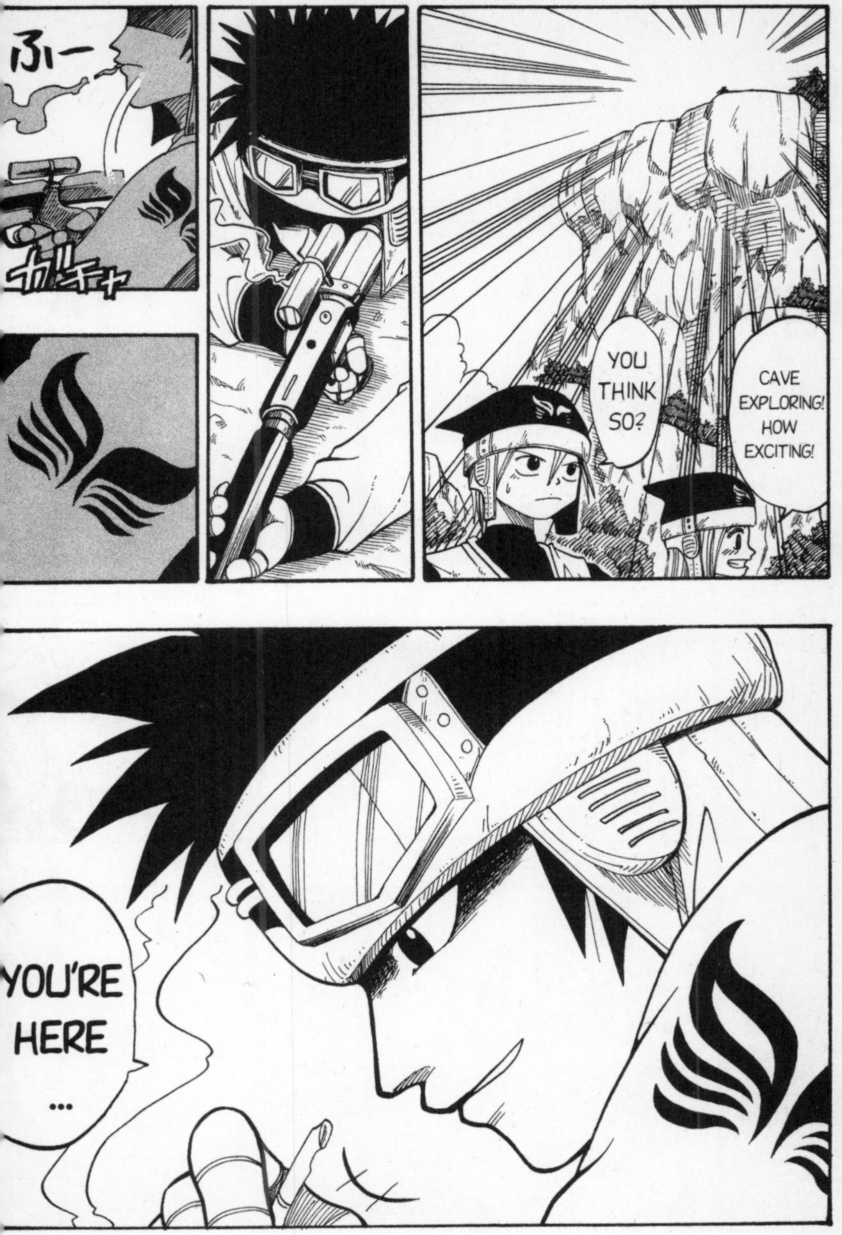
CAVE EXPLORING! HOW EXCITING!
YOU THINK SO?
ふー
ガチャ
YOU'RE HERE ...

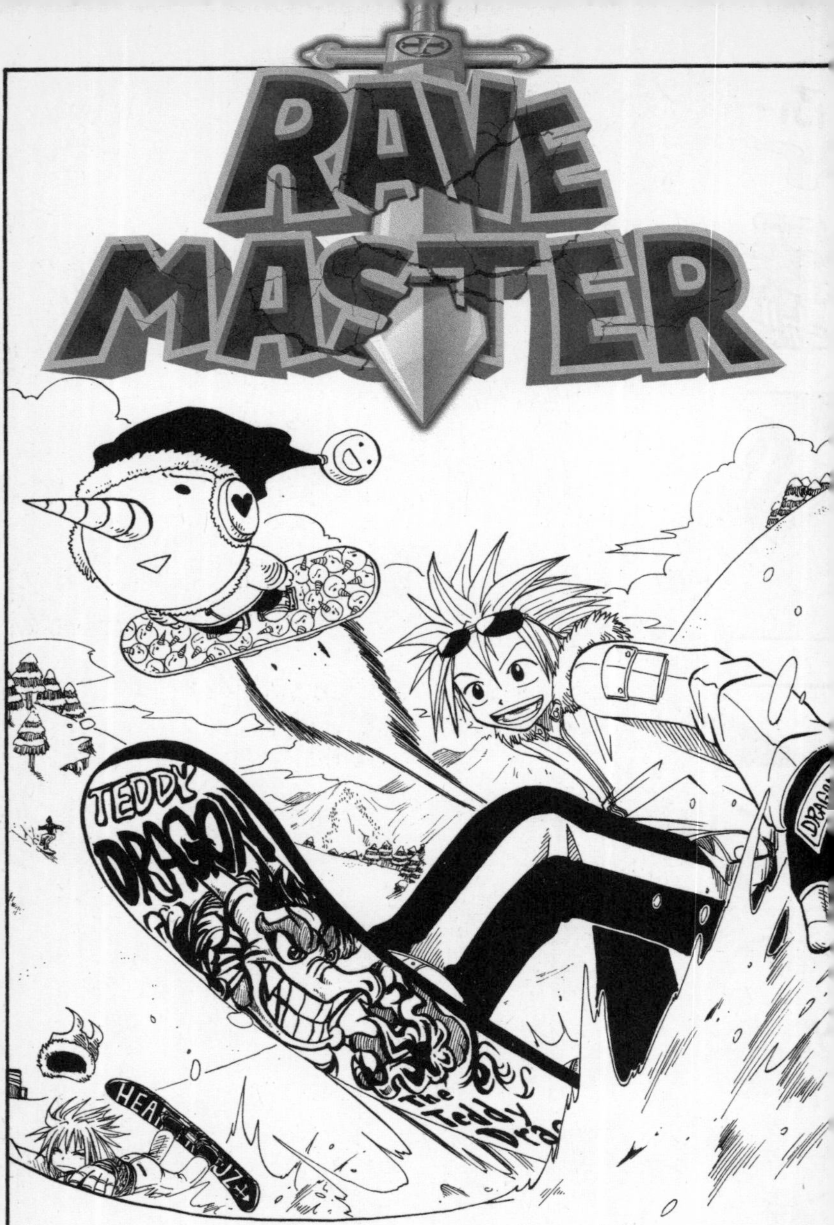
RAVE MASTER
TEDDY
DRAGON

RAVE: 27 ✠ Fade to Black

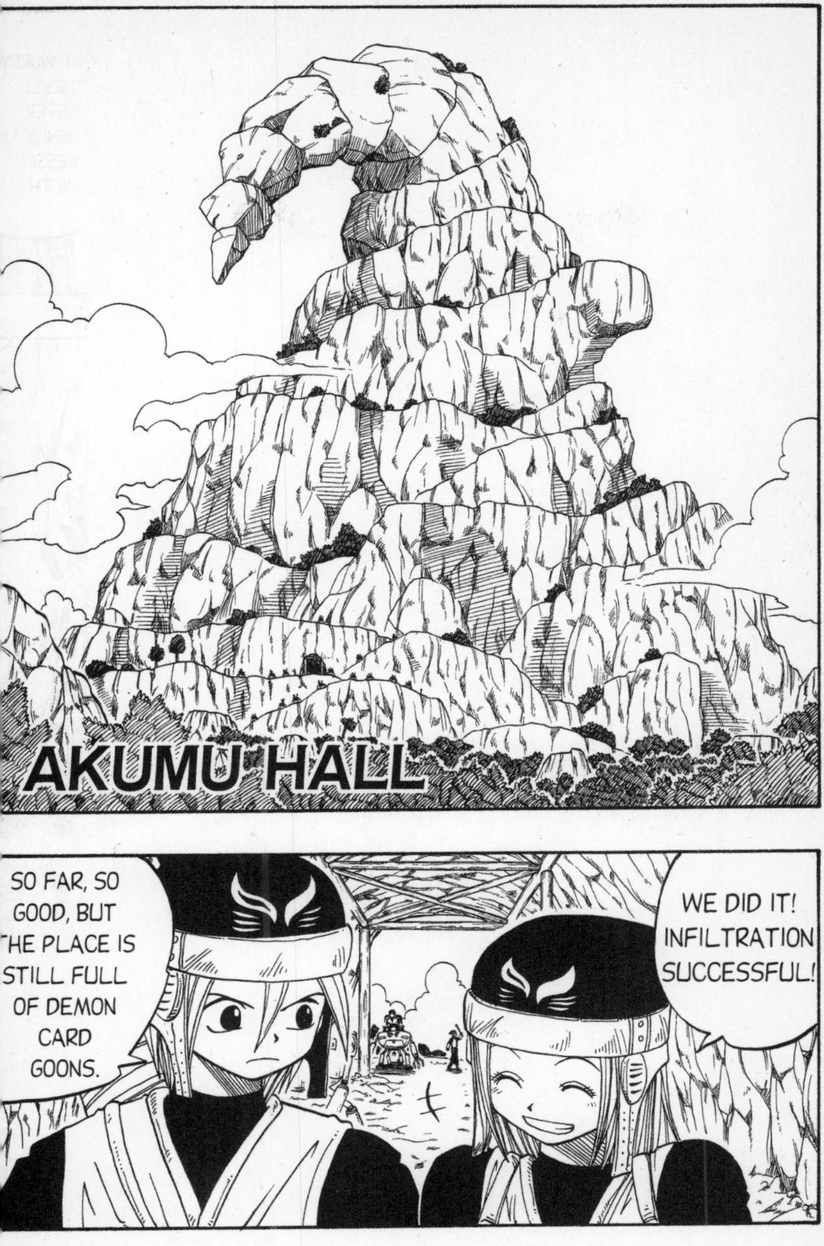
AKUMU HALL
WE DID IT! INFILTRATION SUCCESSFUL!
SO FAR, SO GOOD, BUT THE PLACE IS STILL FULL OF DEMON CARD GOONS.

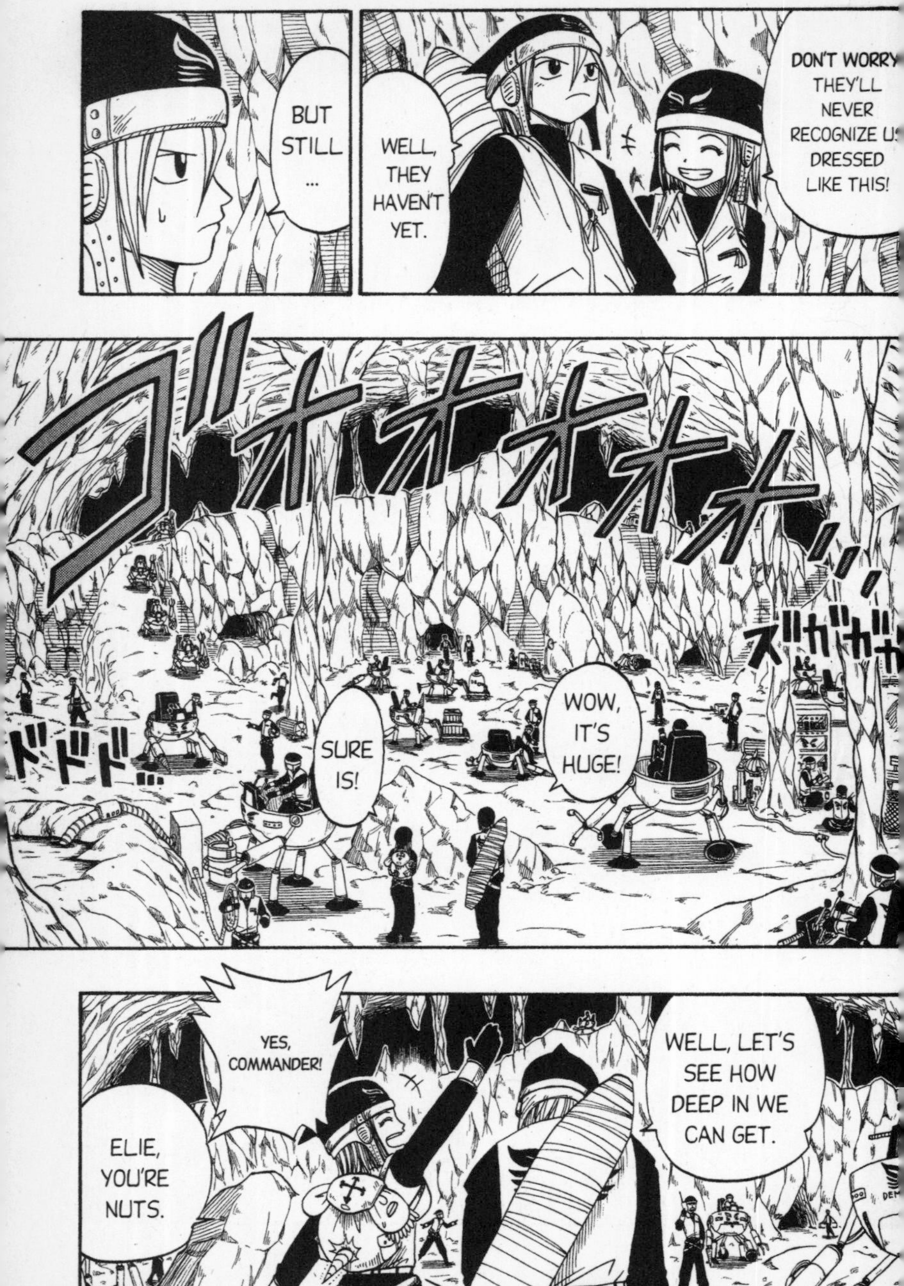
DON'T WORRY THEY'LL NEVER RECOGNIZE US DRESSED LIKE THIS!
WELL, THEY HAVEN'T YET.
BUT STILL ...
ゴオオオオ…
ズガガガ
ドドド…
WOW, IT'S HUGE!
SURE IS!
WELL, LET'S SEE HOW DEEP IN WE CAN GET.
YES, COMMANDER!
ELIE, YOU'RE NUTS.

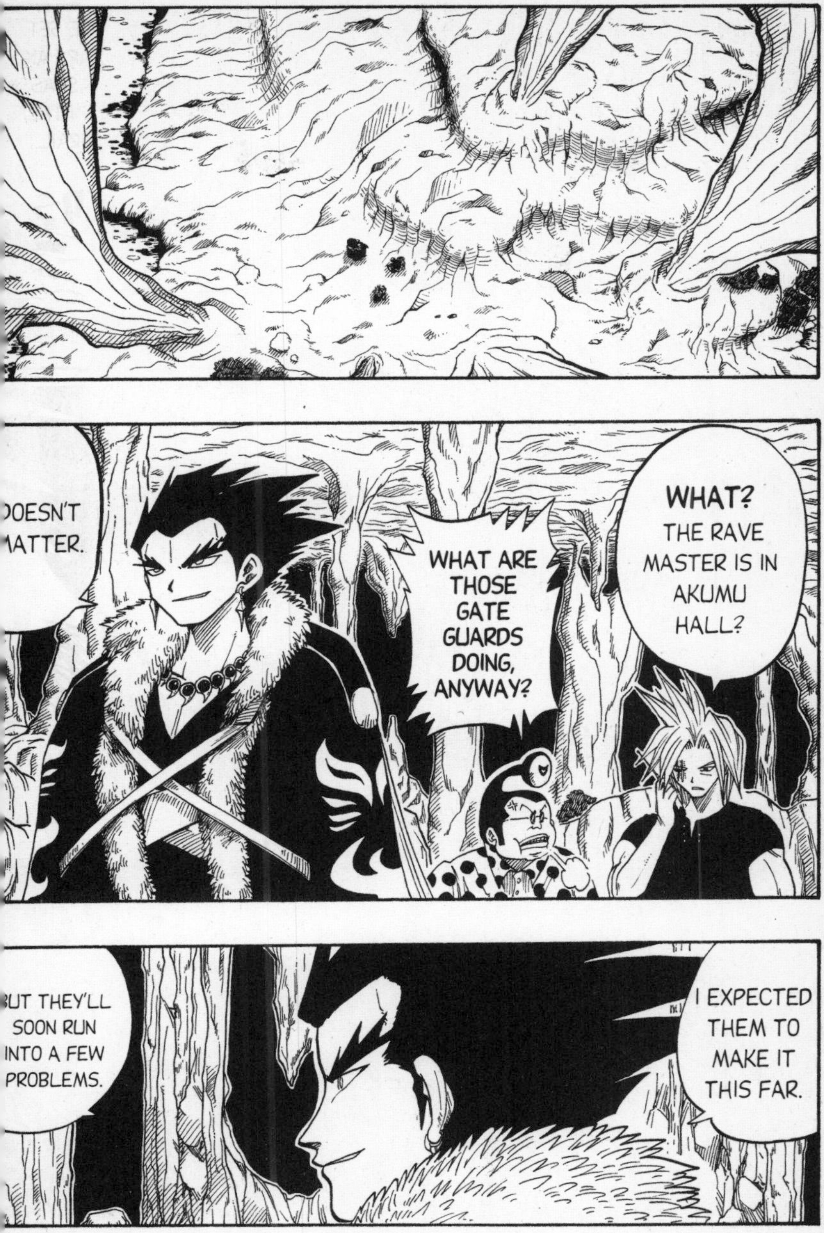
WHAT? THE RAVE MASTER IS IN AKUMU HALL?
WHAT ARE THOSE GATE GUARDS DOING, ANYWAY?
DOESN'T MATTER.
I EXPECTED THEM TO MAKE IT THIS FAR.
BUT THEY'LL SOON RUN INTO A FEW PROBLEMS.

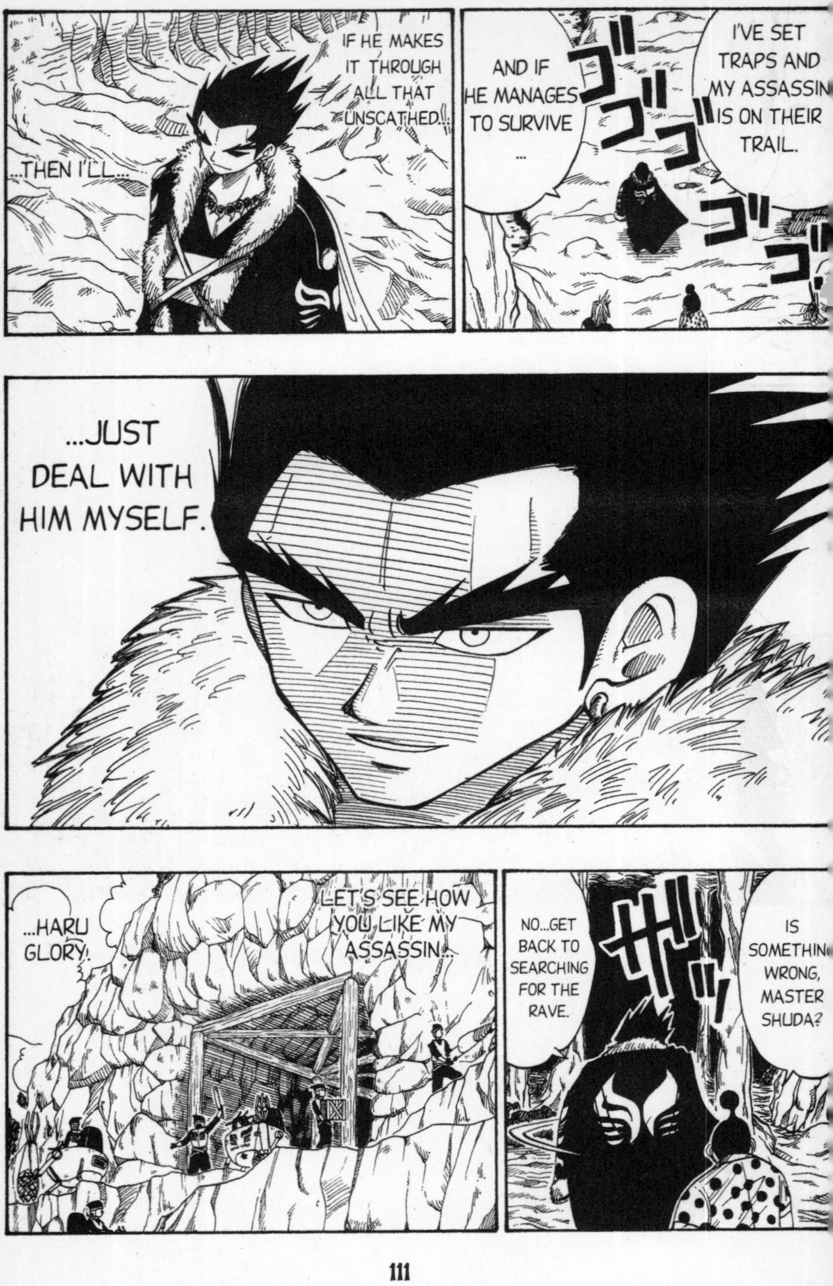
I'VE SET TRAPS AND MY ASSASSIN IS ON THEIR TRAIL.
AND IF HE MANAGES TO SURVIVE ...
IF HE MAKES IT THROUGH ALL THAT UNSCATHED...
...THEN I'LL...
...JUST DEAL WITH HIM MYSELF.
IS SOMETHIN WRONG, MASTER SHUDA?
NO...GET BACK TO SEARCHING FOR THE RAVE.
LET'S SEE HOW YOU LIKE MY ASSASSIN...
...HARU GLORY.

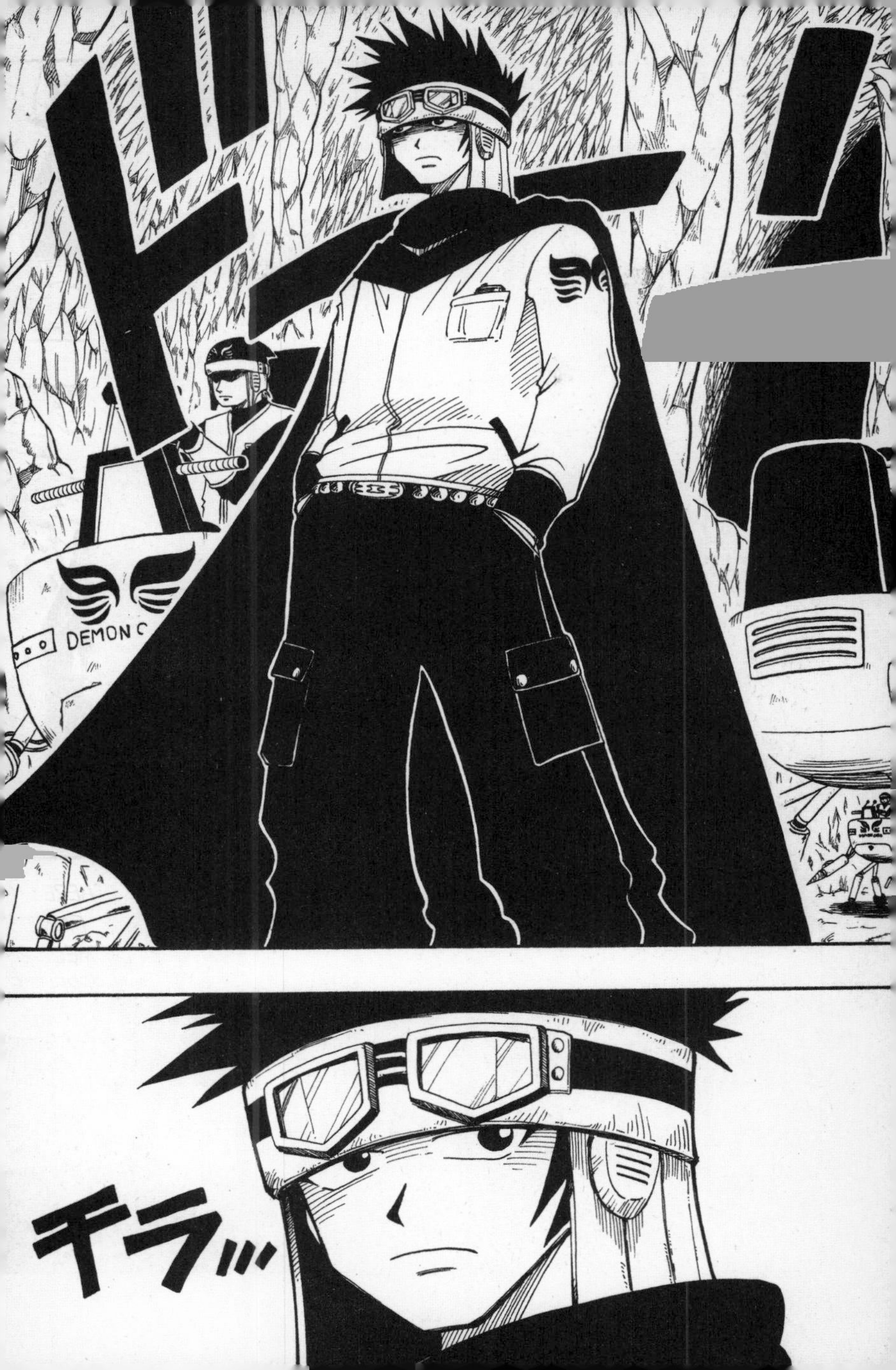
ドーン
DEMON C
チラッ

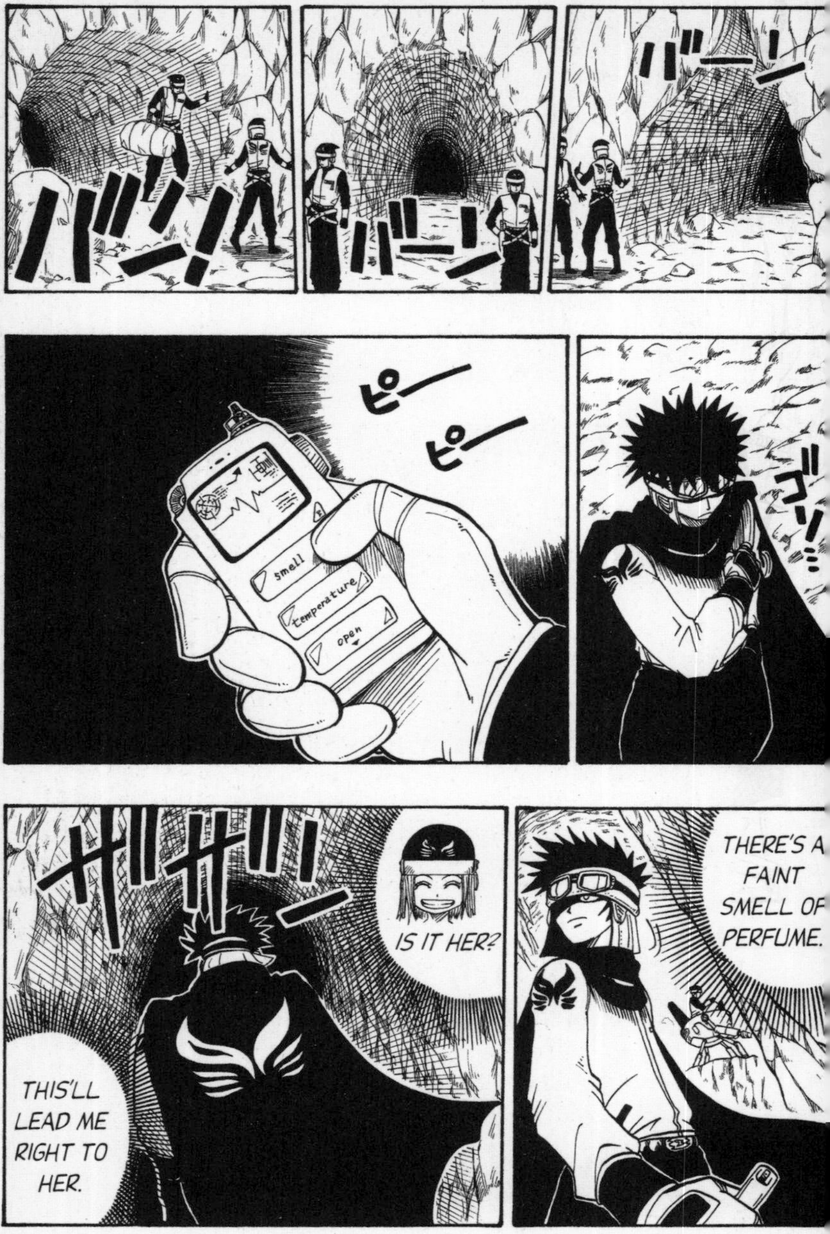
ゴソ
ピー
ピー
smell
temperature
open
THERE'S A FAINT SMELL OF PERFUME.
IS IT HER?
THIS'LL LEAD ME RIGHT TO HER.

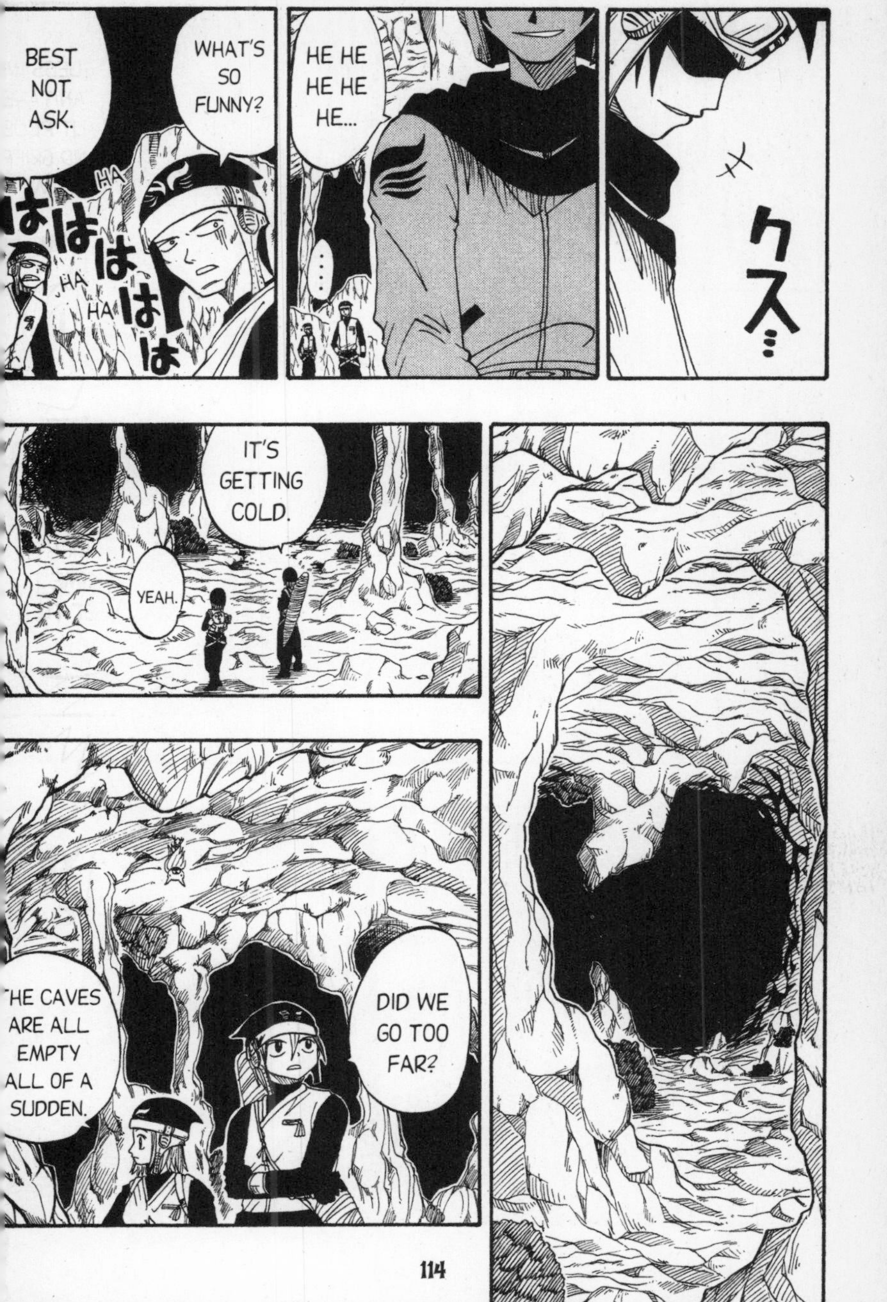
クス
HE HE HE HE HE...
...
WHAT'S SO FUNNY?
BEST NOT ASK.
HA はは HA はは HA はは
IT'S GETTING COLD.
YEAH.
DID WE GO TOO FAR?
THE CAVES ARE ALL EMPTY ALL OF A SUDDEN.

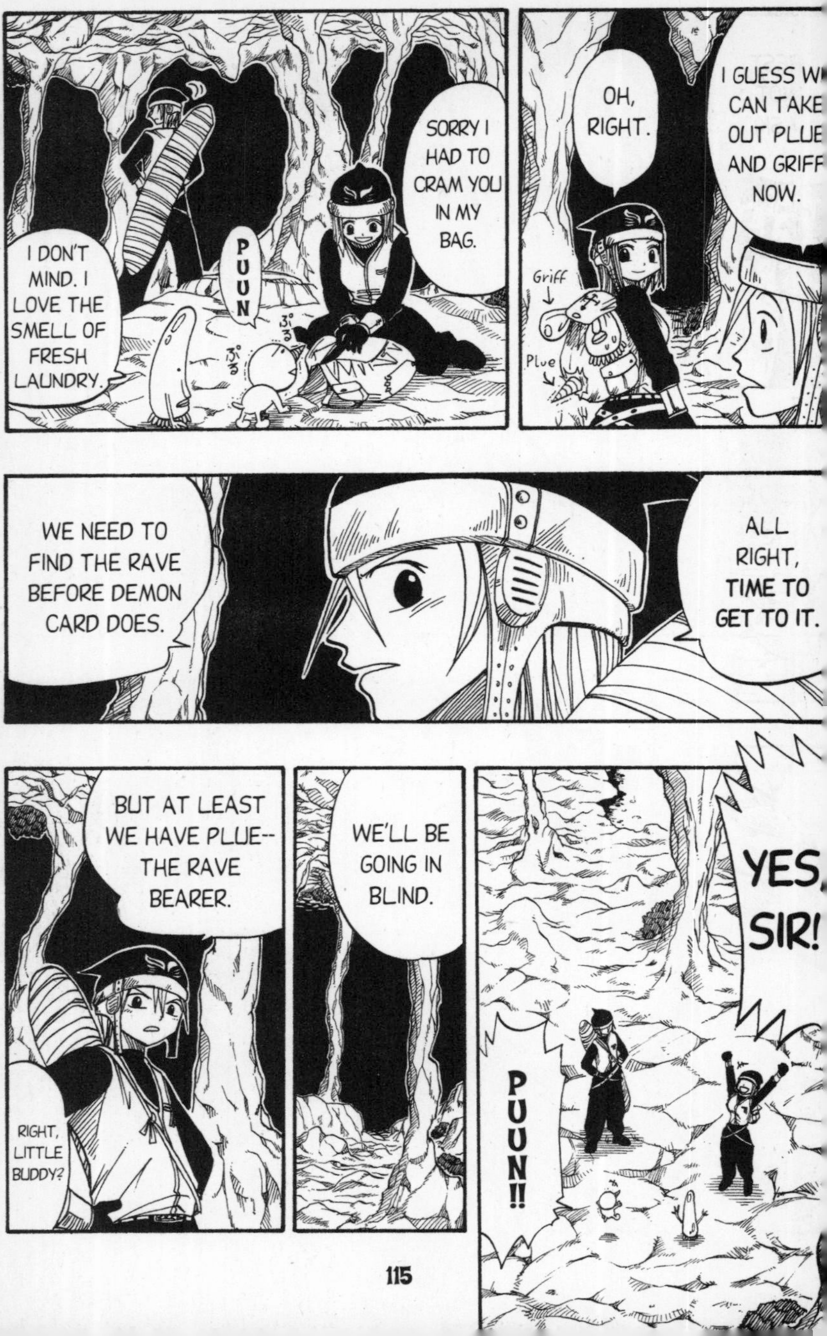
I GUESS W
CAN TAKE
OUT PLUE
AND GRIFF
NOW.
OH, RIGHT.
Griff
Plue
SORRY I HAD TO CRAM YOU IN MY BAG.
PUUN
ぷる ぷる
I DON'T MIND. I LOVE THE SMELL OF FRESH LAUNDRY.
ALL RIGHT, TIME TO GET TO IT.
WE NEED TO FIND THE RAVE BEFORE DEMON CARD DOES.
YES, SIR!
PUUN!!
WE'LL BE GOING IN BLIND.
BUT AT LEAST WE HAVE PLUE-- THE RAVE BEARER.
RIGHT, LITTLE BUDDY?

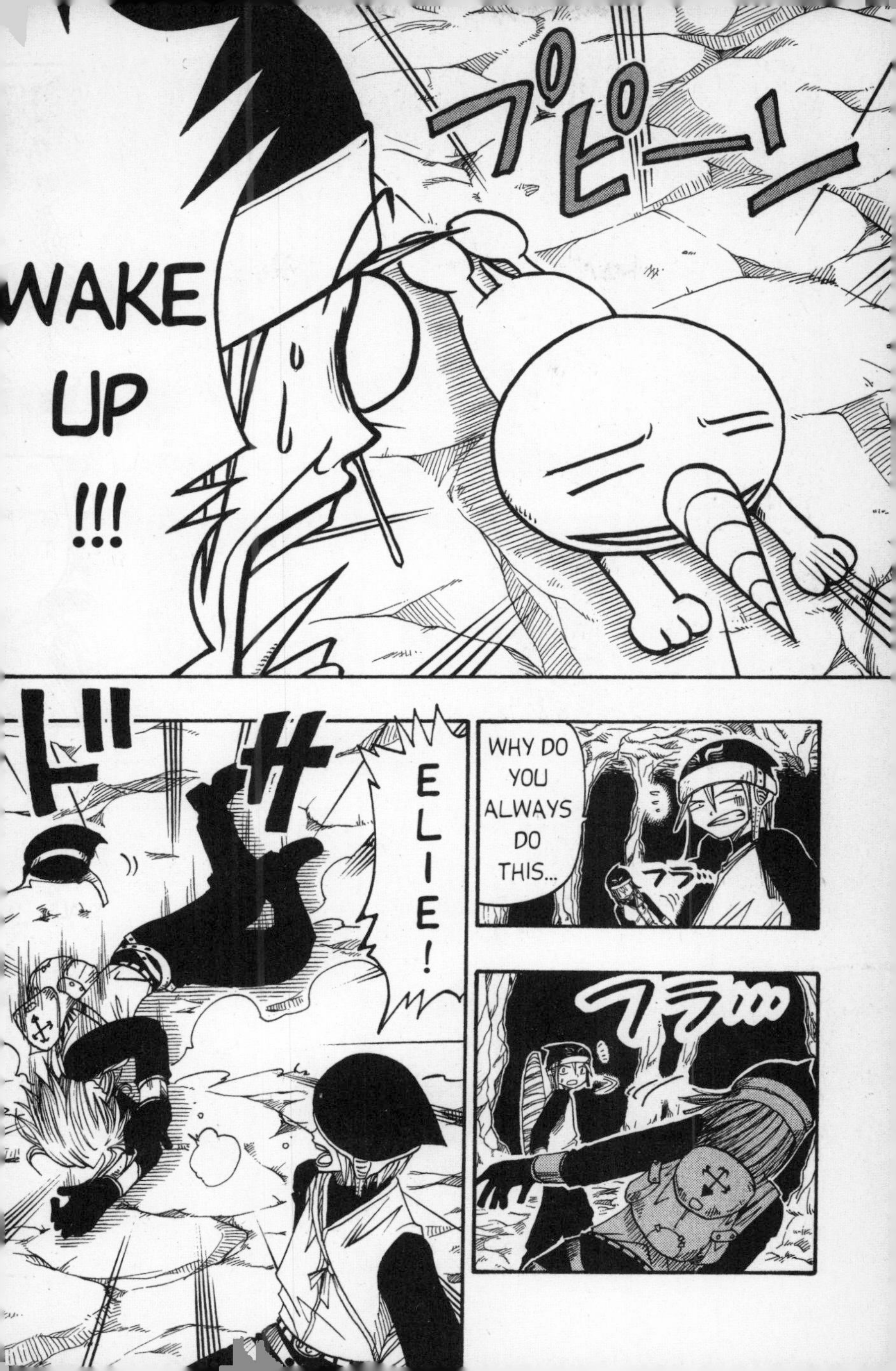

プピーン
WAKE UP !!!
WHY DO YOU ALWAYS DO THIS...
フラ
フラ...
ドサ
ELIE!

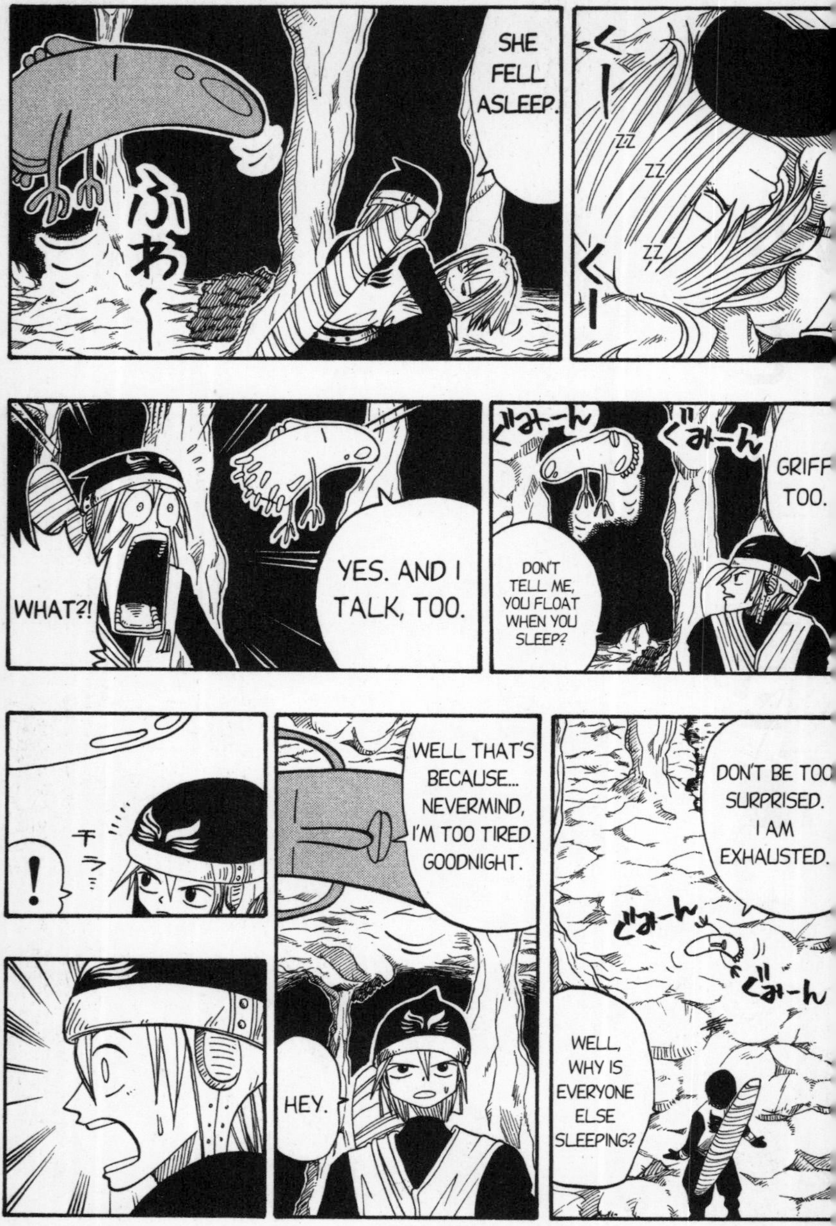
くーくー
SHE FELL ASLEEP.
ふわ〜
GRIFF TOO.
ぐみ〜ん
ぐみ〜ん
DON'T TELL ME, YOU FLOAT WHEN YOU SLEEP?
YES. AND I TALK, TOO.
WHAT?!
DON'T BE TOO SURPRISED. I AM EXHAUSTED.
ぐみ〜ん
ぐみ〜ん
WELL, WHY IS EVERYONE ELSE SLEEPING?
WELL THAT'S BECAUSE... NEVERMIND, I'M TOO TIRED. GOODNIGHT.
HEY.
チラ
!

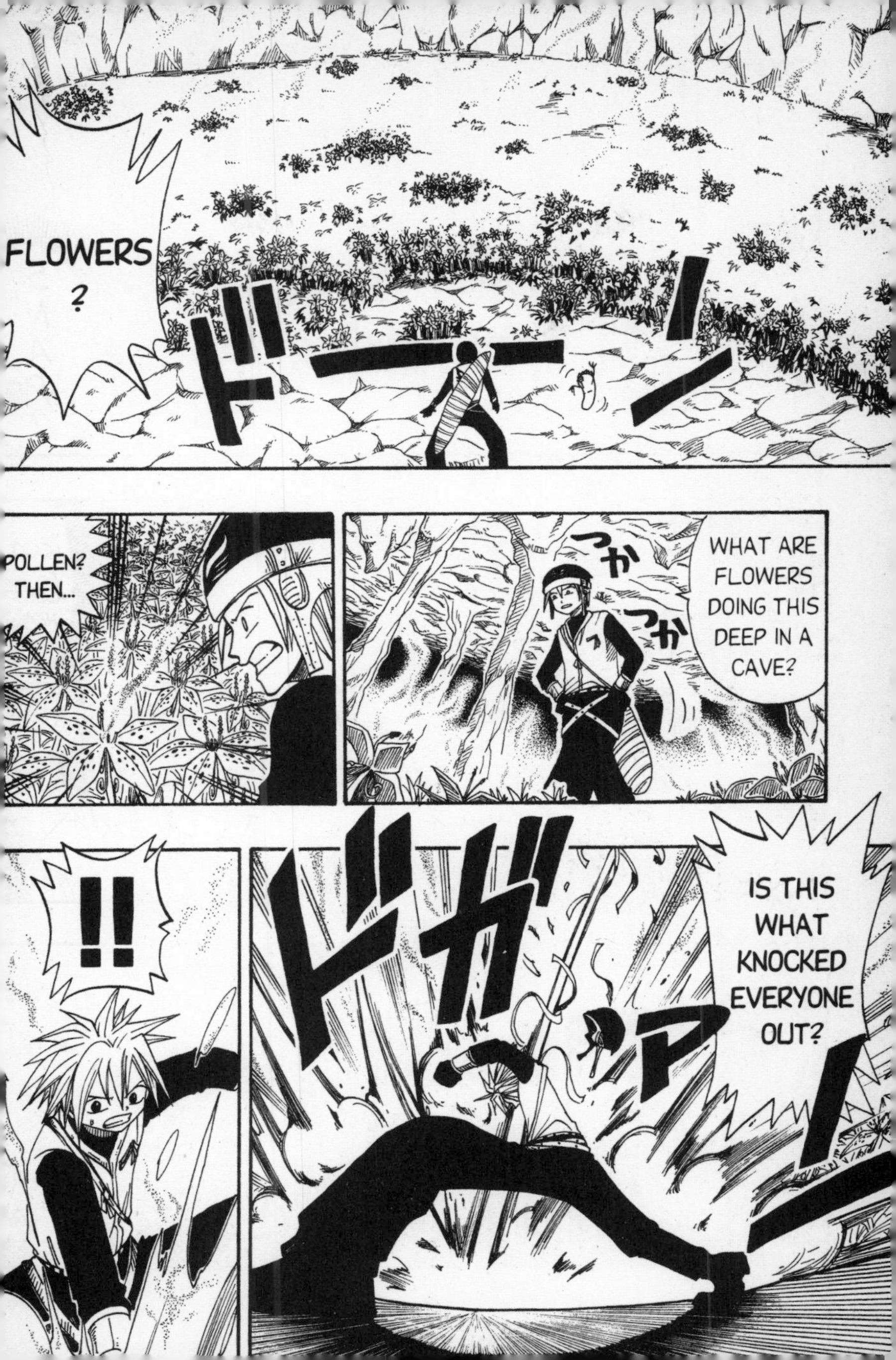
FLOWERS ?
ドーーン
つか
つか
WHAT ARE FLOWERS DOING THIS DEEP IN A CAVE?
POLLEN? THEN...
ドガァー
IS THIS WHAT KNOCKED EVERYONE OUT?
!!

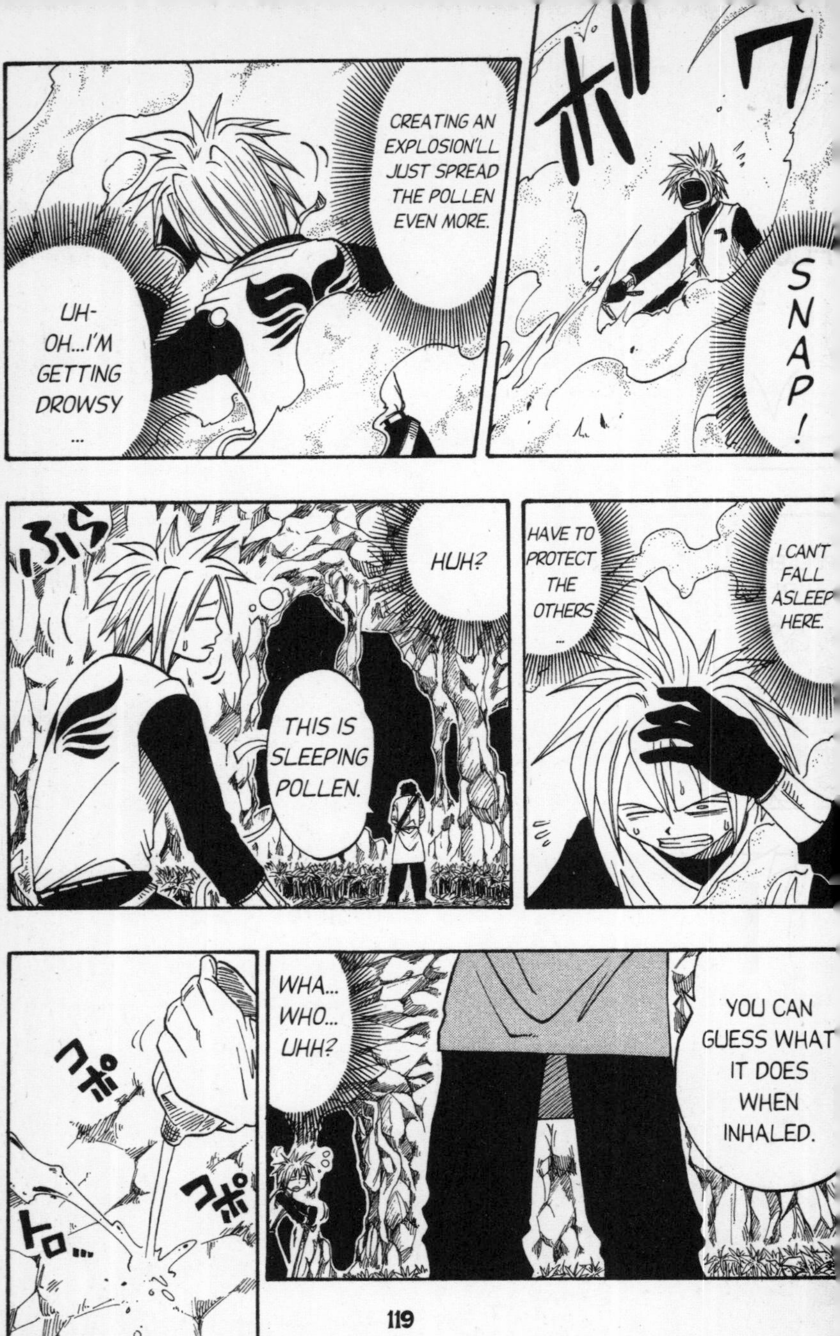
ボワ
SNAP!
CREATING AN EXPLOSION'LL JUST SPREAD THE POLLEN EVEN MORE.
UH-OH...I'M GETTING DROWSY ...
I CAN'T FALL ASLEEP HERE.
HAVE TO PROTECT THE OTHERS ...
HUH?
ふら
THIS IS SLEEPING POLLEN.
YOU CAN GUESS WHAT IT DOES WHEN INHALED.
WHA... WHO... UHH?
コポ
コポ
トロ…

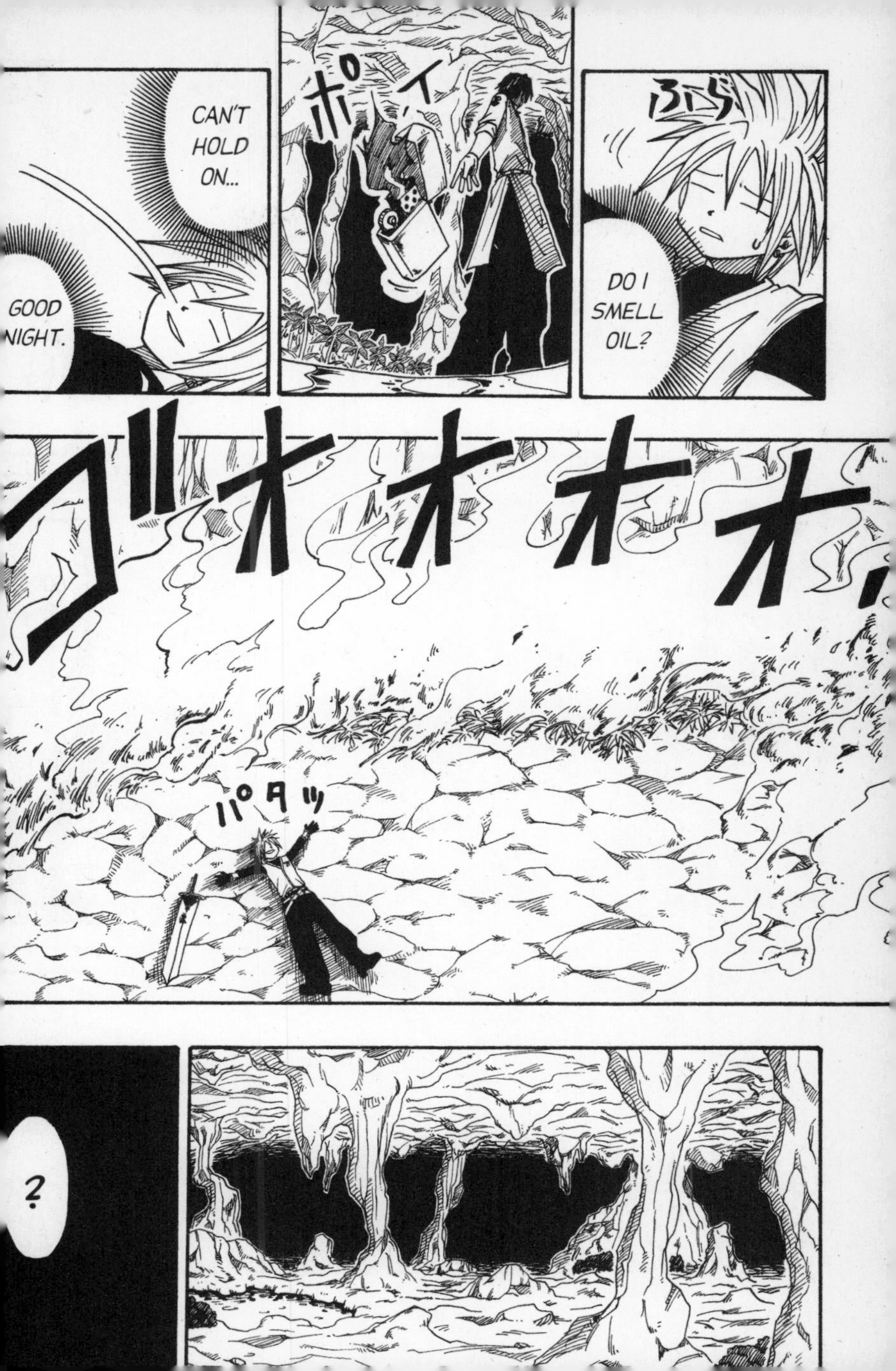
ふら
DO I SMELL OIL?
ポイ
CAN'T HOLD ON...
GOOD NIGHT.
ゴオオオ
パタッ
?

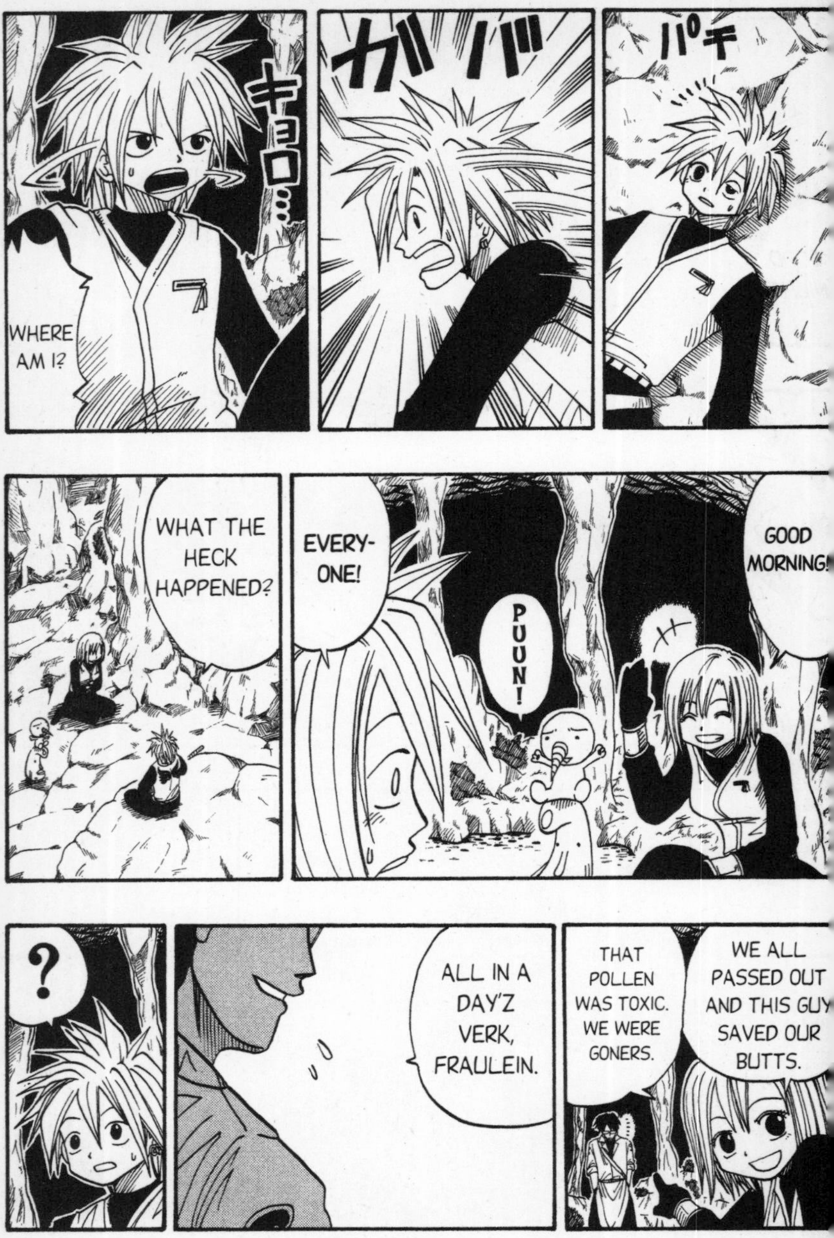
パチ
ガバ
キョロ…
WHERE AM I?
GOOD MORNING!
EVERY-ONE!
PUUN!
WHAT THE HECK HAPPENED?
WE ALL PASSED OUT AND THIS GUY SAVED OUR BUTTS.
THAT POLLEN WAS TOXIC. WE WERE GONERS.
ALL IN A DAY'Z VERK, FRAULEIN.
?

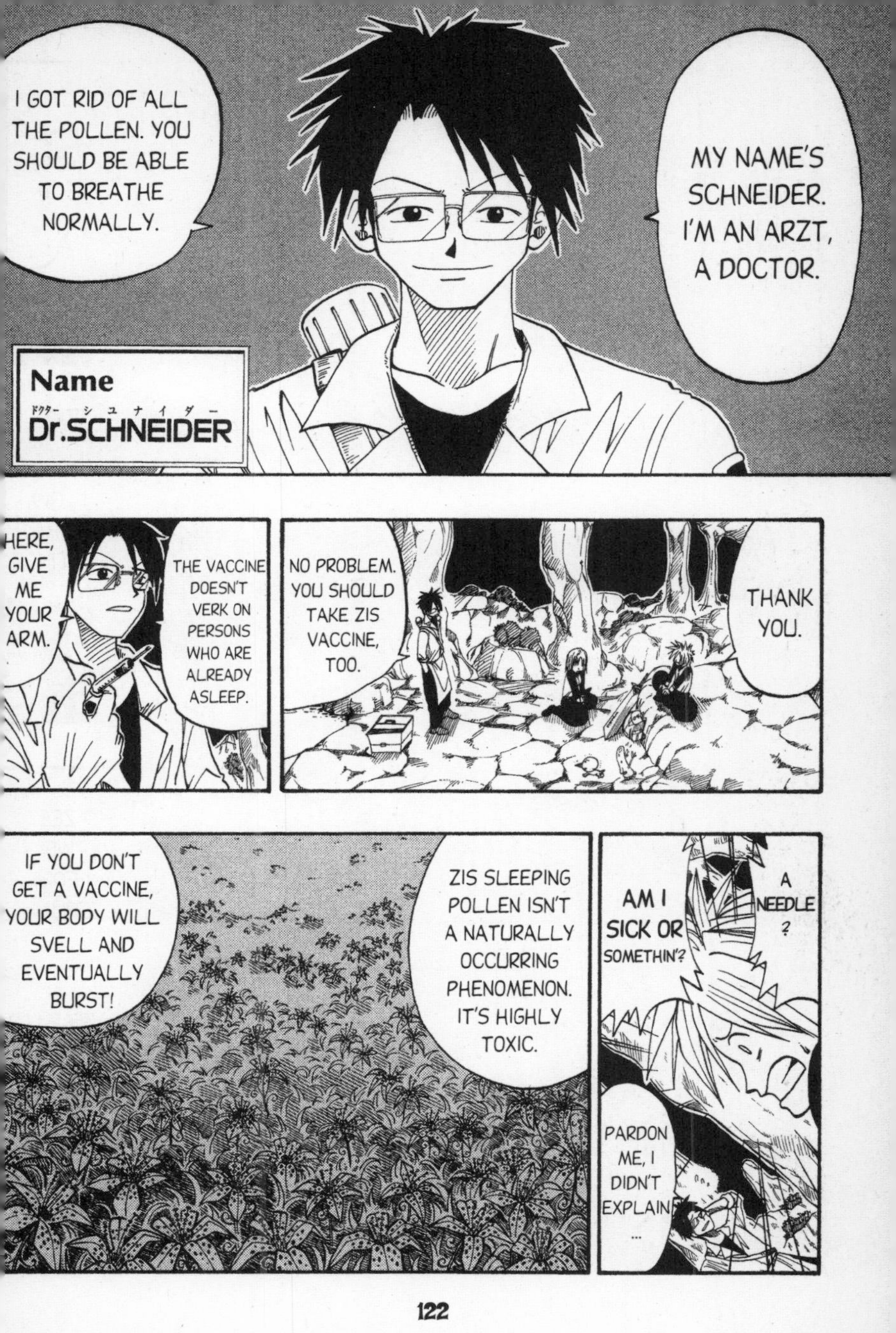
MY NAME'S SCHNEIDER. I'M AN ARZT, A DOCTOR.
I GOT RID OF ALL THE POLLEN. YOU SHOULD BE ABLE TO BREATHE NORMALLY.
Name
ドクター シュナイダー
Dr.SCHNEIDER
THANK YOU.
NO PROBLEM. YOU SHOULD TAKE ZIS VACCINE, TOO.
THE VACCINE DOESN'T VERK ON PERSONS WHO ARE ALREADY ASLEEP.
HERE, GIVE ME YOUR ARM.
A NEEDLE?
AM I SICK OR SOMETHIN'?
PARDON ME, I DIDN'T EXPLAIN...
ZIS SLEEPING POLLEN ISN'T A NATURALLY OCCURRING PHENOMENON. IT'S HIGHLY TOXIC.
IF YOU DON'T GET A VACCINE, YOUR BODY WILL SVELL AND EVENTUALLY BURST!

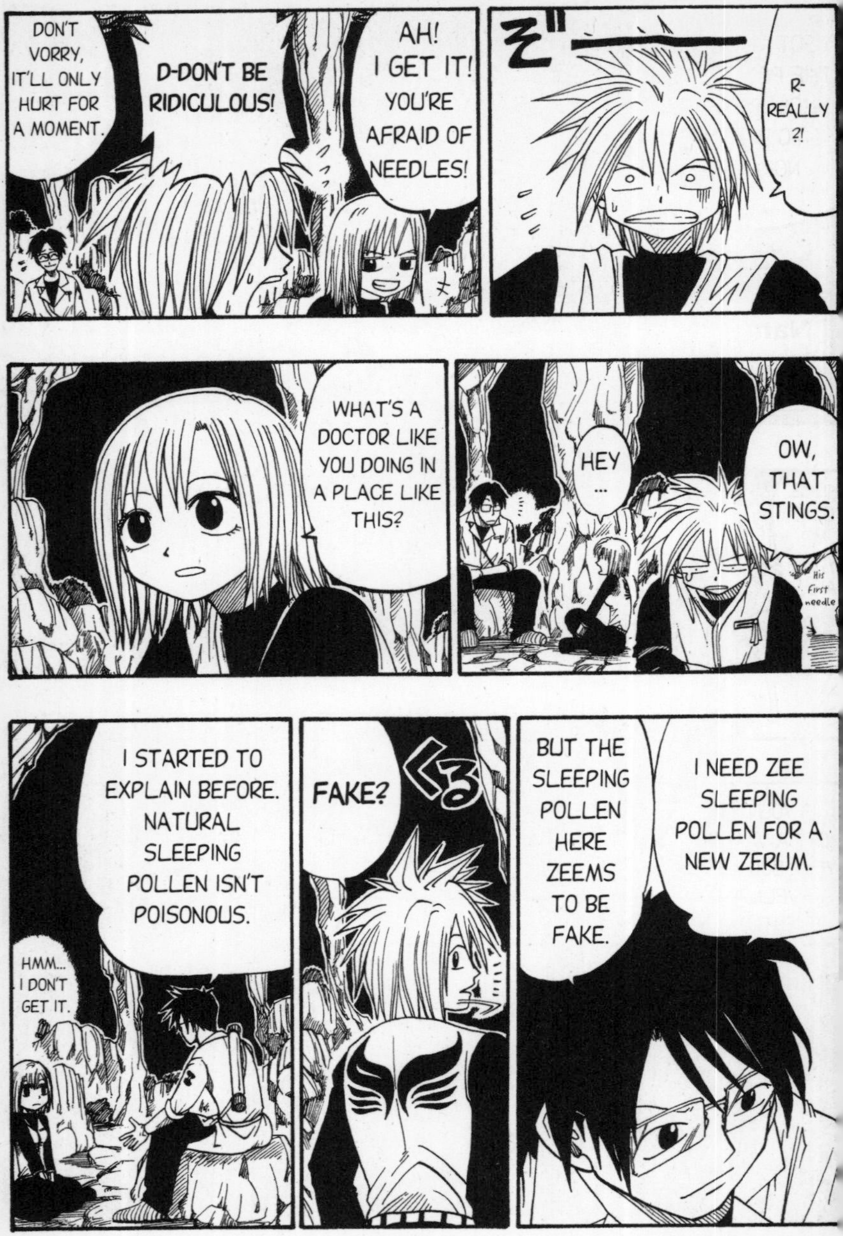
ぞ
R-REALLY ?!
AH! I GET IT! YOU'RE AFRAID OF NEEDLES!
D-DON'T BE RIDICULOUS!
DON'T VORRY, IT'LL ONLY HURT FOR A MOMENT.
OW, THAT STINGS.
His First needle
HEY ...
WHAT'S A DOCTOR LIKE YOU DOING IN A PLACE LIKE THIS?
I NEED ZEE SLEEPING POLLEN FOR A NEW ZERUM.
BUT THE SLEEPING POLLEN HERE ZEEMS TO BE FAKE.
くる
FAKE?
I STARTED TO EXPLAIN BEFORE. NATURAL SLEEPING POLLEN ISN'T POISONOUS.
HMM... I DON'T GET IT.

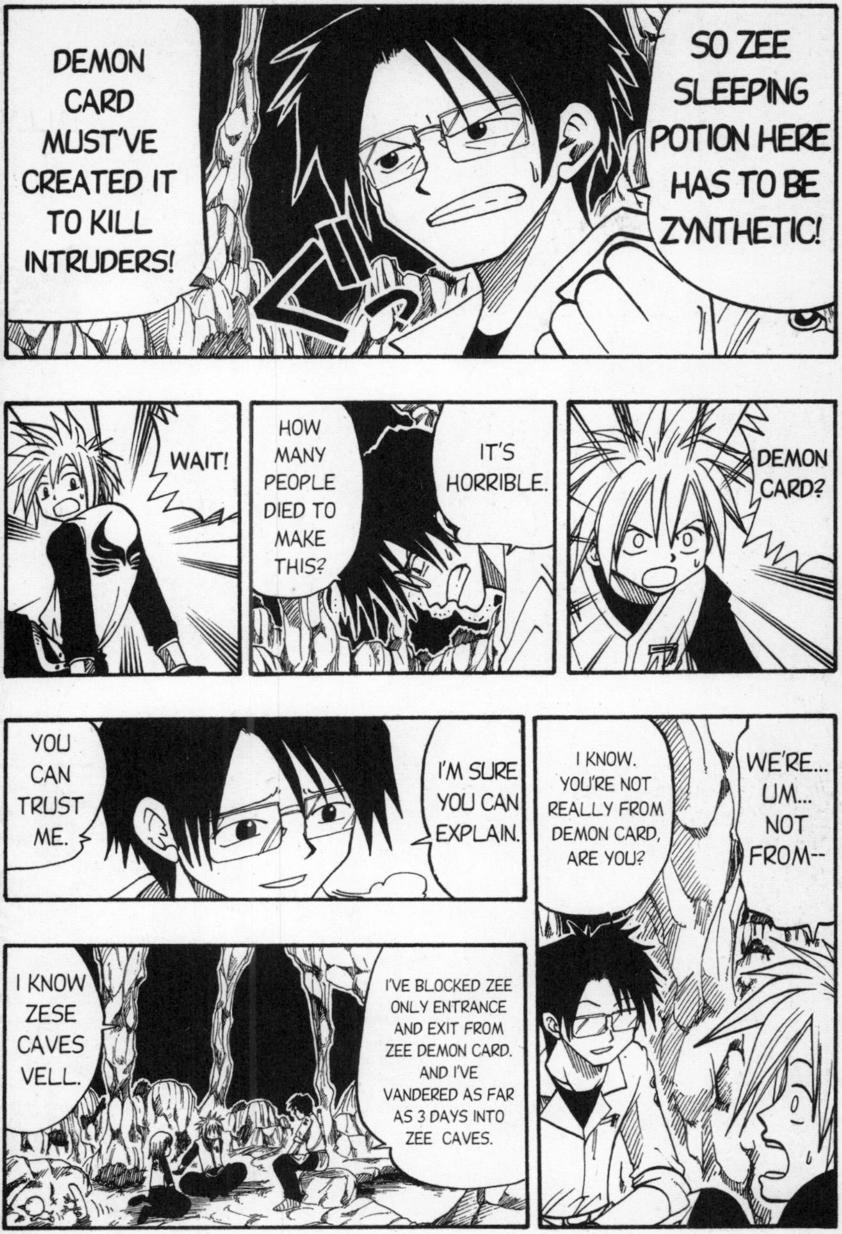
SO ZEE SLEEPING POTION HERE HAS TO BE ZYNTHETIC!
DEMON CARD MUST'VE CREATED IT TO KILL INTRUDERS!
DEMON CARD?
IT'S HORRIBLE.
HOW MANY PEOPLE DIED TO MAKE THIS?
WAIT!
WE'RE... UM... NOT FROM--
I KNOW. YOU'RE NOT REALLY FROM DEMON CARD, ARE YOU?
I'M SURE YOU CAN EXPLAIN.
YOU CAN TRUST ME.
I'VE BLOCKED ZEE ONLY ENTRANCE AND EXIT FROM ZEE DEMON CARD. AND I'VE VANDERED AS FAR AS 3 DAYS INTO ZEE CAVES.
I KNOW ZESE CAVES VELL.

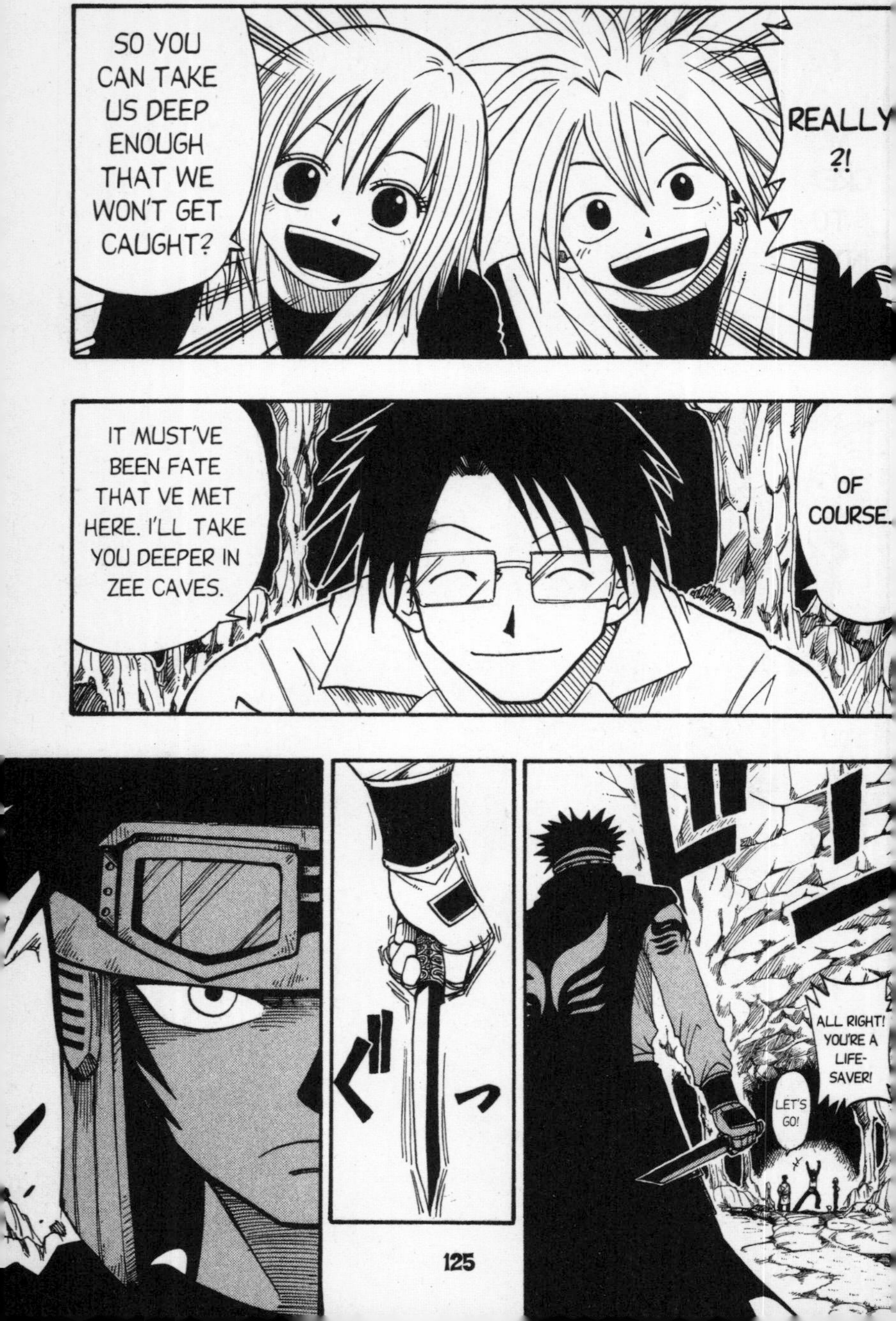
SO YOU CAN TAKE US DEEP ENOUGH THAT WE WON'T GET CAUGHT?
REALLY ?!
OF COURSE.
IT MUST'VE BEEN FATE THAT VE MET HERE. I'LL TAKE YOU DEEPER IN ZEE CAVES.
ALL RIGHT! YOU'RE A LIFE-SAVER!
LET'S GO!
ぐっ

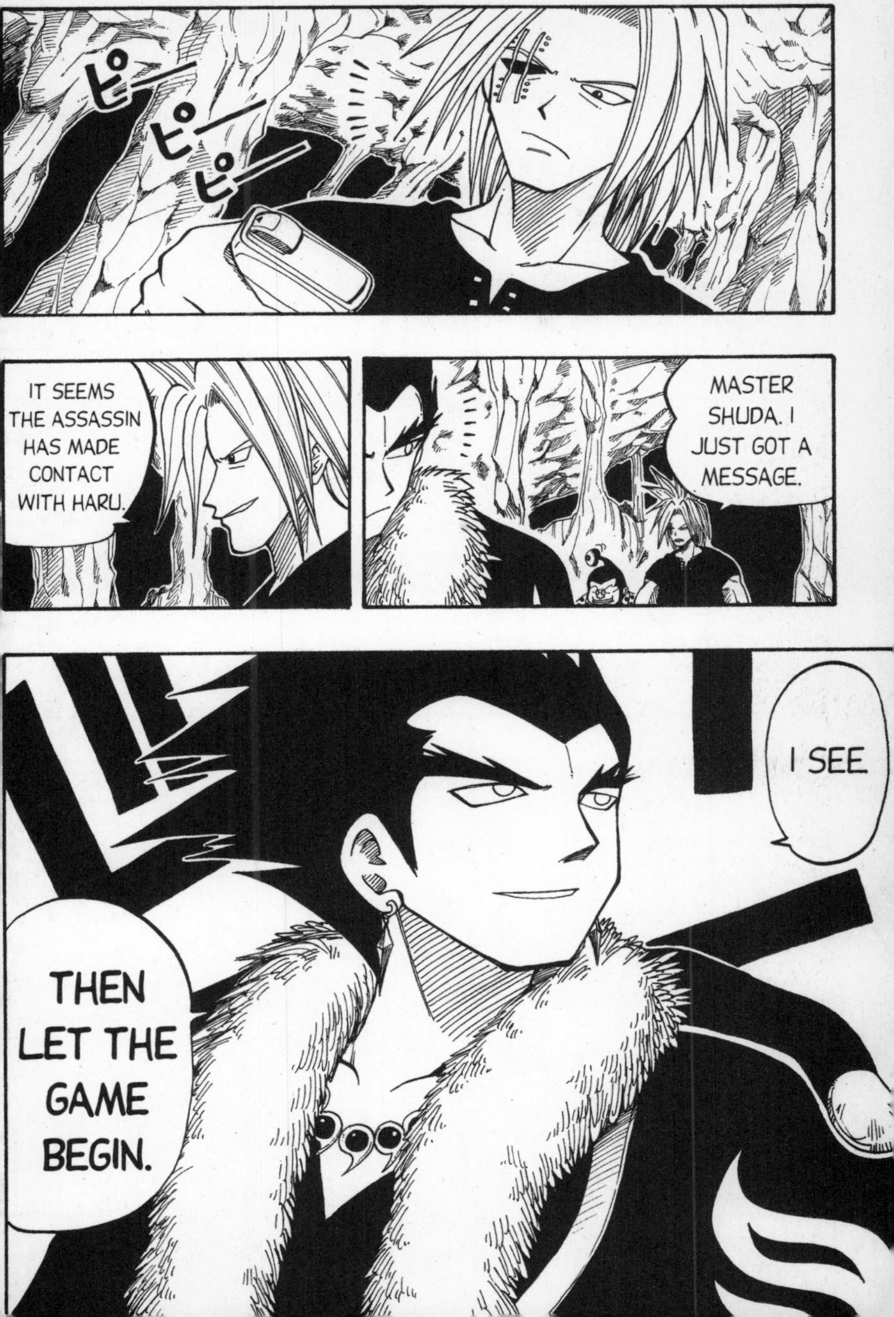
ピー ピー ピー
MASTER SHUDA. I JUST GOT A MESSAGE.
IT SEEMS THE ASSASSIN HAS MADE CONTACT WITH HARU.
I SEE.
THEN LET THE GAME BEGIN.

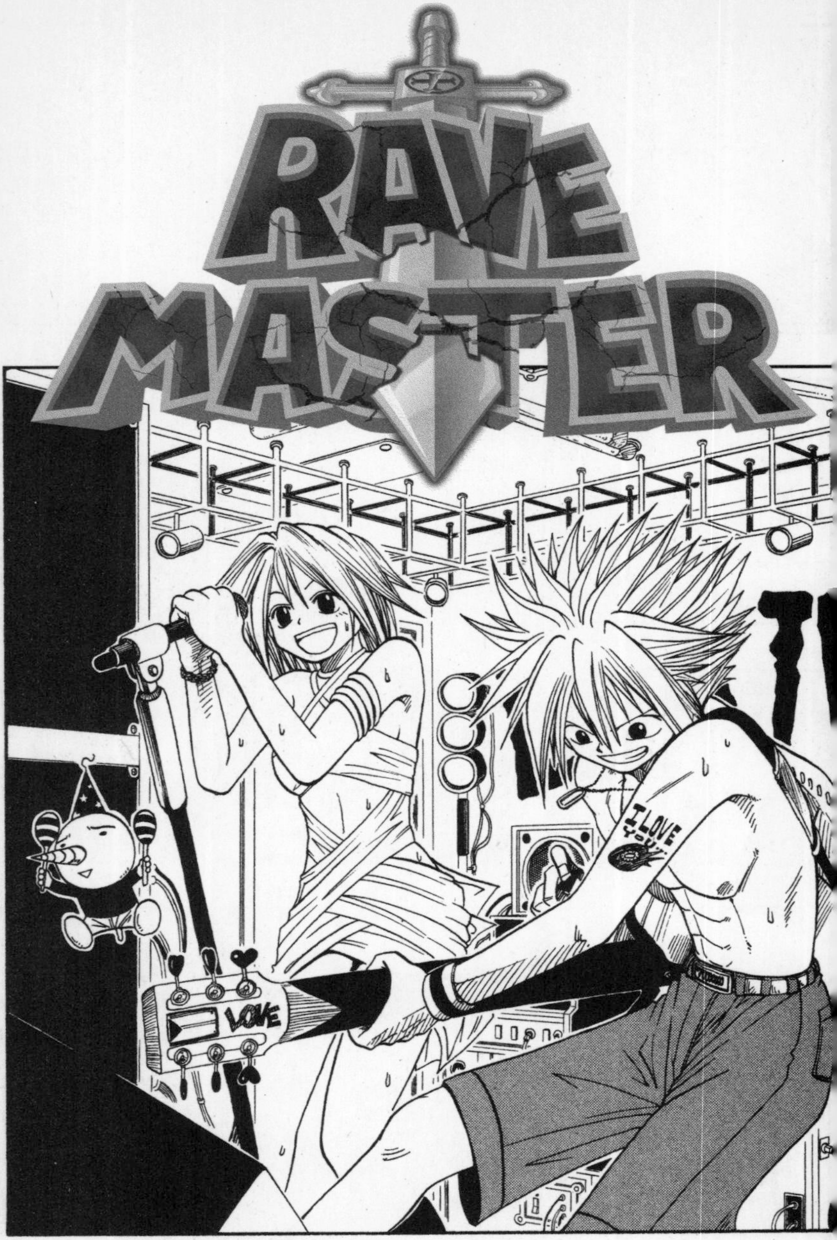
RAVE MASTER
I LOVE YOU
LOVE

RAVE: 28 ✠ Chameleon Panic?!

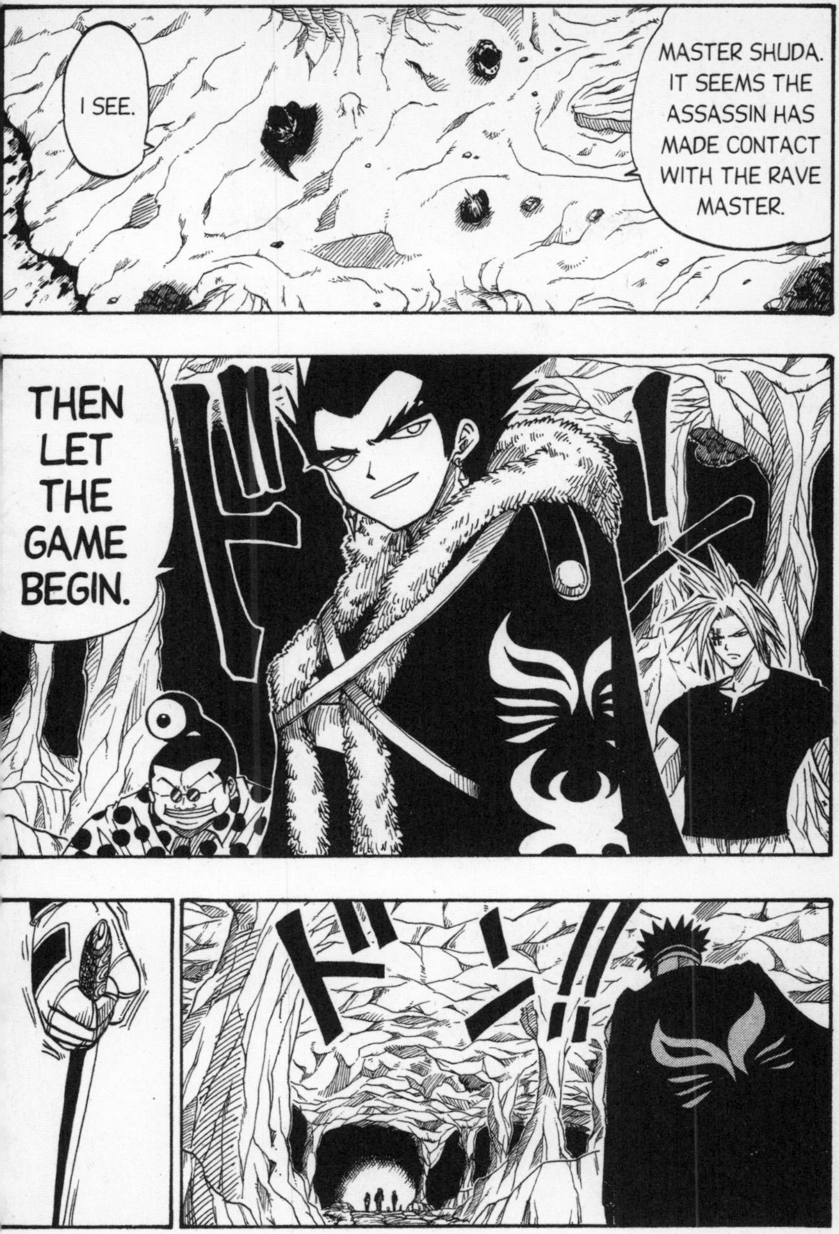
MASTER SHUDA. IT SEEMS THE ASSASSIN HAS MADE CONTACT WITH THE RAVE MASTER.
I SEE.
THEN LET THE GAME BEGIN.

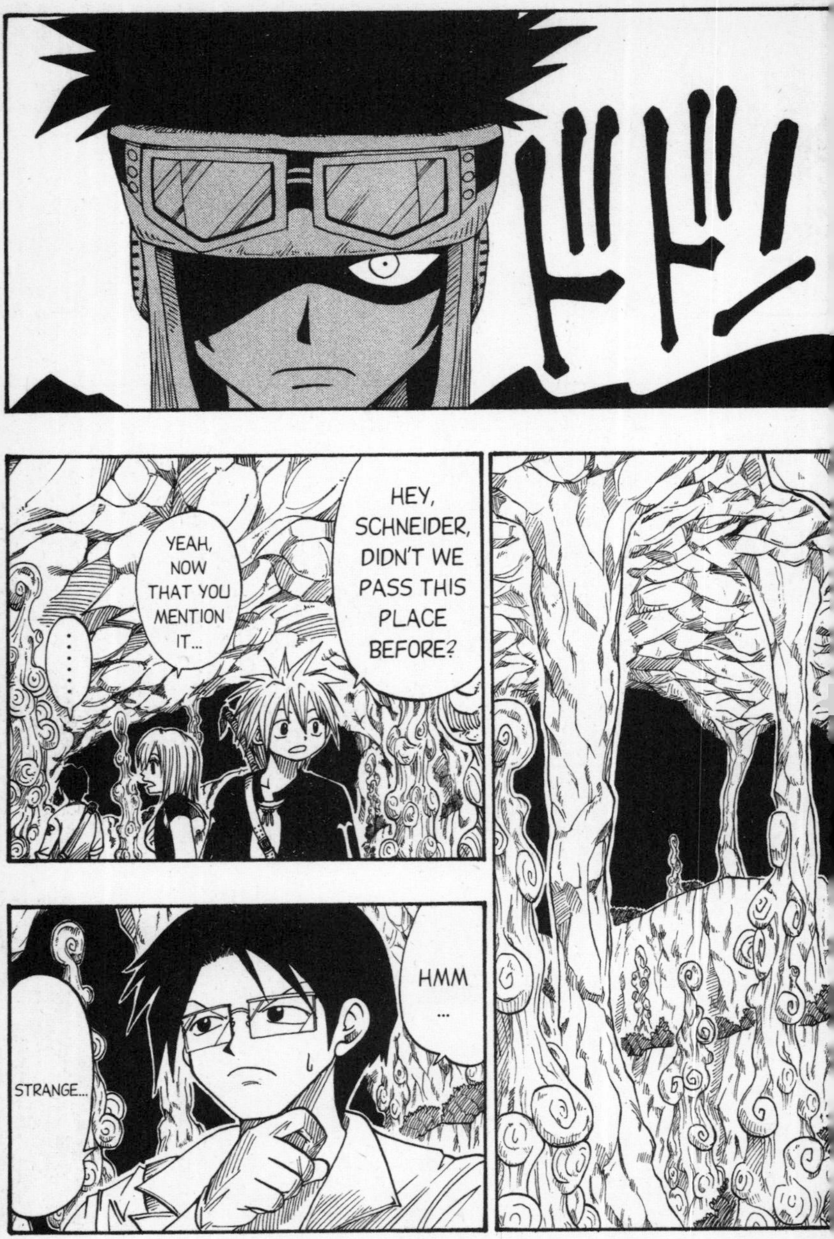
HEY, SCHNEIDER, DIDN'T WE PASS THIS PLACE BEFORE?
YEAH, NOW THAT YOU MENTION IT...
......
HMM ...
STRANGE...

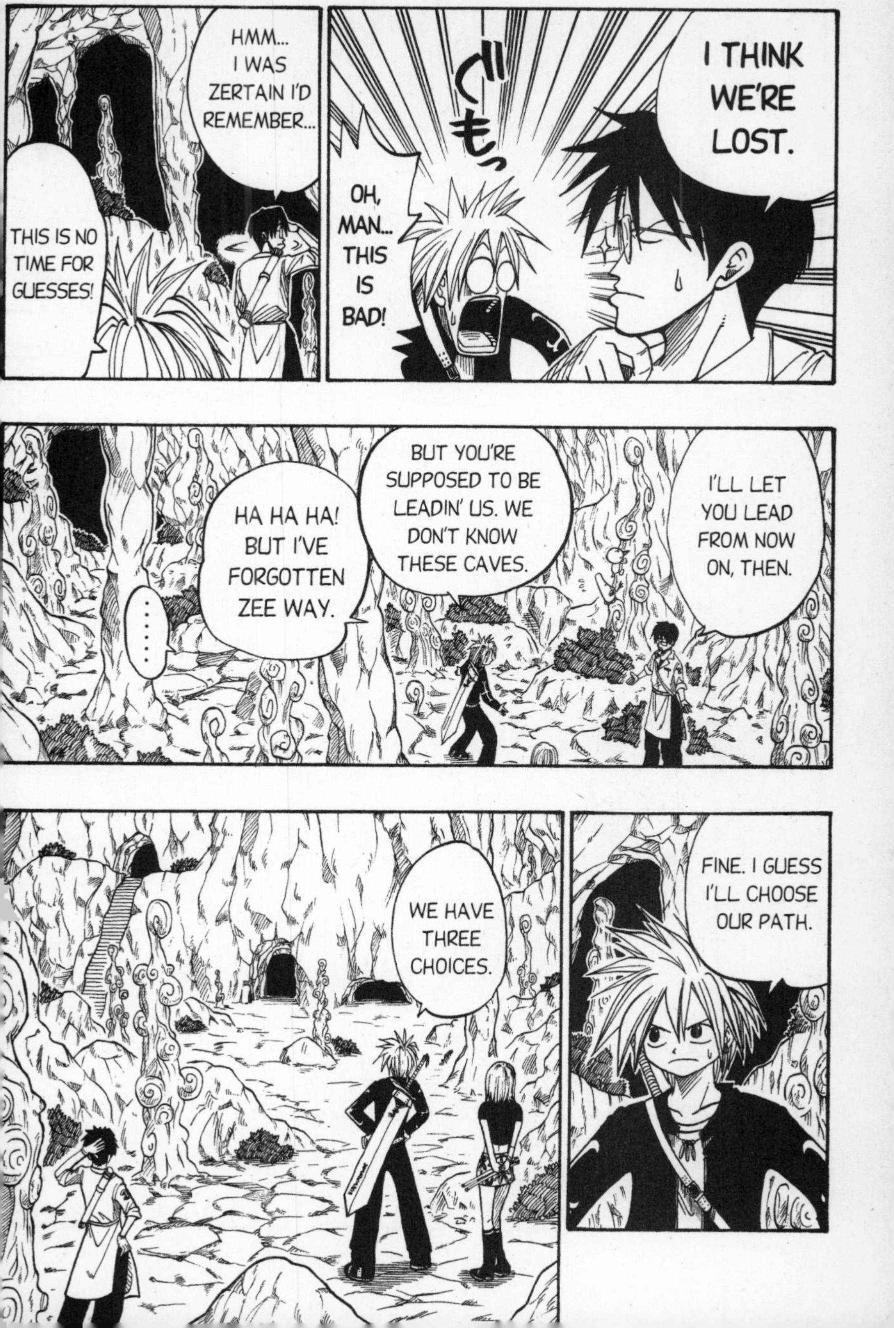
I THINK WE'RE LOST.
ぐもっ
OH, MAN... THIS IS BAD!
HMM... I WAS ZERTAIN I'D REMEMBER...
THIS IS NO TIME FOR GUESSES!
I'LL LET YOU LEAD FROM NOW ON, THEN.
BUT YOU'RE SUPPOSED TO BE LEADIN' US. WE DON'T KNOW THESE CAVES.
HA HA HA! BUT I'VE FORGOTTEN ZEE WAY.
......
FINE. I GUESS I'LL CHOOSE OUR PATH.
WE HAVE THREE CHOICES.
...

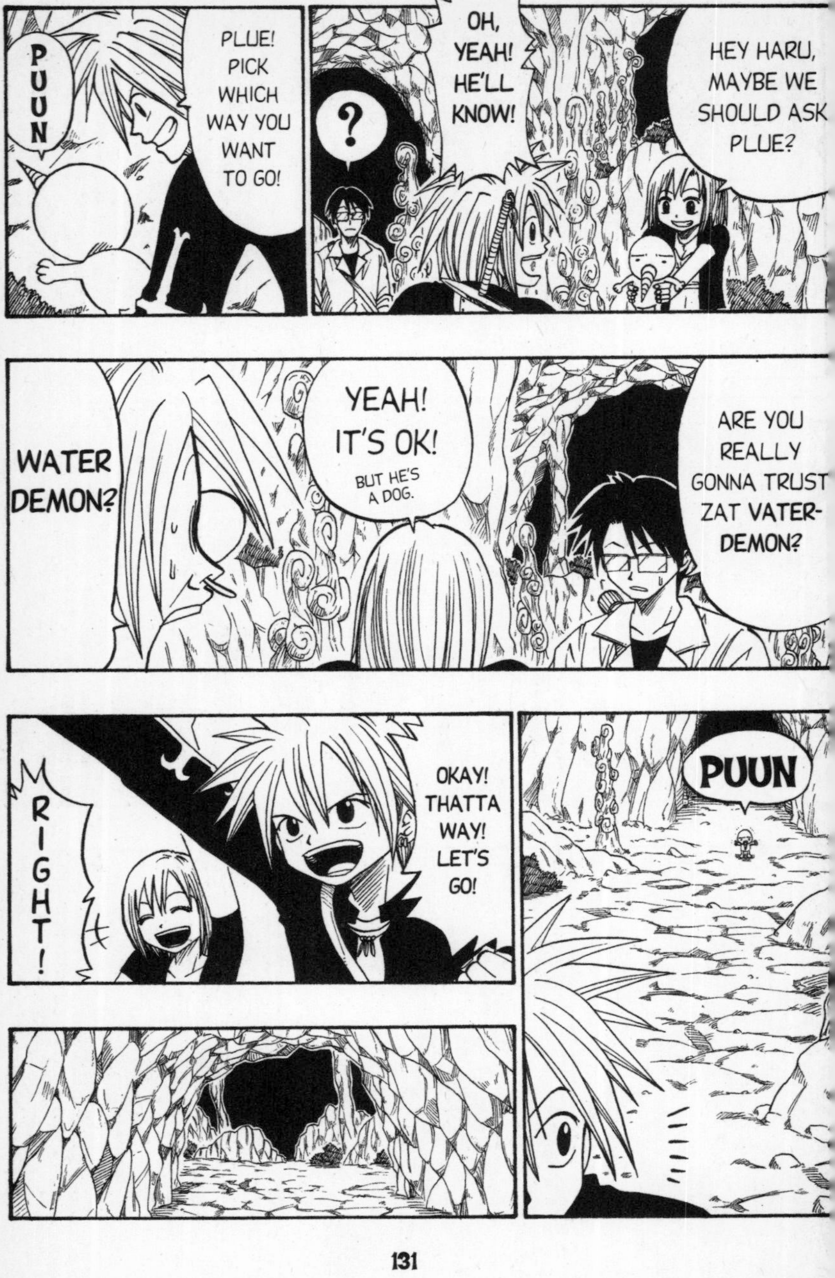
HEY HARU, MAYBE WE SHOULD ASK PLUE?
OH, YEAH! HE'LL KNOW!
?
PLUE! PICK WHICH WAY YOU WANT TO GO!
PUUN
ARE YOU REALLY GONNA TRUST ZAT VATER-DEMON?
YEAH! IT'S OK!
BUT HE'S A DOG.
WATER DEMON?
PUUN
OKAY! THATTA WAY! LET'S GO!
RIGHT!

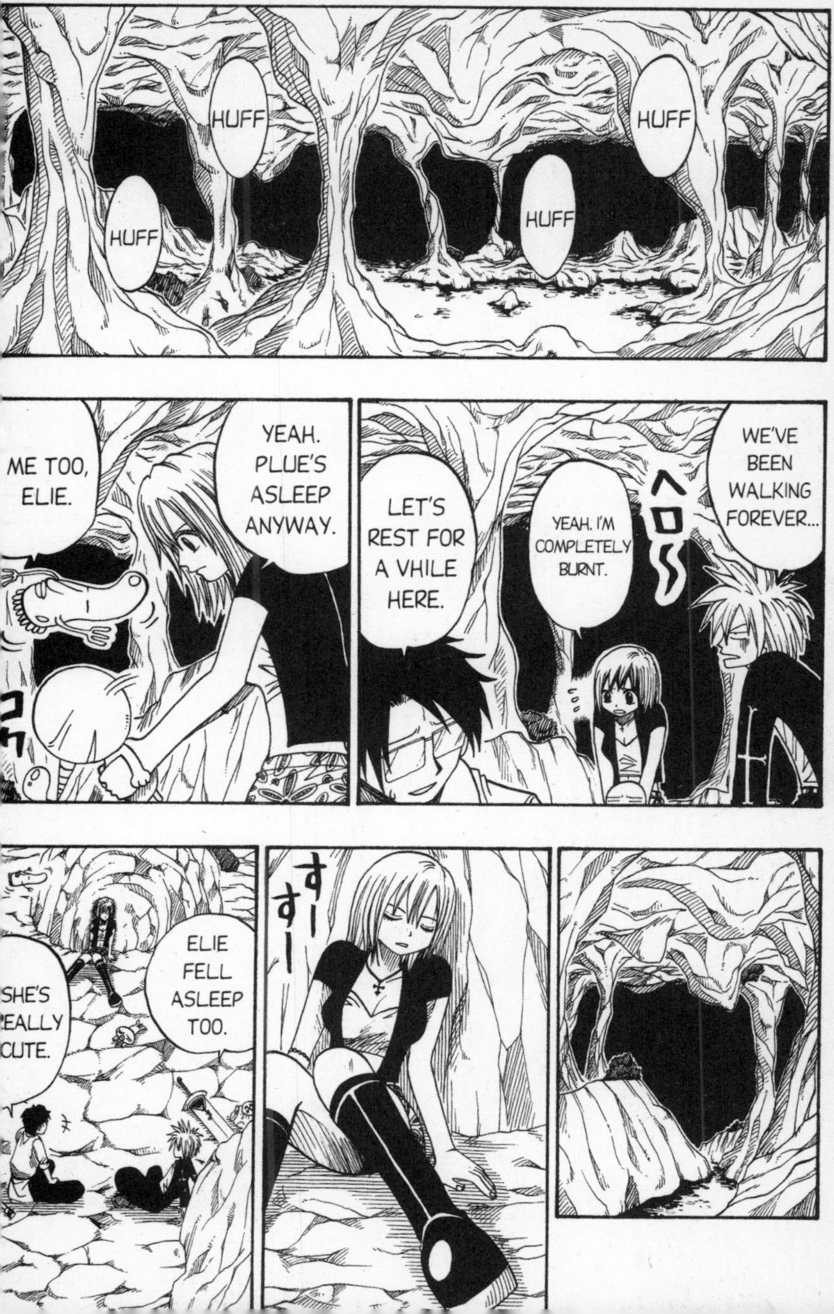
HUFF
HUFF
HUFF
HUFF
WE'VE BEEN WALKING FOREVER...
ヘロ〜
YEAH. I'M COMPLETELY BURNT.
LET'S REST FOR A VHILE HERE.
YEAH. PLUE'S ASLEEP ANYWAY.
ME TOO, ELIE.
コク
すーすー
ELIE FELL ASLEEP TOO.
SHE'S EALLY CUTE.

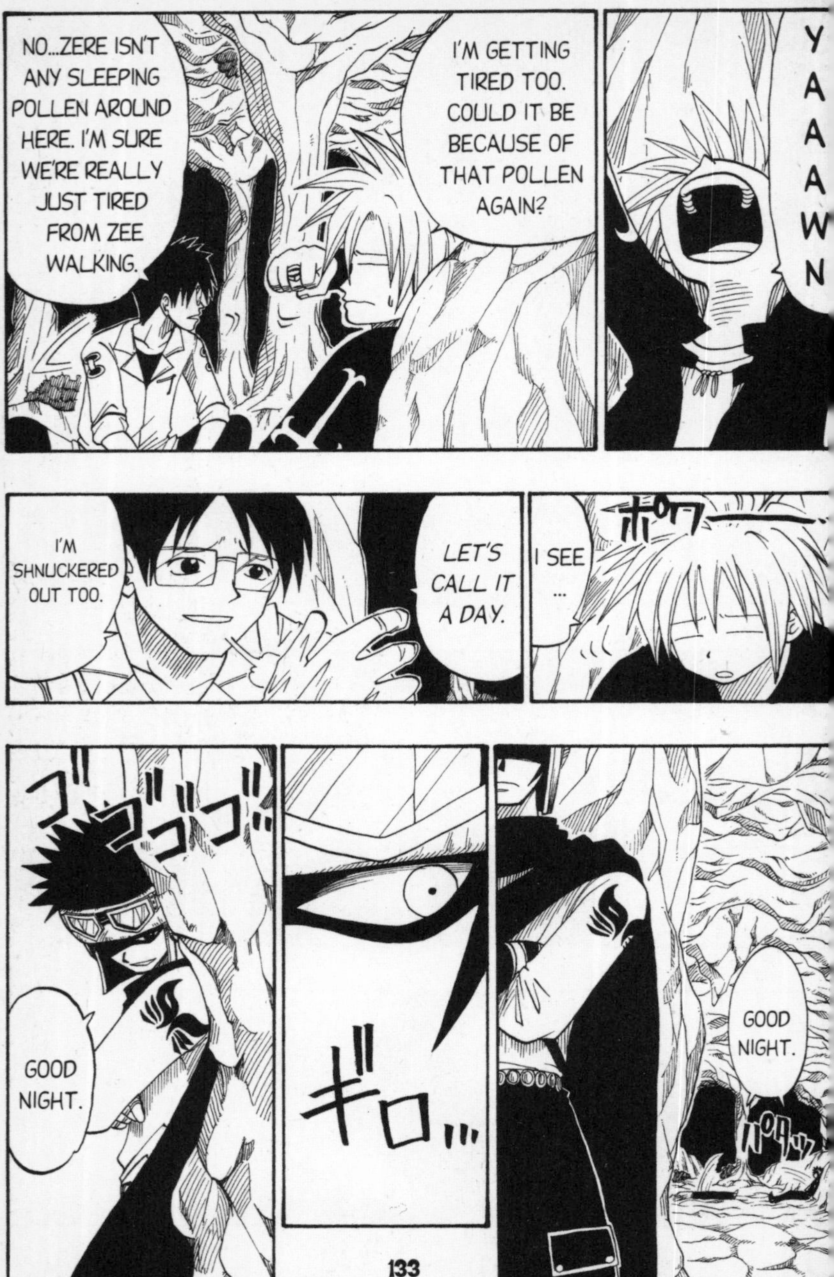

YAAAWN
I'M GETTING TIRED TOO. COULD IT BE BECAUSE OF THAT POLLEN AGAIN?
NO...ZERE ISN'T ANY SLEEPING POLLEN AROUND HERE. I'M SURE WE'RE REALLY JUST TIRED FROM ZEE WALKING.
I SEE ...
LET'S CALL IT A DAY.
I'M SHNUCKERED OUT TOO.
GOOD NIGHT.
ギロ
GOOD NIGHT.

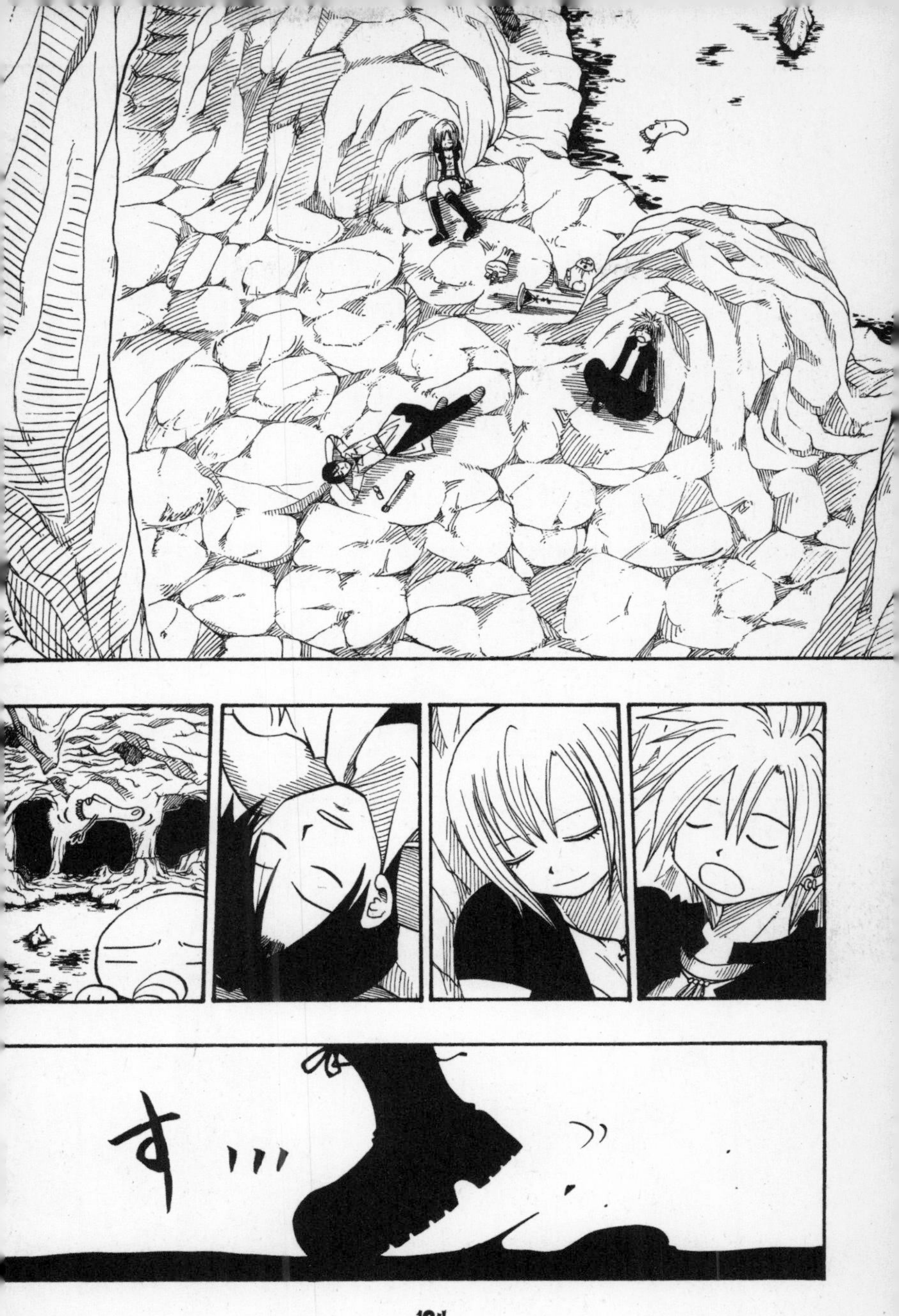
す

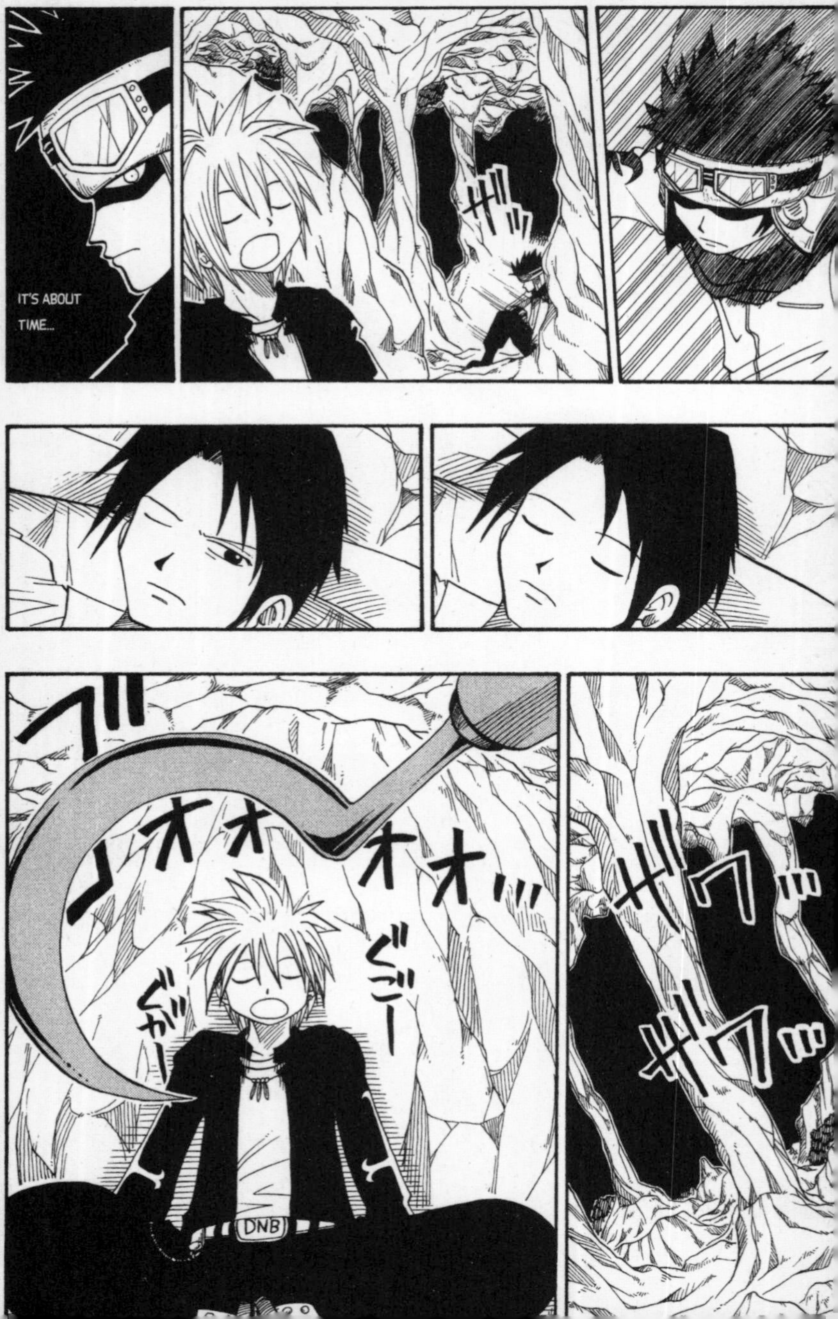
ザッ
IT'S ABOUT TIME...
ザワッ
ザワッ
ブゥンオオオオッ
ぐごー
ぐがー

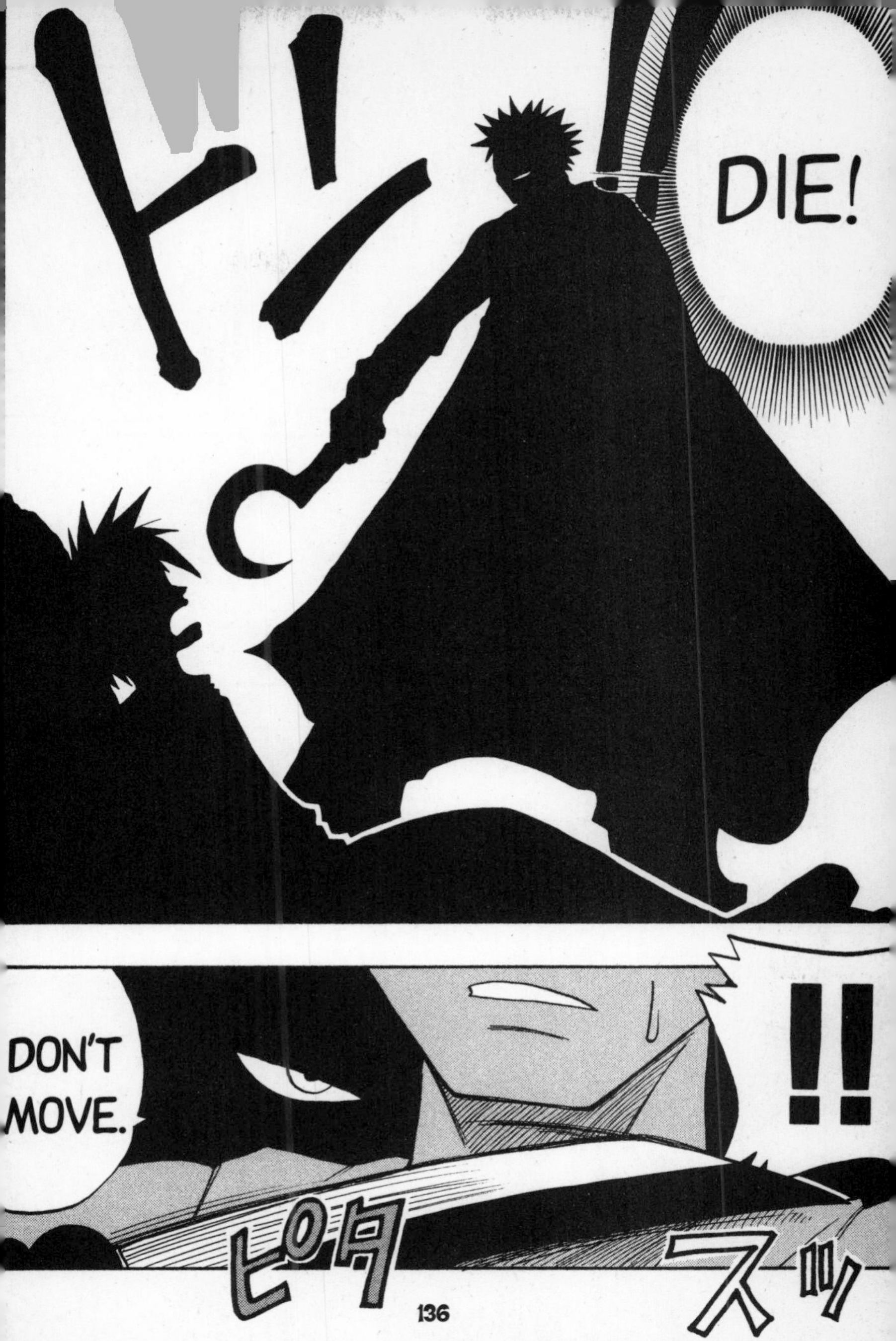
DIE!
!!
DON'T MOVE.
スッ
ピタ

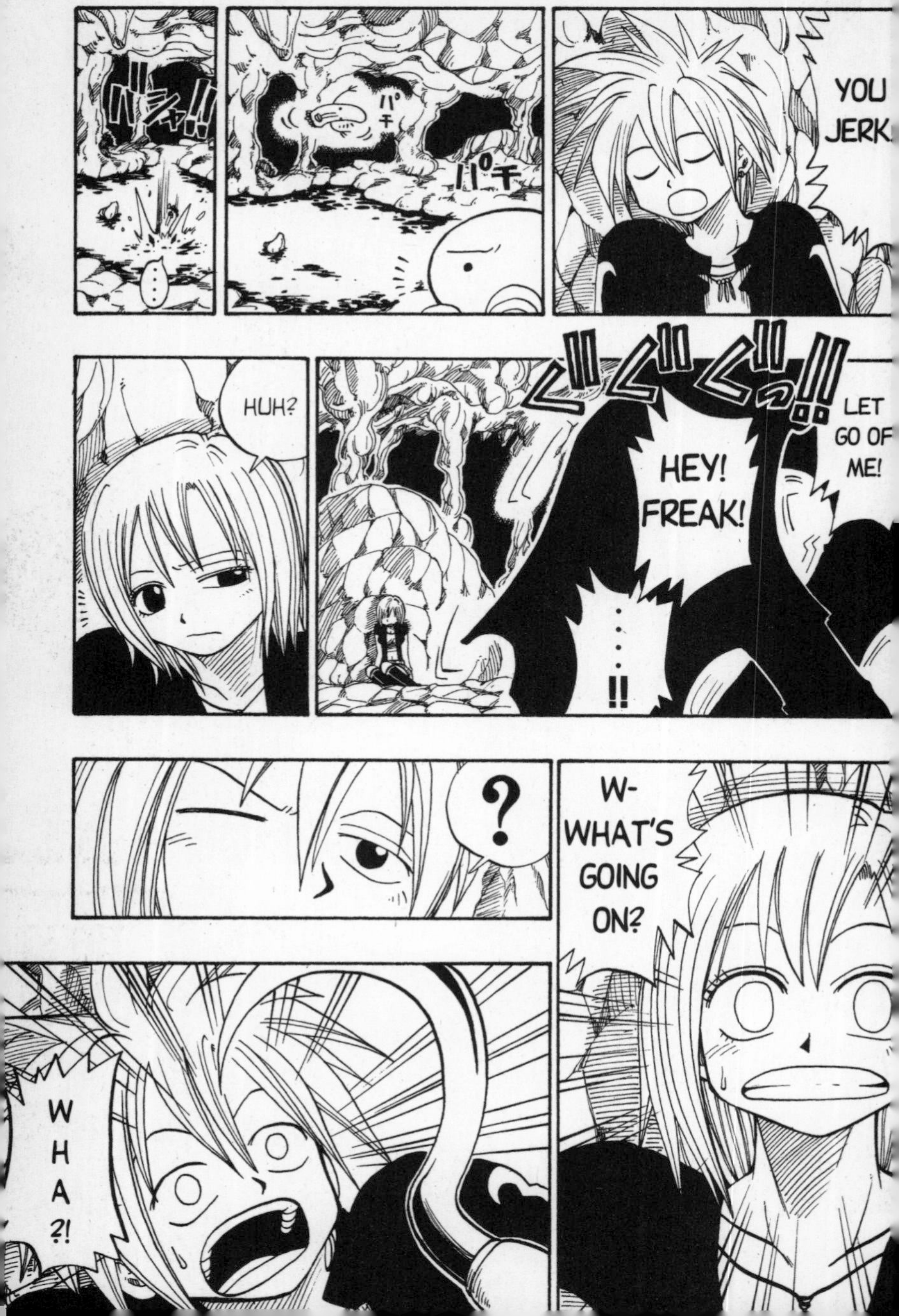
YOU JERK!
パチ
パチ
バシャ!!
...
ぐいぐいっ!!
LET GO OF ME!
HEY! FREAK!
...!!
HUH?
W- WHAT'S GOING ON?
?
WHA?!

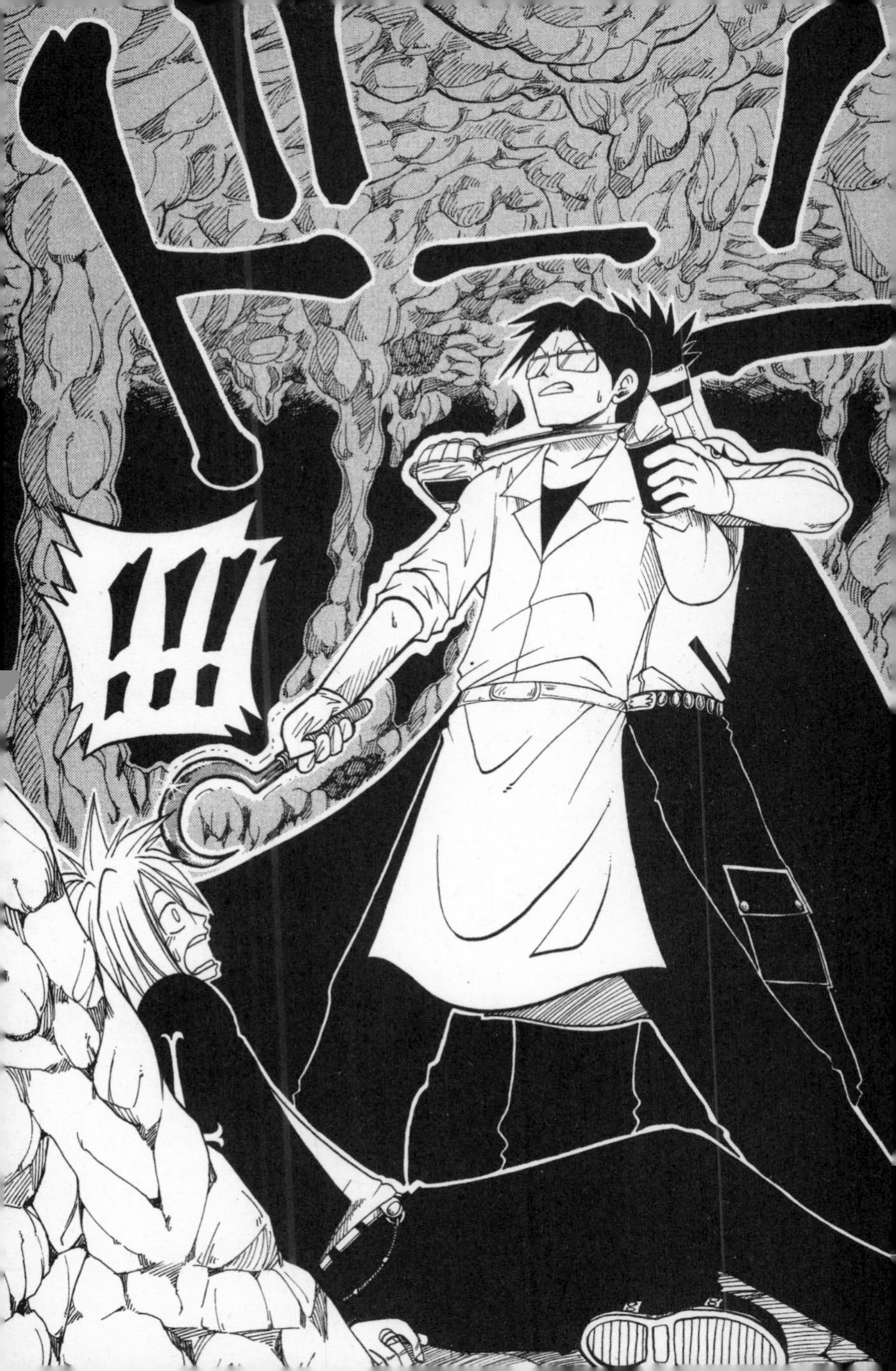
ドーン
!!!

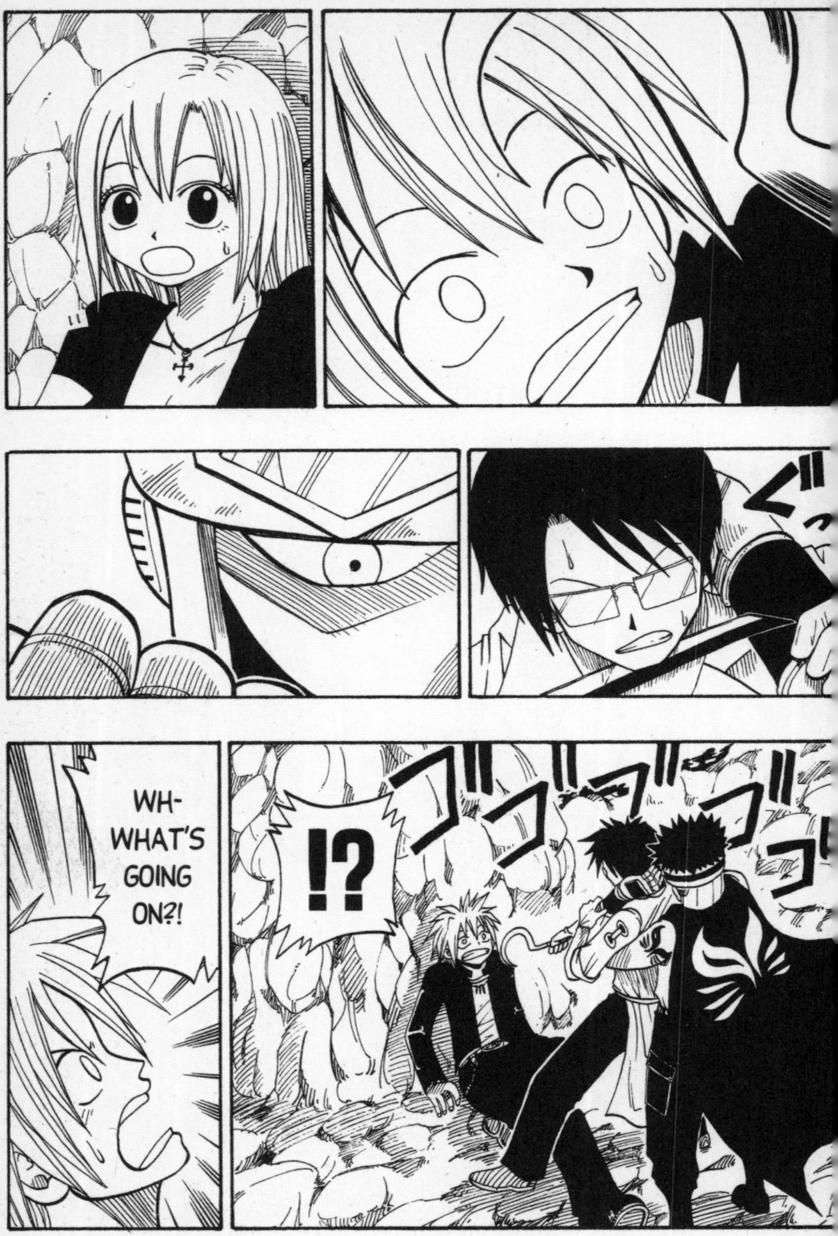
ぐっ
ゴゴゴゴゴ
!?
WH- WHAT'S GOING ON?!

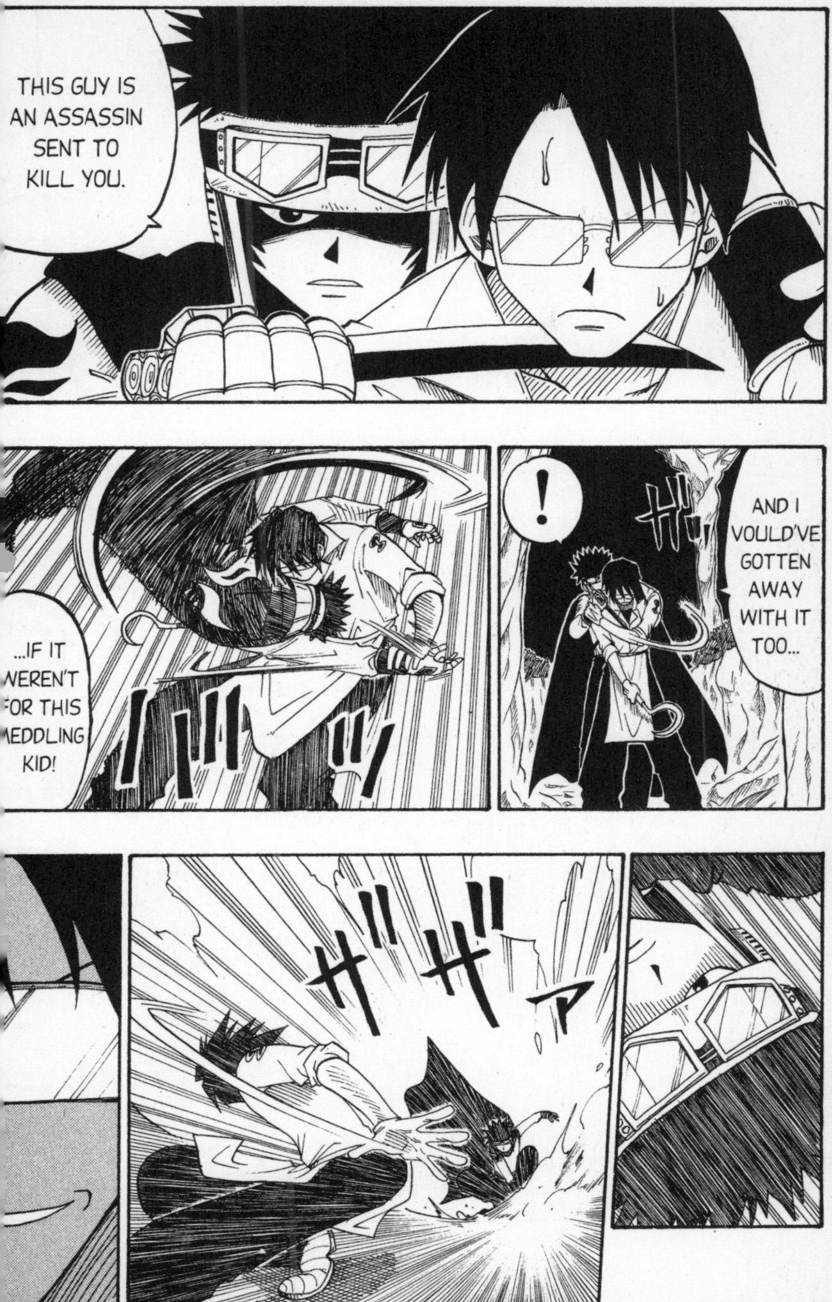
THIS GUY IS AN ASSASSIN SENT TO KILL YOU.
!
AND I WOULD'VE GOTTEN AWAY WITH IT TOO...
...IF IT WEREN'T FOR THIS MEDDLING KID!

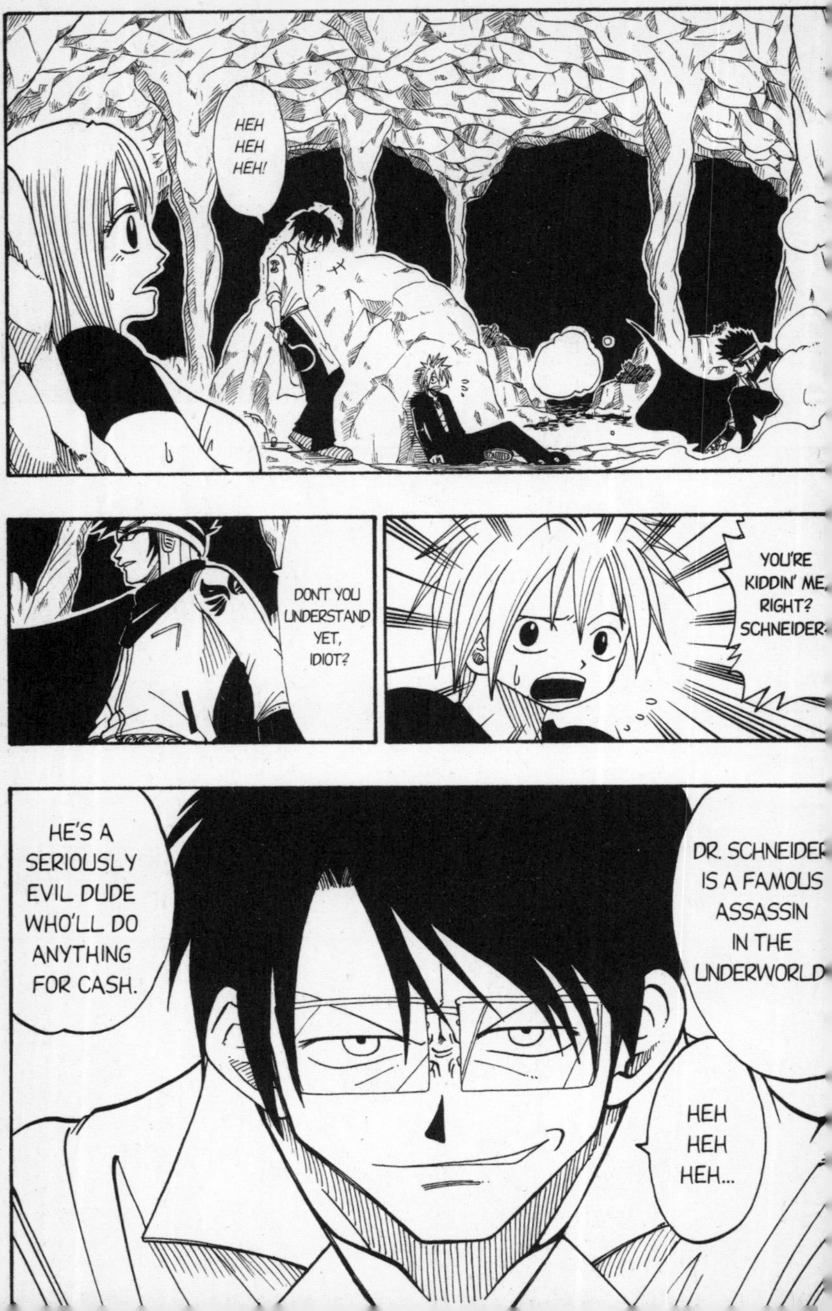
HEH HEH HEH!
YOU'RE KIDDIN' ME, RIGHT? SCHNEIDER
DON'T YOU UNDERSTAND YET, IDIOT?
DR. SCHNEIDER IS A FAMOUS ASSASSIN IN THE UNDERWORLD
HE'S A SERIOUSLY EVIL DUDE WHO'LL DO ANYTHING FOR CASH.
HEH HEH HEH...

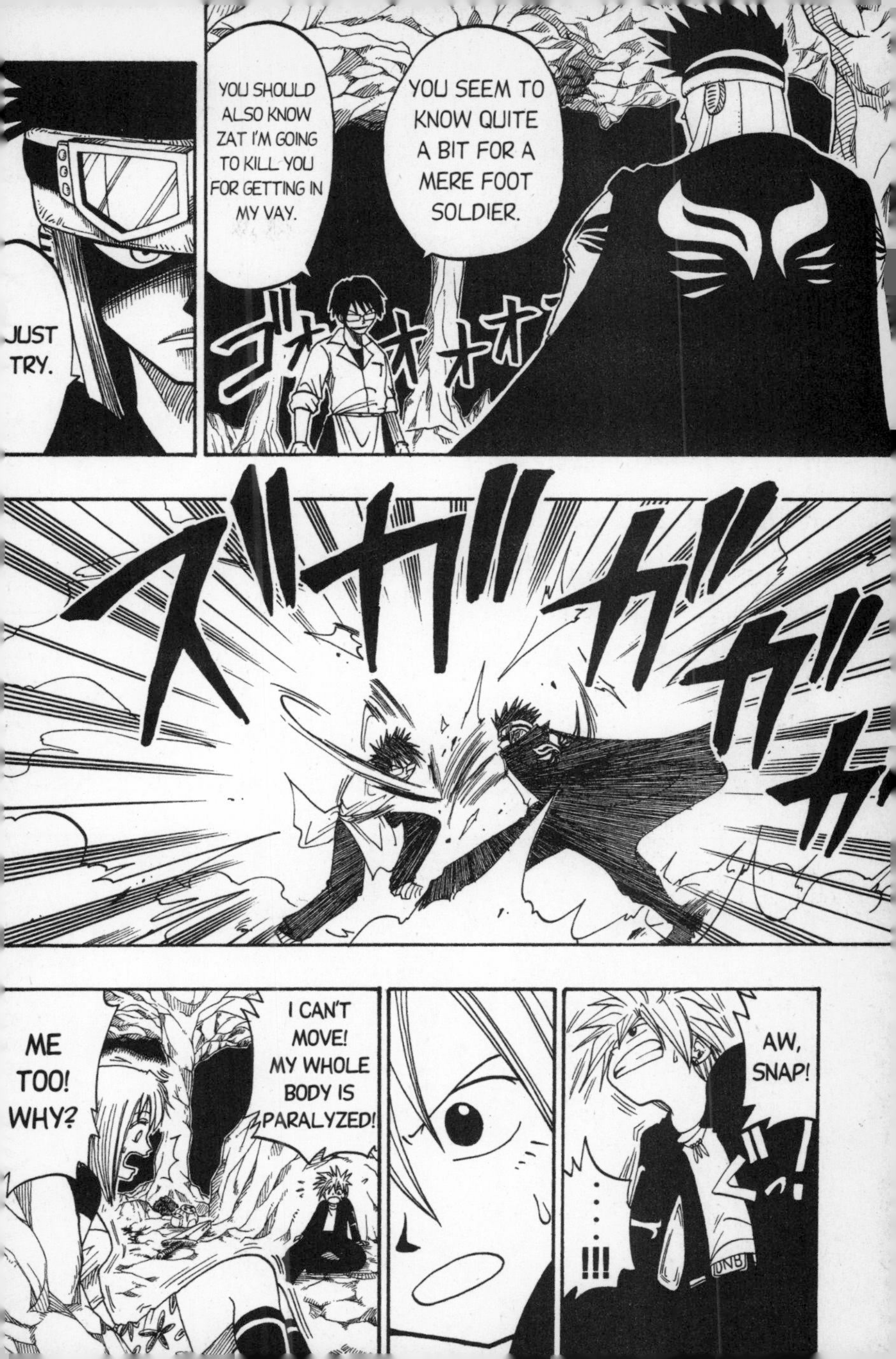

YOU SEEM TO KNOW QUITE A BIT FOR A MERE FOOT SOLDIER.
YOU SHOULD ALSO KNOW ZAT I'M GOING TO KILL YOU FOR GETTING IN MY VAY.
JUST TRY.
AW, SNAP!
......!!!
I CAN'T MOVE! MY WHOLE BODY IS PARALYZED!
ME TOO! WHY?

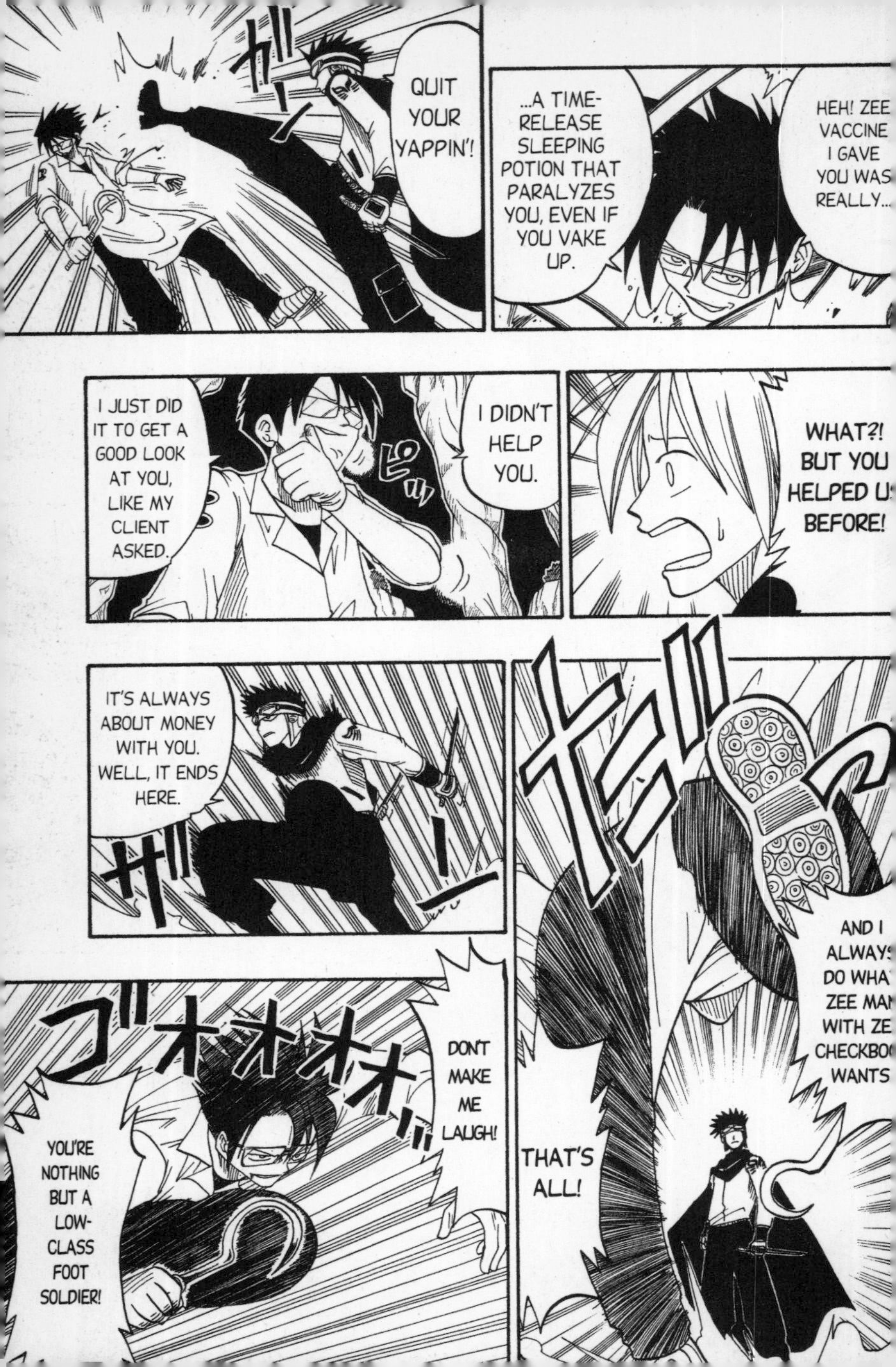
HEH! ZEE VACCINE I GAVE YOU WAS REALLY...
...A TIME-RELEASE SLEEPING POTION THAT PARALYZES YOU, EVEN IF YOU VAKE UP.
QUIT YOUR YAPPIN'!
WHAT?! BUT YOU HELPED U BEFORE!
I DIDN'T HELP YOU.
I JUST DID IT TO GET A GOOD LOOK AT YOU, LIKE MY CLIENT ASKED.
AND I ALWAY DO WHA ZEE MA WITH ZE CHECKBO WANTS
THAT'S ALL!
IT'S ALWAYS ABOUT MONEY WITH YOU. WELL, IT ENDS HERE.
DON'T MAKE ME LAUGH!
YOU'RE NOTHING BUT A LOW-CLASS FOOT SOLDIER!

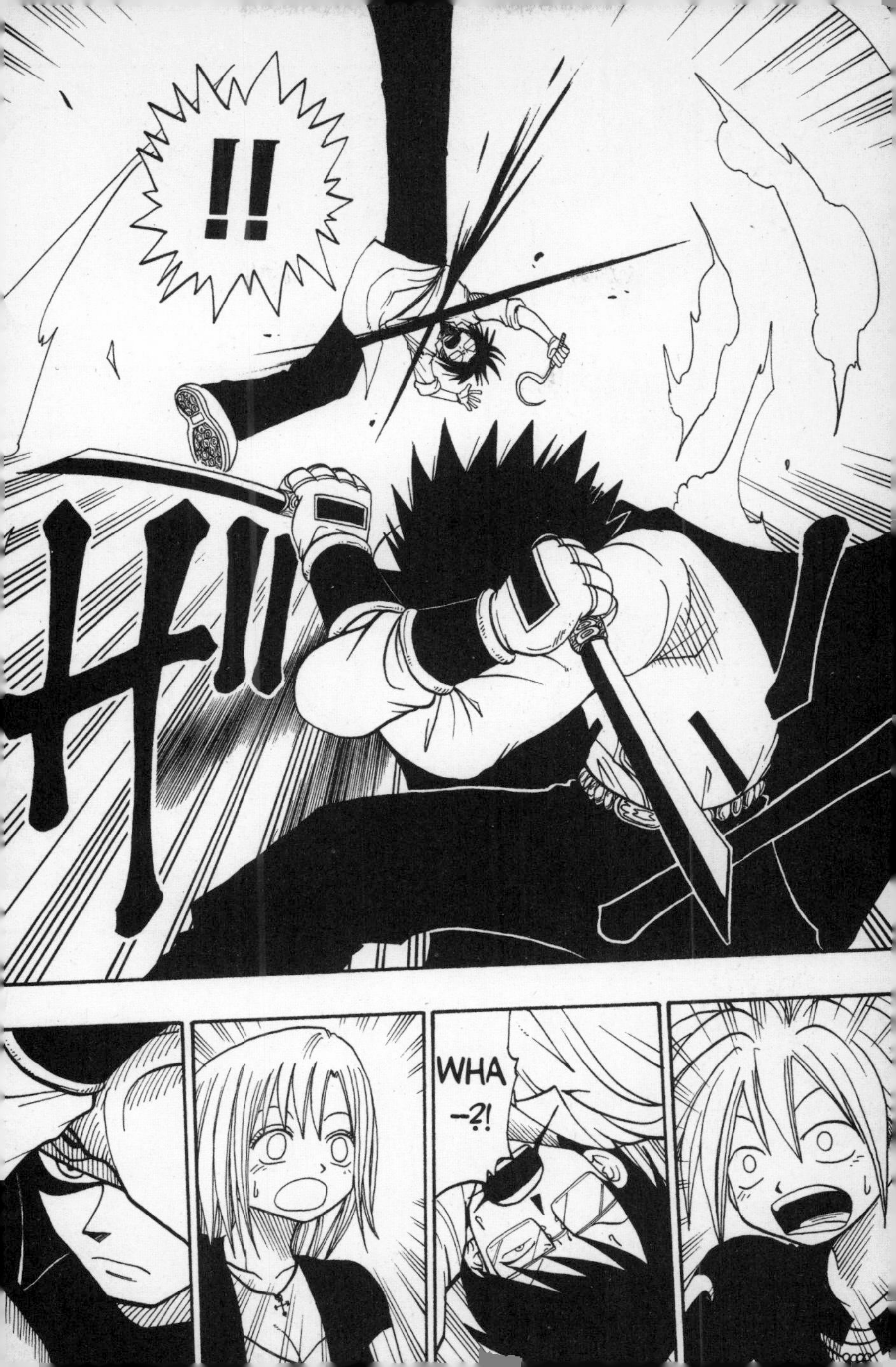
!!
WHA --?!

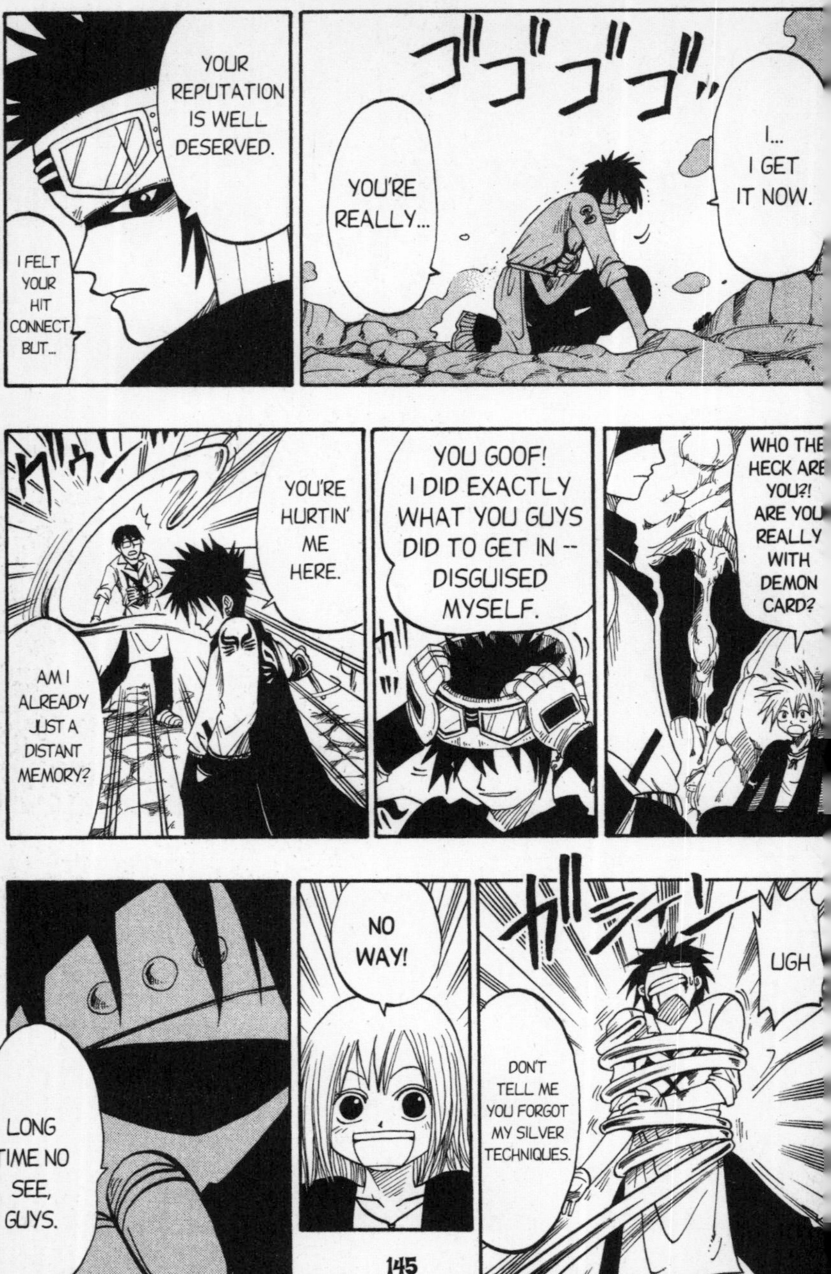
I... I GET IT NOW.
YOU'RE REALLY...
YOUR REPUTATION IS WELL DESERVED.
I FELT YOUR HIT CONNECT BUT...
WHO THE HECK ARE YOU?! ARE YOU REALLY WITH DEMON CARD?
YOU GOOF! I DID EXACTLY WHAT YOU GUYS DID TO GET IN -- DISGUISED MYSELF.
YOU'RE HURTIN' ME HERE.
AM I ALREADY JUST A DISTANT MEMORY?
UGH
DON'T TELL ME YOU FORGOT MY SILVER TECHNIQUES.
NO WAY!
LONG TIME NO SEE, GUYS.

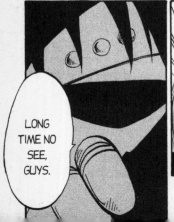

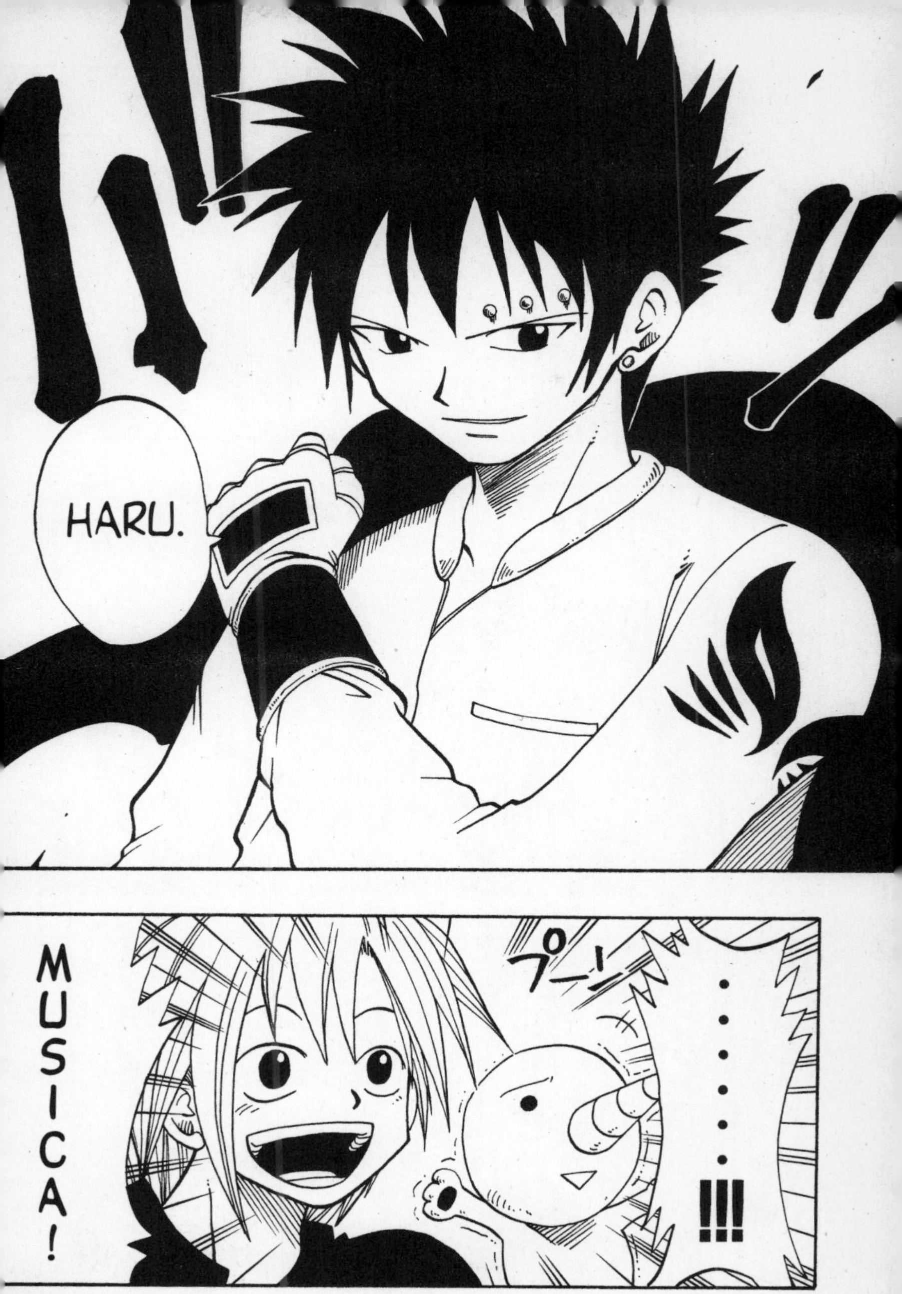
HARU.
......!!!
プー!
MUSICA!

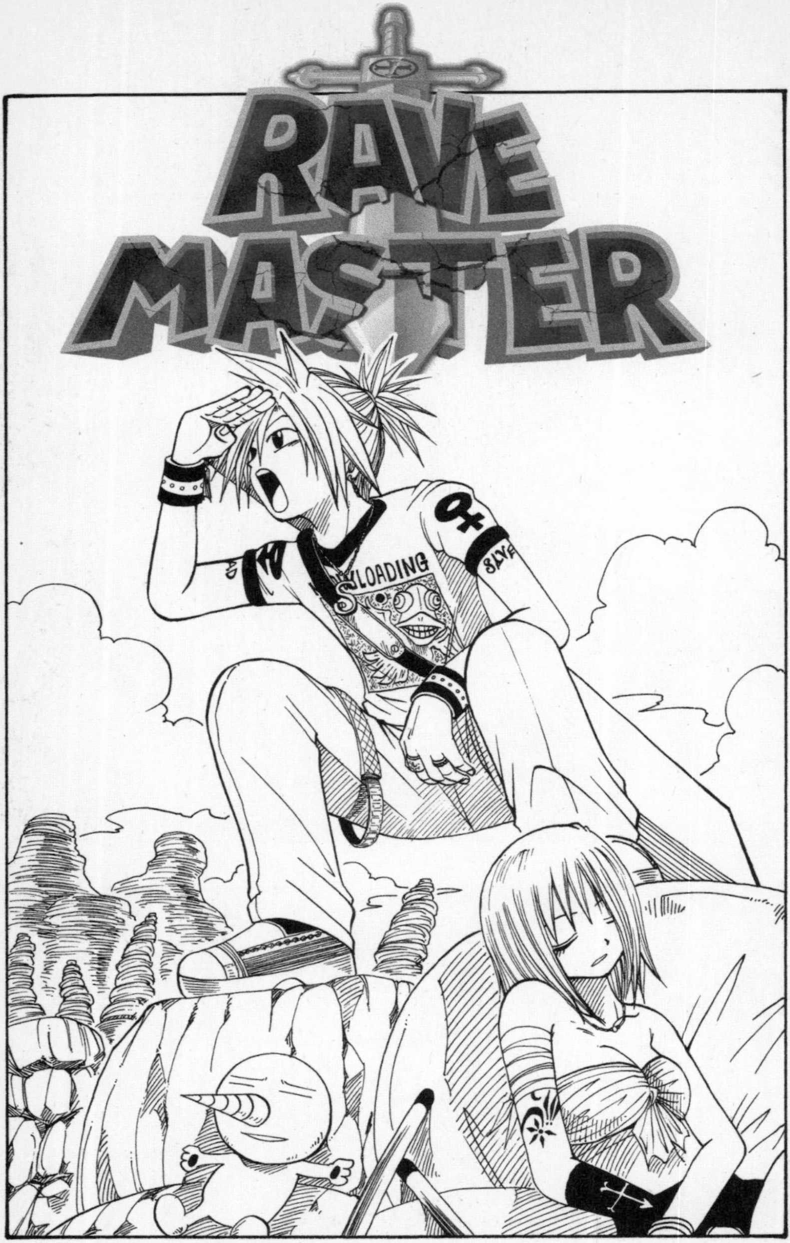
RAVE MASTER
LOADING

RAVE: 29 ✠ Open Sesame?!

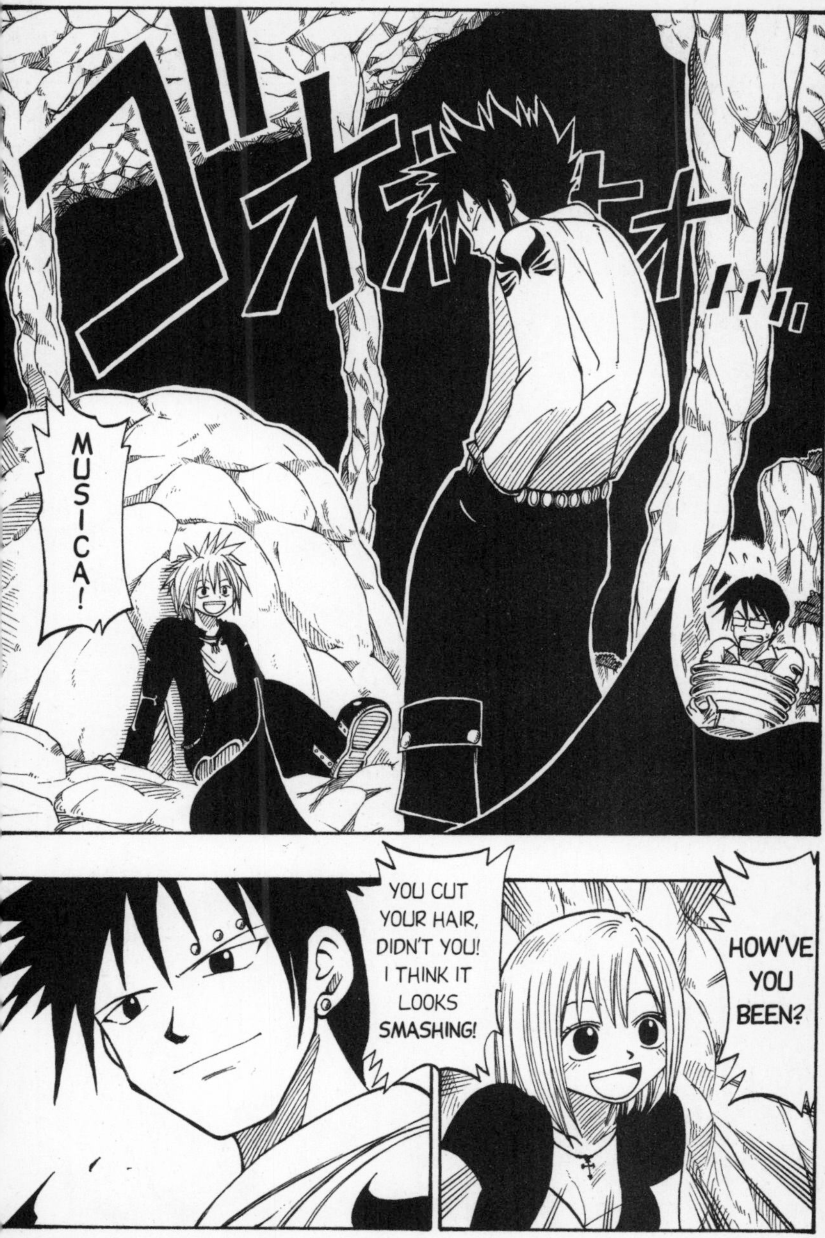
MUSICA!
HOW'VE YOU BEEN?
YOU CUT YOUR HAIR, DIDN'T YOU! I THINK IT LOOKS SMASHING!

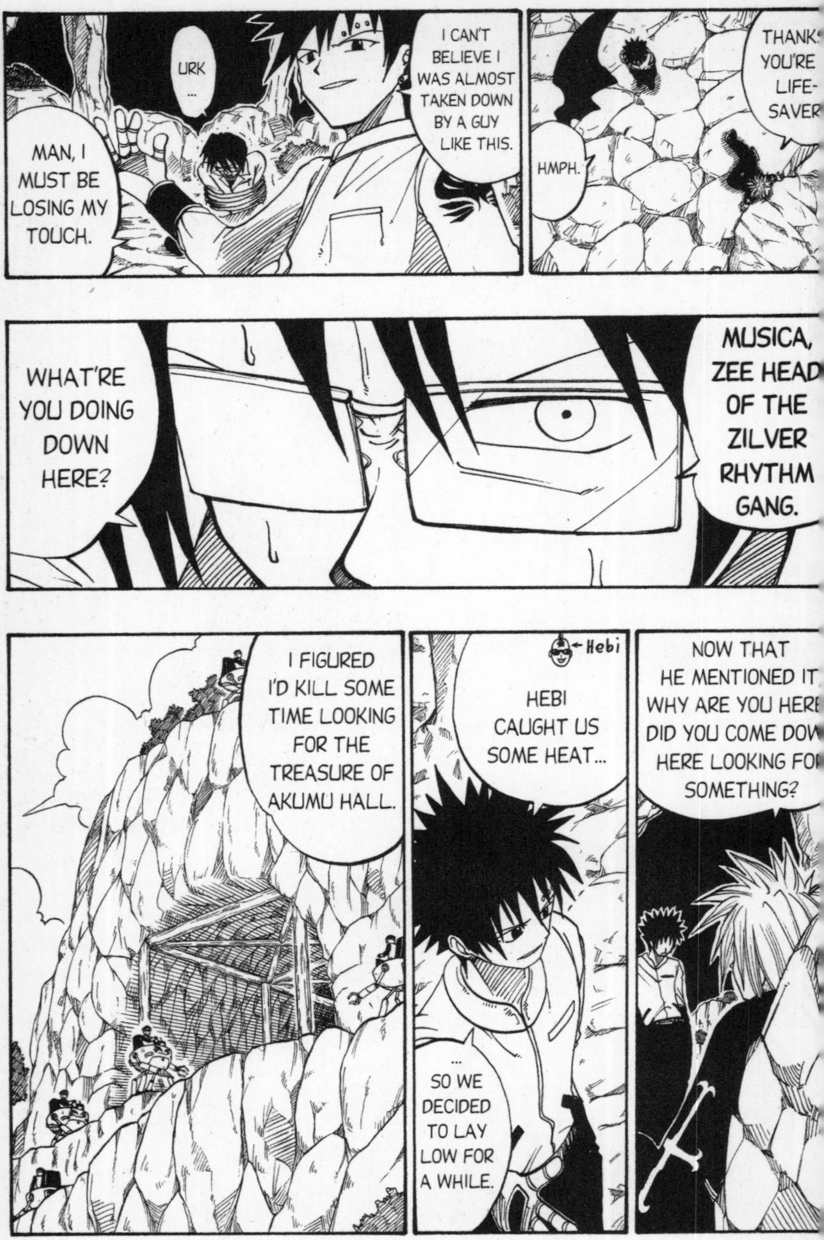
THANKS YOU'RE LIFE-SAVER
HMPH.
I CAN'T BELIEVE I WAS ALMOST TAKEN DOWN BY A GUY LIKE THIS.
URK ...
MAN, I MUST BE LOSING MY TOUCH.
MUSICA, ZEE HEAD OF THE ZILVER RHYTHM GANG.
WHAT'RE YOU DOING DOWN HERE?
NOW THAT HE MENTIONED IT WHY ARE YOU HERE DID YOU COME DOW HERE LOOKING FO SOMETHING?
Hebi
HEBI CAUGHT US SOME HEAT...
... SO WE DECIDED TO LAY LOW FOR A WHILE.
I FIGURED I'D KILL SOME TIME LOOKING FOR THE TREASURE OF AKUMU HALL.

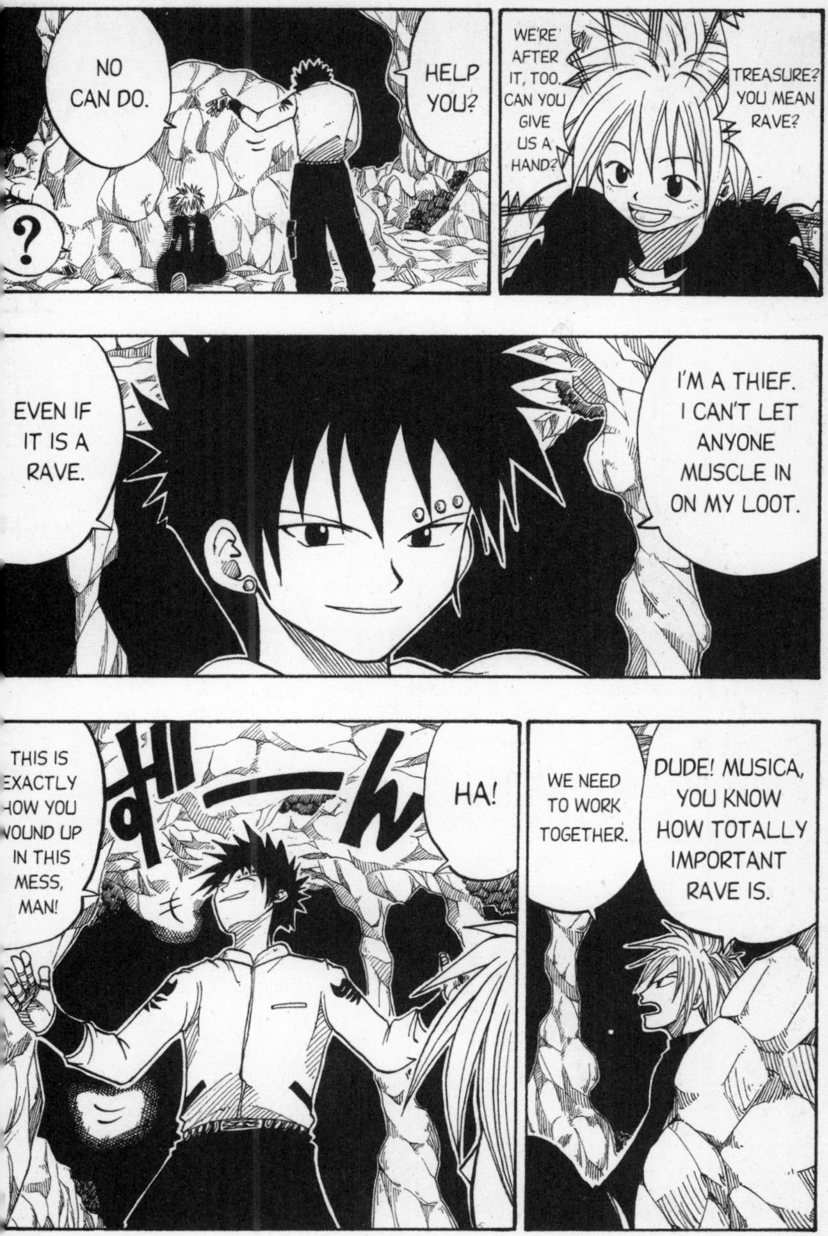
TREASURE? YOU MEAN RAVE?
WE'RE AFTER IT, TOO. CAN YOU GIVE US A HAND?
HELP YOU?
NO CAN DO.
?
I'M A THIEF. I CAN'T LET ANYONE MUSCLE IN ON MY LOOT.
EVEN IF IT IS A RAVE.
DUDE! MUSICA, YOU KNOW HOW TOTALLY IMPORTANT RAVE IS.
WE NEED TO WORK TOGETHER.
HA!
THIS IS EXACTLY HOW YOU WOUND UP IN THIS MESS, MAN!

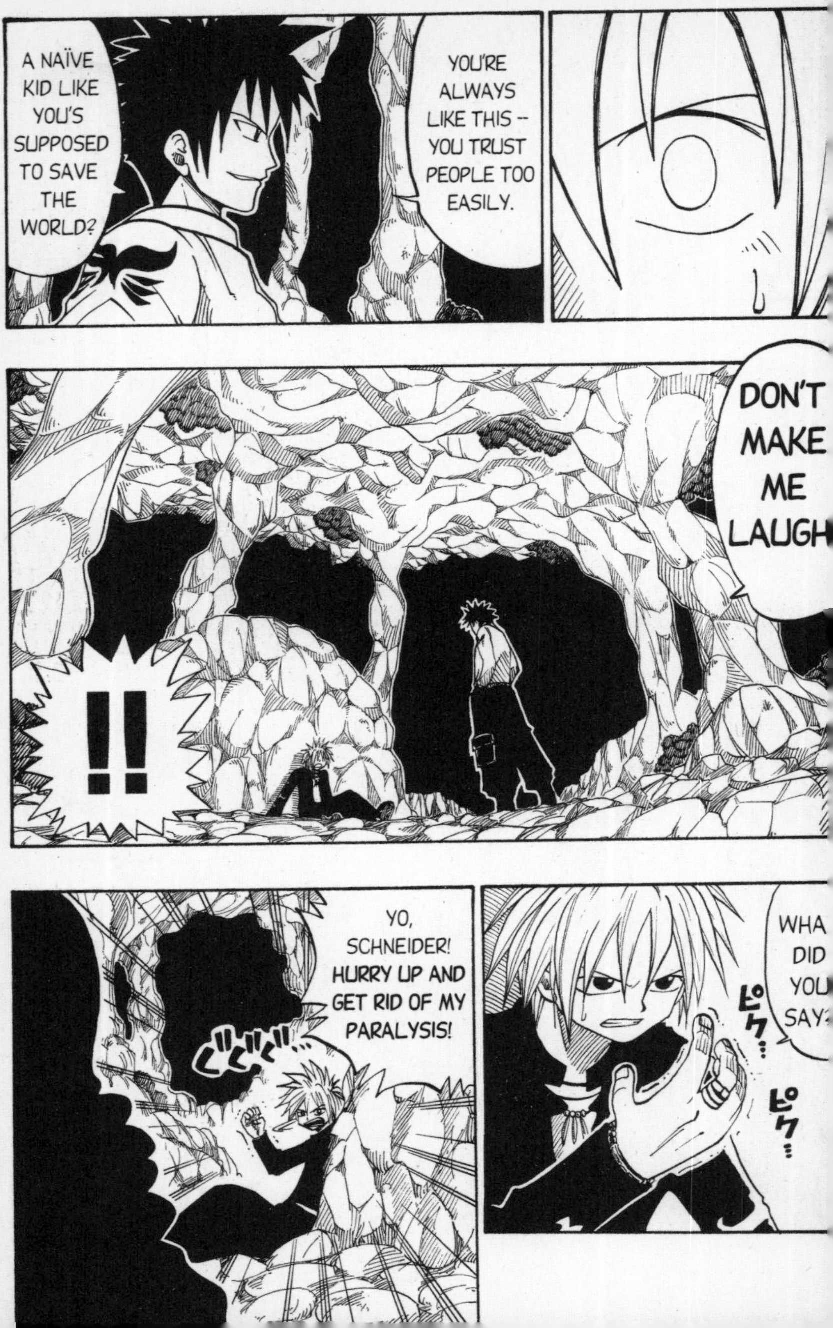
YOU'RE ALWAYS LIKE THIS -- YOU TRUST PEOPLE TOO EASILY.
A NAÏVE KID LIKE YOU'S SUPPOSED TO SAVE THE WORLD?
DON'T MAKE ME LAUGH
!!
WHA DID YOU SAY
ピク
ピク
YO, SCHNEIDER! HURRY UP AND GET RID OF MY PARALYSIS!
ぐぐぐ...

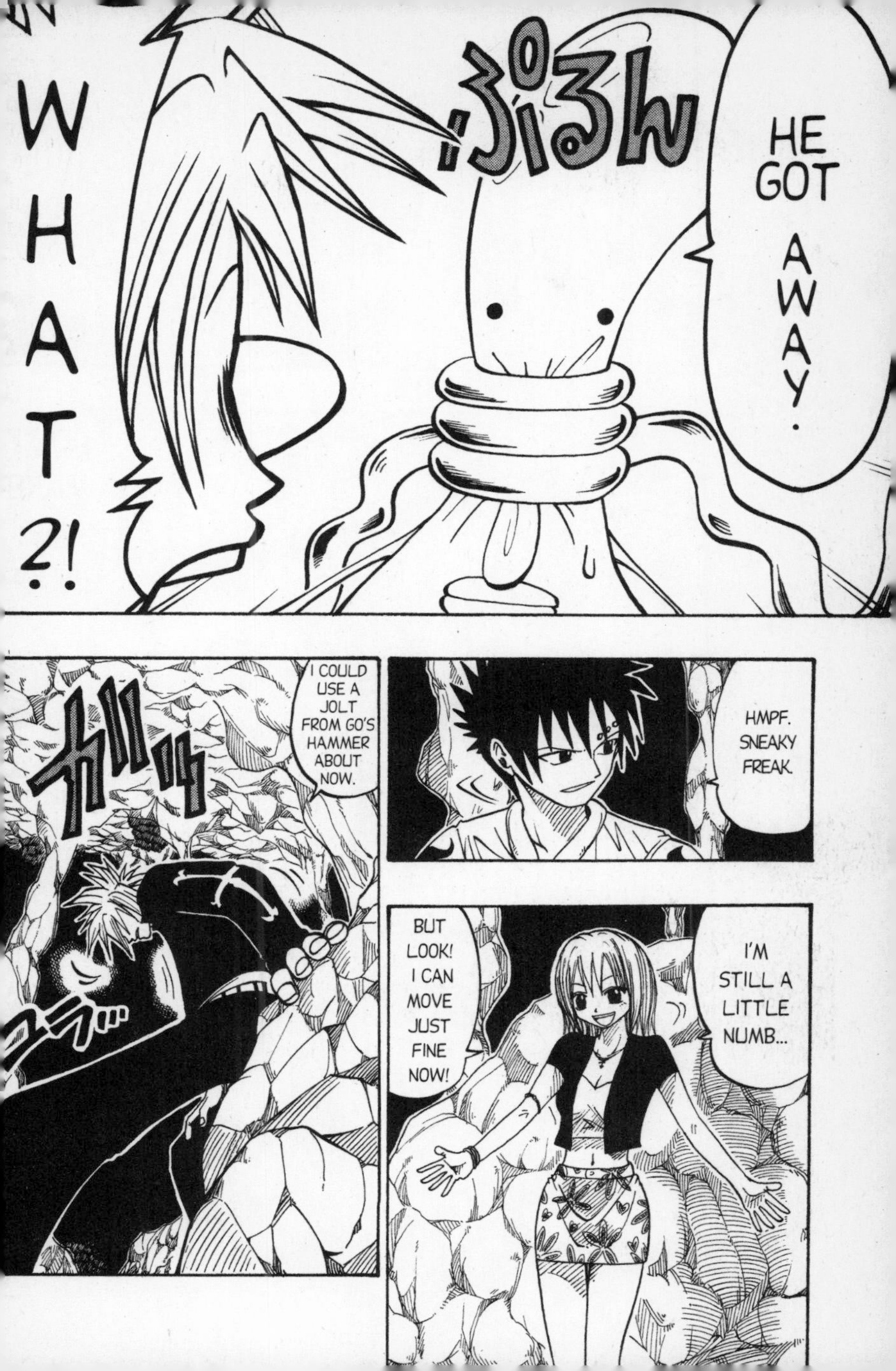
HE GOT AWAY.
WHAT?!
HMPF. SNEAKY FREAK.
I'M STILL A LITTLE NUMB...
BUT LOOK! I CAN MOVE JUST FINE NOW!
I COULD USE A JOLT FROM GO'S HAMMER ABOUT NOW.

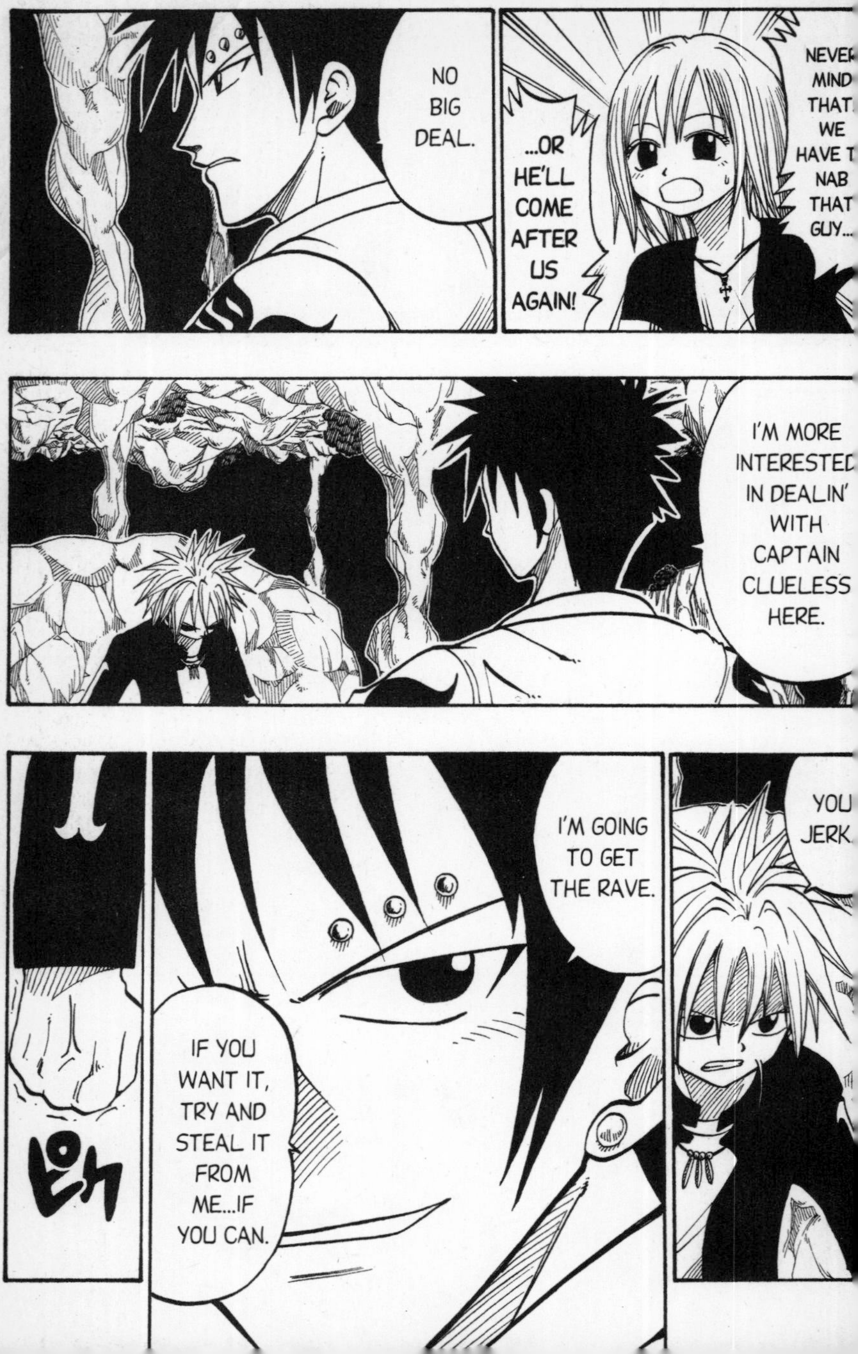
NEVER MIND THAT. WE HAVE T NAB THAT GUY...
...OR HE'LL COME AFTER US AGAIN!
NO BIG DEAL.
I'M MORE INTERESTED IN DEALIN' WITH CAPTAIN CLUELESS HERE.
YOU JERK.
I'M GOING TO GET THE RAVE.
IF YOU WANT IT, TRY AND STEAL IT FROM ME...IF YOU CAN.

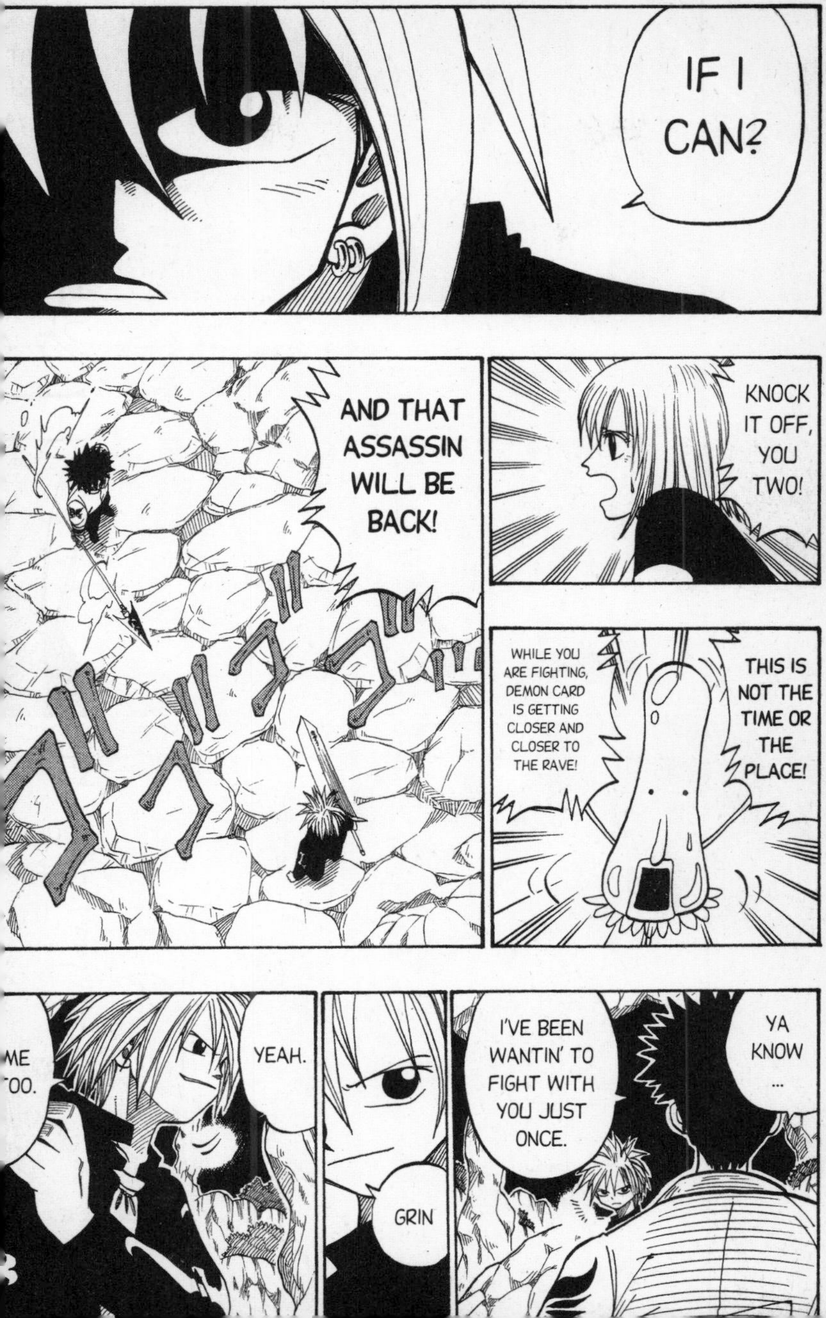
IF I CAN?
KNOCK IT OFF, YOU TWO!
THIS IS NOT THE TIME OR THE PLACE!
WHILE YOU ARE FIGHTING, DEMON CARD IS GETTING CLOSER AND CLOSER TO THE RAVE!
AND THAT ASSASSIN WILL BE BACK!
YA KNOW ...
I'VE BEEN WANTIN' TO FIGHT WITH YOU JUST ONCE.
GRIN
YEAH.
ME TOO.

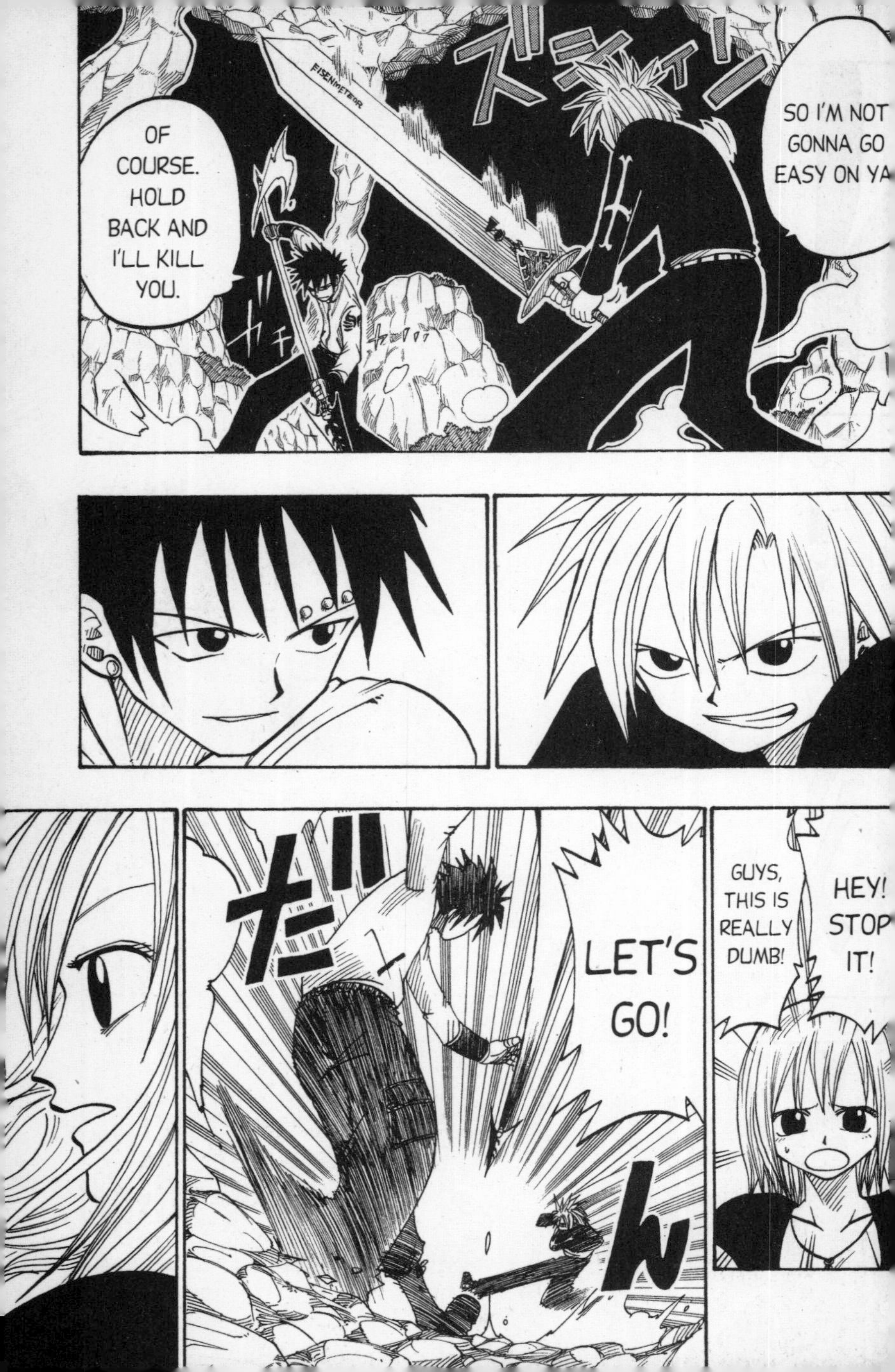
SO I'M NOT GONNA GO EASY ON YA
EISENMETEOR
OF COURSE. HOLD BACK AND I'LL KILL YOU.
HEY! STOP IT!
GUYS, THIS IS REALLY DUMB!
LET'S GO!

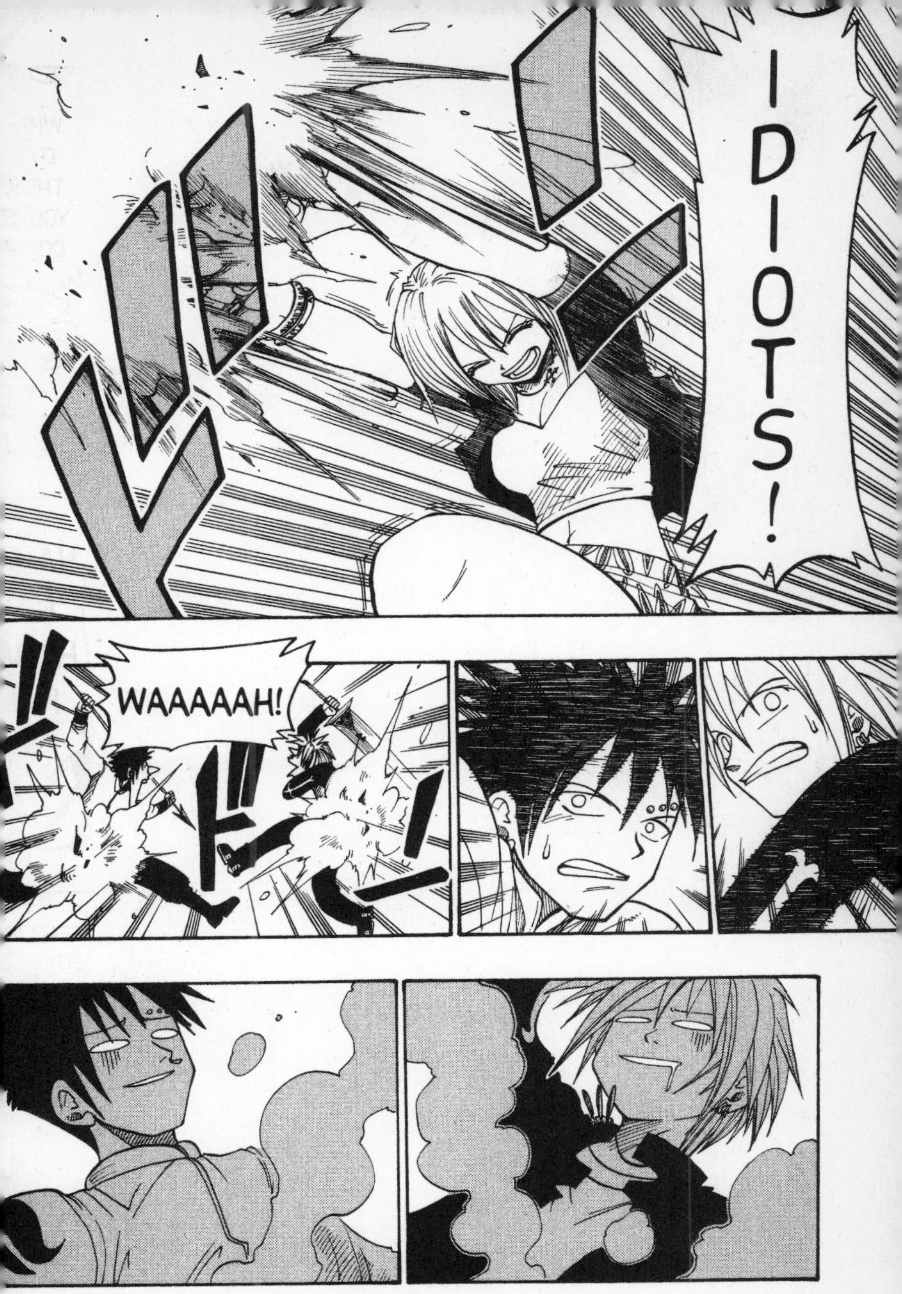
IDIOTS!
WAAAAAH!

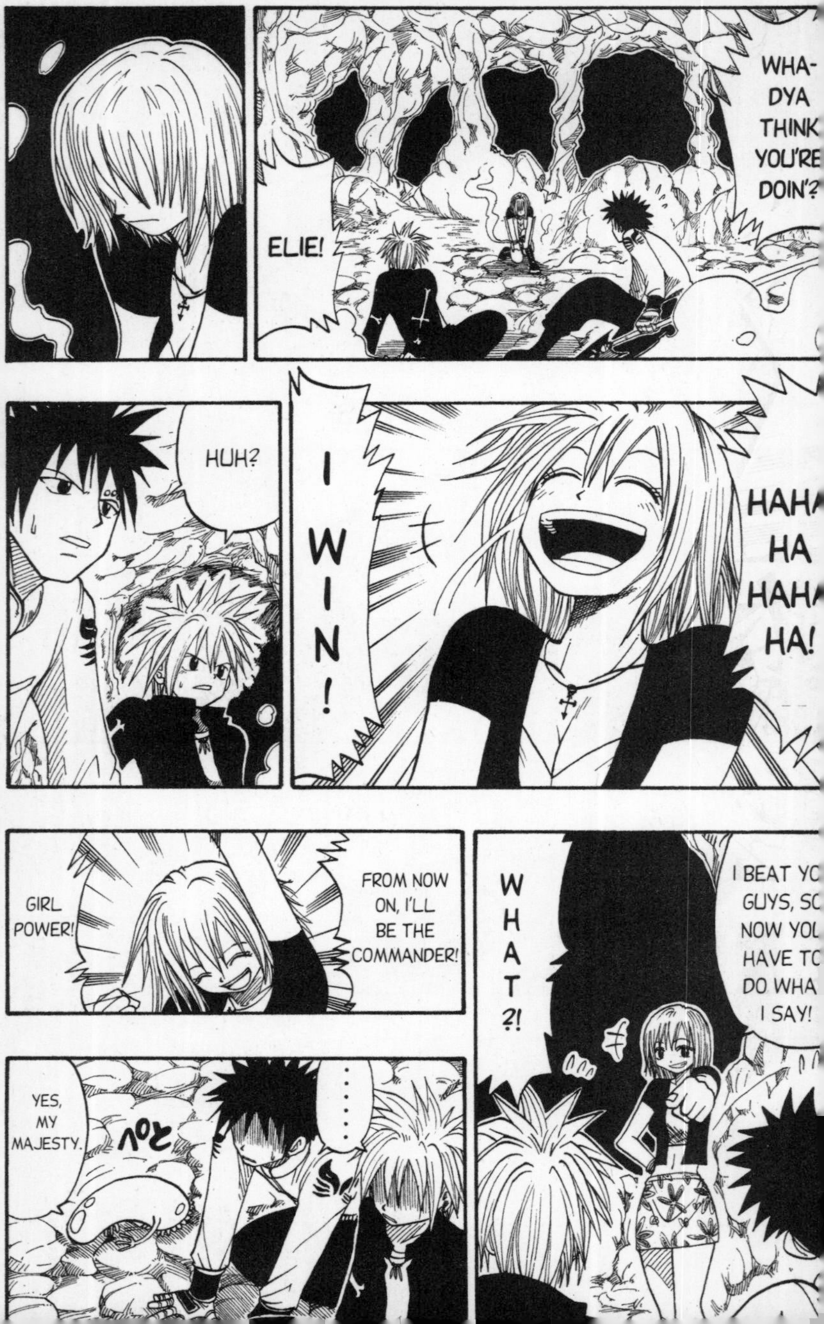
WHA-DYA THINK YOU'RE DOIN'?
ELIE!
HAHAHA HA HAHAHA HA!
I WIN!
HUH?
I BEAT YO GUYS, SO NOW YOU HAVE TO DO WHA I SAY!
WHAT?!
FROM NOW ON, I'LL BE THE COMMANDER!
GIRL POWER!
......
YES, MY MAJESTY.

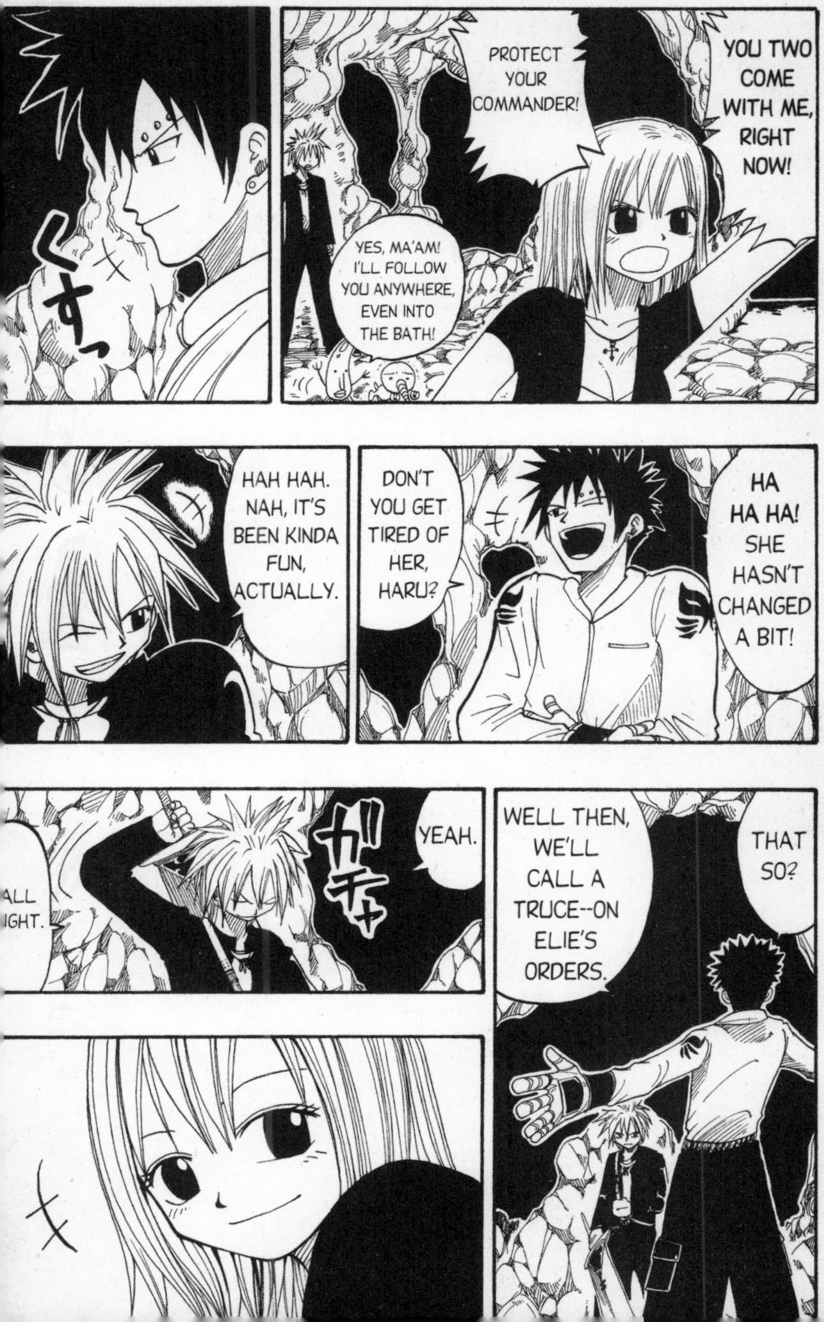
YOU TWO COME WITH ME, RIGHT NOW!
PROTECT YOUR COMMANDER!
YES, MA'AM! I'LL FOLLOW YOU ANYWHERE, EVEN INTO THE BATH!
くすっ
HA HA HA! SHE HASN'T CHANGED A BIT!
DON'T YOU GET TIRED OF HER, HARU?
HAH HAH. NAH, IT'S BEEN KINDA FUN, ACTUALLY.
THAT SO?
WELL THEN, WE'LL CALL A TRUCE--ON ELIE'S ORDERS.
YEAH.
ガチャ
ALL IGHT.

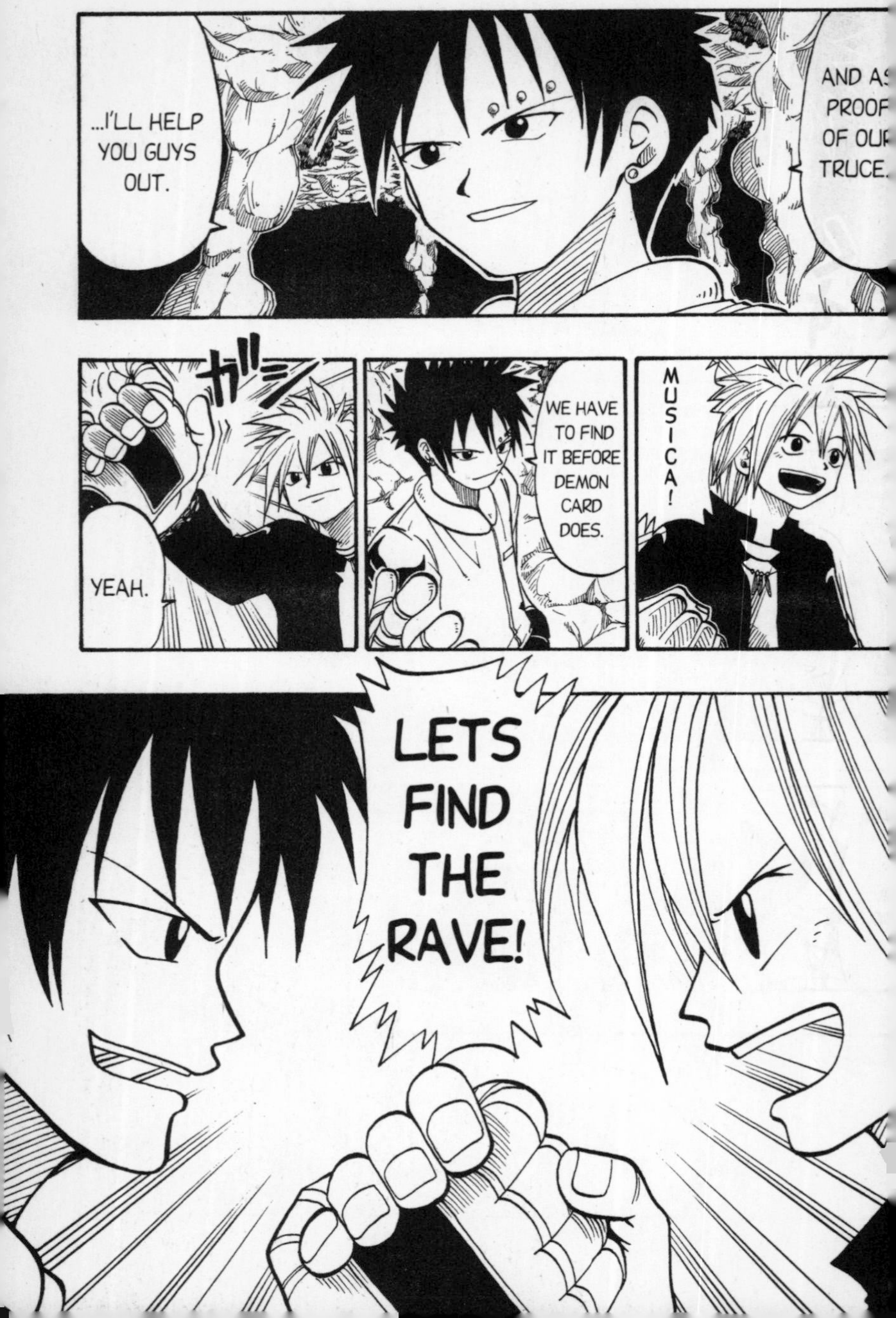
AND AS PROOF OF OUR TRUCE.
...I'LL HELP YOU GUYS OUT.
MUSICA!
WE HAVE TO FIND IT BEFORE DEMON CARD DOES.
ガッ
YEAH.
LETS FIND THE RAVE!

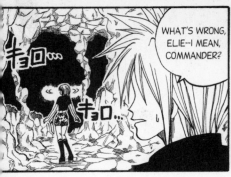

WHAT'S WRONG, ELIE--I MEAN, COMMANDER?

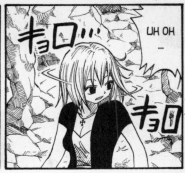

UH OH...

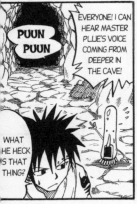

PUUN PUUN

EVERYONE! I CAN HEAR MASTER PLUE'S VOICE COMING FROM DEEPER IN THE CAVE!

WHAT THE HECK IS THAT THING?

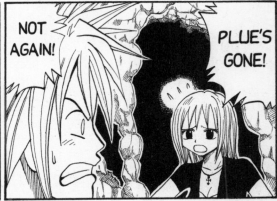

NOT AGAIN!

PLUE'S GONE!

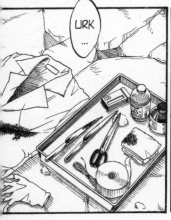

URK...

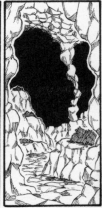

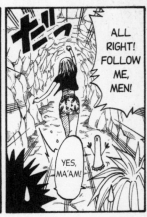

ALL RIGHT! FOLLOW ME, MEN!

YES, MA'AM!

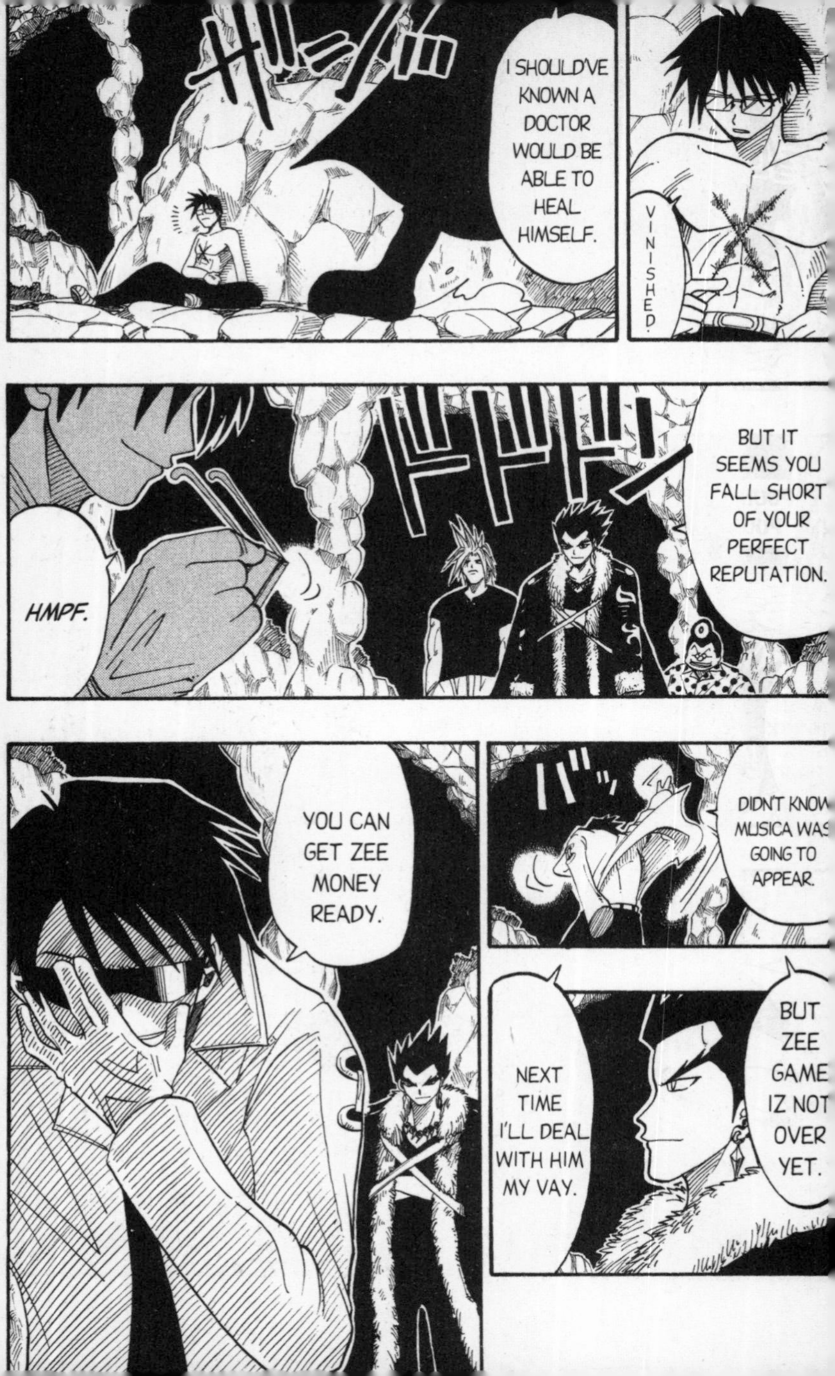
VINISHED.
I SHOULD'VE KNOWN A DOCTOR WOULD BE ABLE TO HEAL HIMSELF.
BUT IT SEEMS YOU FALL SHORT OF YOUR PERFECT REPUTATION.
HMPF.
DIDN'T KNOW MUSICA WAS GOING TO APPEAR.
BUT ZEE GAME IZ NOT OVER YET.
NEXT TIME I'LL DEAL WITH HIM MY VAY.
YOU CAN GET ZEE MONEY READY.

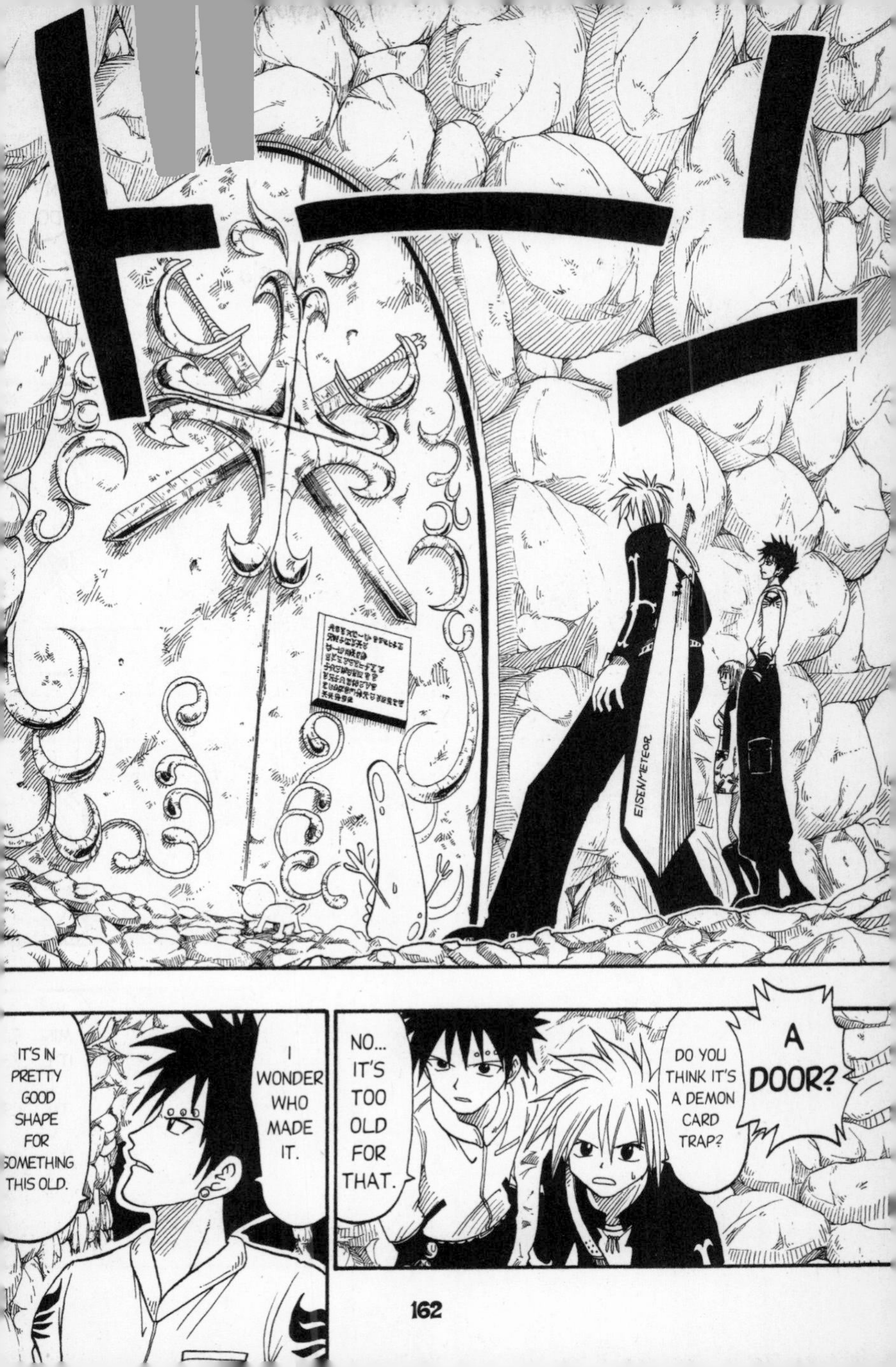
EISEN/METEOR
A DOOR?
DO YOU THINK IT'S A DEMON CARD TRAP?
NO... IT'S TOO OLD FOR THAT.
I WONDER WHO MADE IT.
IT'S IN PRETTY GOOD SHAPE FOR SOMETHING THIS OLD.

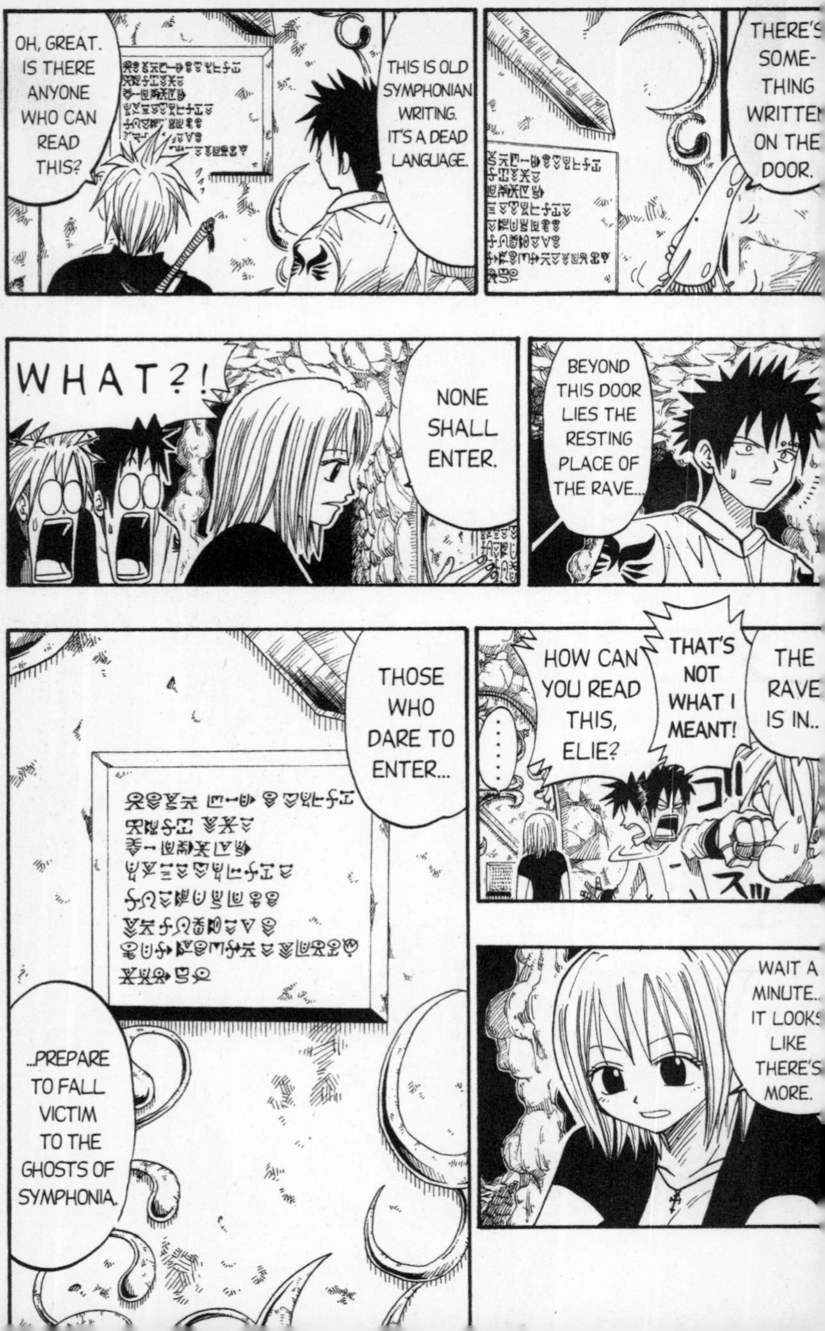
THERE'S SOME-THING WRITTEN ON THE DOOR.
THIS IS OLD SYMPHONIAN WRITING. IT'S A DEAD LANGUAGE.
OH, GREAT. IS THERE ANYONE WHO CAN READ THIS?
BEYOND THIS DOOR LIES THE RESTING PLACE OF THE RAVE...
NONE SHALL ENTER.
WHAT?!
THE RAVE IS IN..
THAT'S NOT WHAT I MEANT!
HOW CAN YOU READ THIS, ELIE?
......
コッ
スッ
WAIT A MINUTE... IT LOOKS LIKE THERE'S MORE.
THOSE WHO DARE TO ENTER...
...PREPARE TO FALL VICTIM TO THE GHOSTS OF SYMPHONIA.

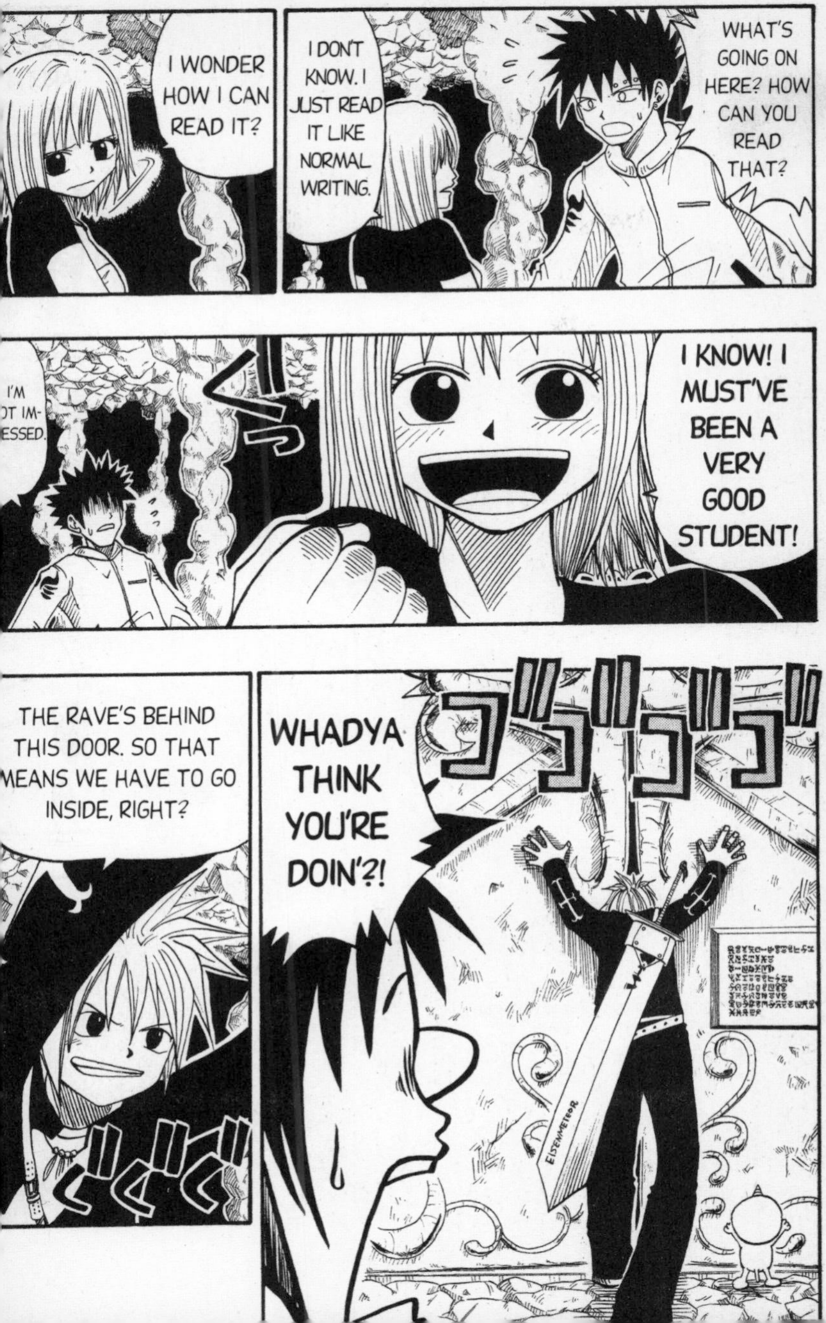
WHAT'S GOING ON HERE? HOW CAN YOU READ THAT?
I DON'T KNOW. I JUST READ IT LIKE NORMAL WRITING.
I WONDER HOW I CAN READ IT?
I KNOW! I MUST'VE BEEN A VERY GOOD STUDENT!
I'M OT IM- ESSED.
WHADYA THINK YOU'RE DOIN'?!
EISENMETEOR
THE RAVE'S BEHIND THIS DOOR. SO THAT MEANS WE HAVE TO GO INSIDE, RIGHT?

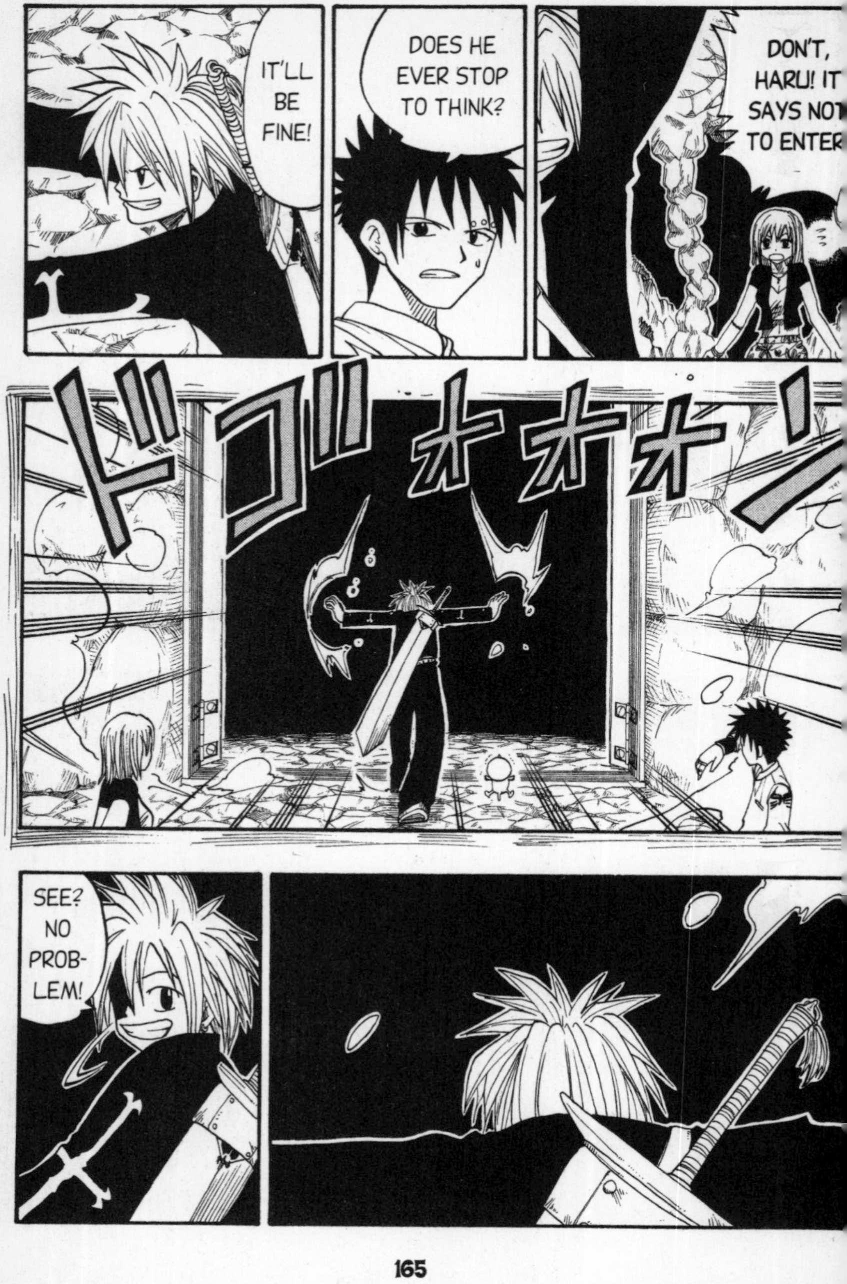
DON'T, HARU! IT SAYS NOT TO ENTER
DOES HE EVER STOP TO THINK?
IT'LL BE FINE!
ドゴオオオン
SEE? NO PROB-LEM!

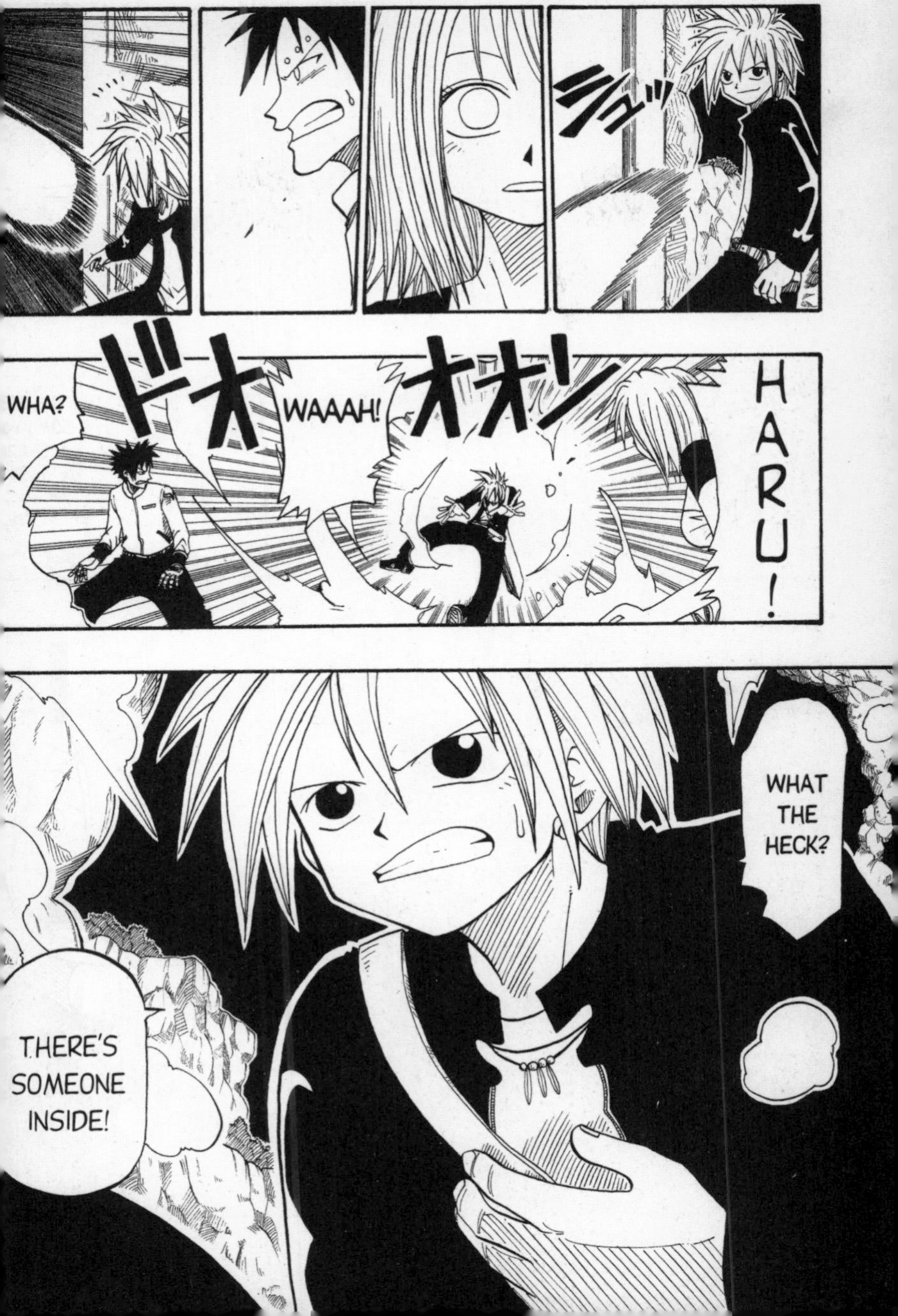

シュッ
HARU!
ドオオオン
WAAAH!
WHA?
WHAT THE HECK?
THERE'S SOMEONE INSIDE!

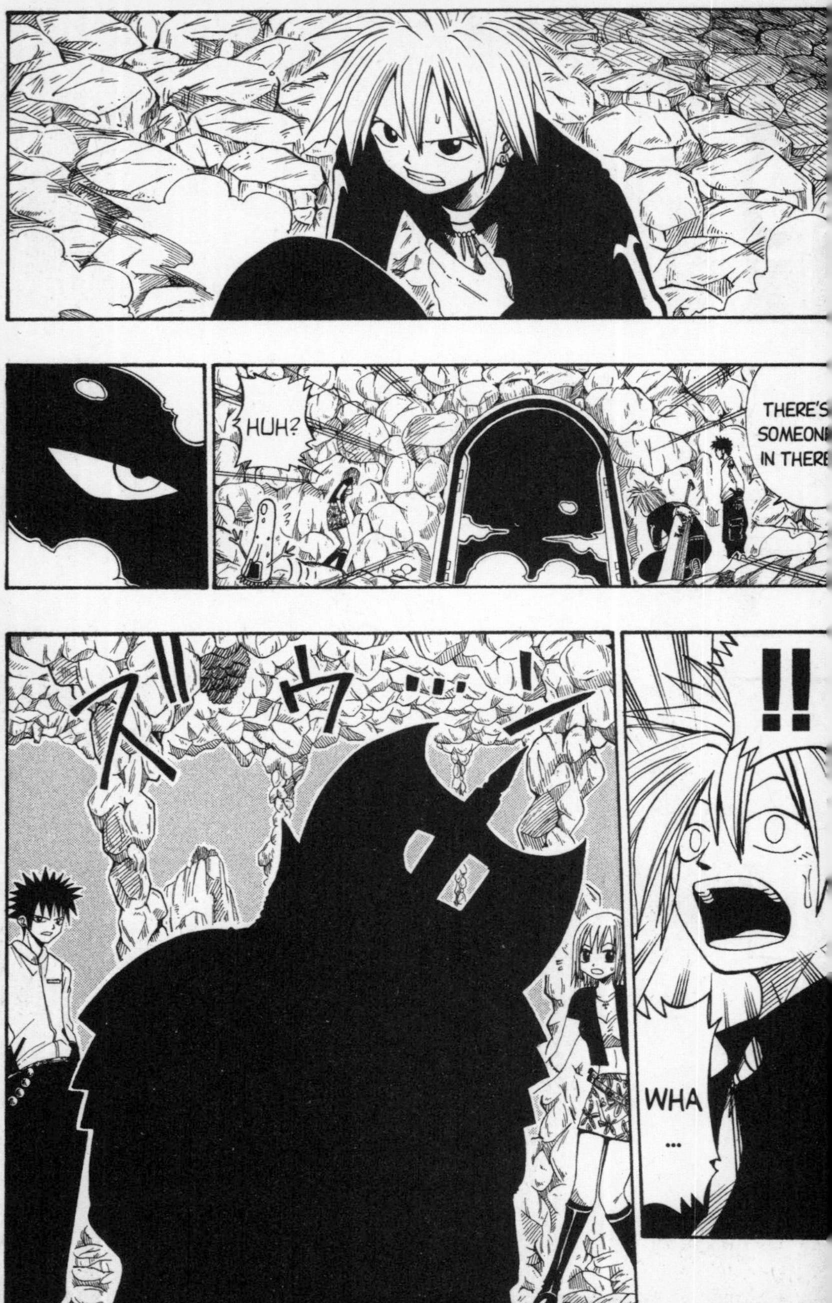
THERE'S SOMEONE IN THERE
HUH?
!!
WHA
...

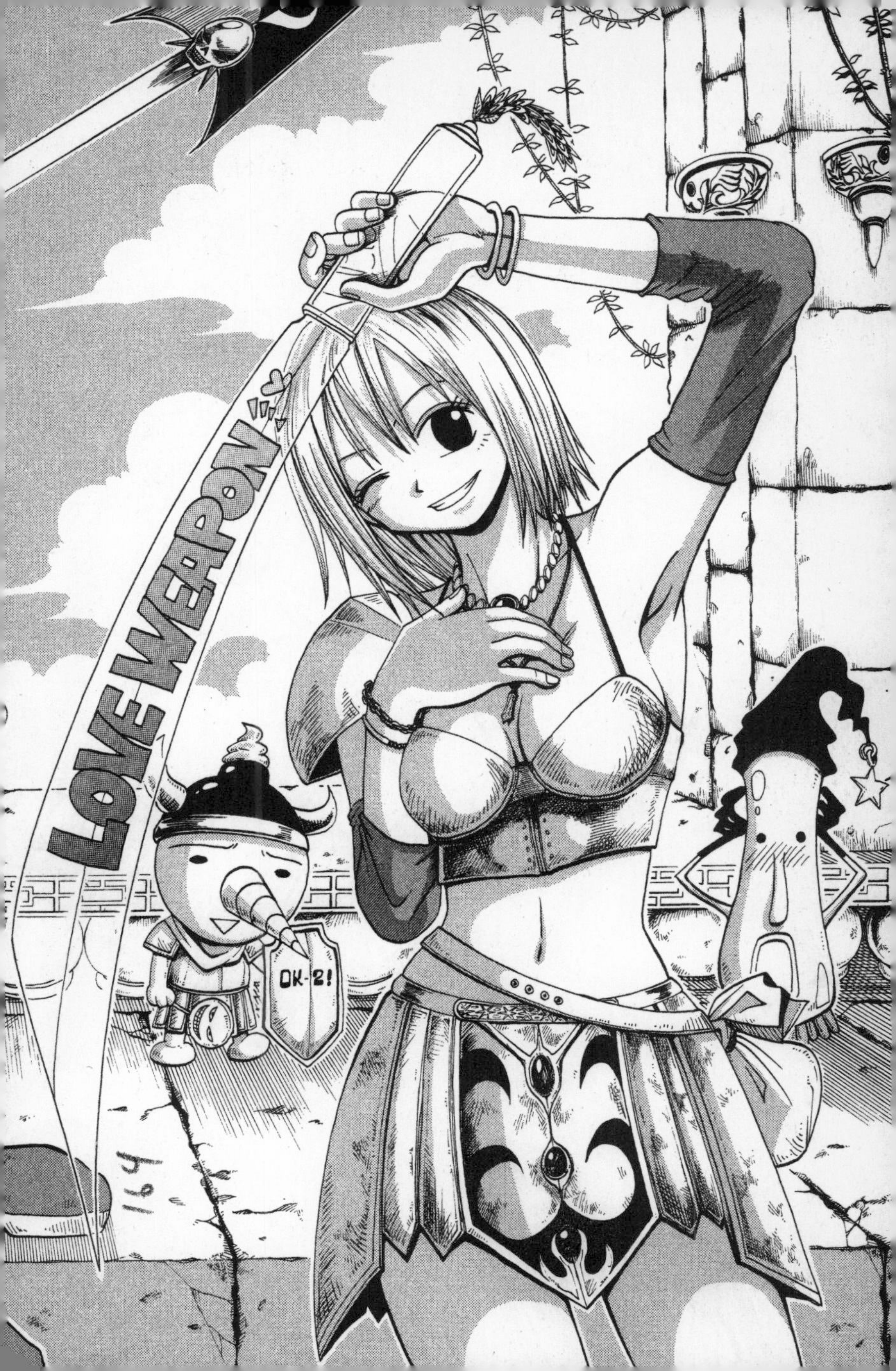
LOVE WEAPON
OK-2!

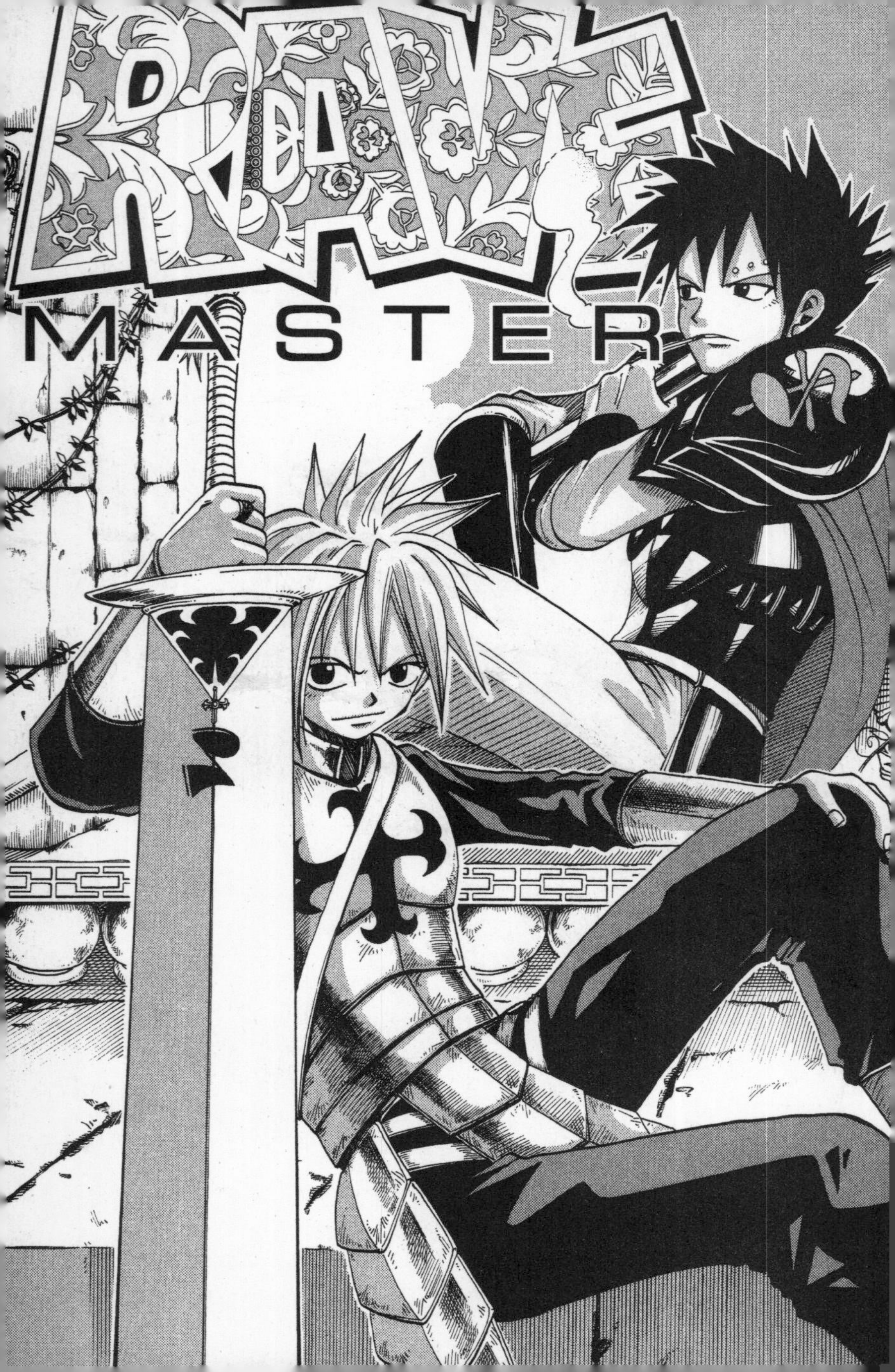
RAVE
MASTER

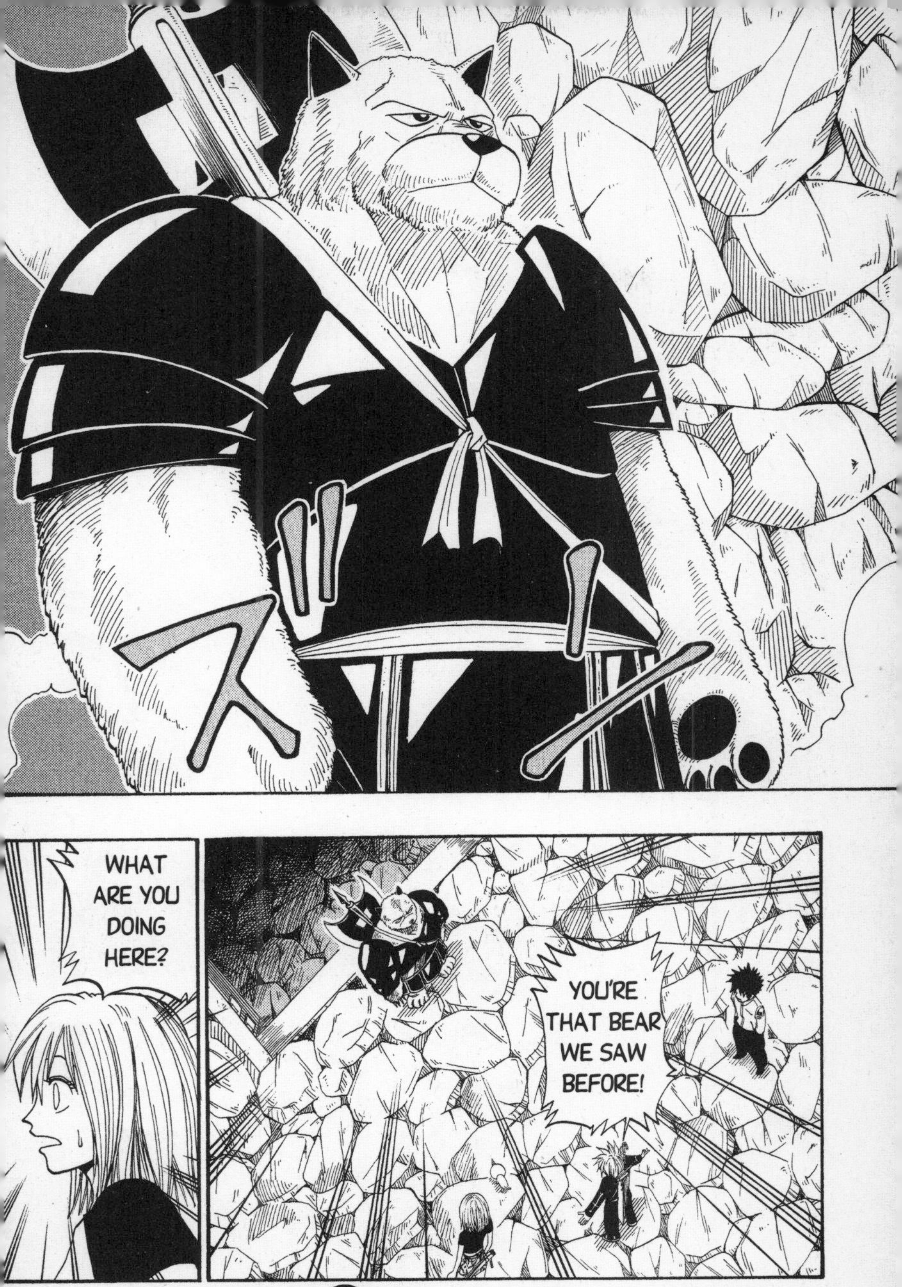
YOU'RE THAT BEAR WE SAW BEFORE!
WHAT ARE YOU DOING HERE?

RAVE:30 ✠ The Truth About Rave

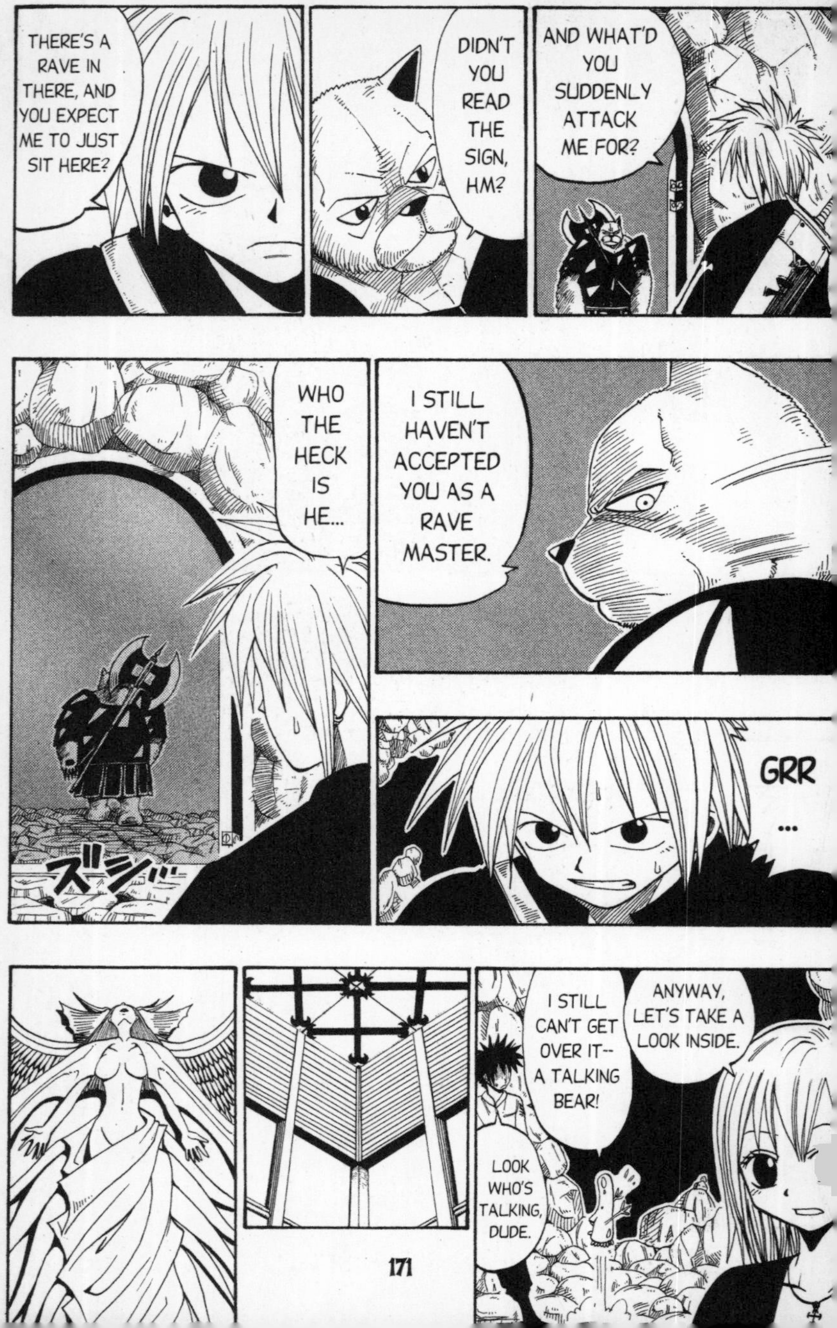
AND WHAT'D YOU SUDDENLY ATTACK ME FOR?
DIDN'T YOU READ THE SIGN, HM?
THERE'S A RAVE IN THERE, AND YOU EXPECT ME TO JUST SIT HERE?
I STILL HAVEN'T ACCEPTED YOU AS A RAVE MASTER.
GRR ...
WHO THE HECK IS HE...
ズシッ
ANYWAY, LET'S TAKE A LOOK INSIDE.
I STILL CAN'T GET OVER IT-- A TALKING BEAR!
LOOK WHO'S TALKING, DUDE.

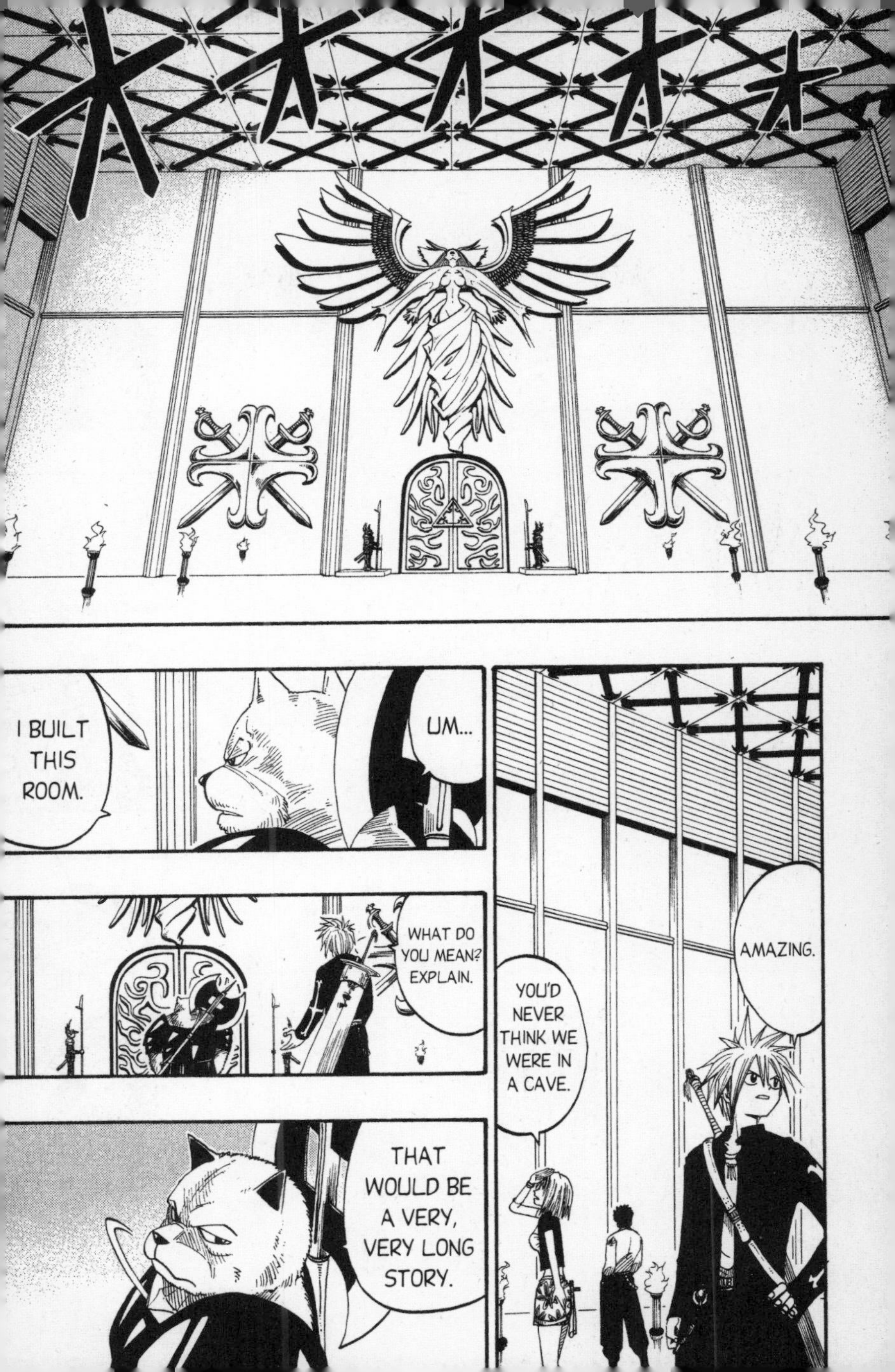
AMAZING.
YOU'D NEVER THINK WE WERE IN A CAVE.
UM...
I BUILT THIS ROOM.
WHAT DO YOU MEAN? EXPLAIN.
THAT WOULD BE A VERY, VERY LONG STORY.

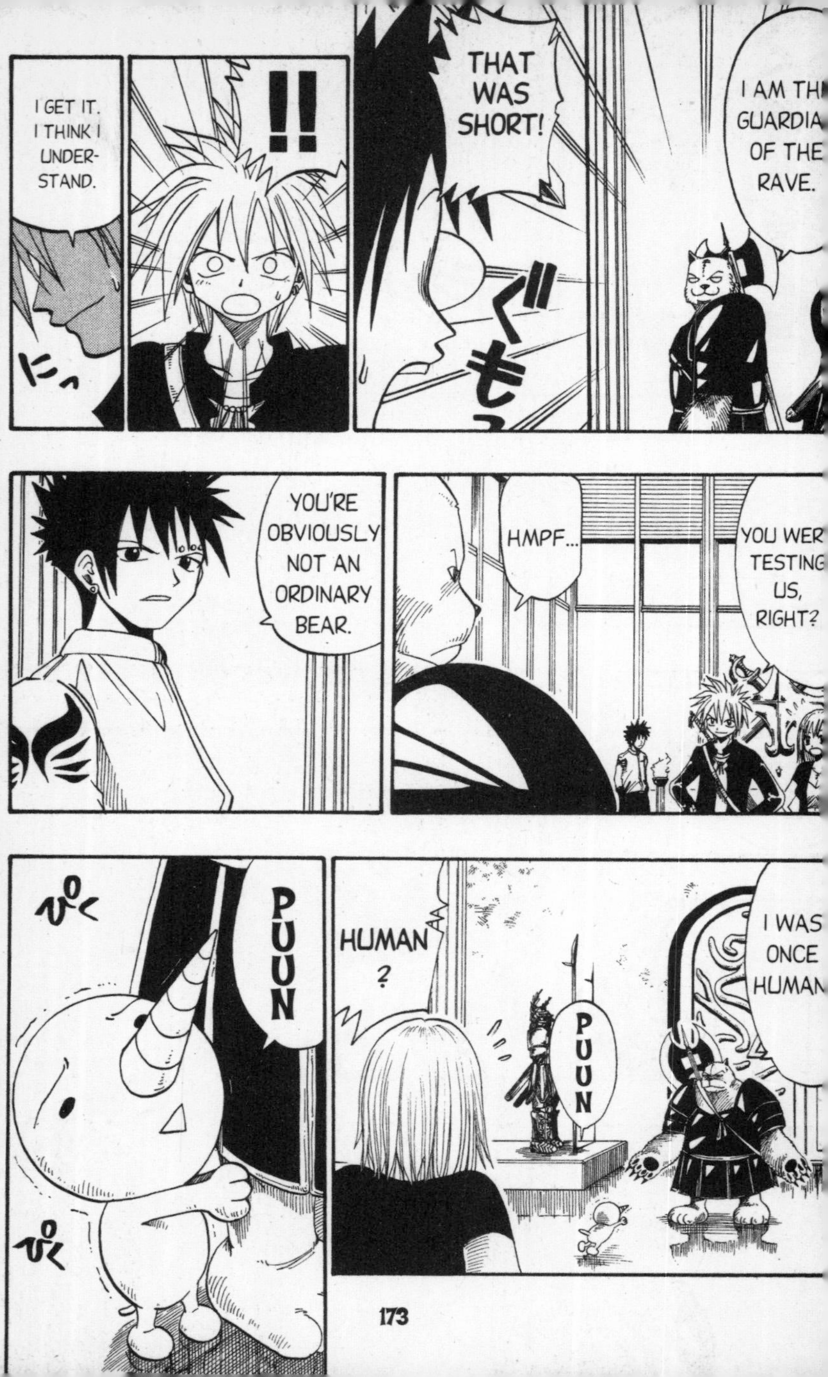
I AM TH GUARDIA OF THE RAVE.
THAT WAS SHORT!
ぐも
!!
I GET IT. I THINK I UNDER-STAND.
にっ
YOU WER TESTING US, RIGHT?
HMPF...
YOU'RE OBVIOUSLY NOT AN ORDINARY BEAR.
I WAS ONCE HUMAN
PUUN
HUMAN ?
PUUN
ぴく
ぴく

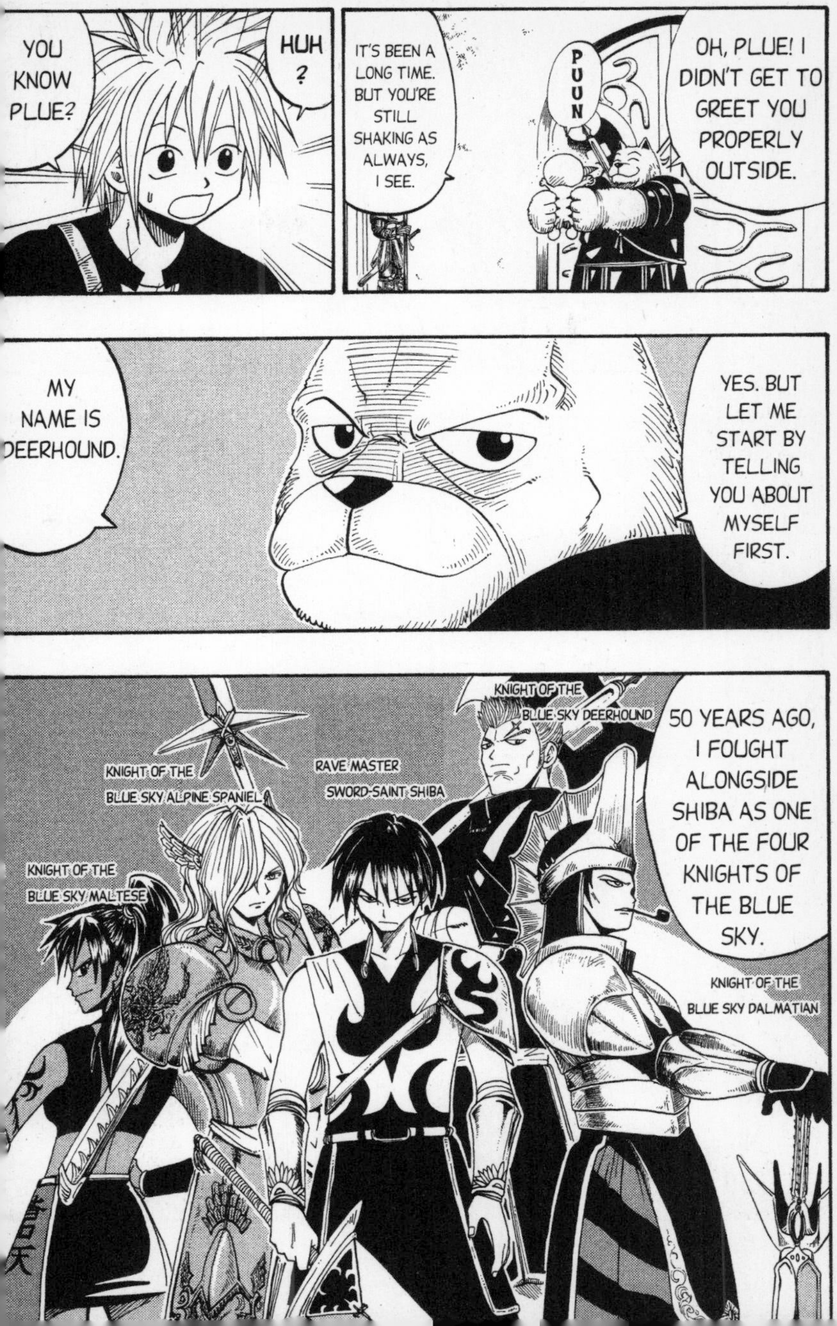
OH, PLUE! I DIDN'T GET TO GREET YOU PROPERLY OUTSIDE.
PUUN
IT'S BEEN A LONG TIME. BUT YOU'RE STILL SHAKING AS ALWAYS, I SEE.
HUH ?
YOU KNOW PLUE?
YES. BUT LET ME START BY TELLING YOU ABOUT MYSELF FIRST.
MY NAME IS DEERHOUND.
50 YEARS AGO, I FOUGHT ALONGSIDE SHIBA AS ONE OF THE FOUR KNIGHTS OF THE BLUE SKY.
KNIGHT OF THE BLUE SKY DALMATIAN
KNIGHT OF THE BLUE SKY DEERHOUND
RAVE MASTER SWORD-SAINT SHIBA
KNIGHT OF THE BLUE SKY ALPINE SPANIEL
KNIGHT OF THE BLUE SKY MALTESE

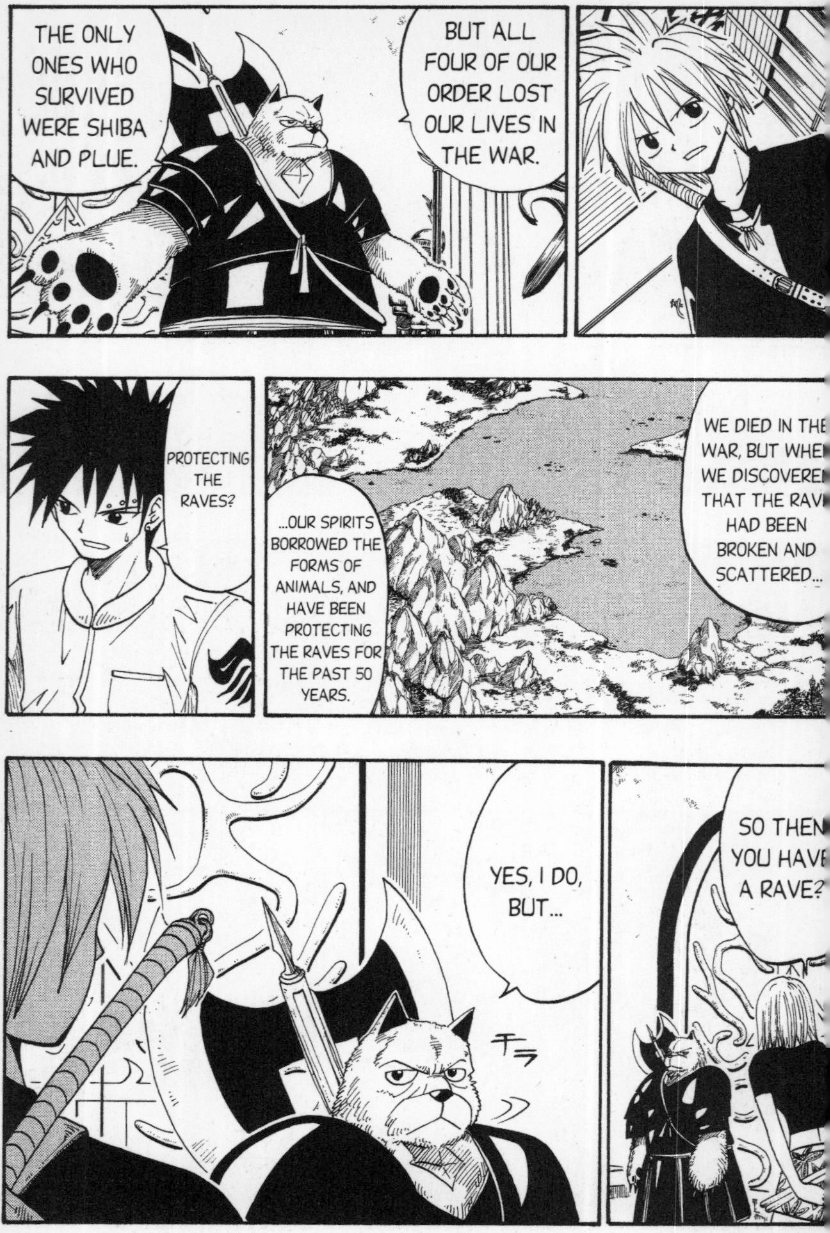

BUT ALL FOUR OF OUR ORDER LOST OUR LIVES IN THE WAR.
THE ONLY ONES WHO SURVIVED WERE SHIBA AND PLUE.
WE DIED IN THE WAR, BUT WHE WE DISCOVERE THAT THE RAV HAD BEEN BROKEN AND SCATTERED...
...OUR SPIRITS BORROWED THE FORMS OF ANIMALS, AND HAVE BEEN PROTECTING THE RAVES FOR THE PAST 50 YEARS.
PROTECTING THE RAVES?
SO THEN YOU HAVE A RAVE?
YES, I DO, BUT...
チラ

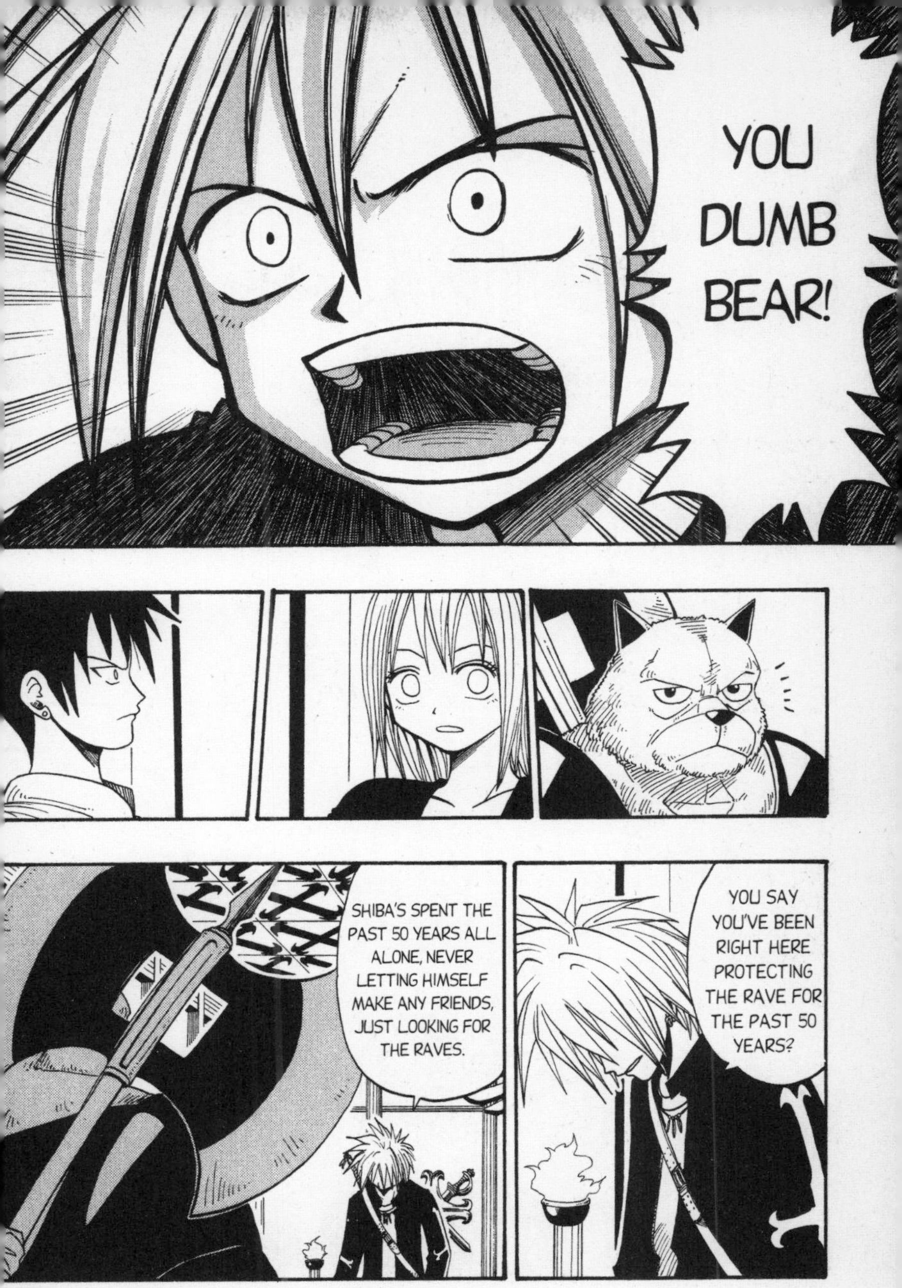
YOU DUMB BEAR!
YOU SAY YOU'VE BEEN RIGHT HERE PROTECTING THE RAVE FOR THE PAST 50 YEARS?
SHIBA'S SPENT THE PAST 50 YEARS ALL ALONE, NEVER LETTING HIMSELF MAKE ANY FRIENDS, JUST LOOKING FOR THE RAVES.

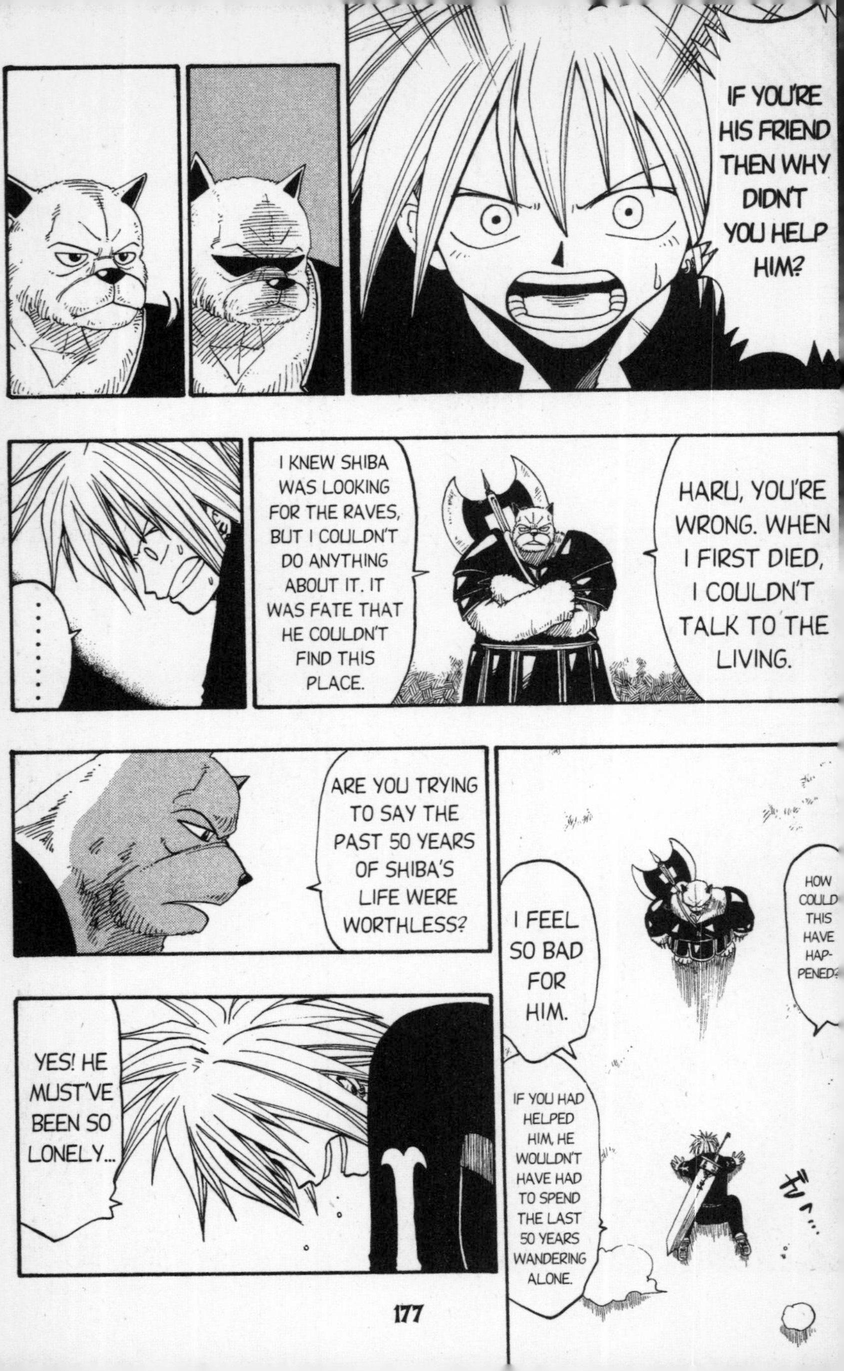
IF YOU'RE HIS FRIEND THEN WHY DIDN'T YOU HELP HIM?
HARU, YOU'RE WRONG. WHEN I FIRST DIED, I COULDN'T TALK TO THE LIVING.
I KNEW SHIBA WAS LOOKING FOR THE RAVES, BUT I COULDN'T DO ANYTHING ABOUT IT. IT WAS FATE THAT HE COULDN'T FIND THIS PLACE.
....
HOW COULD THIS HAVE HAP-PENED?
I FEEL SO BAD FOR HIM.
IF YOU HAD HELPED HIM, HE WOULDN'T HAVE HAD TO SPEND THE LAST 50 YEARS WANDERING ALONE.
ARE YOU TRYING TO SAY THE PAST 50 YEARS OF SHIBA'S LIFE WERE WORTHLESS?
YES! HE MUST'VE BEEN SO LONELY...

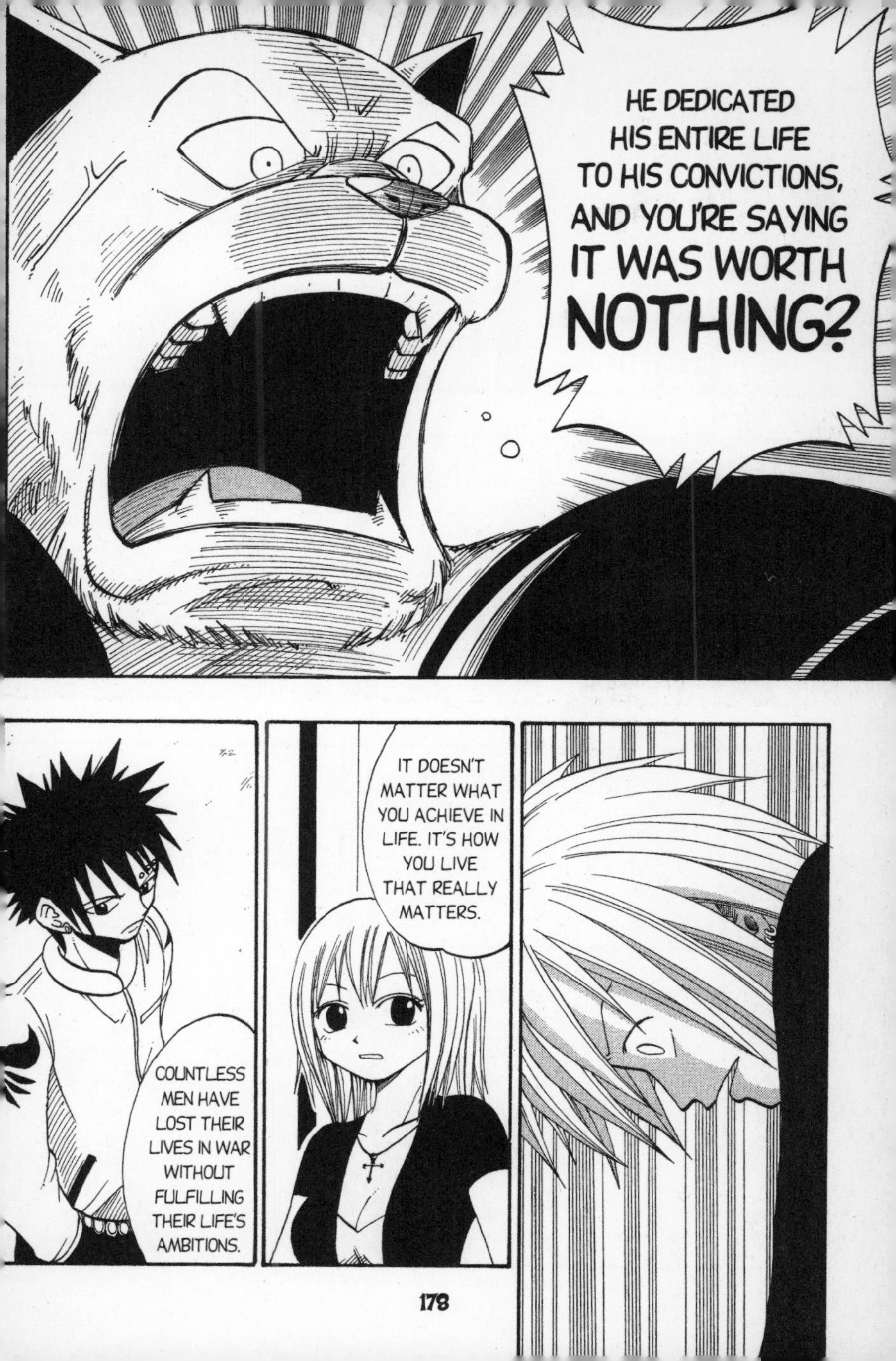
HE DEDICATED HIS ENTIRE LIFE TO HIS CONVICTIONS, AND YOU'RE SAYING IT WAS WORTH NOTHING?
IT DOESN'T MATTER WHAT YOU ACHIEVE IN LIFE. IT'S HOW YOU LIVE THAT REALLY MATTERS.
COUNTLESS MEN HAVE LOST THEIR LIVES IN WAR WITHOUT FULFILLING THEIR LIFE'S AMBITIONS.

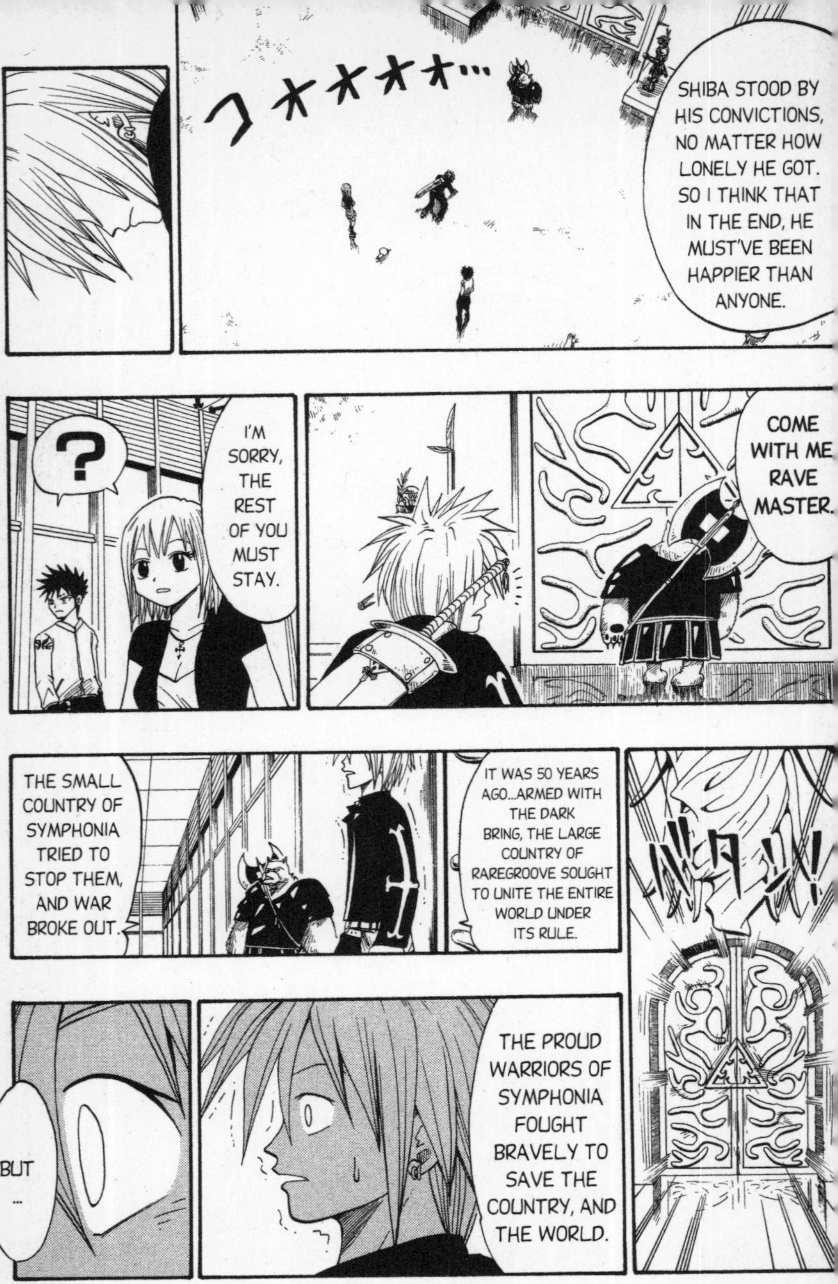
SHIBA STOOD BY HIS CONVICTIONS, NO MATTER HOW LONELY HE GOT. SO I THINK THAT IN THE END, HE MUST'VE BEEN HAPPIER THAN ANYONE.
COME WITH ME, RAVE MASTER.
?
I'M SORRY, THE REST OF YOU MUST STAY.
IT WAS 50 YEARS AGO...ARMED WITH THE DARK BRING, THE LARGE COUNTRY OF RAREGROOVE SOUGHT TO UNITE THE ENTIRE WORLD UNDER ITS RULE.
THE SMALL COUNTRY OF SYMPHONIA TRIED TO STOP THEM, AND WAR BROKE OUT.
THE PROUD WARRIORS OF SYMPHONIA FOUGHT BRAVELY TO SAVE THE COUNTRY, AND THE WORLD.
BUT ...

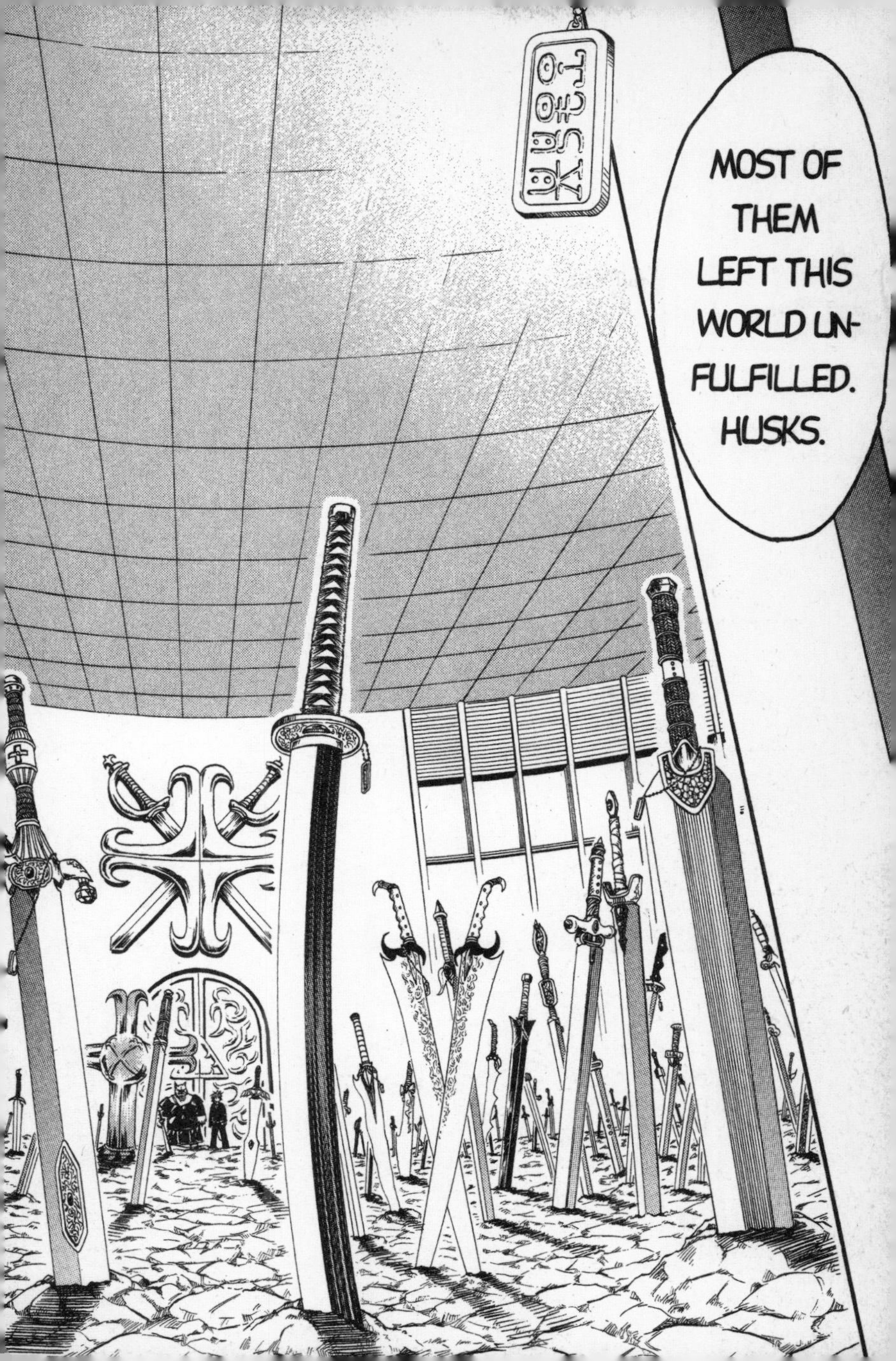
MOST OF THEM LEFT THIS WORLD UN-FULFILLED. HUSKS.

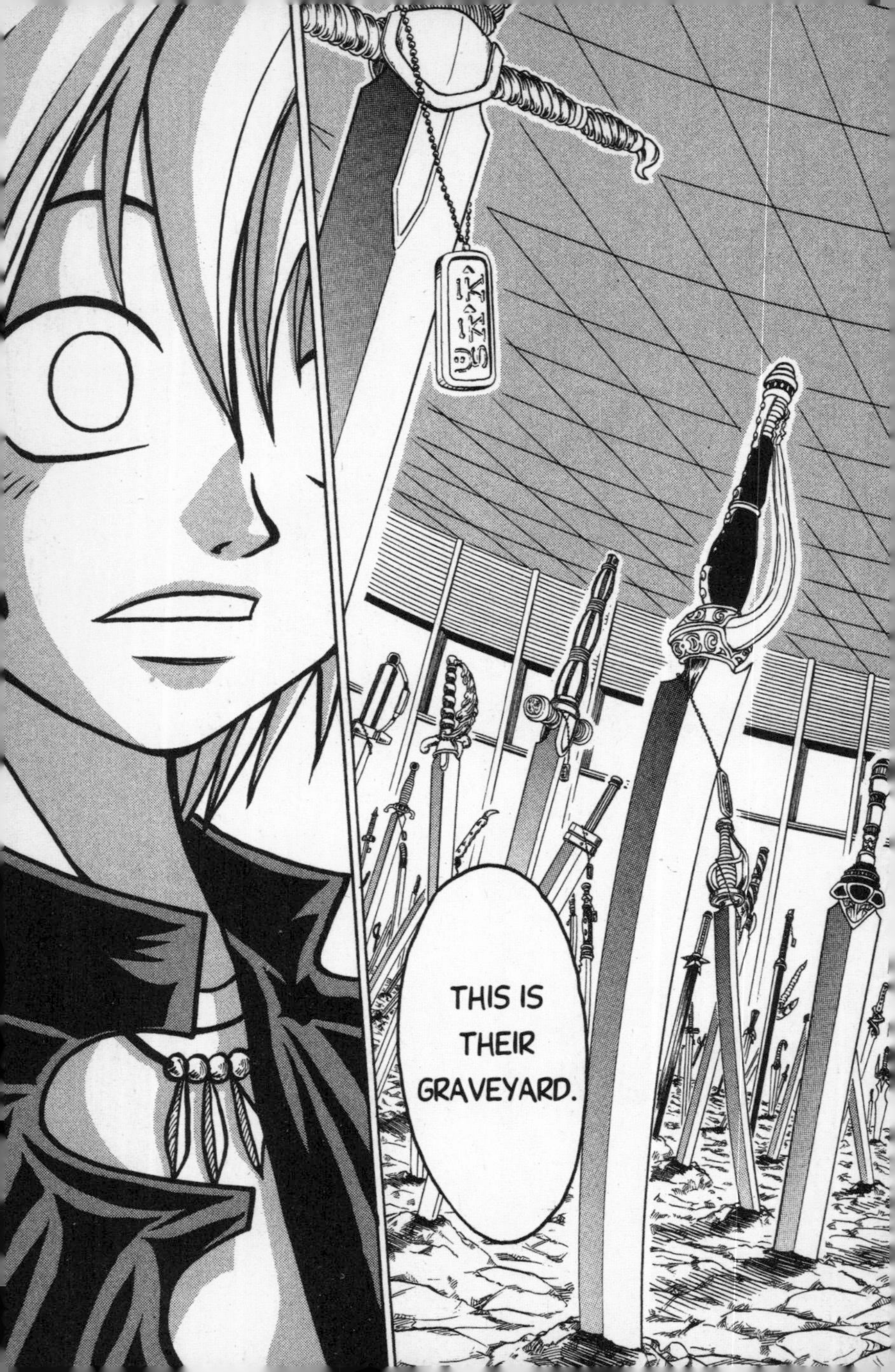
THIS IS THEIR GRAVEYARD.

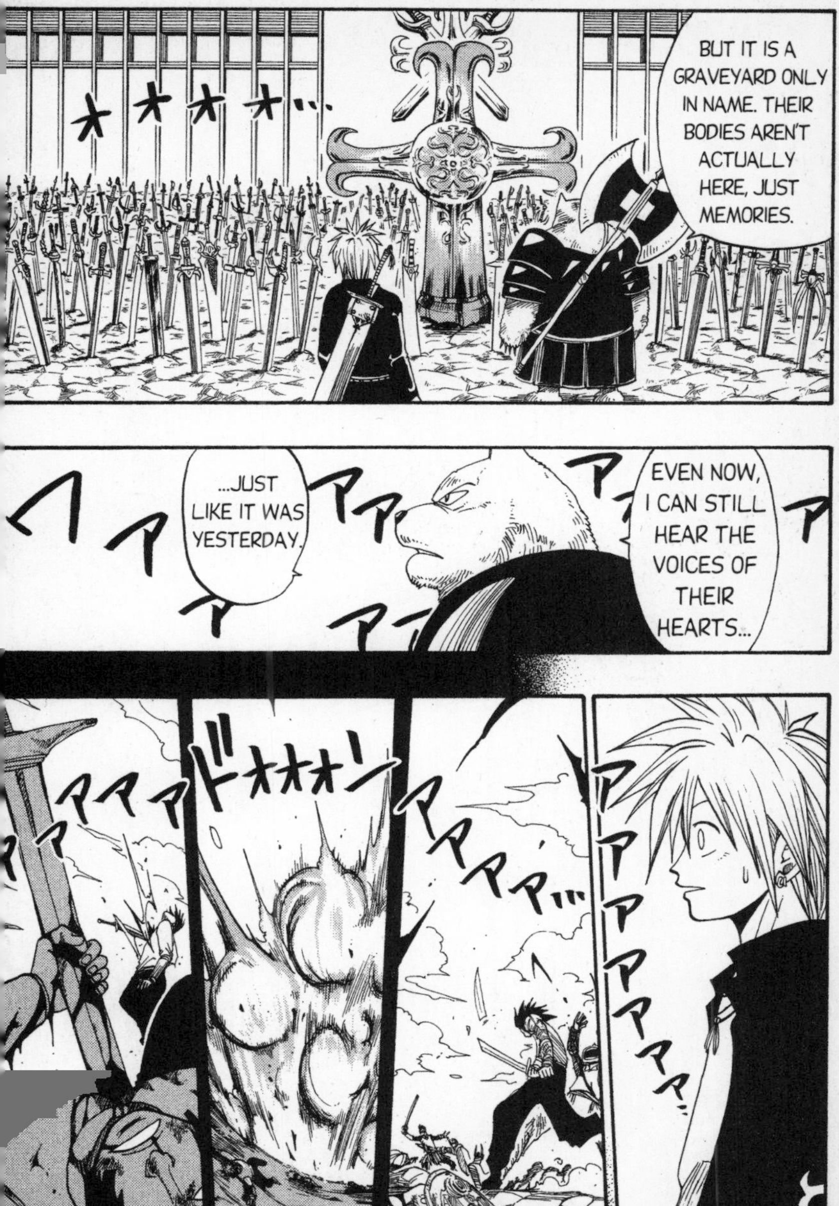
BUT IT IS A GRAVEYARD ONLY IN NAME. THEIR BODIES AREN'T ACTUALLY HERE, JUST MEMORIES.
オオオオ…
EVEN NOW, I CAN STILL HEAR THE VOICES OF THEIR HEARTS...
...JUST LIKE IT WAS YESTERDAY.
ドォォォン

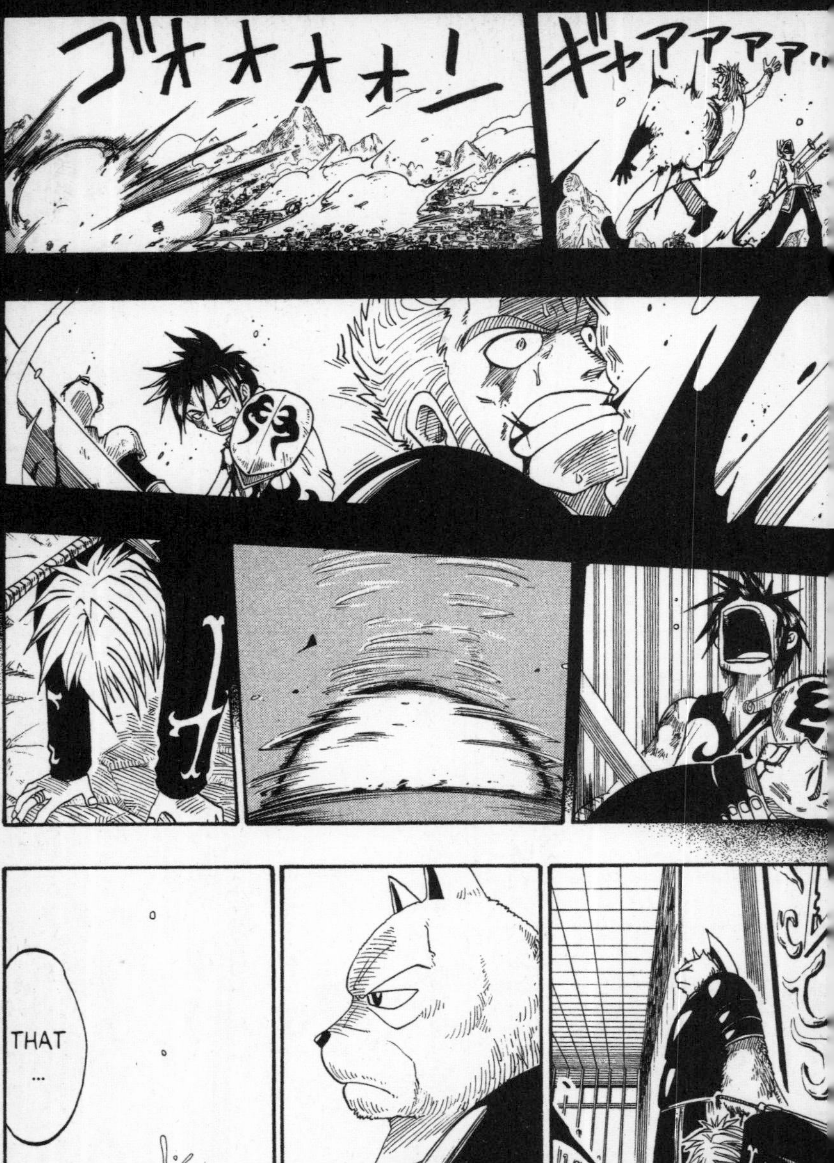
ギャアアアァ"
ゴオオオオーン
THAT
...

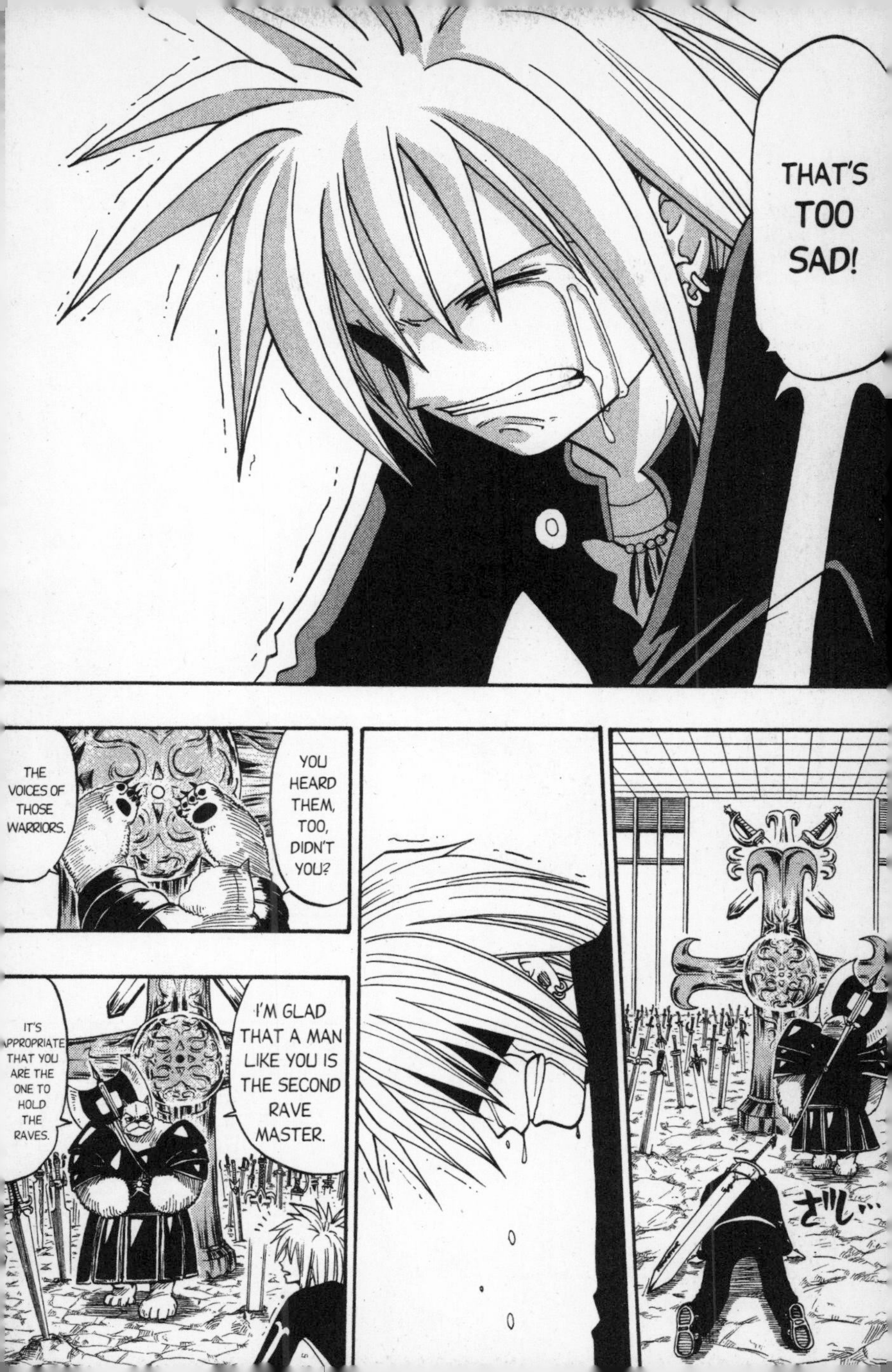
THAT'S TOO SAD!
YOU HEARD THEM, TOO, DIDN'T YOU?
THE VOICES OF THOSE WARRIORS.
I'M GLAD THAT A MAN LIKE YOU IS THE SECOND RAVE MASTER.
IT'S APPROPRIATE THAT YOU ARE THE ONE TO HOLD THE RAVES.

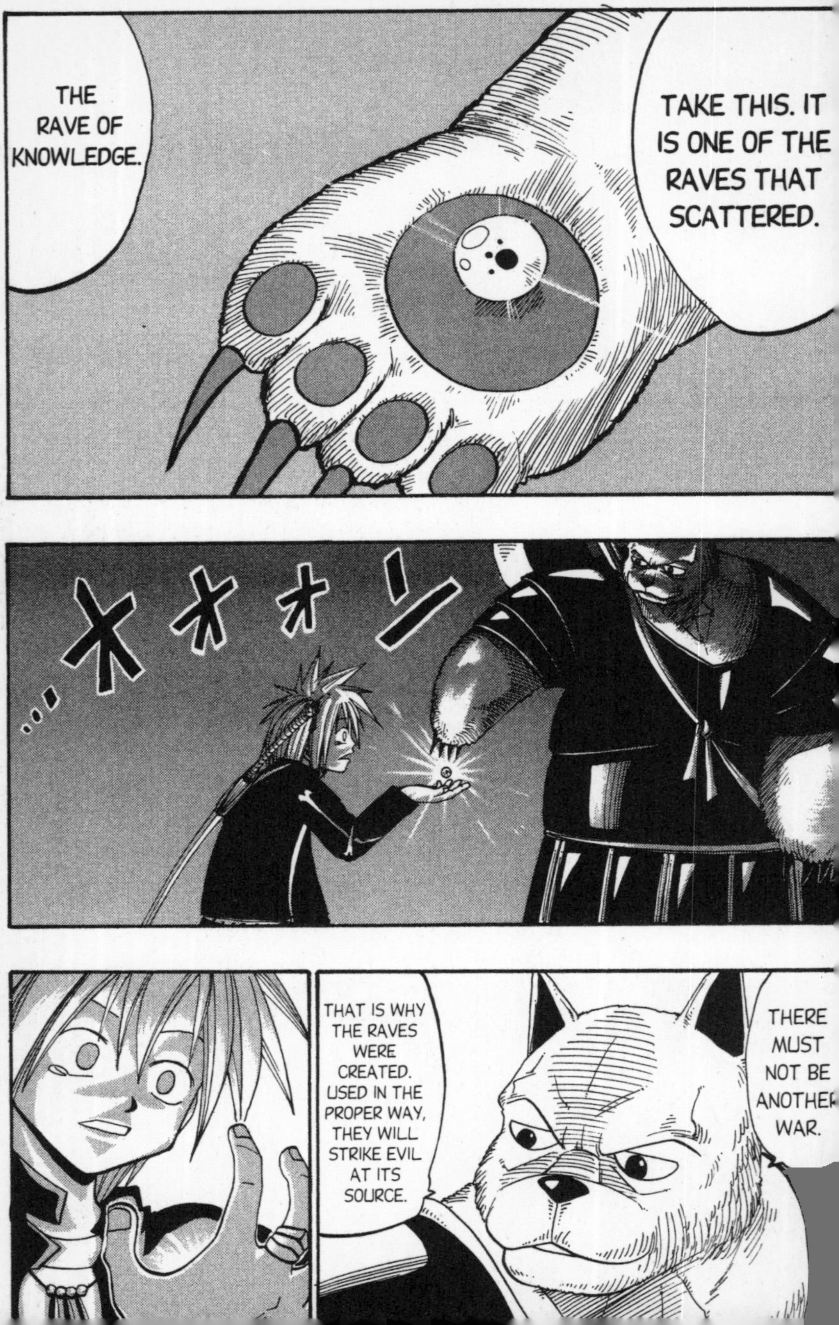
TAKE THIS. IT IS ONE OF THE RAVES THAT SCATTERED.
THE RAVE OF KNOWLEDGE.
...ホオォン
THERE MUST NOT BE ANOTHER WAR.
THAT IS WHY THE RAVES WERE CREATED. USED IN THE PROPER WAY, THEY WILL STRIKE EVIL AT ITS SOURCE.

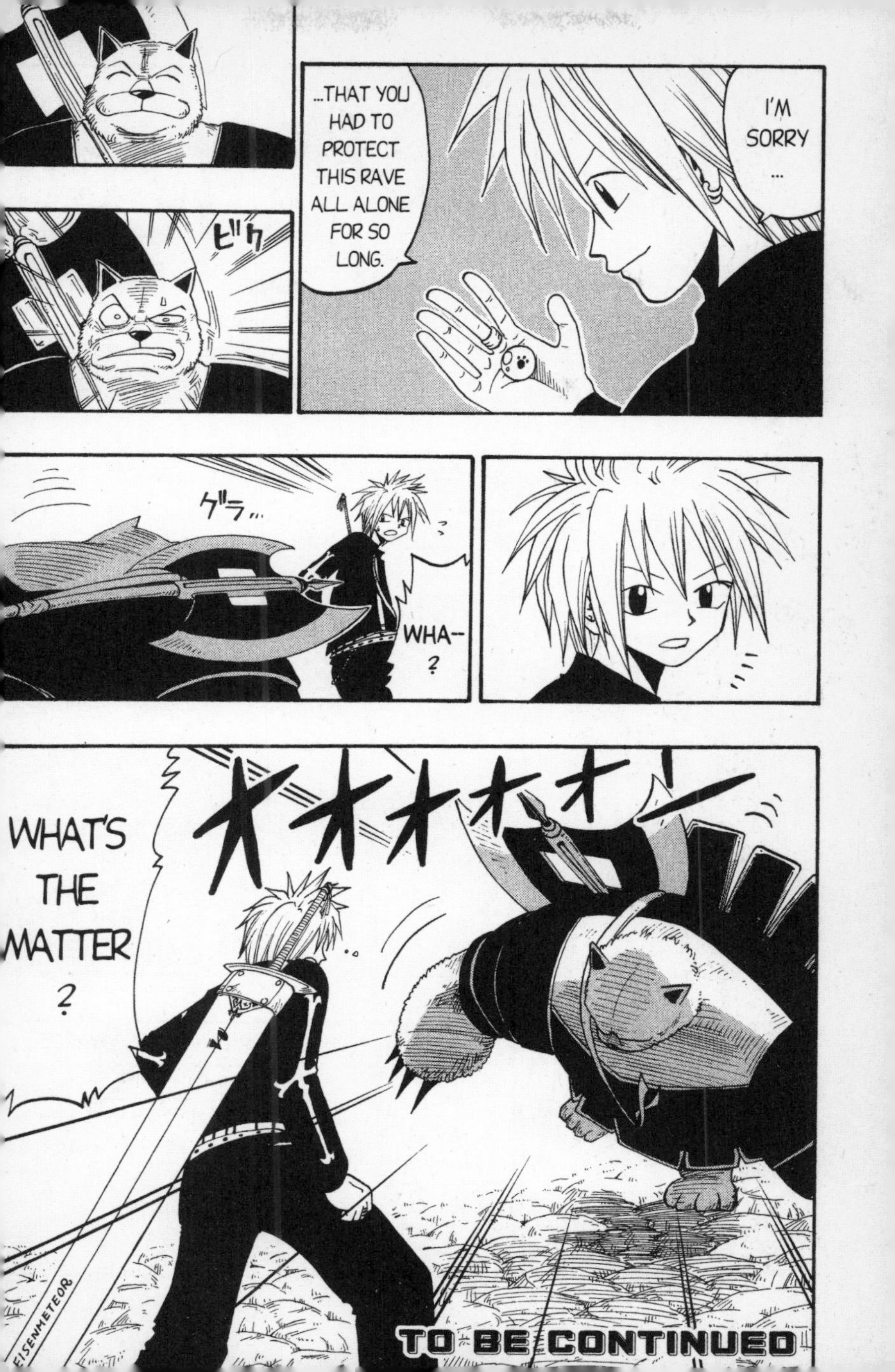

I'M SORRY ...
...THAT YOU HAD TO PROTECT THIS RAVE ALL ALONE FOR SO LONG.
ビク
グラ…
WHA--?
オオオオオー
WHAT'S THE MATTER?
EISENMETEOR
TO BE CONTINUED

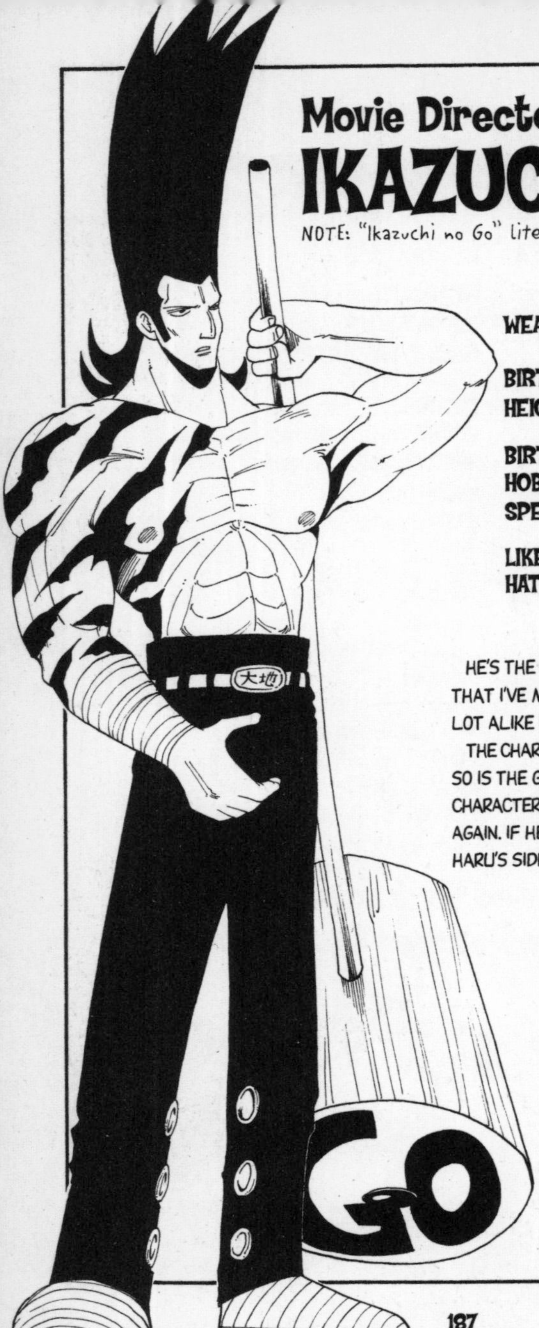
大地
GO

Movie Director:

IKAZUCHI NO GO

NOTE: "Ikazuchi no Go" literally means "Go of thunder."

WEAPONS: THUNDER HAMMER & DARK BRING (ANGRY BLITZ)
BIRTHDAY/AGE: SEPTEMBER 15, 0040 / 26
HEIGHT/WEIGHT/BLOOD TYPE: 199 CM / 82 KG / O
BIRTHPLACE: EXPERIMENT
HOBBIES: LOOKING IN A MIRROR
SPECIAL SKILLS: SEEMS TO BE A FIRST-RATE MOVIE DIRECTOR
LIKES: MOVIES, PANDAS
HATES: CRITICS

HE'S THE SECOND CHARACTER (AFTER GEMMA) THAT I'VE MODELED AFTER A FRIEND. THEY'RE A LOT ALIKE IF I DO SAY SO MYSELF.

THE CHARACTER IS PRETTY DUMB, AND ACTUALLY, SO IS THE GUY I MODELED HIM AFTER. HE'S THE CHARACTER I MOST WANT TO SHOW UP IN THE STORY AGAIN. IF HE DOES SHOW UP AGAIN, WILL HE BE ON HARU'S SIDE?

REPRESENTATIVE WORK:
"HELLO, BOBBY"

HAPPY SMILEY MOVIE AWARDS:
◎ BEST PICTURE
◎ BEST DIRECTOR
AND 7 OTHER AWARDS

Go's girlfriend:
ROSA THE ACTRESS

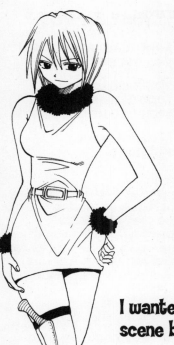

WEAPONS: DANCING FANGS
BIRTHDAY/AGE: JULY 10, 0047 / 19
HEIGHT/WEIGHT/BLOOD TYPE:
   167 CM / 48 KG / B
BIRTHPLACE: EXPERIMENT
HOBBIES: WATCHING PRO WRESTLING
SPECIAL SKILLS: DANCING
LIKES: MUSCLES
HATES: COCKROACHES

I PUT HER IN JUST TO FIGHT WITH ELIE (LAUGHS).
ACTUALLY, I WANTED TO DO A SORT OF TAG-TEAM BATTLE WITH HARU & ELIE VS. GO & ROSA. BUT I REALLY DIDN'T THINK IT WOULD BE SUCH A GOOD IDEA TO PUT BOYS AND GIRLS AGAINST EACH OTHER. ANYWAY, DON'T YOU THINK GO AND ROSA MAKE A GOOD COUPLE?

I wanted to draw a romantic scene between Go and Rosa...

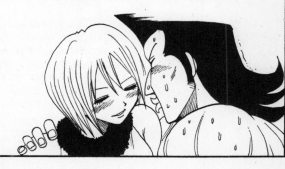

Rave Guardian: KUMA

(ONE OF THE KNIGHTS OF THE BLUE SKY, DEERHOUND)

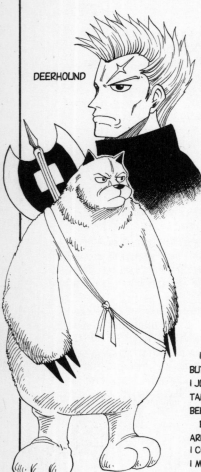

DEERHOUND

Deerhound
(9988 - 0016 / DIED AT AGE 28)

WEAPONS: BATTLE AXE (REGA HOLY)
HEIGHT/WEIGHT/BLOOD TYPE:
206 CM / 94 KG / A
HOBBIES: READING ROMANCE NOVELS
SPECIAL SKILLS: BATTLE AXE
LIKES: WAR
HATES: PEACE

Kuma
(♂)

WEAPONS: BATTLE AXE (REGA HOLY)
BIRTHDAY/AGE: ?
HEIGHT/WEIGHT/BLOOD TYPE:
200 CM / 215 KG / ?
HOBBIES: READING ROMANCE NOVELS
SPECIAL SKILLS: CATCHING FISH IN THE RIVER
LIKES: PEACE
HATES: WAR

I HAD KUMA'S BACKGROUND DECIDED FROM THE START. BUT YOU MUST BE WONDERING WHY I CHOSE A BEAR. WELL, I JUST THOUGHT IT'D BE COOL IF THERE REALLY WERE TALKING BEARS! THAT'S ALL. A TALKING GIRAFFE WOULD'VE BEEN GOOD TOO.

BY THE WAY, ALL OF THE KNIGHTS OF THE BLUE SKY ARE NAMED AFTER DOGS. WHY DOGS, YOU ASK? WELL, I COULD HAVE NAMED THEM AFTER TYPES OF GIRAFFES. I MEAN, I'M NOT HUNG UP ON GIRAFFES OR ANYTHING.

WHAT?! COME ON, GIRAFFES ARE CUTE!

Head of the Silver Rhythm gang:
SILVERCLAIMER MUSICA
(Part 2)

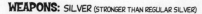

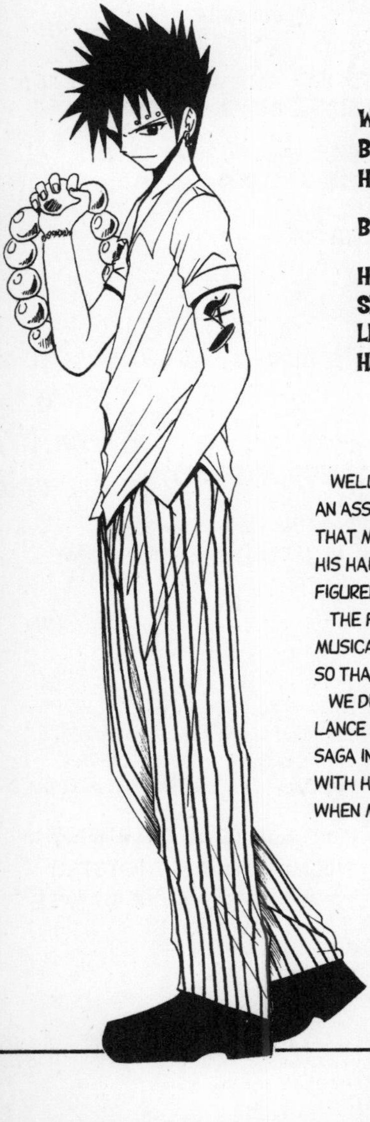

WEAPONS: SILVER (STRONGER THAN REGULAR SILVER)
BIRTHDAY/AGE: MAY 20, 0048 / 18 *
HEIGHT/WEIGHT/BLOOD TYPE:
174 CM / 61 KG / 0
BIRTHPLACE: BORN IN PUNK STREET,
RAISED IN BLUES CITY
HOBBIES: MAKING SILVER ACCESSORIES
SPECIAL SKILLS: MACKIN' ON LADIES, STEALING
LIKES: GIRLS, ARCADES
HATES: GUYS WHO PICK ON GIRLS

WELL, LOOKS LIKE SCHNEIDER'S BEEN EXPOSED AS
AN ASSASSIN (LAUGHS). AND IT LOOKS LIKE NO ONE KNEW
THAT MUSICA WAS AFTER HIM. OF COURSE NOT...HE CHANGED
HIS HAIR...A ROUND OF APPLAUSE FOR THOSE OF YOU WHO
FIGURED IT OUT.

THE FANS HAD MIXED REACTIONS TO THE CHANGE IN
MUSICA'S HAIR. HEH HEH. BUT THE MAJORITY APPROVED,
SO THAT'S A RELIEF.

WE DIDN'T SEE MUCH OF HIM IN ACTION DURING THE
LANCE SAGA, BUT HE'LL HAVE A BIG PART IN THE SHUDA
SAGA IN THE NEXT VOLUME. PEOPLE SEEM TO BE HAPPY
WITH HIS RETURN. I WAS NEARLY BURIED IN FAN LETTERS
WHEN MUSICA CAME BACK.

*Note: We said he was born on
July 20th in the last volume--
Sorry, we lied. This is his real
birthday.

If You Were PLUE

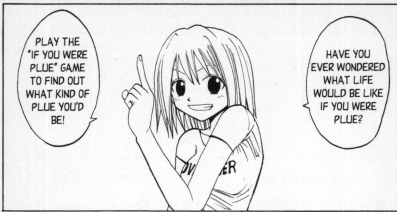

HAVE YOU EVER WONDERED WHAT LIFE WOULD BE LIKE IF YOU WERE PLUE?
PLAY THE "IF YOU WERE PLUE" GAME TO FIND OUT WHAT KIND OF PLUE YOU'D BE!

Hey everybody, if you were Plue, what kind of Plue would you be? Have you ever thought about it? No? That's fine. You can do it now! It's pretty simple. It depends on what your name is. I'll give you an example using the editor Jake Forbes.

① JAKE FORBES

FIRST, WRITE OUT YOUR FIRST AND LAST NAME.

② J A K E F O R B E S
↓ ↓ ↓ ↓ ↓ ↓ ↓ ↓ ↓ ↓
10 1 11 5 6 13 16 2 5 17

NEXT, ASSIGN A NUMBER FROM 1-26 TO EACH LETTER OF YOUR NAME. A -- 1, B -- 2, C -- 3, D -- 4, E -- 5 AND SO ON THROUGH THE ALPHABET, UP TO Z-- 26.

③ 10+1+11+5+6+13+16+2+5+17
= 86

NEXT, ADD ALL OF THE NUMBERS UP. THE LAST DIGIT IN THE TOTAL IS YOUR NUMBER. IN OUR EXAMPLE, JAKE FORBES' NUMBER IS 6. WHEN YOU HAVE YOUR NUMBER, TURN THE PAGE TO FIND OUT WHAT KIND OF PLUE YOU ARE! (GO ON TO NEXT PAGE)

THIS IS FOR THOSE OF YOU WHO HAVE TOO MUCH TIME ON YOUR HANDS!

F YOU WERE PLUE 2: This is where you use the number you found in the last page!

1. Regular Plue

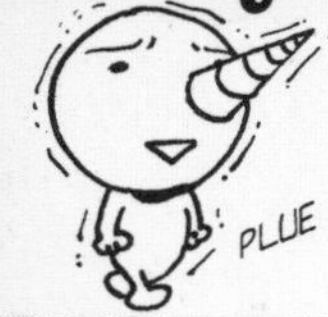
PLUE

JUST A REGULAR PLUE. HE CAN WALK ON TWO LEGS EVEN THOUGH HE'S A DOG, BUT THAT'S NORMAL FOR HIM. YOU'RE JUST LIKE THE PLUE IN THE SERIES.

2. Eating Plue

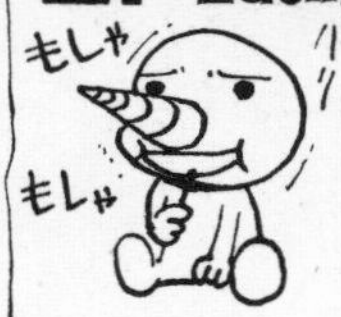

YOU LIKE EATING. YOU'RE HAPPIEST WHEN YOU'RE EATING. BE CAREFUL YOU DON'T GET FAT.

3. Sleeping Plue

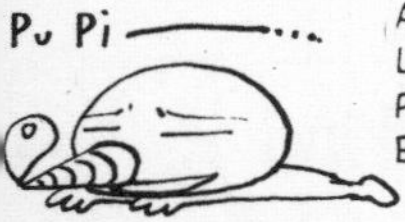
Pu Pi

AREN'T YOU GOING TO BE LATE? EVEN IF YOU WERE PLUE, YOU'D DO NOTHING BUT SLEEP.

4. Drowning Plue

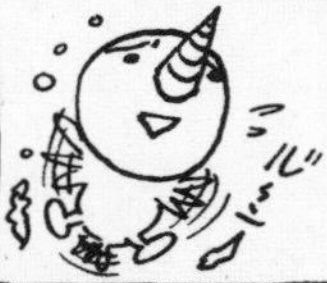

YOU TRY YOUR DARNDEST TO DO WHAT YOU CAN'T, LIKE TRYING TO CROSS THE OCEAN WHEN YOU CAN'T EVEN SWIM. YOU'RE ALWAYS UP FOR A CHALLENGE.

5. Curious Plue

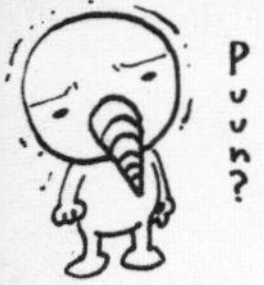
Puuun?

IT'S GREAT TO BE CURIOUS AND HAVE LOTS OF INTERESTS, BUT IT CAN ALSO GET YOU IN TROUBLE. BE CAREFUL.

6. Withered Plue

PLUE LOOKS SO FUNNY WHEN HE'S ALL WITHERED. BUT I'M SURE YOU'LL MAKE A FINE PLUE.

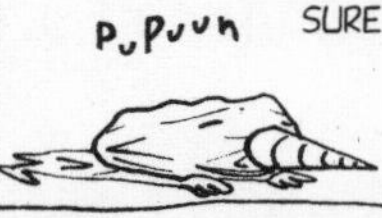
PuPuun

7. Hungry Plue

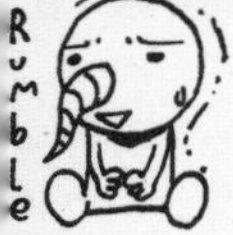
Rumble

EAT SOMETHING. YOU REALLY NEED TO EAT. YOUR NOSE IS WITHERED. YOU SHOULD MAKE FRIENDS WITH PEOPLE WHO ARE "EATING PLUE."

8. Crying Plue

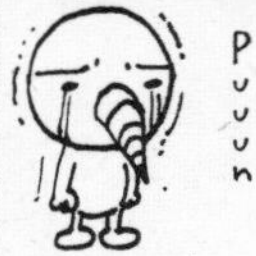
Puuun

CHIN UP. IF YOU DO NOTHING BUT CRY, YOU'LL MISS THE FUN THINGS IN LIFE. I'M SURE YOU'D LOVE SMILING TOO.

9. Cosplay Plue

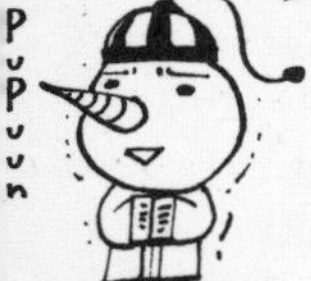
PuPuun

YOU'RE THE PLUE THAT I SOMETIMES DRAW IN THE MARGINS DOING DIFFERENT THINGS. YOU SHOULD GIVE COSPLAY A TRY.

0. Griff?

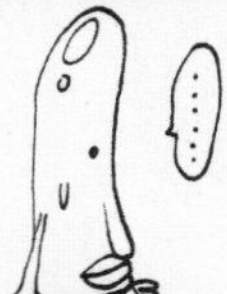
...

SORRY, BUT YOU'RE NOT PLUE, YOU'RE GRIFF. IT'S PRETTY RARE, SO YOU SHOULD BE PROUD. BUT YOU'VE GOT A DIRTY MIND.

RAVE RAVE BACKGROUND MATERIALS

Demon Card Digging Machine 1-A

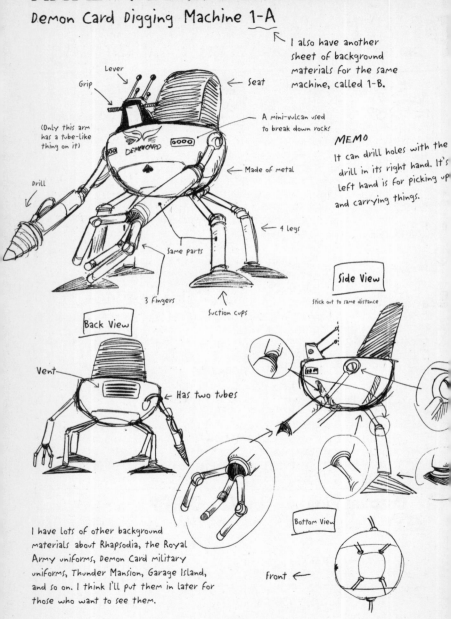

I also have another sheet of background materials for the same machine, called 1-B.

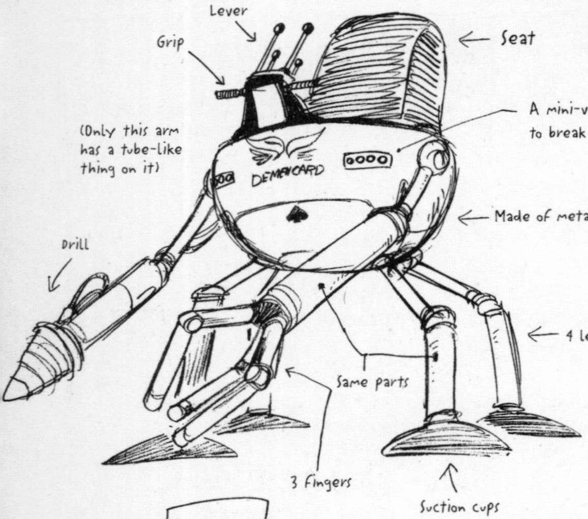

Lever
Grip
Seat
A mini-vulcan used to break down rocks
(Only this arm has a tube-like thing on it)
DEMONCARD
Made of metal
Drill
4 legs
Same parts
3 fingers
Suction cups

MEMO

It can drill holes with the drill in its right hand. It's left hand is for picking up and carrying things.

Back View

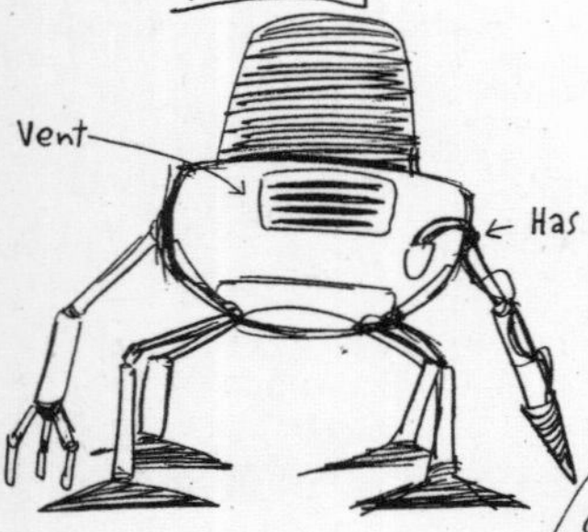

Vent
Has two tubes

Side View

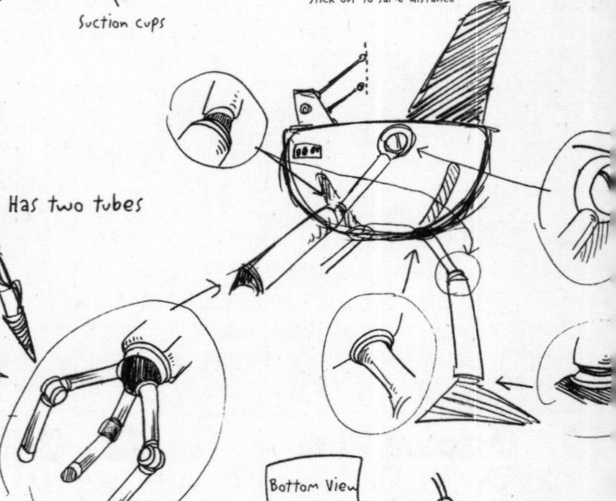

Stick out to same distance

Bottom View

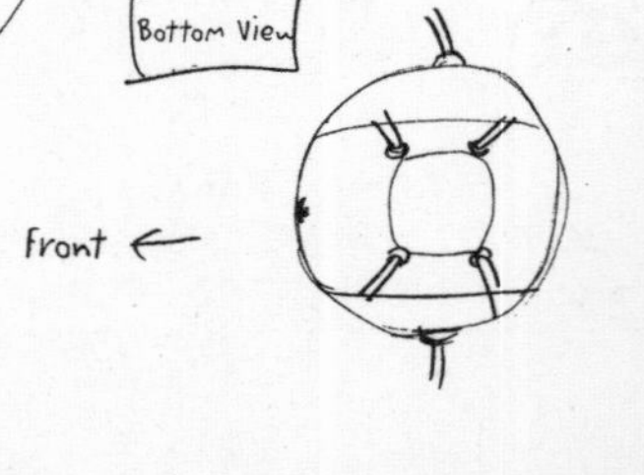

Front

I have lots of other background materials about Rhapsodia, the Royal Army uniforms, Demon Card military uniforms, Thunder Mansion, Garage Island, and so on. I think I'll put them in later for those who want to see them.

"Afterwords"

FIRST OFF, EXCUSES. I'M SORRY, BUT RAVE 0077 WON'T BE APPEARING IN THIS VOLUME. I APOLOGIZE TO EVERYONE WHO WAS LOOKING FORWARD TO IT. PEOPLE MIGHT COMPLAIN, "SOMETHING LIKE THAT CAN'T TAKE YOU MORE THAN AN HOUR TO DRAW!" WELL, THAT MAY BE TRUE, BUT IT TAKES MUCH LONGER THAN THAT FOR ME TO THINK OF WHAT TO DRAW! YUP! THIS IS MY EXCUSE. ACTUALLY, THINGS HAVE BEEN REALLY BUSY FOR ME IN THE DRAWING DEPARTMENT AS I HAD TO DO DOUBLE INSTALLMENTS OF *RAVE MASTER* FOR *WEEKLY SHONEN MAGAZINE*, PLUS SOME EXTRA COLOR PAGES FOR THE MAGAZINE. THIS WAS THE SECOND TIME I DID TWO CHAPTERS AT ONCE FOR THE MAGAZINE (THE FIRST WAS FOR CHAPTERS 10 & 11). DOING THAT, AND GETTING THINGS DONE FOR THE GRAPHIC NOVEL EDITION IS ABSOLUTELY THE WORST. BUT I ENJOY DRAWING, SO IT'S ALL GOOD. IT'S HARD, BUT IT'S FUN. THAT'S THE BEST. I'LL PROBABLY BE ABLE TO PUT RAVE 0077 IN THE NEXT VOLUME. AND AGAIN, I'M REALLY SORRY EVERYONE!

WHOA, THAT'S LONG! I'M HIRO MASHIMA, A MANGA ARTIST WHO PUTS GAGS INTO HIS HANDWRITING. WHAT DID YOU THINK OF *RAVE MASTER* VOLUME 4? WHEN I LOOK OVER IT AGAIN, I REALIZE THAT THE ART IS CHANGING REALLY FAST (LAUGHS)! LIKE IN CHAPTERS 28 - 30. ALL OF A SUDDEN, I THOUGHT, "I WANNA DRAW WELL!!" SO I USED "GET BACKERS" AND SUCH AS A REFERENCE AND TRIED CHANGING THE ART A BIT. I WAS A LITTLE HESITANT TO CHANGE THE DESIGNS I HAD BEEN USING FOR A WHILE, SO IT WAS A LITTLE TOUGH, BUT I'M STILL GOING TO KEEP LOOKING FOR WAYS TO IMPROVE MY ART. I WANT TO GET BETTER AT DRAWING.

BY THE WAY, I'VE GOTTEN LETTERS THAT I USED AN "R" INSTEAD OF AN "L" IN "EXPLOSION." AND OF COURSE, "L" IS THE CORRECT SPELLING. I MADE A MISTAKE AND PUT "R"!(EDITOR'S NOTE: WE FIXED THIS FOR THE ENGLISH EDITION). A LOT OF ENGLISH COMES UP IN THE RAVE WORLD, BUT I DON'T REALLY KNOW ENGLISH ALL THAT WELL, SO I MAKE A LOT OF MISTAKES, EVERYONE. DON'T TRUST A SINGLE WORD OF ENGLISH OR ANY OTHER FOREIGN LANGUAGE IN *RAVE MASTER!* (LAUGHS)

OH AND BY THE WAY, PLUE IS GOING TO BE IN "GET BACKERS"! I'M TOUCHED! THANK YOU SO VERY MUCH, MR. AYAMINE! CAN I CALL YOU MY BIG BRO?

SPECIAL THANKS
TO "KATAGE" FOR HELPING ME WITH CHAPTER 25
TO "DOKE" FOR HELPING ME WITH CHAPTER 28
AND TO ALL THE READERS!

NEXT TIME IN RAVE MASTER!

Raver Boi

Haru's a boy
Elie's a girl
And together they're going on a quest
She's from Punk Street
He's Master of Rave
There's much more to say
He needed her
She'd never turn him down 'cause she needed him as well
And all of their friends
Like Plue with his nose
They all lent a hand, and they wear funky clothes

He was a Raver boy
He met a Blue Sky boy
But was he good enough for him?
Kuma had a fuzzy face
But Haru'd better brace
'Cuz a surprise attack's gonna end their mirth

50 years ago
Kuma was a great knight
But now he's a bear—quite a "grizzly" sight
He guards a Rave
Now who does he see
The new raver boy—Haru Glory
They ought to be friends
But Shuda comes round
With his flying ship
That tears out of the ground
Elie tags along
As the fight takes to the sky
She'll battle a weirdo who shoots goo from his eye

He was a Raver boy
She said "wait for me, boy"
But was he good enough to be
A Rave Master Lord
With the Ten-Powers Sword
Do Elie and the others know what he's worth?

They'll stick with the Raver boy
They'll say "we're coming with you, boy"
Musica's back with the show
Griff will take them on the road
Plue will lead them with his nose
And Elie's memories still aren't known

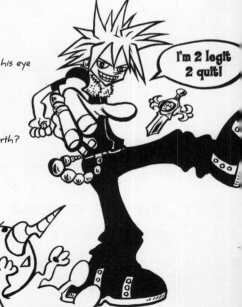

I'm 2 legit 2 quit!

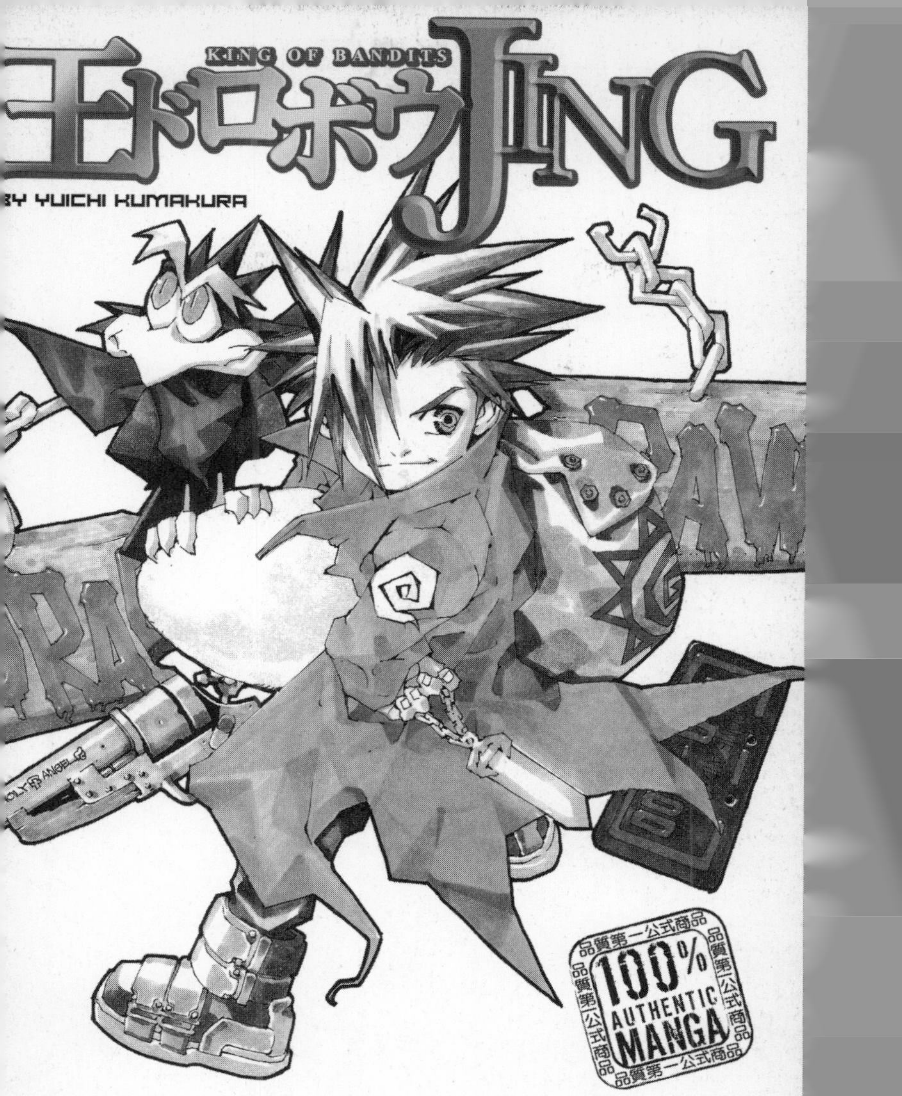
KING OF BANDITS
王ドロボウ JING
YUICHI KUMAKURA
100% AUTHENTIC MANGA
品質第一公式商品

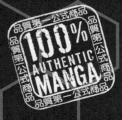

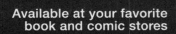

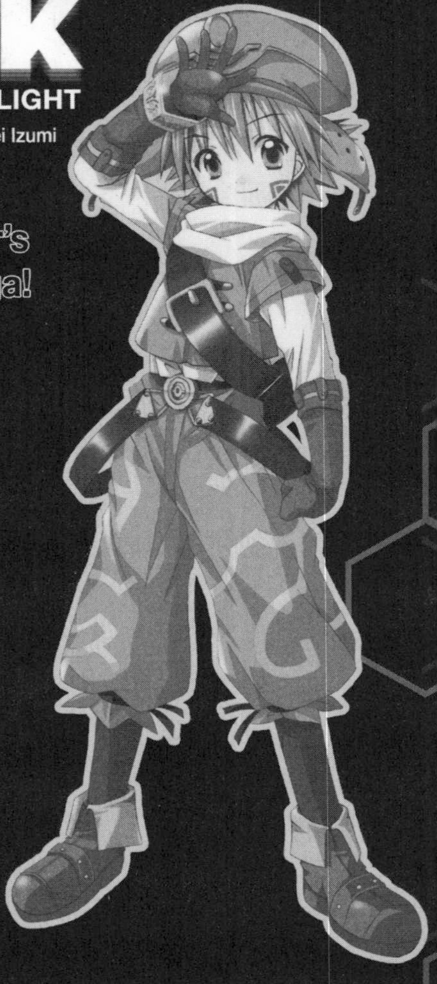

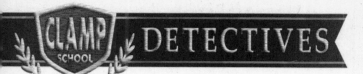

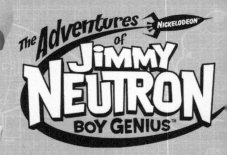

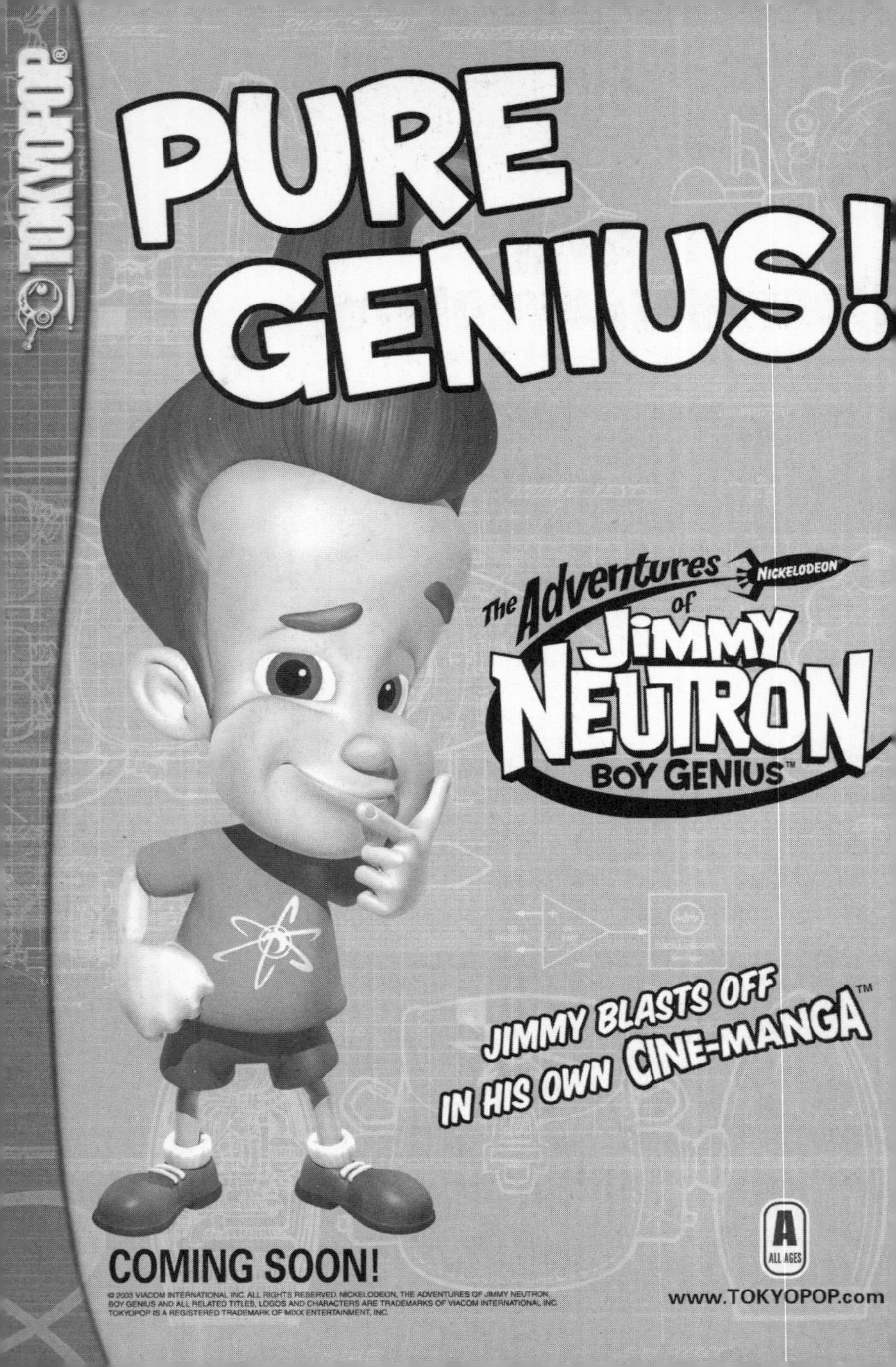

STOP!

This is the back of the book.
You wouldn't want to spoil a great ending!

This book is printed "manga-style," in the authentic Japanese right-to-left format. Since none of the artwork has been flipped or altered, readers get to experience the story just as the creator intended. You've been asking for it, so TOKYOPOP® delivered: authentic, hot-off-the-press, and far more fun!

DIRECTIONS

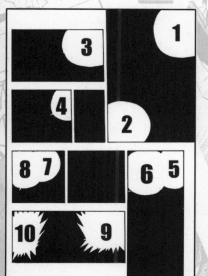

If this is your first time reading manga-style, here's a quick guide to help you understand how it works.

It's easy... just start in the top right panel and follow the numbers. Have fun, and look for more 100% authentic manga from TOKYOPOP®!

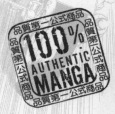

100% AUTHENTIC MANGA